The Western Islands Handbook

The Western Islands Handbook

David Perrott

KITTIWAKE

Published by
Kittiwake Press
3 Glantwymyn Village Workshops, Machynlleth,
Montgomeryshire SY20 8LY

Seventh edition (formerly titled '*Guide to the Western Islands of Scotland*', first edition 1986)

Care has been taken to be accurate.
The publishers cannot accept responsibility for any errors which may appear, or their consequences.
Some islands have been visited or re-visited by the author more recently than others. If you would like to help keep this book up to date, please send your comments to the above address.

Please remember that much land, and many islands, are private. Their inclusion does not imply any right of public access. Roads and tracks indicated are not necessarily rights of way. If in doubt, seek permission first.

Photographs by the author except on pages: 9, 15, 18 (bottom), 54, 56, 58, 60, 63, 93, 95, 97, 111, 123, 124, 125, 127, 129, 130, 131 and 166. We wish to thank Caledonian MacBrayne for the use of one of their photographs on the cover (picture 4)

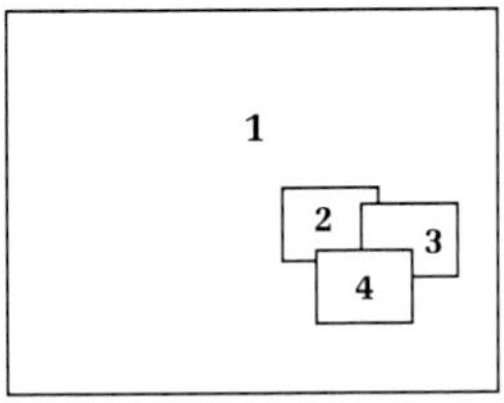

Cover photographs:
1 The Sound of Barra
2 Isle Ornsay, Skye
3 Glen Brittle, Skye
4 Brodick, Arran

Produced on an Apple Macintosh using Works, Photoshop, Streamline, Freehand and QuarkXPress.
The typeface is Melior.

Film output by
Litho Link, Welshpool, Montgomeryshire

Printed by
MFP Design & Print, Manchester

A catalogue record for this book may be found in the British Library

ISBN 9511003 9 4
7/2.0/3.98

Introduction

The Western Islands of Scotland are a remote and beautiful part of Europe, with their own history, their own unique way of life and, especially in the Outer Hebrides, their own language. The purpose of this book is to give you background information before you go, and to guide you once you are there.

The text, which sets each island in context historically and scenically, describes all the places of interest, as if on a guided tour. Photographs and drawings give a visual impression, and all the ferry services are noted. Each island has a map to familiarise you with the lie of the land. The content is arranged geographically, in order that you may identify other islands in the vicinity and learn about those as well.

This book is now in its seventh edition. In response to readers comments, it now includes the splendid Clyde islands of Bute, Cumbrae and Arran, a separate group from those to the west of Kintyre, but one which will amply repay exploration.

When you visit the islands, please bear in mind that the weather, whilst generally mild, can be extremely changeable – calm, sunny and warm one day, a force eight gale the next – so be prepared with suitable clothing, and plan an alternative itinerary just in case it rains. The author's personal experience (and to some extent statistics confirm this) suggests May and June are usually the best months to go, with more calm sunny weather and, of course, very long daylight hours. As an added bonus, at that time of year the dread Scottish midge will not *usually* be active.

Whilst the *Outer* Hebrides rarely seem to be busy, you should bear in mind that late July and August on

Skye and Mull can become quite hectic. With the road bridge to Skye now open, this most famous of islands could easily become a holiday centre to rival the Lake District. So if you *have* to go during high summer, use this book to explore off the beaten track, where you will still find places to call you own, if only for a day. *And* take plenty of insect repellent.

Within the text of this book, and listed on page 172, are the locations of Tourist Information Centres in the area. These are without doubt the best and most up-to-date source of information regarding ferries and boat trips, charters to remote islands, local crafts, opening times, restaurants and accommodation. Staffed by people who live in the area, they will be pleased to help you, and their local knowledge is without equal.

As you travel, on foot or by bike, by car, motorcycle, coach, boat or aeroplane, please respect the lifestyle and activities of those who live on the islands. Care always for wildlife, natural habitats, beaches and countryside in what still remains one of the most untouched regions of Europe.

Contents

ATLANTIC OCEAN
Flannan Isles
St Kilda
THE OUTER HEBRIDES
LEWIS
Stornoway
The Minch
Handa
The Summer Isles
Ullapool
Shiant Isles
Tarbert
Scalpay
Harris
Leverburgh
Berneray
Otternish
North Uist
Lochmaddy
The Little Minch
Monach Islands
Benbecula
South Uist
Lochboisdale
Ludag
Eriskay
Barra
Eoligarry
Vatersay
Castlebay
Mingulay
The Sea of the Hebrides
Uig
Rona
Portree
Raasay
SKYE
Sconser
Kyleakin
Kyle of Lochalsh
Kylerhea
Glenelg
Soay
Armadale
Canna
Rum
Mallaig
Eigg
Arisaig
THE SMALL ISLES
Muck
Fort William
Kilchoan
Coll
Tobermory
Tiree
Lochaline
Treshnish Isles
Fishnish
Lismore
Ulva
MULL
Craignure
Staffa
Oban
Iona
Fionnphort
Seil
Isles of the Sea
Luing
Scarba
Colonsay
Oronsay
Jura
Port Askaig
Colintraive
Wemyss Bay
Kennacraig
Rothesay
Islay
Largs
Bute
Claonaig
Port Ellen
Gigha
Tayinloan
Lochranza
Ardrossan
Arran
Brodick
Davaar
Ailsa Craig
Sanda

The Western Islands of Scotland

The Outer Hebrides

Western Isles. With an area of 716,000 acres and a population of 29,600 this archipelago, 130 miles long, lies in a crescent about 40 miles off the north-west mainland of Scotland. Its west coast is pounded by the unbroken force of the North Atlantic. The name Hebrides is derived from the Norse *Havbredey,* the 'isle on the edge of the sea'. Consisting mainly of Lewisian gneiss, it is said to be the oldest known fragment of Europe. There are over 200 islands in the group, but of these only 13 are now inhabited, with about 80 per cent of the population living on Lewis and Harris.

Of the many physical aspects setting these islands apart from the rest of Scotland perhaps the most memorable is the quality of the light. Reflected off the clear water of the surrounding sea it accentuates edges and heightens colours with its luminosity. Other times the dark storm clouds come in procession from the west, or the sea mist envelopes everything. The climate is mild, with no extremes of temperature or rainfall but the wind blows strongly two days in three, especially in the north.

Most visitors to the Outer Hebrides approach from the east. The first impression is that of a barren, rock-strewn land, broken by flooded glaciated valleys, narrow and steep sided. But if the approach were from the west, the first sight would be of long white beaches, backed with fertile grassland grazed by cattle and dotted with cottages. Between these two contrasting coasts lies peat moor and a landscape which, although appearing devoid of trees, has most types present. Over 800 plant species have been recorded on the islands.

There are many prehistoric stone structures throughout the islands, the most famous being the stone circles at Callanish, built about 4000 years ago when the climate was drier and warmer, and the inhospitable peat bogs were less extensive.

The patterns of human population are very different between the northern and southern islands. Harris and the Isle of Lewis (together with Barra) reached their zenith in 1911 (35,000 people) due to the quite exceptional circumstances surrounding the herring fisheries. The pattern of North and South Uist is more comparable with that of the rest of the islands of Scotland, reaching over 14,000 in 1841, then succumbing to the clearances. Much land is still held by absentee landlords, being left fallow for sporting activities.

Today the Outer Hebrides is the last major stronghold of the Gaelic language (the Gàidhealtachd), due probably to the physical distance of the islands from the mainland. In the Outer Hebrides a life-style and culture have survived that elsewhere has virtually disappeared. Gaelic, once the subject of derision on the mainland, is now actively promoted in the Outer Hebrides in the face of the insidious influence of television.

Lewis, Harris and North Uist are Protestant, South Uist and Barra are Roman Catholic, and Benbecula is a mixture of the two. There is no friction between the two religious communities – in fact the geography of the Sound of Harris has caused North Uist to have more contact with its Roman Catholic neighbours than with Lewis and Harris.

The main body of Protestants belong to the Free Presbyterian Church, with its strict observance of the Sabbath: Stornoway on Lewis is a major stronghold of the Lord's Day Observance Society. On Sunday, on the Protestant islands, all the bars, restaurants and shops close, making it difficult for those in bed-and-breakfast accommodation, public transport ceases and people go out only to attend church services, during which no hymns are sung. Sundays on South Uist and Barra are altogether a more lively affair.

The traditional form of entertainment is still the ceilidh, originally meaning gossiping house but more recently a gathering with music.

The Outer Hebrides appeal to visitors as a perfect place to get away from it all. There is a Hebridean saying that reflects the atmosphere of these islands: 'When God made time, he made plenty of it.' The people are friendly and helpful towards tourists, but they have done little to provide organised facilities. There is no need. Nature endowed the islands with lochs full of salmon and trout and sea fishing of equal quality. It provided rugged scenery under wide open skies. The west coast has beaches the equal of any in Europe, deserted even on warm days. The seas are clear and clean, but naturally, a little cold. Archaeologists will find some of the finest sites in the country, and ornithologists can seek out rare and unique species. There is even a bumble bee – *Bombus Jonellus var. Hebridensis* – found nowhere else. As part of its policy of preserving the Gaelic language, the Western Islands Council has installed Gaelic road signs throughout the islands. A leaflet is available from the local Tourist Information Centres giving the English equivalents – it is a good idea to obtain a copy on arrival.

Isle of Lewis

The name Lewis is derived from *leogach* (pronounced loo-ach) meaning marshy. The largest and most populous island in the Outer Hebrides, with 20,100 inhabitants (and more graduates per head of population than any other part of Britain), it borders Harris to the north of the Forest of Harris, a natural barrier of wild moorland and mountain. The island is made up almost wholly of gneiss, rising to 1885 ft at the summit of Mealisval in the south-west, and to 1874ft at the summit of Beinn Mhor in the south. Much of the gneiss is overlaid with glacially deposited boulder clay. There are small areas of Torridonian sandstone near Stornoway and several hundred acres of granite in the parish of Barvas.

The dominant feature of Lewis is the dark, undulating central peat moor, scattered with hundreds of shallow lochs. Although its appearance is uniform, its sheer size is impressive. Centuries of peat cutting have enlivened the surface of the moor with circles, squares and snaking lines, each cut having a herring-bone pattern. The cutting takes place in the early summer, when the moor becomes alive with families engaged in this work. Later, when the cut peat has dried, it is carried away from the banks in sacks, barrows, car boots and modified tractors and trailers to be used as fuel. Going to the peats is very much a social occasion.

The peat began to form when Neolithic farmers cleared the indigenous woodland, thus destroying a natural means of drainage. Water which would have been absorbed and evaporated by the trees now collected on the poor soil. Under the wet and acidic conditions thus created the growth of sedge, moss, grass and heather began to outstrip the rate at which dead plants decompose and the layer of peat – fibrous plant remains – began to form. Lewis peat is a mixture of sphagnum and deergrass which, on some parts of the moor, is still making. The peat in the deeper, blacker layers is a fine fuel, clean and easy to handle when dry, but its calorific value is only two-thirds that of coal. In its natural state the water content can be as high as 90 per cent. The reserves of peat on Lewis have been estimated at 85 million tons, and it is still cut in the traditional way. A good worker, with helpers, can cut 1000 peats a day, which then have to be drained, dried and transported. A crofting family would use around 15,000 each year. The neatly stacked peats – the *cruach* – by the crofts and houses represent a large investment of time and labour and the islanders are justly proud of them.

The main pillars of the Lewis economy are weaving, fishing,

crofting (there are about 3500 small crofts, generally worked on a part-time basis), marine construction, and to some extent tourism. This variety has brought a measure of stability lacking on other islands with less diverse sources of income. If a cold wind blows in one sector of the Lewis economy, as has often been the case in the past, there are others to fall back on.

Known world-wide is Harris Tweed and the centre of production is Lewis. Harris Tweed can only be sold as such if it is made in the Outer Hebrides from virgin Scottish wool, woven on hand-looms in the weavers' own homes. It must also bear the orb trade-mark of the Harris Tweed Association, founded in 1909. The hard-wearing, warm and water-resistant cloth is produced 28/30 inches wide, in rolls of 38 weaver's yards (each being 72 inches). The tweed was originally produced for the crofters' own use until its wider applications were promoted by the wives of the landowners, such as Lady Dunmore of Amhuinnsuidhe Castle, who recognised its exceptional quality and durability.

Attempts to change production methods by using larger power-looms were resisted by the weavers, 95 per cent of whom voted to retain traditional method, not only to protect employment but also to preserve their quality of life and independence. Working at home allows them time to tend the croft, look after the sheep and cut peat. Working in a factory would be far too rigid. Of course some things have changed in the industry. The wool is no longer sheared, dyed with crotal (natural dyes made from lichen) over a peat fire, carded and spun at the croft – all this has been done in the factory at Stornoway since 1934. The prepared wool is delivered to the weaver, and the finished cloth collected by van from the factory. The finished bundles of tweed can be seen lying at the roadside, in all sorts of weather, awaiting collection. Tweed produced by entirely traditional methods is still made by Marion Campbell of Plocrapool, who spins, dyes and weaves in the original way, and has received many accolades for her work, including the British Empire Medal.

The hand-looms are usually housed in small sheds; a rhythmic clacking reveals work in progress. The weaver sits at the loom, his legs providing the power and his hands changing the shuttles. It looks, and is, hard work. There are about 750 such weavers on Lewis and Harris who, together with 400 mill workers, produce some 5 million yards each year, the skill traditionally being passed down the generations, although it can now be learned at the technical college in Stornoway.

The first owners of Lewis were clans of Norse origin. Later, the island became part of Scotland, with the MacLeods being replaced by the Mackenzies of Kintail in 1610, who then held the island until 1844 when Mrs Stewart Mackenzie sold it to Sir James Matheson for £190,000. He invested £500,000 (earned from the China trade) on improvements – draining land, building schools and investing in

ISLE OF LEWIS

new industries. Lord Leverhulme bought the island (along with Harris) in 1918, intending to develop the fishing industry. After spending £875,000 he gave up in 1923. On leaving, he gifted the 64,000-acre parish of Stornoway to the people, to be administered by the elected Stornoway Trust, and offered crofts as free gifts, although only 41 were accepted. Much of the remaining land fell into the hands of speculators and absentee landlords. The slump resulting from his withdrawal caused the emigration of over 1000 able-bodied men to North America, some of whom returned during the Depression of the 1930s.

In the heyday of the herring fishing industry over 1000 boats operated from Stornoway, but the loss of men during World War I and Norwegian competition brought about its eventual demise. The white-fish industry suffered from steam trawlers fishing illegally and destroying the local line-fishing gear. Now, with the aid of loans and grants, the industry is on its feet again with local boats landing white fish and prawns.

The only *town* in the Outer Hebrides, is Stornoway. It is the administrative centre of the Western Isles Authority and has a steadily rising population as a result of migration from the surrounding countryside. On its outskirts there is much new housing to accommodate this influx.

The town has a fresh, cosmopolitan atmosphere, and offers a range of shops, hotels, bars, restaurants and services unique in the Western Isles. It also has a well established Pakistani community – shopkeepers with a working knowledge of Gaelic. The Tourist Information Centre is situated in Cromwell Street.

The fine natural harbour provides shelter in all conditions, and is host to the local and visiting fishing boats and traders as well as the Caledonian MacBrayne ferry *Isle of Lewis* from Ullapool. The lifeboat based here is responsible for one of the largest areas in the British Isles. A colony of grey seals has also made its home in the harbour. On **Eilean na Gobhail** (goat island) opposite, there are ship-repair facilities and a slipway. To the north of the harbour are the Beasts of Holm. It was on these rocks, at 1.55 on the morning of 1 January 1919, that the steamer *Iolaire,* ferrying Lewis men from Kyle of Lochalsh on the final leg of their journey home from the war, was wrecked. 205 of the 285 on board drowned. Rumours of drunkenness among the crew were rife in the islands until the public enquiry, held in Stornoway the following month, found no evidence whatsoever to support this view.

The 18thC net-loft on North Beach Quay is probably the oldest building still standing in the town. St Peter's Episcopal Church has the prayer book taken by David Livingstone on his travels. Martin's Memorial, the spired church in Francis Street, was built in the 19thC at the birthplace of Sir Alexander Mackenzie, the man who made the first overland crossing of Canada. The police headquarters, the

Lews Castle, Stornoway

Sheriff Court and two hospitals are also situated in the town, along with the Nicholson Institute, a senior comprehensive school founded in 1873 by a Lewisman subsequently killed in Shanghai. There is a sports centre and swimming pool, a golf course and a cinema. The sea fishing in this area is excellent and boat trips are arranged by the local sea-angling club.

To the west of the town is the turreted Lews Castle, built by Sir James Matheson during the 1840s, and surrounded by a square mile of beautiful mixed woodland. These woods, unique in the Outer Hebrides, have been colonised by a wide variety of woodland birds and there is also a large rookery of about 150 nests. What were once private gardens are planted with berberis, azalea, fuchsia and rhododendron. The Stornoway Trust now uses the castle as a technical college, where navigation, weaving, building and engineering are taught.

To the east of Stornoway is the comparatively densely populated Eye Peninsula, known as Point. Stornoway Airport, to the north of the road to Point, was both civil and military (the RAF first came here in 1941), but NATO are now expected to withdraw completely.

At the very western end of Point, by the north shore, stand the walls of the now defunct 14thC St Columba's Church and the graveyard of Ui, an important religious site said to have been built where St Catan had his cell in the 6thC. The graveyard is the burial ground of 19 MacLeod chiefs of Lewis, including Margaret Mackinnon, who was the daughter of Ruari, the chief, and the mother of John, who was the very last abbot of Iona. There is a fine effigy of Roderick MacLeod on the south side of the church and an impressive Celtic stone on the north. The last service was held here in 1828. The rest of the peninsula is of little interest, being undulating moorland shared by crofters and commuters. There are pleasant small beaches near Bayble and Garrabost, and a lighthouse at Tiumpan Head.

North-east of Stornoway the road passes the beaches at Coll and Gress, before ending near Tolsta by Traigh Mhor, a fine sweep of dune-backed sands with caves and stacks nearby. The road to Tolsta was built by Lord Leverhulme, who intended it to become part of a circuit of northern Lewis, connecting with the Port of Ness. North of Tolsta, the coast is inaccessible by car, remaining isolated, lonely and wild.

The road from Stornoway to Barvas crosses the central peat moor, following the north-west course of the River Barvas (a salmon river) until it meets the west coast road. This road, with its scattered crofting/weaving townships, follows a route about a mile inland, and little of interest can be seen without leaving it.

The first impression given by the townships is one of untidiness – old houses are left to crumble while new ones remain not quite finished. Cars stand abandoned right outside front doors, although it must be said that the interiors of the houses are given a great deal of attention and care. What we see has two explanations. The communities are virtually classless and non-competitive in the modern urban sense so there is no desire to impress the neighbours with outside appearances. Secondly, while the people do wish to have new houses, cars, etc., they seem not to want to make a clear break with the past, so old things that have served them well are left to just fade away.

It was from the townships of Barvas that the idea of re-seeding the barren moorland spread. Initially the surface of the moor is skimmed, after which lime-rich shell sand, nitrous phosphate and fertiliser are spread, seeds are sown, and worms and bacteria turn the whole lot into soil. Many thousands of acres have been improved in this way under the Crofters Commission Land Improvement Scheme. It raises the grazing potential for sheep 30-fold and, where the reclaimed land adjoins the moorland, the contrast is quite dramatic. In March 1980 Barvas was the scene of a unique referendum to see whether the people wished to have licensed premises in the parish. The idea was defeated and drinking continues in one or two *bothans,* shacks on common ground, tolerated by the police. Strangers are *not* welcome.

The tallest standing stone in the Hebrides, Clach an Trushal, stands overlooking the sea at Ballantrushal. To the east of Loch an Duin at Shader is Steinacleit, a 50-ft diameter burial cairn encircled by stones, in a large oval enclosure. It stands on the skyline and can be reached via a rough track. From Dell to Port of Ness there are many crofts and the land is green and sandy. On the coast, between Dell and Eoropie, are several small sandy bays, from which the natural arch at Roinn a'Roidh can be seen. Just beyond the arch is **Luchruban,** the tidal 'pigmy's isle'. Its claim to occupation by small

Clach an Trushal, the tallest standing stone in the Hebrides

people is unfounded, as the bones found here were more likely the remains of food consumed by the occupant of an ancient stone cell, the remnants of which can still be seen. It is from the small harbour at Port of Ness that the men of the district leave every August to bring back guga (young gannet), considered quite a delicacy, from Sula Sgeir, 41 miles to the north.

The most northerly village in the Outer Hebrides is Eoropie. The key to the restored 12thC Church of St Moluag (Teampull Mholuidh), in a field to the north, can be obtained from the store.

The red brick lighthouse and white foghorn tower at the Butt of Lewis, which became automatic in April 1997, stand above the rocky northern tip of the island. 44 miles north-north-east is the tiny island of Rona (North Rona), and 200 miles north are the Faeroes. To the south-east of the Butt is the attractive tiny Port Sto.

Heading south-west from Barvas the road passes Loch Mor Barvas, a refuge for wildfowl, before reaching Arnol. At the far end of the township is The Black House museum. This *tigh dubh,* last occupied in 1964, has walls six-feet thick, with a roof of thatch over turf, weighted with ropes and stones. A peat fire burns in the centre of the floor, and there is no chimney. These structures were warm, dry and quiet when the wind outside howled. Visitors see authentic room settings, including straw-lined box beds. Arnol stands at the edge of the machair (see Harris), where the crofts are divided by stone dykes. The original settlement, along with others on this western seaboard of Lewis, was closer to the sea, on a site occupied since the 1stC AD, but winter storms and the exhaustion of the peat beds resulted in re-siting during the 18thC. Nearby Loch na Muilne, a mill loch, powered several of the township's water-mills.

By the roadside at Bragar there is a whalebone arch some 20-ft high – suspended from it is the harpoon that killed the whale. The children of Shawbost, the next village, made a splendid folk museum for the 1970 Highland Village Competition which is now housed in a converted church to the south of the road.

By the coast at Carloway is the village of Garenin. At the end of the road, above a sheltered shingle bay, this the last remaining street of black houses in Lewis (in fact, some are white houses – *tigh geal* – the dry stone walls having been cemented, and the roofs tarred). The last family left here about 1973. The buildings are now being actively preserved by the Garenin Trust, and one has been converted into a Hebridean Hostel by the Gatliff Trust. It is expected that all will be restored by the year 2000.

Doune Carloway is a well-preserved broch with the tallest part of the wall standing over 22ft high and a diameter of 47ft. The galleries, staircase and entrance can be clearly seen, and the view from it is superb. A new visitor centre is being constructed here.

The main road now heads south along the side of East Loch Roag, which is scattered with low-lying islands. Between Carloway and Breasclete the land becomes more hilly with many small lochs. Tucked away by the shore is the pretty village of Tolsta Chaolais. What was once the shore station for the Flannan Isles lighthouse stands in Breasclete. The fish drying plant here is now used for research into and manufacture of anti-cancer drugs and pharmaceuticals, using vegetable and fish oil derivatives.

At the head of East Loch Roag is Callanish, site of a stone circle erected almost 5000 years ago – older, in fact, than Stonehenge. The monoliths make a rough Celtic cross 405ft north to south, 140ft east to west. 47 are now left, the tallest over 15ft high, and within the central circle is a cairn where the remains of a cremation were found. It was not until 1857, when five feet of peat was dug away, that the original height and extent of the stones was seen. Various theories exist regarding their true purpose – at present the astro-archaeologi-

cal one seems the most credible. Professor Gerald Hawkins, an American astronomer, has used a computer to verify 12 significant astronomical alignments, one of the main ones being mid-summer moonset, south along the main avenue, over Clisham on Harris. Whereas Stonehenge seems to relate to the sun, Callanish seems to relate to the moon. There is still much more research to be done before firm conclusions can be drawn and such studies will have to include the many other smaller stone circles in the area which also align with Callanish. A local legend claims that the stones are really giants, petrified by St Kieran for refusing to be christened. The new visitor centre here is open daily.

After Garynahine, the main road traverses the central moorland on its way to Stornoway, a minor road leaving it to head south-west to Great Bernera and Uig, and soon crossing the Abhainn Grimersta river, which is fed by the remote Loch Langavat and acknowledged as one of the best salmon rivers in Europe. To the north is the hilly and loch-strewn island of **Great Bernera** in Loch Roag. It is the largest of over 40 islands in the loch, the other notable ones, all uninhabited, being **Little Bernera, Vuia Mór, Vacsay** which had a population of nine in 1861, **Pabay Mór** (population of 17 in 1861) where there are the remains of a church, and **Drasay** which once had a population of two. This whole area surrounding Loch Roag is, without doubt, one of the most attractive parts of Lewis. The many freshwater lochs make good fishing for brown trout, and the mountains to the south-west are the haunt of golden eagles, peregrine falcons and buzzards. Great Bernera is a lobster-fishing centre and, in 1972, a fish-processing plant was built at Kirkibost on the east side. The name most common on the island is MacDonald, said to be descendants of a watchman who was given the island as reward for his services to the MacAulays of Uig. The bridge was opened in 1953 after the islanders threatened to construct a causeway themselves by dynamiting the cliffs.

There is a small sheltered beach, facing Little Bernera, beyond the deserted village of Bosta. Archaeologists have uncovered a circular dwelling on Bost beach which probably dates from the Iron Age and is now hopefully to be scheduled as a National Monument. It was originally believed to be a single wheelhouse home, but more dwellings have now been uncovered. Dating from 300AD, it is thought to have been occupied by the 'rabbit people'. Eventually it is planned to open the site to the public, with artifacts from here being displayed in the museum in Bernera.

To the north-west is the island of **Bearasay,** retreat of Neil MacLeod, who defeated the Fife Adventurers (merchants who tried to take over the island in the 16thC to exploit the herring fishing), but who later turned pirate and was eventually executed.

To reach Uig the road passes round Little Loch Roag through typical peat and rock scenery. At Carishader, on the west shore of Loch

Traigh na Berie, Lewis

Roag, the scenery again becomes attractive. Behind Miavaig the road passes through the surprisingly lovely, steep-sided, green and rocky Glen Valtos – a glacial meltwater channel. A minor road completes a circuit of Cliff, Valtos, Reef and Uigen. There are superb beaches here, especially the dune-backed shell sands of Traigh na Berie, sheltered by Pabay Moy and Vacsay. To the north of Glen Valtos is the township of Aird Uig, and Gallan Head. The Flannan Isles are 21 miles north-west into the Atlantic.

The Uig Sands are beautiful – wide, clean, flat and well sheltered – access is good, and the grassland at the back of the beach is flat enough for a football pitch. The whole is overlooked by the cream-painted and slated Uig Lodge and the superbly sited school at Timsgarry. A hand-carved walrus-ivory chess set of Norse origin dating back to about 1150 was found in 1831 at Ardroil, by a herdsman whose beast uncovered it in the dunes. Parts of the set are now in the British and the Scottish National Museums. The Brahan Seer, Kenneth MacKenzie, was born at Uig, and became famous for his detailed prophesies.

The view inland from Uig, along the glen between Mealisval and Tahaval, is a dramatic and refreshing change from the peat moors of the north. The road ends at Brenish. Beyond here was Tigh nan Cailleachan Dubh (house of the black old woman), a Benedictine convent possibly associated with Iona. To the south is **Mealasta Island,** lying about half a mile off the coast, where the mountains drop steeply to the sea.

To the south of Stornoway is the parish of Lochs, aptly named as, in parts, there seems to be more water than land. It is best seen early or late in the day when the water appears like mercury against the dark peat moor. The coast here is steep and rocky with no beaches, and narrow sea lochs cut deeply into the land – Loch Seaforth, for example, brings salt water some 12 miles inland.

The most rewarding areas of this parish are well off the main road. To the north of Loch Erisort lies the smaller inlet of Loch Leurbost with the villages of Leurbost, Crossbost, Ranish and Grimshader all attractively sited to the north and linked by a loop road. The seaward end of the lochs are littered with small islands.

Further south, a minor road connects with Keose and the alginate factory, where seaweed collected from around the island is processed. Alginate from here apparently went to the moon – fire-proofing the astronauts' notepads. Beyond the crofting township of Balallan, which straggles along the road for two-and-a-half miles, a splendid road sign names no less than 11 villages to be found by following the route along the southern shore of Loch Erisort to Cromore, Marvig and Lemreway. The first habitations to be passed are Habost, Kershader and Garyvard, all refreshing places, with grass, conifers and rowan.

At Cromore, **Eilean Chaluim Chille,** with its ruined church dedicated to St Columbia and small burial ground, can be seen. The main road finishes at Lemreway, situated at the back of a bay sheltered by **Eilean Iubhard.**

To the south of Loch Erisort and to the east of Loch Seaforth, is the treeless Park (or Pairc) deer forest, where herds of red deer roam freely. It was here, in 1887, that one of the last uprisings of the Crofters' War (which began with the Battle of the Braes on Skye) took place. The crofters, desperate for more land, killed 200 deer to draw attention to their plight – and entertained invited journalists to roast venison in order to obtain wide coverage by the press. The leaders of the Deer Raid were later tried and found not-guilty of mobbing and rioting. The 57,000 acre estate is still privately owned and is used for hunting, fishing and little else.

The whalebone arch at Bragar

Harris

With a population of 2200, Harris is separated from Lewis by the deep intrusions of Loch Seaforth and Loch Resort, and six miles of mountainous and treeless deer forest, rising to a height of 2622ft at the summit of Clisham, the highest point in the Outer Hebrides. North Harris is separated from South Harris by the narrow neck of land at Tarbert, where two sea lochs almost cut the island in two.

Gneiss, the rock of the Outer Hebrides, is nowhere more apparent than on Harris, always visible even if covered here and there with peat or water or strewn with boulders. It is only on the west coast that a narrow border of machair brings some relief. Machair is the low-lying, sometimes undulating, land behind the dunes and the stabilising fringe of marram grass. It consists of as many as 50 types of flowering plants among grass, growing on wind-blown shell sand. Its fertility is enhanced by animal dung and the spreading of seaweed manure. It is easily damaged by overgrazing and the erosive effects of rabbits and of wheeled vehicles.

Untilled, the soil forms a layer about six inches thick, uniform and free from stones. With cultivation and the addition of seaweed it often reaches a depth of 12 inches. The wind is constantly spreading fresh shell sand over the machair – a natural dressing of lime. On these gneiss islands, the fertile machair is a vital land resource. In early summer, when in flower, it is brilliantly coloured and is so heady with perfume that it is said it can flavour the milk of grazing dairy cattle. Against the blue sea and the white shell-sand beaches, it is magical.

The people of Harris, although said to have the same Norse ancestry as Lewis, have a different dialect, with fewer words of Norse derivation and spoken with a softer lilt. The island was held by the MacLeods of Harris from the time of the Norse surrender in the 13thC until 1779, when it was sold to Captain Macleod of Berneray. He invested in a fishing industry for the island, building the harbour at Rodel and numerous roads, as well as restoring Rodel church and planting many trees. The Earl of Dunmore purchased Harris in 1834, later selling the north to Sir Edward Scott in 1868 and the south to Lord Leverhulme in 1919. After the latter's scheme to revitalise the island and its fishing industry failed in 1923, much of the land was sold to absentee landlords who sold off assets, built by Lord Leverhulme, with scant regard for the indigenous population. Eventually some of the land that was cleared in the 19thC was purchased by the Government and returned to the crofters.

East Loch Tarbert, Harris

Before the Clearances the population had risen far beyond that which the land could reasonably support and living standards were intolerably low. Such were the pressures that lazybeds, strips of fertile soil built by hand on top of the rock and used for growing potatoes and oats, were stretching 500ft up the hillsides in places. In the 19thC depopulation was seen as the only possible way of raising living standards.

The main occupations today are crofting, weaving (Harris Tweed originated here but the centre of production is now Lewis), knitting, fishing and little else. As a result, depopulation continues steadily, with many young people leaving to find employment elsewhere.

Tarbert is the largest village. There are shops, some selling knitwear and tweed, a post office, hotel and ferry terminal. The Caledonian MacBrayne ferry *Hebridean Isles* links with Uig on Skye, and the ferry *Loch Bhrusda* links Leverburgh with Otternish (Newtonferry) on North Uist. The Tourist Information Centre is open during the summer, and there is hostel accommodation at Kyles Stockinish (SYHA) and Rhenigidale (Gatliff Trust).

NORTH HARRIS

East Loch Tarbert is littered with many rocks and islands, the largest of which are **Scotasay**, which had a population of 20 in 1911 but is now deserted, and the thriving Scalpay, reached via the ferry from Kyles Scalpay. The road to the ferry winds along the north side of the loch, past crofts forged out of the barren ground. Many now have well-tended gardens – in one, two small palm trees grow. A path from Urgha leads north along Laxadale Lochs to Maaruig on Loch Seaforth.

To the north of West Loch Tarbert are the high bare mountains of the Forest of Harris. On the shore, beneath Clisham, is Bunavoneadar where there are the remains of a whaling station built by Norwegians about 1912. It was utilised by Lord Leverhulme as part of his revitalisation scheme, being finally abandoned in 1930.

The narrow road winds around the head of Loch Meavaig, where the view north along the glen, between the steep and craggy sides of Oreval (2172ft) and Sron Scourst (1611ft), is quite dramatic. In a beautiful and isolated position above the township of Meavaig stands the corrugated-iron school, neat, tidy and painted cream. Here the children learn and play looking out towards **Soay Beag, Soay Mór** and **Taransay**, a fine prospect.

Beyond Cliasmol, with its maze of lazybeds, is the baronial-style Amhuinnsuidhe Castle (pronounced Ah-vin-soo-ee), standing by the pretty inlet of Loch Leosavay. Built by the Earl of Dunmore in 1868, the castle is of attractive warm-grey stone imported into Harris. The road approaches the castle through white gates and passes the where the waters of Loch Leosaid tumble into the sea. Here, in June and July, salmon can be seen leaping. The west entrance to the grounds is through a fine archway, beyond which there is a sturdy terrace of stone houses and stables. The castle gardens are planted with shrubs and lilies, and pheasants wander among the trees. It was at Amhuinnsuidhe Castle in 1912 that James Barrie, the Scottish author and dramatist, conceived of the drama *Mary Rose,* inspired, it is said, by one of the small islets in Loch Voshimid, four-and-a-half miles to the north-east.

Most of this part of Harris, including the castle, is privately owned. The herds of red deer that roam the hills are carefully protected, the lochs are rich with salmon and trout, and golden eagles and ravens haunt the peaks. The castle is available for weekly lets to those who can afford it.

A mile inland from Amhuinnsuidhe, Loch Chliostair feeds a new hydroelectric power station which supplies most of Harris. The arch dam built here was the first of its type in the Outer Hebrides. The road proceeds north-west through an area of peat before reaching the small crofting community of Hushinish. To the west of the superb beach, low cliffs of rose-coloured gneiss shelter guillemots, shags and fulmars. Cattle and sheep graze behind the dunes. When a strong southerly wind blows, the sands spread everywhere, sometimes burying the road. A short distance to the north a small pier serves the island of **Scarp,** first settled around 1810, but abandoned by its last remaining crofters on 2nd December 1971. The population peaked at 160 in 1901 – in the 1940s the population was still over 100, but the cottages are now used only as holiday homes. This rocky island rises to a height of 1011ft in the north; the 'village' is sheltered from the prevailing winds by a smaller hill in the east of the island. In 1934, well before the army brought its missiles to South Uist, an experiment was conducted here by Gerhard Zucha to see if mail could be sent to and from Scarp by rocket. On the first firing, celebrated with a special stamp issue, the projectile exploded on impact and most of the mail was damaged. The service ceased. Several small islands lie offshore. Five miles to the south-west is the low-lying islet of **Gasker,** which has a seal colony.

SOUTH HARRIS

The eastern coastline, known as Bays, is broken with narrow sea lochs and many small islands; inland the gneiss is spattered with hundreds of small lochs. The coast road (or Golden Road, so called because it was so expensive to build) winds through this dramatic heather-clad and rock-strewn landscape where boulders balance precariously on hill slopes and small dwellings nestle in dips and hollows.

Many crofters came here when the fertile land in the west was cleared for sheep, having to grow their food where none had grown before. They collected seaweed and mixed it with peat, arranging the whole in raised beds for drainage. The mixture weathered into compost and, on these lazybeds, oats and potatoes were grown. Gradually the beds were enlarged, running far up the hillsides in places, and the seaweed had to be carried further and further. A few sheep were grazed among the rocks. In the crofters' favour was the broken coastline which provided shelter for their boats and enabled them to catch herring and lobster, and the freshwater lochs which supplied trout.

But life was never easy, and neither was death. So intractable is the ground that the dead had to be taken to the west coast for burial. Here we are privileged to see a land where men and women have literally forged their existence on bare inhospitable rock and the sight is an inspiration. Now that life is a little easier, there is time to grow a few flowers by the croft – a fine sight amongst these bare hills.

At Drinishader, to the west of East Loch Tarbert, Mrs Alex MacDonald wove tweed that was presented to the Queen, Elizabeth II. Beyond Grosebay is Kyles Stockinish where a youth hostel overlooks **Stockinish Island.** The small inlet on the island is used as a lobster pond.

From Loch Flodabay the Shiant Isles can be seen 18 miles to the north-east, their tall cliffs rising steeply from the sea. After Loch Finsbay the road rises around the foot of Roinebhal (1506 ft) from

South Harris, looking towards Roinebhal

which the whole panorama of the coast and the lochs can be seen. There is now the prospect of a 'super quarry' here, a project causing the usual arguments between those in favour of the creation of local jobs and those concerned about the degradation of a fragile environment. If the project goes ahead, most of the mountain will be quarried away over a period of sixty years, leaving a vast new harbour.

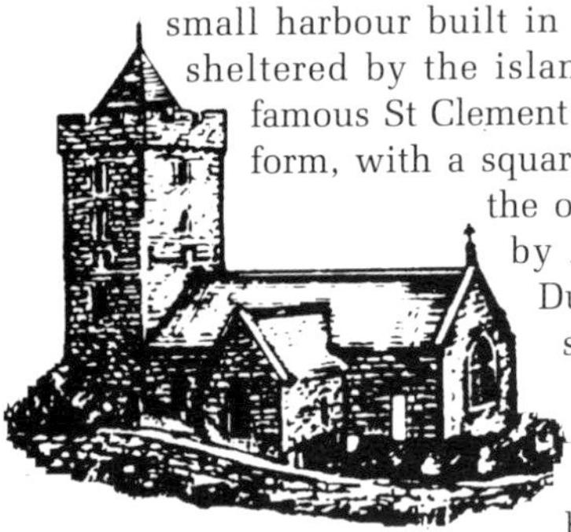

The village of Rodel, a mile or so north of Renish Point, has a small harbour built in the late 16thC by Captain Macleod, sheltered by the island of Vallay and overlooked by the famous St Clement's Church, the plan of which is cruciform, with a square central tower, making it unique in the outer isles. It was built in about 1500 by Alasdair Crotach, 8th MacLeod of Dunvegan in Skye, using mellow green sandstone, some imported from Mull. His effigy, sculpted in 1528, lies in a fine arched recess tomb, beautifully and simply carved. The church has been twice restored, in 1787 and 1873. Regrettably, the Rodel Hotel stands empty and forlorn.

Two-and-a-half miles north-west of Rodel, through Gleann Shranndabhal, is Leverburgh, formerly Obbe. The name was changed when Lord Leverhulme tried to revolutionise the fishing industry here. He chose Obbe, on the Sound of Harris, because it gave equal access to both the waters of the Atlantic and the Minch, so that his boats could always find sheltered water in which to fish. He planned to blast away many of the rocks and skerries that make the waters of the sound so treacherous, and he built factories and houses for his workers. The initial catches of herring exceeded expectation but the project never really worked well. He sold out in 1923, and within two years all activity had stopped. A small passenger ferry crosses the sound to Berneray and Newtonferry on North Uist.

At the eastern end of the South of Harris are the small green islands of **Gilsay, Lingay, Scaravay** and **Groay**. The two largest islands in the Sound are **Killegray**, which once had a population of five, and **Ensay**, which once supported 15 people. Both have houses still standing, and attractive beaches. On Ensay there is a private Episcopal chapel by the house, with a fine oak door carved by Robert Thompson of Kilburn in North Yorkshire, and Viking relics have been uncovered. In summer these two islands are grazed by sheep, and visited occasionally by the holidaying Royal Family.

After Leverburgh, the road passes through Glen Coishletter. As the summit is reached acres of glorious cream shell sand come into view, sheltered by the great bulk of Chaipaval to the west, rising to 1201ft. It is an extremely pleasant walk through the crofting land and up to the top. The view is splendid – on a clear day St Kilda can be seen some 45 miles to the west and the Skye Cuillins 50 miles south-east. The small island of **Coppay**, which has a seal colony, can be seen one-and-a-half miles to the west. The Scarista Hotel, opened in 1978, offers fresh food and comfortable accommodation.

The road along the west coast crosses the machair behind the beaches. The crofts look prosperous, with sheep and cattle grazing nearby. The beach at Borve is excellent; at its southern end there is a standing stone. Standing in a hollow sheltered by woods planted by the Earl of Dunmore, Borve Lodge was occupied by Lord Leverhulme during his time on the island. A mile offshore is the handsome island of **Taransay** – two large humps joined by a narrow neck of dunes – where cattle and sheep can be seen grazing by the shore. Its settlement of Piable once had a population of 76, which gradually dwindled until the last family left in 1942, although it was later re-inhabited and once again abandoned in 1974. The school, by the landing, closed in 1935. Taransay once had two chapels, one dedicated to St Taran, where women were buried, the other to St Keith, where men were interred. It is said that a mixed burial in one of the grave yards resulted in a body being found on the surface the following morning. In the south west is Aird Vanish, a lonely place with sea caves and a wild storm beach.

There are more fine creamy shell sands at Traigh Seilebost, backed by a spit of dunes, which in turn are backed by the estuarine sands of Traigh Luskentyre. On the northern shore, behind the dunes, is the township of Luskentyre.

The road skirts the southern side of the estuary, passing saltings and then crossing a causeway before climbing between the South Harris Forest and the wild hills to the south. The view back towards Taransay is magnificent, especially when the sea thrift is in bloom.

South Harris is an area of stark contrasts and is worthy of much exploration. There are fine rough walks along the harsh eastern seaboard and through the central hills and lochs. In summer, if the wind drops and the sun shines, the beaches on the west, backed by the machair in flower, are perfect for a day by the sea. The whole is unspoiled, undeveloped and uncrowded.

Scalpay

Situated off Harris at the mouth of East Loch Tarbert, Scalpay has a population of about 380 and the main industry is fishing – once for herring, but now for prawns. All the habitations are on the western seaboard and the pressure of so many people on the land resulted in extensive lazybed cultivation, although most are now unused. A fine natural harbour is situated in the north-west with another on the west. On **Eilean Glas,** in the far south-east, there has been a lighthouse since 1788 – the first in the Western Isles but now superseded by a 19thC light. This is now automatic. The original keepers houses, built of Aberdeen granite by Robert Louis Stevenson's grandfather, are now let to holiday visitors.

The Scalpachs are a tight-knit and vigorous community with a strong attachment to their little island. Enlightened leadership and modest and timely investments in new equipment have allowed them to maintain their viability during periods of considerable change in the fishing industry. Bonnie Prince Charlie came here, on his way to Stornoway, after his defeat at Culloden in 1746. Donald Campbell, a farmer, gave him refuge and the use of his boat.

A new £7 million, 325-yards-long, bridge, completed in the autumn of 1997 and also carrying a new water main, has now made a *permanent* connection with Harris.

North Uist

With a population of 1800, and an area of 75,000 acres, this is a low-lying island, deeply incised in the east by the sea and so liberally endowed with freshwater lochs that half the area is covered by water, reflecting so much light that colours seem to glow and shimmer in the sun. Rising from this anglers' paradise are North and South Lee (860ft and 922ft respectively) and, further south, Eaval (1138ft), the highest point on the island. In the north and west a few low hills give way to wide sandy bays with tidal islands, backed by tracts of machair, particularly attractive in the spring and early summer. With no high ground in the west, the prevailing winds blow unchecked.

After the period of Norse occupation, North Uist was ruled by the MacRuairidhs, followed by the MacDonalds of Sleat (Skye) whose official title was confirmed by James IV in 1495. They held the island until 1855, when it was sold to Sir John Powlett Ord who split the estate. It is now all owned by the enterprising Lord Granville, a cousin of the Queen.

In the early 19thC there were almost 5000 people living on the island, but a decline in population over the last 160 years has continued. Evictions were carried out around 1850 under the direction of Lord MacDonald of Sleat, whose conduct as a landowner did him little credit. Police constables were brought to the island, cottages were burned and a bloody fight took place between the police and the crofters near Malaclete. The church minister was conspicuous by his absence during this time.

In recent years the economy has been fairly well balanced, with a spread of activities including crofting, fishing, the production of alginates, weaving and knitting, and bulb-growing has also been tried. A more recent venture is scallop farming. The crofts on North Uist are generally quite large, enabling them to be worked as a primary means of income, rather than on the part-time basis common elsewhere. There was once a large herring fishing fleet centred on Loch Maddy, but today the fishing industry is concerned mainly with lobsters and crabs, and is based on Grimsay. The alginate factory, opened in 1957, is at Sponish on Loch Maddy where local collectors bring seaweed for processing. Knitwear and tweed are produced both on an individual and collective basis. Look out for the 'Sea/Sky Chamber' on a site overlooking the sea. It was built by Sussex artist Chris Drury.

The islanders have been Protestant since the late 18thC, sharing their religion, strangely, with their more distant neighbours across the Sound of Harris rather than with the Catholics of South Uist and

North and South Lee, North Uist

Barra. The different religious communities live in total harmony.

The complex area of lochs in the east, both salt and fresh, and the salmon, sea trout and brown trout they contain, are a major attraction to anglers. Fishing is controlled by the North Uist Estate and the Newton Estate. A good place to start enquiries is the hotel at Lochmaddy, the main village and terminal for the Caledonian MacBrayne ferry *Hebridean Isles* from Uig (Skye). As well as the hotel, there are shops, a bank, post office, school and small hospital. The position of the village, which has a population around 300, at the back of Loch Maddy, is very attractive. There are two theories regarding the derivation of *maddy*. One claims it is from the two dog (maddy) shaped rocks at the entrance to the loch, the other that the loch is rich in a certain kind of shellfish called, in Norse, maddies. The village is the natural centre for touring the island and for fishing. A new arts centre and museum by the old harbour slipway now illustrates many facets of the island's history, with many fine photographs, exhibits and artifacts.

By the road, to the north-west, Blashaval rises to 358 ft. On its western slope are three standing stones called Na Fir Bhreige, the false men, said to mark the graves of three spies who were buried alive. The north side of Loch Maddy is reached across a narrow neck of land, and there are fine views over the many islands in the loch towards North and South Lee. The east coast of the promontory has a few small hills, and to the north, in the Sound of Harris, are the islands of **Sursay, Tahay, Vaccasay** and **Hermetray.** It was on the last that Charles I planned to establish a fishing station, but the outbreak of the Civil War brought the scheme to a premature end.

In Clachan Sands, to the west of the Newtonferry road, are the remains of the pre-Reformation church of St Columba and a burial

Shillay
Pabbay
SOUND OF HARRIS
SOUTH HARRIS
Leverburgh
Haskeir Islands
Boreray
Berneray
Udal
Vallay
Newtonferry
Griminish Point
Tigharry
Hosta
Malaclete
Hermetray
Hougharry
Loch nan Geireann
Balranald
NORTH UIST
LOCHMADDY
Paible
To Uig, Skye
Kirkibost Island
South Lee 922'
Loch Eport
Monach Islands
Baleshare
Teampull na Trionaid
Eaval 1138'
North Ford
Grimsay
Airport
Floddaymore
Balivanich
Ronay
Nunton
Rueval 409'
Rossinish
BENBECULA
Borve
Liniclate
Eochar
St Peter's Port
Wiay
South Ford
Army Missile Range
Loch Bee
Loch Càrnan
West Gerinish
Our Lady of the Isles statue
Howmore
Loch Skipport
Verran Island
Loch Druidibeg
Hecla 1988'
Ormiclate
Ormiclate Castle
UIST
Beinn Mhor 2034'
Rubha Ardvule
Bornish
Flora MacDonald's birthplace
Milton
Loch Eynort
SOUTH
Stuley
Daliburgh
Kilpheder
LOCHBOISDALE
Calvay
Orosay
To Oban & Mallaig
Garynamonie
Pollachar
Ludag
SOUND OF BARRA
ERISKAY
BARRA
0 Miles 10
To Oban & Mallaig

ground. Just behind Port nan Long is the broch, Dun an Sticir, last occupied in 1602 by Hugh MacDonald of Sleat (*see* Duntulm, Skye). The causeway to it can still be seen, but the building is now little more than a pile of stones. The easy climb to the summit of Beinn Mhor (625 ft), is well worthwhile; looking to the south-west the contrast between the loch-strewn east and the machair in the west can be clearly seen. At the northern tip of North Uist is the ferry port of Otternish, where the Caledonian MacBrayne ferry *Loch Bhrusda* connects with Berneray and Leverburgh on South Harris.

Of the three large islands visible from here – Berneray, Pabbay and Boreray – only the first is still inhabited (see below).

Pabbay, four-and-a-half miles off North Uist was once known as the granary of Harris. It once supported a population of over 300 who produced, among other things, whisky. The island was cleared for sheep and is now run as a farm from Berneray. It has a small herd of red deer and rises to a height of 643 ft on the northern side. On the southern shore is an old burial ground. A mile to the north are the small islands of **Shillay,** where grey seals breed.

Boreray, two-and-a-half miles north-west of Newtonferry, is one-and-a-half miles long by one mile wide, the highest point being 184 ft, and it has a large central loch. In 1841 it supported a population of 181, but it was evacuated by request in 1923, although one family changed its mind at the last minute, obtaining a holding of 87 acres. Until quite recently it was still being farmed by a resident family. Coins from the reign of James IV have been found in the sands.

The main road of North Uist skirts its north coast, passing between the white sands surrounding the tidal island of **Oronsay** and Loch nan Geireann. On one of the islands in the loch, Eilean-an-Tighe, the remains of a neolithic potter's workshop have been found. Acknowledged to be the earliest such example yet found in Western Europe, its size indicates it must have served quite a wide area. North Uist is rich in ancient sites; standing stones, stone circles and chambered cairns are spread profusely over the island. To the north of Grenitote, on the narrow peninsula of sand and machair, a team of archaeologists have excavated at Udal a site occupied from the Bronze Age until the Clearances. In the sea cliffs at the northern tip, Aird a'Mhorain, an incised cross and some cup marks (Bronze Age carvings of ritual significance) have been found. A freshwater spring here is known as the Well of the Cross. In the shallow waters of Loch Olavat, by Griminish, a submerged 5000 year old Neolithic village has been discovered, with timbers and foundations still appearing to be virtually intact.

The tidal island of **Vallay** (which had a population of 59 in 1841) is reached across the white sands of Vallay Strand. The fine grey-stone house on the island was built by Erskine Beveridge and is now the property of the North Uist Estate.

At the north-west corner of North Uist is Griminish Point, where there is a natural rock arch 30 ft high. Eight miles west-north-west are **Haskeir Island** and **Haskeir Eagach,** a small group with stacks and arches, frequented by grey seals and puffins. Lewis Spence based his book *Island of Disaster* around Haskeir Eagach, the most southerly of the group.

In Loch Scolpaig a small castellated folly stands on a green islet. It was built by Alex MacLeod, chamberlain to the MacDonald estates, who also erected the conspicuous Latin cross half a mile south-west at Kilphedder in 1830, after it was unearthed in a burial ground nearby. Beyond Loch Hosta (said to cover another drowned village) there is a vast area of dunes, and the small beach at Traigh Stir, opposite the loch, is quite beautiful. In the cliffs at Tigharry is the Kettle Spout, a spouting cave.

To the west of Balranald House, once the seat of the MacDonalds of Griminish, is the RSPB's Balranald Reserve. The varied habitat here includes the tiny island of **Causamul,** two miles offshore, a seal nursery and refuge for the winter duck population, and beaches, dunes, machair, marshes and freshwater lochs. A notable rarity often seen here is the red-necked phalarope. Access to the reserve is restricted; the summer warden resides at Goular, near Hougharry.

Tigharry, Hougharry and Paible are the main west-coast communities, an area of well-kept crofts and grazing land. Many of the graves of North Uist's nobility are to be found in the churchyard at Hougharry. Inland, on the southern slope of South Clettraval (436 ft), is Cleatrbhal a'Deas, a wheelhouse and chambered cairn.

To the south of Paible there are wide expanses of white sand around the tidal dune islands of **Kirkibost Island** (across the sands from the solid, square Westford Inn) and the larger **Baleshare** reached by a causeway. Its name means East Township – West Township was swept away by the same exceptional tide that widened the Sound of Pabbay, and also isolated the Monach Isles (eight miles west of Baleshare) once fordable at low tide. There are extensive beaches on Baleshare, and the remains of Christ's Temple. Hugh MacDonald of Baleshare is thought to have introduced the kelp industry (kelp, when burned, produces alkali) to the Hebrides in about 1735, which resulted in a period of prosperity until it collapsed in the first half of the 19thC.

The most important ecclesiastical remains on North Uist are at Carinish in the extreme south-west. Here stands the fine ruin of Teampull na Trionaid, a medieval monastery and college thought to have been founded by Beathag, daughter of Somerled, in the early 13thC, and later enlarged by the wife of John MacDonald of Islay, first Lord of the Isles, in 1350. It was rebuilt in the 16thC, destroyed after the Reformation, and rebuilt again in the 19thC. Many chiefs sent their sons to be educated here. Alongside is Teampull Clan A'Phiocair, the chapel of the Macvicars, teachers at the college. Close by are the Slochdanan cup marks and Feithe na Fala, the Ditch of

Teampull na Trionaid, North Uist

Blood, scene of a battle in 1601 between the MacLeods of Harris and the MacDonalds of Uist.

The main road south connects with Benbecula, but not before passing right through a stone circle on a slight rise, half a mile from Carinish. To the south of Loch Eport, the road through the small community of Locheport passes the five chambered cairns and stone circle of Croineubhal Craonaval, before finishing about one-and-a-half miles from the steep and rocky western side of Eaval, which can only be climbed via its eastern slope (Loch Obisary cuts off any approach from the north and west). The view from its summit is more than adequate compensation for the steep climb.

The road to the north of Loch Eport passes Ben Langass (295ft), the only hill between Clachan and Lochmaddy. Conspicuous on its slope is Langass Barp, a neolithic chambered cairn which, although partially collapsed, can, with care, be entered. Around the western side of the hill can be found Pobull Fhinn, Finn's People, a stone circle above Loch Langass.

The western tip of the low-lying island of **Grimsay** is linked to North Uist (and Benbecula) by the causeway opened in 1960. Prior to its opening, the sands of Oitir Mhor (north ford) could be crossed at low tide, although not without risk as the tide rises swiftly. Grimsay is a lobster-fishing centre, with a large storage facility built in 1968. Live lobsters can be taken to the airport four miles away to arrive fresh in the fish markets within a few hours.

To the east of Grimsay the largest of several islands is **Ronay,** rising to a height of 377 ft, and uninhabited since the 1920s, although it once supported 180 people before being cleared in 1831. Fishermen were buried by the Lowlander's (St Michael's) Chapel.

Hostel accommodation is available at Lochmaddy (SYHA) and Claddach Baleshare (Gatliff Trust).

Berneray

This splendid island, a favourite holiday haunt of HRH Prince of Wales since 1987, is three miles long and one-and-a-half miles wide. The population of about 140 live in well-kept, white-painted houses on the eastern side. Although lying close to North Uist, it forms part of the Parish of Harris and is still privately owned. The island is green (there is no peat) with superb beaches. Prior to the 16thC it was almost connected to Pabbay, but strong tides swept the sands away. The people are crofters, lobster fishermen and knitters and support a campaigning and active community council. At the heart of the island is the new community centre, well known for its rousing ceilidhs. A small café is run here, and there are toilets. An excellent tea room is situated on the road to the car ferry terminal.

The oldest building on the island is the Gunnery of LacLeod, birthplace of the Gaelic scholar Norman MacLeod. The nearby school has one teacher and 15 pupils. The church to the north was built by Telford in 1827. Close by the community centre is the Chair Stone, in legend a place of execution. A standing stone, Clach Mhòr, overlooks Traigh Bhulrgh, on a sacred site associated with Saint Columba and Saint Maolrubha. The Giant MacAskill's house stood by the southern shore. Born in 1825, he stood fully 7ft 9ins tall in perfect proportion. In 1849 he toured with Barnum & Bailey's Circus. There is a post office and shop on the island, and a minibus service. The Caledonian MacBrayne ferry *Loch Bhrusda* connects with Otternish on North Uist and Leverburgh on Harris, and calls at the new harbour, maintaining regular links with Berneray's larger neighbours. Work on a new £8.6 million causeway linking Berneray to North Uist is planned, and is hoped to be completed by the year 2000. The Gatliff Trust has a Hebridean Hostel on the island.

Benbecula

Benbecula's name derives from *Beinn a'bhfaodhla* (mountain of the fords), a reminder of days when the island was the stepping stone between the Uists. It is low-lying and wind-swept, with machair in the west and peat moorland in the east where the coast is deeply cut by sea lochs. The whole island is liberally endowed with freshwater lochs, making it, like its neighbours, a rewarding place for anglers and ornithologists.

There is a solitary hill, Rueval, a prominent landmark rising to 409 ft just north of the island's centre. On the south-east side of the hill is the cave where Bonnie Prince Charlie hid on 25 and 26 June 1746 while waiting for Flora MacDonald to organise his escape (see South Uist and Skye). The intrepid pair finally went over the sea to Skye from Rossinish, east of here. The easy walk to the top of Reuval is an excellent way to see the island, laid out beneath you like a map.

The indigenous population, a harmonious mixture of Protestant and Catholic numbering 1300 (plus 500 military personnel), have recently enjoyed a measure of prosperity thanks to the presence of the army at Balivanich. Whether these benefits will be long-term, and anything other than material, remains to be seen. The army base was established in 1958; in 1971 the missile range on South Uist and attendant facilities were expanded at a cost of £22 million. Initially, and understandably, there was local resistance to the military presence, but a vigorous local campaign secured disturbance payments. Now the base has become an accepted part of the island's life to a degree that would leave a considerable vacuum were the Ministry of Defence to decide it was no longer needed.

Balivanich is the centre of activity on Benbecula – a cluster of regimented houses with a large NAAFI supermarket, shops, garages and other services, as well as a council office. To the north is the airfield, established by the RAF during World War II and now serving as an important link in the communications of these islands, with regular flights to Stornoway and Glasgow. It is manned by a small contingent of RAF technicians.

A main road crosses the island from north to south, but more interesting is the west-coast route which passes through the tidy crofts and farms. South of Balivanich is the Culla beach, beautiful cream sands backed by dunes, and behind these are the ruined walls of the 14thC Nunton Chapel. It was from Lady Clanranald at Nunton House that Bonnie Prince Charlie obtained his disguise as Betty Burke before leaving with Flora MacDonald from Rossinish on 28 June 1746. The road continues by the shore to Borve, where the ruined walls of the 14thC castle, once a Clan Ranald stronghold and occupied until 1625, stand in a field. To the south-west of the road are the barely visible remains of a chapel that once belonged to the castle. The MacDonalds of Clanranald held the island until 1839, when it was sold to Colonel Gordon of Cluny (*see* South Uist), whose family and trustees owned the island until 1942.

The impressive new community school at Liniclate educates 570 pupils from the surrounding islands, who previously had to board out on the Isle of Lewis. Facilities open to the public include a 25 metre swimming pool, a games hall, library, museum, theatre and cafeteria. From Liniclate a minor road heads south-east to the pier at Peter's Port, with another road branching north to Loch Uiskevagh. The south-east coast here is in complete contrast to the west with many small coves and rocky islands, the largest being **Wiay**, a bird sanctuary, which in 1861 had a population of six, but has been uninhabited since 1901. The pier at Peter's Port was built in 1896; it was then found that there was no road to it, and access by sea was dangerous. Later a causeway and a road were built, but the pier was hardly ever used – and remains a planner's folly. The main road passes through Creagorry, with its hotel and large food store, before crossing O'Reagan's Bridge (built in 1943 to serve the airfield) over the sands of South Ford to South Uist.

South Uist

The second largest island in the Outer Hebrides, having an area (including Benbecula and Eriskay) of 90,000 acres and a population of 2280, South Uist has a mountainous spine running almost the full length of its eastern side, rising to 2034ft at the summit of Beinn Mhor (Big Mountain, but known until the 19thC as Geideabhal, Goat Mountain, by the locals) and to 1988ft at the summit of Hecla. Four sea lochs cut deep into the east coast: Loch Boisdale, Loch Eynort, Loch Skipport (joining with the non-tidal Loch Bee to make the north-east tip virtually an island) and Loch Sheilavaig. The west coast has 20 miles of virtually unbroken beach, white shell sand backed by dunes and the springy grass of the machair, making for excellent coastal walking, usually with an invigorating salty breeze blowing off the clear, blue Atlantic. Between the mountains and the machair there is peaty moorland with many freshwater lochs, rich with salmon, sea trout and brown trout; however, fishing is strictly controlled. Here and there are deserted black houses, often looking more organic than man-made.

The main sources of income are crofting, fishing, fish and shellfish farming, alginates and the missile range. Seaweed is processed at North Lochboisdale, the wrack or tangle being collected from the east-coast bays, where great heaps are cast up after storms. Collection is done on a part-time basis, although the factory provides some full-time employment. The weed is also collected by crofters for their own use as fertiliser.

The Royal Artillery range is situated in the area west of West Gerinish and Loch Bee. It provides both direct employment, and work generated by the needs of the 500 or so military personnel. The islanders and soldiers are on good terms; compensation has been paid for land taken and disturbance caused, and, when the range is not in use, the grazing is made available.

The Hebrideans of South Uist are mainly Roman Catholic – small roadside shrines are visible evidence of this – and thus Sundays are a more lively affair than those on the Protestant islands further north.

The only village on the east coast is Lochboisdale (population 300) where the Caledonian MacBrayne ferry *Clansman* from Oban and Barra, and the *Lord of the Isles* from Mallaig and Barra, call. There are shops, a hotel, bank, school, police station and Tourist Information Centre. The village straggles westwards to Daliburgh, with crofts seemingly everywhere and cottages built quite often on rocky outcrops with scant regard for shelter – where the land is poor, the dwelling had to be built on the least fertile part of the croft.

Colonel Gordon of Cluny, who bought the island together with Benbecula and Eriskay from the MacDonalds of Clanranald (descendants of Ranald, the son of John, first Lord of the Isles) in 1838, was a particularly insensitive man. He cleared the islands for sheep, evicting crofters and forcing emigration. A few were given land, which was too poor for sheep, on Eriskay. During this period over 1000 emigrants left Lochboisdale on *The Admiral,* only to arrive in America destitute. Some of those evicted took to the hills, pursued by police. Between 1841 and 1861 the population of South Uist fell from 7300 to 5300. Later militant action by the crofters won them their present holdings. Today the whole 90,000 acre South Uist Estate is still privately owned.

At the mouth of Loch Boisdale is the island of **Calvay,** with a ruined 13thC castle where Bonnie Prince Charlie took refuge from the king's soldiers on 15 June 1746, and an automatic light replacing the original built in 1857. There is one main north-south road on South Uist which runs wide and straight beside the machair. It reveals little of the true character of the island, the most interesting parts of which are to be found by walking or driving down the narrow roads to the west and, occasionally, to the east.

South of Daliburgh, where there is a hospital, the main road finishes at Pollachar, the 'bay of the standing stone'. There is an inn here, with fine views towards Barra. South-west of Daliburgh, near Kilpheder, are the remains of a wheelhouse dating from the 2ndC AD, excavated in 1952. It has a circular plan, the hearth being the hub and stone piers at the rim supporting the spokes – wooden rafters. It was probably used as a farm house. Where the track from Kilpheder breaks into three near the sea, take the middle track. Over the dunes is a beautiful white beach. Further south along the main road, on a slight rise, is the church of Our Lady of Sorrows, built by the Barra priest Calum McNeil in 1963. The Garrynamonie school nearby will be long remembered for Frederick Rea, headmaster between 1890-1913, who refused to acknowledge Gaelic and taught only in English.

At Mingary, to the east of the road, a track leads to Barpa

Loch Skipport, where the steamers once called

Mhingearraidh, a chambered cairn with a ring of pillar stones standing prominently on the slope of Reineval. Just north of Milton, a cairn and plaque inside low, ruined walls marks the birthplace of Flora MacDonald, the young woman who helped Bonnie Prince Charlie after his defeat at Culloden. The Prince left the mainland on 24 April 1746 with a price of £30,000 on his head. After many exploits in the Outer Hebrides, including being chased by a man o'war, and a three-day drunken debauch, he met Flora MacDonald, who agreed to help him. The Prince, disguised as Flora's maid 'Betty Burke', left Benbecula in a small boat for Skye on 28 June 1746. The ruin is worth visiting for its romantic associations and splendid view.

About two miles north of Milton, a minor road ends at Rubha Ardvule, the most westerly point on the island. This promontory contains a small lochan, the haunt of many waterfowl. Beneath the shingle there is said to be an old Norse stone causeway, revealed once when exposed by a storm. By Loch Bornish there is a small Roman Catholic church with a simple and dignified interior, the only decoration being behind the altar. Archaeologists working on a settlement here, dating from the 4th–9thC, have discovered fragments of bone containing letters in ogham script. Only half-a-dozen such examples have been found in Scotland. The minor road north through the crofts can be followed to Ormiclate Castle, a fine ruin standing in a farmyard. The unfortified building took seven years to build and burned down seven years later, on the eve of the Battle of Sherrifmuir in 1715, where the builder, Ailean MacDonald of Clanranald, was mortally wounded. Much still remains to be seen, including an armorial plaque in the north wall. Its site, overlooking the Atlantic, is superb.

Hecla and Beinn Mhór, South Uist

The little church near the west coast at Howmore has an unusual central communion pew and a fine interior. Nearby are the remains of Caibeal Dhiarmaid church (dedicated to St Columba), Caibeal nan Sagairt and Teampull Mor. On an islet in Loch an Eilein are the few remains of Caisteal Bheagram, a small 15th or 16thC tower. There is a Gatliff Trust hostel (under restoration) at Howmore, near the church.

The ridge between the peaks of Beinn Mhor and Hecla dominates the area; a walk along the top is a fine energetic day's work with, of course, excellent views, including Skye and the Cuillins to the east. On the southern slope of Beinn Mhor, beneath the lower summit of Spin (1168ft) is the wooded glen of Allt Volagir, full of birch and hazel, and brightened with violets and bluebells in the spring and Scottish primrose and Alpine gentian in summer.

The Loch Druidibeg Nature Reserve (total area 4145 acres) is just to the north of Drimsdale, stretching for four miles inland from the sandy shore, through the dunes and lime of the machair to the acid peat moorland around the loch. The shore of the loch is broken with many small peninsulas which, together with innumerable small islets, make an ideal habitat for many types of waterfowl. It is now the most important (and one of the last remaining) breeding grounds in the British Isles of the native grey lag goose. Also of interest is the differing flora of the two soil types; for instance the shallow calcareous lochs and marsh of the machair have a richer vegetation than their counterparts in the acid peat. A rarity, the American pondweed, has its only natural distribution in the British Isles in the Uists. A permit is required to visit the reserve.

The road east to Loch Skipport, along the northern edge of the reserve, is well worth exploring. The country is rugged heather, peat and boulders, with a small clump of conifers and rhododendrons hiding around a corner as a pleasant surprise. The road finishes with a steep descent to the decayed pier (built 1879) in the sheltered waters of Loch Skipport, where the steamers once called. The lighthouse at Rudha Ushinish became operational in 1857 and is now automatic. To the south is Nicolson's Leap, where legend has it that he leapt a 50ft gap to the stack holding the Clanranald Chief's son in his arms, after a liaison with the chief's wife. From this perch he bargained with his pursuer, and ultimately jumped, with the boy, into the sea below.

Beyond the nature reserve, the army missile range begins to make its presence felt. Firing, if you are there at the time (there are frequent periods of apparent inactivity), often results in sharp bangs and flashes over the sea. The longer-range missiles are tracked from St Kilda, over 40 miles to the north-west (*see* page 54).

On the slope of Rueval, The Hill of Miracles, is the 30-ft granite statue of Our Lady of the Isles by Hew Lorimer, erected in 1957 to commemorate Marian Year. The tall pillar-like Madonna and child look towards the missile range, and is itself overlooked by the range control installation (known as space city) at the summit.

The road crosses Loch Bee on a causeway. Mute swans can sometimes be seen on this large expanse of shallow water. It is noticeable that many of the small islets in the lochs throughout the Uists are covered with dense thickets of willow, hazel, rowan, and juniper growing among ferns, all thriving out of the reach of grazing sheep – an indication of what much of the island must have looked like before the hand of man fell so heavily upon it, clearing the trees and introducing sheep.

Eriskay

Eriskay (from the Gaelic *Eirisgeigh,* Eric's isle) is a small island, two-and-a-half by one-and-a-half miles, with a population of 160. The island was made famous worldwide by *The Eriskay Love Lilt* and other beautiful Gaelic melodies which originated here, and by the shipwreck of the *SS Politician,* which inspired Sir Compton Mackenzie's book, *Whisky Galore!* It also has its place in the romantic story of the ill-fated rising of 1745; the half-mile beach of Coilleag a'Phrionnsa on the west is where Bonnie Prince Charlie first set foot on Scottish soil, landing from *Du Teillay* en route from France to the Scottish mainland. The pink sea bindweed (*Calystegia soldanella*) which grows at the back of the beach, and on Vatersay, is said to have spread from seeds dropped by the Prince.

Eriskay belonged to the MacNeils of Barra until 1758, when it passed to the MacDonalds of Clanranald. Eriskay, Barra, Benbecula and South Uist were sold to Colonel Gorden of Cluny in 1838, who cleared the island for sheep but allowed a few evicted crofters to settle on Eriskay as it was too poor for grazing. Like the crofters of Harris, they made lazybeds of seaweed and peat, raised for drainage, on which they grew oats, barley and potatoes.

The main area of settlement is on the north coast, with another small township by the fine natural harbour in the east. The 180 people of this thriving community are Roman Catholic, take great pride in their well-maintained and brightly painted houses, and have a strong attachment to their native island. There is a shop, primary school, post office, church and pub with relics from the *SS Politician.* The main occupations, supplemented with crofting, are fishing (a small fleet takes herring, lobster, prawn and white fish) and the production by the women of hand-knitted sweaters, with patterns peculiar to Eriskay.

The sea around the island is quite shallow and unsuited to large vessels. It was therefore surprising when the 12,000-ton *SS Politician,* bound for New York with 24,000 cases of whisky on board, foundered to the east of Calvay, between Eriskay and South Uist. The islanders felt it their duty to salvage such a valuable cargo, and soon nearly everyone on the island, and some say the livestock as well, was drunk. What is less well known is that several islanders served prison sentences for possession of what was not theirs. Compton Mackenzie based his book *Whisky Galore!,* set on the fictional island of Todday, on these events. The classic Ealing comedy film of the same name was made on Barra in 1948. The seaweed-cov-

Eriskay

ered hulk of the stern of the ship is still visible when the tide is low.

The angelus at St Michael's Church, built in 1903 by Father Allen MacDonald, is rung on a bell recovered from the German battle-cruiser *Derfflinger,* scuttled at Scapa Flow, and the altar base is constructed from the bow of a lifeboat from the aircraft-carrier *Hermes.* Eriskay ponies, used on the island to carry peat and seaweed, are supposedly the nearest thing to a native Scottish breed still surviving. They stand 12 to 13 hands high and have small ears, but whether or not they are a native strain is not clear.

The ruin of Weaver's Castle on **Eilean Leathan** in the **Stack Islands,** off the southern tip, was once the base of the pirate and plunderer of wrecks, MacNeil. A vehicle ferry connects Eriskay with Ludag on South Uist, and a passenger ferry links with Ludag, and Eoligarry on Barra.

Barra

Barra has a population of 1300, and an area of 22,000 acres (including Vatersay). It has been suggested that the name may derive from *Finbar* (St Barr), a 6thC saint. The island is a microcosm of the whole of the Outer Hebrides, with a rocky and broken east coast, fine sandy bays on the west backed with machair, rising to a maximum height of 1260 ft at the tooth-like summit of Heaval. The whole is Archaean gneiss, heavily glaciated. Over 150 species of birds and 400 types of plants have been recorded here – figures comparable with the rest of the Outer Hebrides.

Following the Norse domination of the Hebrides, the MacNeils held Barra from 1427, receiving the charter from Alexander, Lord of the Isles. James IV confirmed this charter in 1495. During the 16thC they raided English shipping, and made forays into Ireland. Although taking no active part in the 1745 rising, the chief of the

Clan MacNeil was implicated in the revolt, imprisoned, but never prosecuted; in 1747 the clan moved to Eoligarry. When in debt in 1838, Roderick MacNeil sold the island to Colonel Gordon of Cluny (who had also bought Benbecula, South Uist and Eriskay), who offered the island to the Government as a penal colony – a further demonstration of his total lack of sensitivity towards the islanders. Deciding he was receiving insufficient rent, he undertook clearances in 1857 with the help of imported policemen, confiscating the crofters' stock and causing many emigrants to arrive destitute in the New World. Later land shortages led to discontent among the remaining crofters, with the result that the large farms were split.

The ancestral home of the MacNeils is the impressive medieval fortress of Kiessimul Castle, built on a rock outcrop in Castle Bay. A high wall encloses a keep, hall and chapel, providing shelter at the expense of any outward prospect. There has been a fortification on this site since the 11thC – the present building dates from the 15thC. In 1937 Robert Lister MacNeil, 45th Chief of the Clan MacNeil, purchased his ancestral home together with 12,000 acres of Barra. An architect, he restored the castle, which has now become a focal point for MacNeils all over the world. He died in 1970 and is buried in the chapel. Enquire at the Tourist Information Centre for details of visiting arrangements.

The basis of the island's economy is crofting, with both sheep and cattle being kept. There is a fishing fleet catching white fish, prawns and lobster.

When James Methuen began using Castle Bay as a port in 1869, at the start of the herring boom, the associated curing and packing industries brought great prosperity. Within 20 years as many as 450 boats, mainly from the east coast of mainland Scotland, were using the harbour, seeming to make a floating bridge to Vatersay. The resident fleet was ill-equipped to compete, but many Barra men were engaged as crew, and by 1911 the population of the island had risen to 2620. During the 1930s the industry declined, being halted finally by the outbreak of the Second World War.

The famous Sea League was formed here by Compton Mackenzie, who was then living on Barra, and John Lorne Campbell of Canna, in 1933, to protect local fishermen from illegal trawling in the Minch by the English. It

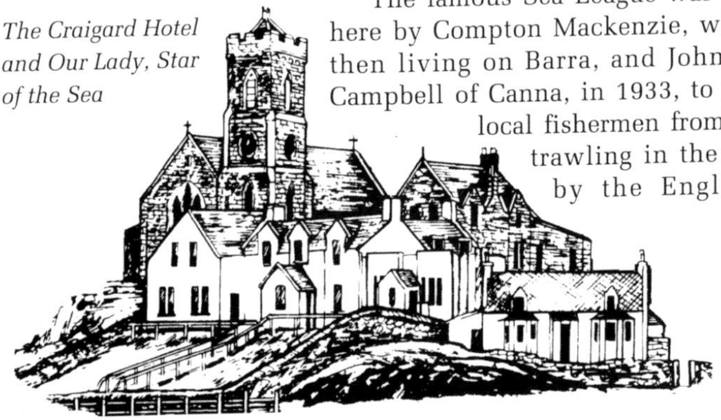

The Craigard Hotel and Our Lady, Star of the Sea

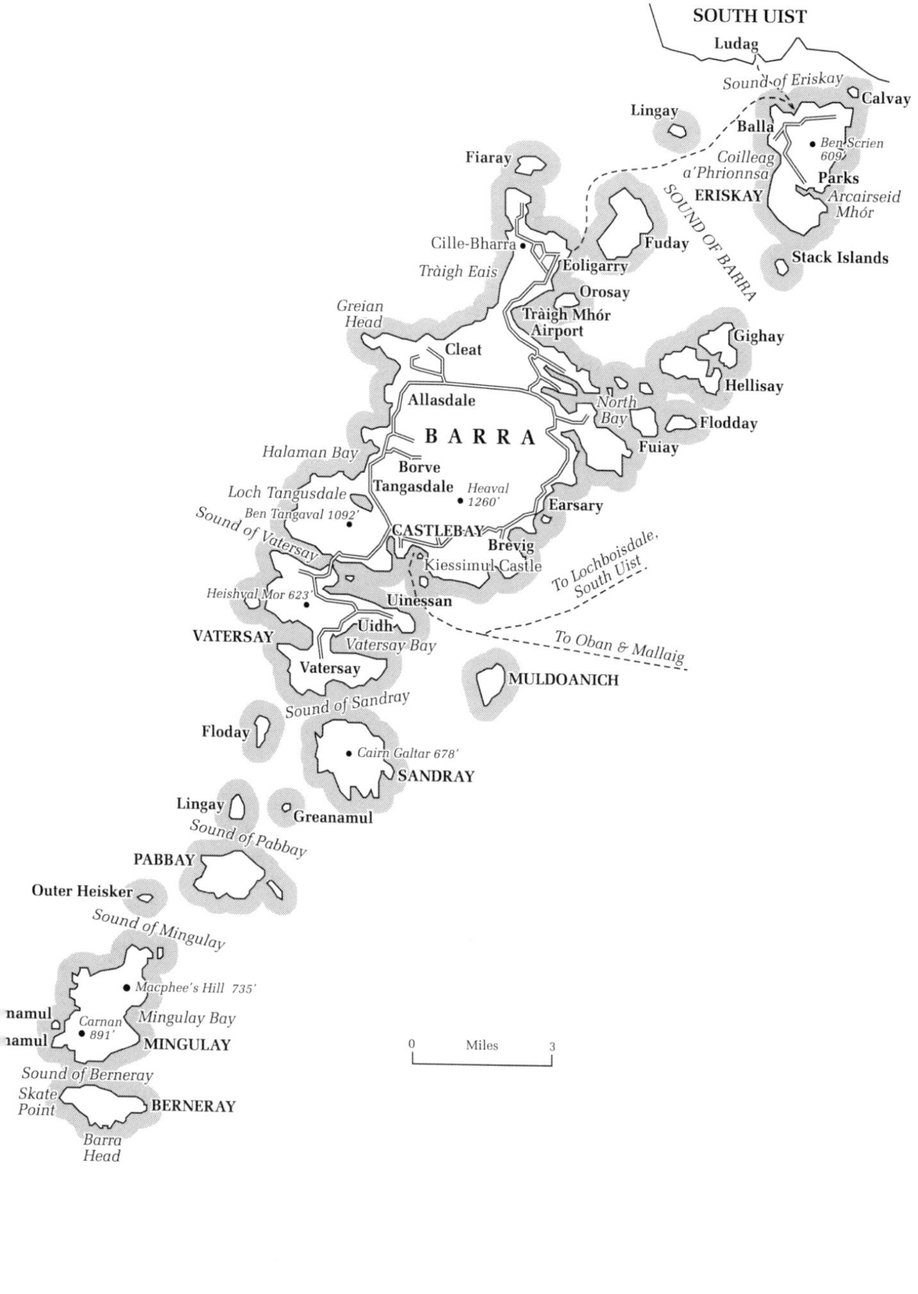
SOUTH UIST
Ludag
Sound of Eriskay
Calvay
Lingay
Balla
Ben Scrien 609'
Coilleag a'Phrionnsa
Parks
ERISKAY
Arcairseid Mhór
Fiaray
SOUND OF BARRA
Fuday
Cille-Bharra
Eoligarry
Stack Islands
Tràigh Eais
Orosay
Tràigh Mhór Airport
Greian Head
Gighay
Cleat
Hellisay
North Bay
Allasdale
Flodday
BARRA
Fuiay
Halaman Bay
Borve
Tangasdale
Heaval 1260'
Loch Tangusdale
Earsary
Ben Tangaval 1092'
Sound of Vatersay
CASTLEBAY
Brevig
Kiessimul Castle
To Lochboisdale, South Uist
Heishval Mor 623'
Uinessan
Uidh
VATERSAY
Vatersay Bay
To Oban & Mallaig
Vatersay
MULDOANICH
Sound of Sandray
Floday
Cairn Galtar 678'
SANDRAY
Lingay
Greanamul
Sound of Pabbay
PABBAY
Outer Heisker
Sound of Mingulay
Macphee's Hill 735'
Mingulay Bay
Carnan 891'
MINGULAY
Sound of Berneray
Skate Point
BERNERAY
Barra Head
0 Miles 3

pressed the Government for protective legislation but came up against stiff opposition from the English fishing lobby. Many young Barra men still go to sea, but now in either the merchant or Royal Navy or to the North Sea.

Other minor employment is found in the production of perfume, and knitwear, and the removal of shell grit from Traigh Mhor, for use as a building material and as chicken feed. This latter activity is the subject of some debate, as it is claimed that the continuing removal of shell is compromising the future use of the beach as the island's airstrip, with it's regular flights to Glasgow.

Most of the people are Catholic, and have been so since St Patrick founded the See of the Isles in the 5thC, which, until the 14thC, was united with the See of Sodor and (Isle of) Man. During the 17thC there was a degree of religious persecution, but the islanders clung steadfastly to their faith. Ministers of the church of Scotland have been present since 1734, and have been, for the most part, servile to the landowners, Rev. Henry Beaston (1847-71) particularly so during Colonel Gordon's clearances. Gaelic is spoken, although all the inhabitants are bilingual. The people are hardworking and unashamed in their pursuit of pleasure in contrast to their counterparts on Lewis. It is a very bright and cheerful place, seven days a week.

The main settlement is Castlebay, served by Caledonian MacBrayne's *Clansman* from Oban and Lochboisdale, and in the summer by the *Lord of the Isles* from Mallaig and Lochboisdale. There are several small hotels, shops, a mobile chip shop, a post office, Tourist Information Centre, a splendid new school incorporating a leisure centre and swimming pool, bank and hospital. A post bus runs to Eoligarry, via the east coast road. Castlebay faces south towards Vatersay, whilst sheltering it from the north is the mountain of Heaval, with a statue of the Virgin and Child, erected in 1954, on its south-east slope. It is not a difficult walk to the top, and the view of the islands to the south is very fine. The large church overlooking Kiessimul Castle, Our Lady, Star of the Sea, was built in 1889. Moored by the castle is the lifeboat, which serves some of the most difficult waters around the coast of Britain.

The other main areas of settlement are North Bay, Eoligarry, Borve and Earsary. Eoligarry, north of Traigh Mhor (known also as the Cockle Strand), is joined to the main body of the island by a neck of dunes. A small passenger ferry operates from the pier here to Eriskay and Ludag on South Uist. Above the grassland is Cille-bharra, the MacNeil burial ground. There are two roofless chapels by the restored church of St Barr, all possibly 12thC; Sir Compton Mackenzie is buried here. The views over the Sound of Barra, scattered with the islands of Fuday, Lingay and Eriskay, towards the mountains of South Uist are quite outstandingly beautiful.

To the north of the long white beach of Traigh Eais, a few stones

Eoligarry, Barra

mark the site of Dun Scurrival, a prehistoric galleried fort. Off the northern-most tip is the low-lying island of **Fiaray**; to the east is the grassy island of **Fuday**, its name possibly deriving from the Norse utey (outside isle). This latter had a population of seven in 1861, although it has been deserted since the turn of the century. It was used for Norse burials, and was the retreat of some of King Haakon's forces after their defeat at the Battle of Largs in 1263.

The coast around North Bay is rocky and deeply indented. On an islet not far from the road stands a statue of St Barr by Margaret Somerville, a local artist, erected in 1975. The largest offshore island, **Hellisay,** had a population of 108 in 1841, but it was last occupied in the 1880s. The name is Norse – caves isle. Beyond Hellisay is **Gighay** (Gydha's isle), rising to a height of 305ft; it also once had a small population. The road along the east coast winds around the many small bays, with lazybeds crammed in everywhere.

The west coast between Greian Head and Doirlinn Head is a series of white sand beaches, with Halaman Bay in the south being outstanding – a magical place at sunset. Behind the sands is the machair, rich with flowers and scent in the spring and early summer. At Allasdale, to the north, are the remains of Dun Cuier. Between Halaman Bay and Castle Bay, a path leads down to Loch Tangusdale (also called Loch St Clair), stocked with trout; the stump of Castle Sinclair, a small square tower, stands on an islet in the loch.

Barra's increasing population has made it possible for all essential services to be enhanced. Even though limited employment prospects for young people leads to a degree of emigration, many are returning and the future should harbour no fears for this particularly bright jewel of the Hebrides. The Gatliffe Trust is planning a hostel on Barra.

Vatersay

This is almost two islands, joined by a narrow neck of dunes and machair, with fine beaches in the bays thus formed. It is joined to Barra by a causeway built at a cost of £3 million. With a total population of 72, the main settlement is in the south – a picturesque shambles of cottages, wooden council houses, abandoned vehicles and grazing cattle. There is a post office and a public call-box here. To the north is the junior school, community centre, chapel and a few scattered cottages all linked by narrow metalled roads.

The economy is based on cattle and sheep. Until the causeway was completed cattle were tethered to boats and swum across to Barra, to be taken by the Caledonian MacBrayne ferry to the market at Oban. Subsequently they were taken by barge.

The population in 1861 was 32, but by 1911 it had risen to 288 due to an influx of immigrants from Barra and Mingulay. After falling to around 70 people and seeming to lose impetus in the early 1970s, it climbed to 100 but has again diminished.

Totally dependent upon Barra for medical services, secondary schooling and entertainment, many of the younger people were moving across the sound to live on the larger island. However, now that the islands are linked by road it is hoped that the population will once again grow.

At the turn of the century Vatersay was run as a single farm by tenants of Lady Gordon Cathcart, who only visited the island once during her 54 years of ownership. This was at a time of severe land shortage on Barra and South Uist. After pressure from the crofters, the Lady grudgingly parted with a small area of land at Eoligarry on Barra. Continuing unrest forced the Congested Districts Board to try to buy land on Vatersay to rent to the crofters. Finally, in desperation, on the 19 August 1906, one crofter, within one day, erected a wooden dwelling on Vatersay Farm, thatched it and lit a fire; under ancient law this gave him title to the land. Others followed suit. These Vatersay Raiders were brought to trial, but were subsequently released after a public outcry. In 1909 the Board finally purchased the whole island and divided it into 58 holdings.

The island rises to 625ft at the summit of Heishival Mor. Off the extreme eastern tip is the small tidal island of **Uinessan**, where once stood the church of Cille Bhrianain, known as Caibeal Moire nan Ceann, the chapel of Mary of the heads – a short-tempered lady who decapitated those who upset her. Two miles to the east, the dark hump of **Muldoanich** rises from the sea. It once had a chapel and

Vatersay Bay

was known in Gaelic as Maol Domhnaich, the island of the tonsured one of the Lord.

To the west of Vatersay, in 1853, 450 emigrants, many of them Hebrideans, lost their lives when the *Annie Jane* was wrecked. To the south of Vatersay all the islands, once known as the Bishop's Isles, are now uninhabited. Enquire at Castlebay TIC for details of trips to see Sandray, Pabbay, Mingulay and Berneray.

Sandray

The name means sand isle. It lies about one-half mile south of Vatersay, rising to a height of 678ft at the summit of Cairn Galtar. A strip of dunes lies parallel to the east coast. In the early 18thC, the island was divided into nine farms; by 1881 the population had fallen to ten, but rose to 41 in 1911 due to resettlement. It had been deserted since 1934. There was once an ancient chapel, known as Cille Bhride, on the island. To the west, are the small islands of **Lingay, Greanamul** and **Flodday,** the last having a natural arch.

Pabbay

Two-and-a-half miles south-west of Sandray, this is one of the many Priest's Isles in the Hebrides, with the summit rising to a height of 561ft, steep sea cliffs and a massive arched overhang. In 1881 the population was 26, with the settlement being on the eastern side above a shell sand beach. On 1 May 1897 all the able-bodied men were lost in a fierce storm at sea whilst long line fishing. The Mingulay boat survived the same storm. The island is now deserted. On the north-east corner are the remains of Dunan Ruadh, the red fort, and above Bagh Ban there was once a chapel and burial ground – still remaining are three cross-marked stones and one with a cross, a crescent and a lily. All are possibly Pictish. Some small islands lie to the south-west.

Mingulay

Taking its name from the Norse for big isle, Mingulay lies two-and-a-half miles south-west of Pabbay, and is two-and-a-half miles by one-and-a-half miles. It was once owned by MacNeil of Barra, who took care of his tenants – finding new wives for widowers, new husbands for widows, and making good the loss of any milking cow. The remains of the settlement can be seen on the east side, above the sandy Mingulay or Village Bay; the population peaked at 150 in 1881 when the island had its own new school building in the capable hands of John Finlayson, who had trained as a Free Church minister, but decided top spend his life with the Roman Catholic people of these southerly isles. Finlayson loved his life on this remote island, enjoying fishing and taking a great interest in the wildlife of the island. School inspectors often commented on the superb displays of sea shells, birds eggs and wild flowers which they found on their annual inspections. He died on the island in 1904. Sadly the population fell rapidly in the 1900s when many of the inhabitants joined the Vatersay Raiders. By 1912 the population abandoned the island, and it is now deserted. The priest's house is maintained, and the school house still stands, complete with privy-block.

On the western side, the sea cliffs are magnificent, Biulacraig being a sheer 700ft. Islanders once climbed these crags to harvest seabirds' eggs. There are many seabirds, including a large puffin colony, nesting among the ledges, stacks and caves. Two islets off the west coast, **Arnamul** and **Lianamul,** were once grazed by sheep, the latter being reached by a rope bridge.

The highest point is Carnan, rising to 891ft. Macphee's Hill (735ft) is named after a rent collector who landed on the island and found all the inhabitants dead from the plague. His companions rowed away in fear, leaving the unfortunate man on his own for a year, but MacNeil of Barra gifted him some land when the island was resettled. A Bronze Age stone cist (burial chamber), Crois an t'Suidheachain, has been uncovered on the island. Sheep are farmed on the island from Barra. Landings by small boat are easiest at the north end of Village Bay.

Berneray

The southernmost island of the Outer Hebrides and known as Barra Head, its tall sea cliffs (over 600ft at Skate Point) take the full brunt of the Atlantic waves, unbroken by shallow water. After severe gales, small fish are sometimes found on the grass at the top, and in 1836 a 42-ton rock was moved five feet by the force of a storm.

At the western end stands the Barra Head lighthouse, 680 ft above sea level, marking the end, or the beginning, of the Outer Hebrides. Granite to build the tower was quarried on the island. Near the lighthouse are the remains of two promontory forts. In 1881 the population was 57; now that the lighthouse is automatic, the island is unpopulated. The name Berneray is from the Norse, Bjorn's isle. 2000 miles to the west is Newfoundland.

The Hebridean Outliers

Although not served by any regular ferry services, these islands are a fascinating group. A visit to any one of them is a truly memorable experience, and will certainly repay the effort involved in getting there.

Flannan Isles

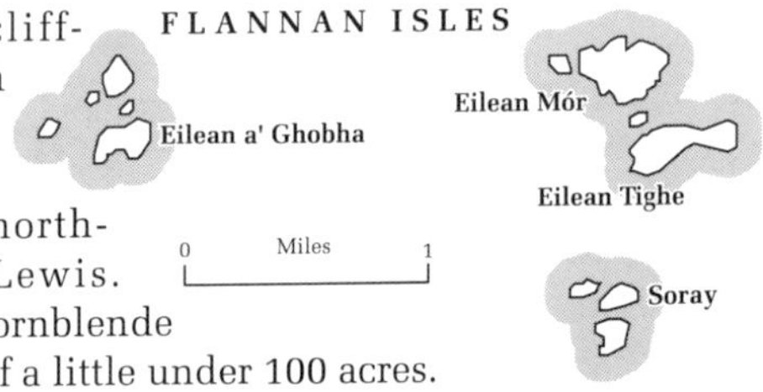

These are a group of cliff-bound islands also known as The Seven Hunters, rising steeply from the sea to 288ft, 21 miles north-west of Gallan Head, Lewis. They are composed of hornblende gneiss, and have an area of a little under 100 acres.

On the largest island, **Eilean Mór** (38 acres), are the remains of the 8thC Chapel of St Flannan, and a lighthouse built 1899 by D. & C. Stevenson of Edinburgh – the scene of a mystery rivalling that of the *Marie Celeste*. On the night of 15 December 1900, a passing steamer, the *Archer*, reported to the Northern Lighthouse Board that the light was out. The *Hesperus* was sent to investigate. The landing party could find no trace of the three keepers: James Ducat, Thomas Marshall and Donald MacArthur. Ducat's logbook was complete up to 13 December, and a slate continued the record to 9.00 am. on the 15th. Ducat's and Marshall's oilskins were gone, a meal of cold meat, pickles and potatoes for three lay untouched, and one chair was knocked over.

The weather at the time of the disappearance was foul, to the extent that a crane was torn from its foundations 100ft above sea level, and a concrete structure was demolished. The logbook told of damage to the west landing, an inlet finishing in a cave, called Skiopageo. The most common theory is that Ducat and Marshall went to inspect this landing. MacArthur, seeing a freak wave coming, ran to warn them. The wave burst into the inlet, exploded in the cave and swept all three away.

The story became well known

in the early 1900s with the publication of Wilfred Gibson's poem Flannan Isle: 'Three men alive on Flannan Isle/Who thought on three men dead.' The light is now automatic. An old rail track, used for transporting fuel, climbs steeply up the cliffs to the tower.

During the 16thC the MacLeods of Lewis used to visit the Flannans to hunt wild sheep and collect seabirds' eggs after performing an elaborate rite of prayer, and not calling anything by its proper name. Today a few sheep are still grazed on the grassy tops by Lewis crofters.

Shiant Isles

The name comes from *Na h-eileanan seunta* (the enchanted isles) and are known locally as Eileanan Mora, the Large Isles. This is a small group ten miles east-north-east of Scalpay, Harris. **Garbh Eilean** (rough island) and **Eilean an Tighe** (home island) are jointed by a narrow neck of land; the third island is **Eilean Mhuire** (Mary's island). On the north and east sides there are spectacular sea cliffs of columnar basaltic formation rising to over 400ft. Compared with the ancient gneiss of the Outer Hebrides, this is young rock, a geological relative of the islands of Staffa and Mull. The soil is rich and fertile on the top, where there are the remains of dwellings.

After the end of the 18thC a shepherd's wife and son fell from the cliffs whilst chasing sheep, and the daughter died in the same way while collecting eggs. In 1845 a whole family fell to their death while hunting sea birds on the cliffs of Garbh Eilean. An old man and his daughter were the last to live here. When he died it was ten days before the girl could row to Lewis for help. The islands were owned at one time by Sir Compton MacKenzie, who renovated the house on Eilean an Tighe and spent time there during the summer writing. In 1937 they were sold to the author and publisher, Nigel Nicolson, for £1500.

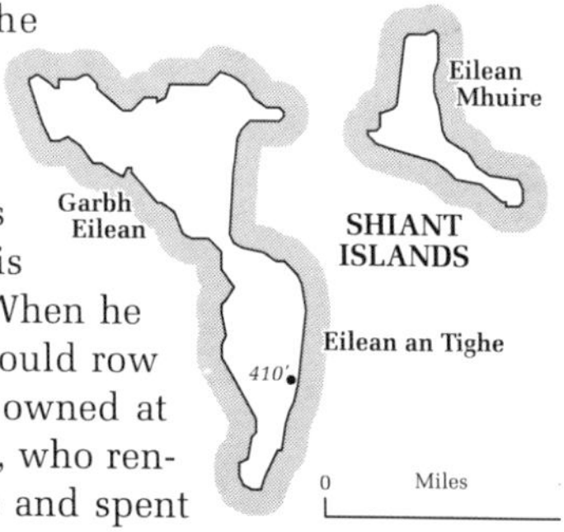

The islands support large colonies of puffins (which burrow into the cliffs), guillemots and wintering barnacle geese. The scree at the foot of the cliffs harbours many brown rats, and the islands are grazed by sheep.

A boat can be hired from Tarbert or Scalpay to visit the Shiants, but beware of the legendary Blue Men of the Minch, who live in the

Sound of Shiant and are said to be not particularly friendly. The Rev. John Gregorson Campbell, minister on Tiree between 1861-91, can vouch for this. He claimed to have seen one: 'a blue covered man with a grey face floating half out of the water'.

St Kilda

This is a spectacular group of islands and stacks, 41 miles west-north-west of Griminish Point, North Uist, owned by the National Trust for Scotland and designated a World Heritage Site. The origin of the name *Kilda* is not clear, since there is no known saint called Kilda. The Norse for well is kelda, and it is thought that 17thC Dutch map-makers became confused with the holy associations of wells, and added the 'St'. It may equally refer to *skildir*, a Norse word meaning shield, possibly describing the shape of the cliffs as they would have appeared from the sea to the east. The largest island, **Hirta,** has an area of 1575 acres. The name Hirta seems to derive from the old Gaelic 'irt', or death. Whether this association is from the romantic idea of the sun setting over it, or the more sinister possibility of being shipwrecked there, is open to conjecture.

Soay and **Dun** close by are 244 and 79 acres respectively, with **Boreray** (189 acres), **Stac an Armin** (13 acres) and **Stac Lee** (96 acres) forming a separate group four miles north-east. All the islands are formed from volcanic rock – granite and gabbro – rising to a height of 1397ft at the grassy summit of Conachair, Hirta; 1225ft at the summit of Soay; and 1260ft on Boreray. Exposure to the full erosive force of the Atlantic has resulted in sheer sea cliffs over 1000 ft high, the most magnificent in Britain. At the base of these walls of rock are many caves, stacks and arches – note especially that in Geo na h-Airde, the most spectacular natural arch on the islands. In the Boreray group, Stac an Armin (627ft) is the tallest monolith in the British Isles.

St Kilda was inhabited for possibly 2000 years by a hardy and, for the majority of that time, self-sufficient community, until the evacuation in 1930. It is known that the Vikings visited these islands. Their original settlement was at Glen Bay on the north side, where there are shielings (summer grazings with rudimentary shelters) to be seen. The most recent population centre was at Village Bay, with some remains of a previous settlement behind. Arable land was enclosed by a dyke. Among the dwellings, and scattered up the mountain slopes, are cleitean – small dry-stone and turf-roofed structures used for storing dried sea birds, which were the St Kildan's staple diet.

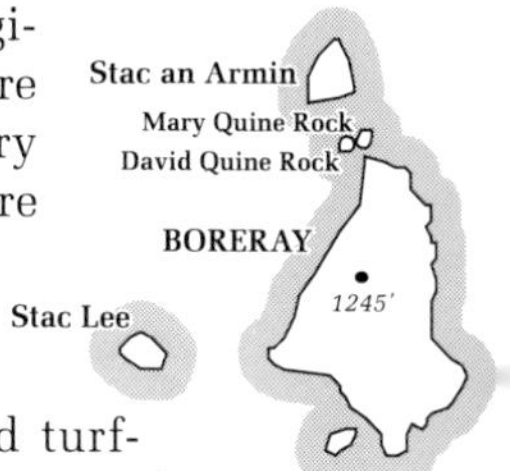

The earliest buildings at Village Bay were pulled down for the building of new black houses in 1830. The present cottages along the main street, six of which are now restored, are of the but-and-ben type, built about 1860. To the east of the houses are the manse (occupied by the army), the school (built 1899) and the church (built in the 1830s), all lovingly restored by working parties recruited by National Trust for Scotland and which have been coming here during the summer for many years. A great occasion took place on 1st June 1993, when a party arrived from Stornoway for the first wedding in the church since 1928.

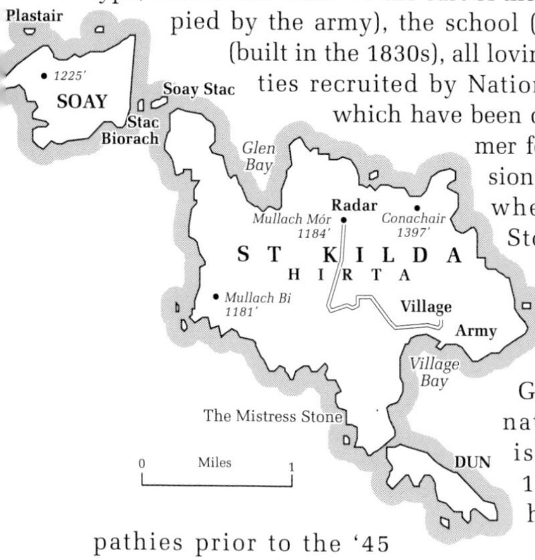

The remains of one rude hut are known as Lady Grange's House – an unfortunate woman exiled on the island for eight years from 1734 for threatening to reveal her husband's Jacobite sympathies prior to the '45 Rising. She died in 1745 and is buried at Trumpan, on Skye.

The population of St Kilda numbered 180 in 1697, but there was a steady decline from this peak, with several low points during cholera and smallpox outbreaks. From the 1750s to the early 1920s the community numbered over 70.

The islands were owned by the MacLeods of Harris and Dunvegan (in Skye) who were given them by a successor of Ranald, son of John, Lord of the Isles. Rent was paid by the St Kildans in the form of tweed, feathers, wool, dairy produce, stock, oil and grain. A steward was appointed by the MacLeods, and his deputy lived on the island, and once a year the steward himself visited to collect the rent.

The islanders held in common ownership everything that was vital to their existence, and all produce was shared. Each day the St Kilda Parliament would meet, latterly outside the post office, to dis-

The St Kilda Parliament, circa. 1926

cuss the day's tasks. With no one man having ascendancy over the others, these discussions could go on all day, with nothing decided. There was no insobriety, but among the men there was a marked fondness for tobacco. Crime was unknown.

Along with the usual crofting activities such as peat cutting, tending the stock, fishing, harvesting, building, sewing, spinning and weaving, the Kildan men collected thousands of sea birds and their eggs. Working in teams using horse-hair ropes, they scaled the terrifying cliffs and stacks (including those of Boreray, a hazardous boat journey away) in their stockinged feet, with remarkably few accidents. Their ankles became thick and strong, and their toes prehensile. They took young gannets, puffins (for their feathers only) and most importantly, fulmars, the bodies of which provided oil for their lamps and for export – one-half pint of oil from each bird. Typical yearly harvests might be 5000 gannets, 20,000 puffins, 9000 fulmars. After plucking the feathers were sorted, and the carcasses salted and packed for storage in the cleitean. Nothing was wasted – even the entrails were used as manure.

There were said to be two tests of climbing ability and agility used by the St Kildans. Young men had to scale Stac Biorach, 236ft high, in Soay Sound, regarded as the stiffest climb in the group; and, before marriage, each suitor had to balance on one heel on the mistress stone at the south-west of St Kilda, perched high above the sea, while grasping his other foot with his hands. This supposedly proved his prowess as a collector of food.

Apart from the ravages of contagious disease, the population was a healthy one, although it is not surprising that dyspepsia was common as their diet consisted largely of the oily flesh of sea birds. Perhaps the most tragic disease to afflict the island was 'eight-day

Stac an Armin and Boreray

sickness' *tetanus infantus,* which claimed eight out of every ten children born in the years before 1838. Various church ministers claimed it to be God's will, and the island people accepted this. Fortunately the Rev. Angus Fiddes did not. He took a course in midwifery and returned to St Kilda in the 1890s determined to eradicate the disease. He found that St Kildans traditionally coated the severed umbilicus of an infant with a mixture of fulmar oil and dung, and were loathe to change their ways. After a protracted battle with the islands' knee woman, who performed this rite, he demonstrated that by using sterile and antiseptic methods this centuries-old blight could be eradicated.

The arrival of the first tourists aboard the steamship *Glen Albyn* in July 1834 marked the start of the St Kildan's increased dependence on the outside world, and their subsequent decline. They sold cloth, skins and birds' eggs and used the money thus earned to buy food, clothing and tobacco. This commerce, a new factor in their economy, depended on good communications with the mainland – communications that were difficult to maintain due to the weather conditions and their situation en route to nowhere.

During the latter part of the 19thC the St Kildans relied on the prevailing westerly winds to carry messages requesting help to the main Hebridean islands. They fashioned small wooden boats with masts and sails, or used inflated sheeps' bladders, with the letters enclosed in bottles. Later, a loose arrangement was made with trawlermen to convey messages and mail. The post office on the island was opened in 1899, but there were never any scheduled deliveries or collections.

Other factors influencing the eventual evacuation were education, which began in earnest in 1884 and taught the young people that there might be a better life elsewhere, and a series of resident ministers who inspired such religious zeal that the islanders were in church every day of the week, at times when they should have been growing food or collecting eggs.

After the community nearly starved in 1912 a wireless transmitter was installed the following year, although it soon broke down. It was repaired and used during World War I, resulting in a German submarine shelling the island on 18 May 1918, destroying the store and damaging the church, but harming no one. The submarine was later captured by an armed trawler. A cannon, which can be seen to the east of the army camp, was later positioned to guard the bay. It was never fired.

Finally, a decision was taken and the island was evacuated on 19 August 1930, when 36 St Kildans left on HMS *Harebell,* with those cattle and sheep that could be rounded up following on the *Dunara Castle*, a ship which had been bringing tourists since 1875. Most of the St Kildan men, on leaving an island with no trees, were found work with the Forestry Commission.

Scottish Natural Heritage now manages the islands, which are Britain's premier sea-bird breeding station, in partnership with the National Trust for Scotland. It has been estimated that 37 per cent of the total world gannet population is to be found there, particularly on Stac an Armin and Stac Lee. There were 50,050 nests at the last count, as well as 62,780 fulmar nests, the largest single British colony, and 230,500 puffin burrows. Figures on the storm petrel are not clear, but the colony is thought to be one of the largest. Also to be found breeding are Manx shearwater, Leach's petrel, razorbill and the very aggressive great skuas (or bonxies), which have about 85 territories. In addition there are 7830 Kittiwake nests, 22,700 guillemots and 3800 razorbills, but only seven species of land birds breeding on the group, including the St Kilda wren, a sub-species. There is also a species of long-tailed field-mouse, which is a sub-species of the mainland field-mouse, although the St Kilda house-mouse died out soon after the evacuation.

Between 600 and 2000 Soay sheep (the population is cyclical) roam free on St Kilda; they are a primitive species similar to those kept by neolithic farmers. Where the sheep cannot graze, the vegetation on Dun is particularly lush. On Boreray the sheep left by the St Kildans, blackface and Cheviot crosses, have reverted to a wild state. Over 130 flowering plants occur, including some mountain types influenced by the cool climate. Blue whales have recently been tracked in the seas around the islands. Wind speeds of 130 mph at sea level have been recorded.

Since 1957, the army maintained a base of 15 men plus civilian technicians to run the radar on top of Mullach Mor, but this has now been handed over to civilian control. Missiles are fired from the range on North Uist and tracked by the installation here. The National Trust for Scotland were helped in their work by the soldiers, and their presence was greatly appreciated by the resident summer warden.

Those who have spent 24 hours or more on, or have sailed to, St Kilda can join the exclusive St Kilda Club. Artefacts and memorabilia of the St Kildans can be seen in a small museum in one of the cottages. You can visit the 'Puff Inn' for a lively evening (takings over £3000 per week during the summer!) and stamps and souvenirs can be bought at the small store (but now the army has gone – please check). Sadly the St Kildans themselves are no more – a community which became an administrative inconvenience and a charge upon mainstream society has been lost for ever for want of many of the things that were provided by the army. Those wishing to land on the island *must* first contact the National Trust for Scotland. Charter boats from Oban make regular visits during the summer, and berths are often available if booked in advance.

Monach Islands

Also known as Heisker, these are a group of four small islands about eight miles west of Baleshare, South Uist, with a total area of 836 acres. The two main ones, **Ceann Iar** and **Ceann Ear** (where there was once a convent) are joined at low tide.

On **Shillay**, the most westerly, there is a red brick lighthouse, built in 1864 but disused since 1942; at one time a crude light was maintained by monks who inhabited the islands. In the 16thC, sands that were passable at low tide between the Monachs and North Uist were swept away by the same exceptional tide that formed the Sound of Pabbay.

The islands have long been populated. Before 1810 over 100 people lived there, but over-grazing

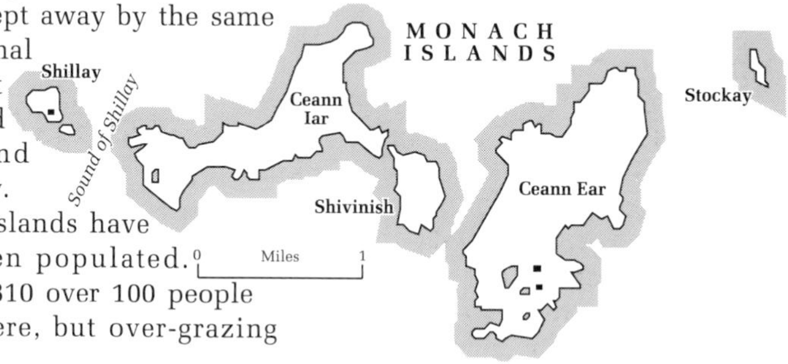

weakened the stabilising grass, and a disastrous storm blew the top soil away and the people left. By 1841, 19 people were re-established, and in 1891 over 100 people were again living on the group with their own post office and school. The numbers then began to dwindle and the last crofters left in 1942; the only cottage still habitable is privately owned. Occasionally the islands are visited by lobster fishermen. A cairn on Ceann lar marks the grave of Lieut. R.N.R. MacNeill, who drowned as a result of *H.M.A. Laurentic* striking a mine on 25 January 1917 off Northern Island. Superstitious sailors believe a drowned body will drift home – in the case of Lieut. MacNeill this was indeed the case, since Ceann Iar is the traditional clan home.

The Monachs are now a National Nature Reserve, and permission to land must be obtained from the North Uist Estate, Lochmaddy, and from the warden at Loch Druidibeg. The habitat is a prime example of shell sand, dune and uncultivated machair over gneiss; the rock rises only to a little over 60ft. Barnacle and white-fronted geese winter here, and arctic, common and little terns, fulmars and herons may also be seen. The reef of **Stockay** is a grey-seal nursery.

The North West

These islands lie just off Scotland's most remote coast. Rich in bird-life, they have varied and sometimes quite unexpected histories.

Handa Island

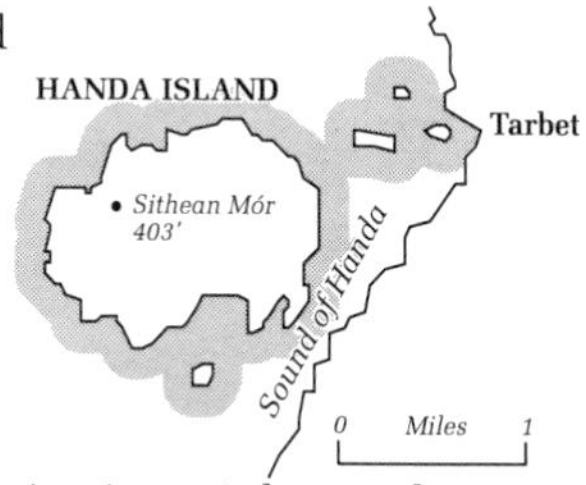

Highland. This mainly cliff-bound island of 766 acres consists of a Torridonian sandstone outcrop standing off a Lewisian gneiss foreland, less than a mile south-west of Tarbet. The sea cliffs on the north and west rise to 400ft, and there is an impressive rock known as the Great Stack, resting on three pillars. The interior is mainly rough pasture, peat bog and heather. It was once inhabited by seven families who had a 'queen' and, as on St Kilda, the menfolk used to hold a daily parliament to decide the work. The people emigrated to America during the potato famine of 1848. Handa was used as a burial place by mainlanders to save the corpses from the attentions of scavenging wolves.

Although privately owned, Handa is run as a nature reserve by the RSPB who maintain a warden during the summer. It is designated as an SSSI. 141 species of birds have been recorded, with 35 breeding regularly. Of most importance are the colonies of sea birds – indeed Handa is the most important UK breeding site for guillemots, with 70,000 pairs being recorded. The last white-tailed sea eagles nested here in 1864, and of great notoriety was an eccentric albino oystercatcher with a deformed bill, which died on 9 July 1967 and is now in the Royal Scottish Museum, Edinburgh. 216 species of plants have been recorded plus more than 100 species of mosses. Small plantations of lodgepole pine and alders have been established, and there are many rabbits. The colony of large brown rats, possibly introduced by the Vikings, had reached plague proportions by 1997, so over *3 tonnes* of rat poison was used to try to eradicate them

A bothy is available to those who wish to stay on the island (book with the RSPB in Edinburgh), and day visits can be made via a local boatman in Tarbet (not Suns). A modest landing fee is charged.

Summer Isles

Highland. These are a group of islands and skerries spread over 30 square miles, lying north-west of Loch Broom, consisting of Torridonian sandstone covered with peat.

The largest island in the group is **Tanera Mór**, with an area of 804 acres. In 1881 its population numbered 119 people, who lived in the settlements by The Anchorage, one of the best natural harbours in the north-west. The population declined until, in 1931, the last tenants left. Sir Frank Fraser Darling farmed the island between 1939 and 1944, and wrote about this period in his book *Island Farm.* Then once again it was deserted until the mid-1960s, when the Summer Isles Estate decided to restore many of the cottages and the schoolhouse as holiday accommodation. The permanent population now numbers about 10, and 250 sheep are grazed. The Summer Isles Post Office, which issues its own stamps (recognised by the Post Office) for conveying mail to the mainland, and the Offshore Islands Philatelic Society are both run from Tanera Mór.

Between the two settlements of Ardnagoine and Garadheancal are the remains of a fishing station at Tigh-on-Quay founded in 1783 by Roderick Morison of Stornoway and John Mackenzie of London, whose business thrived when the seas were full of herring; there were other stations on **Isle Ristol** and Isle Martin. Barrels of the salted fish were exported as far afield as

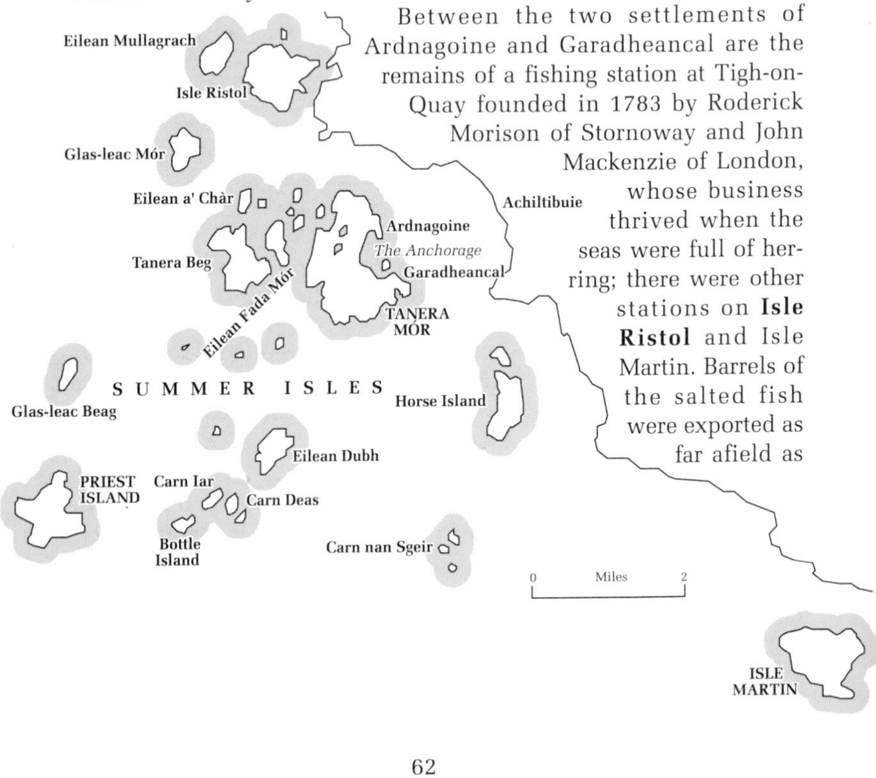

The Summer Isles photographed from Priest Island. on 24th May, 1927.

West Indies, and as many as 200 vessels were at one time to be seen anchored in the bay. During the 19thC the island was a centre for the illicit distilling of whisky. Tanera Mor rises to 405ft at the summit of Meall Mor, affording fine views as far as the Outer Hebrides. Holiday accommodation can be booked through the Summer Isles Estate, and a regular ferry operates from Achiltibuie. There are facilities for boating, sailing and fishing among other things, amid excellent scenery and seclusion.

The island of **Tanera Beg**, to the west, has a beach of coral sand, rare in this area. **Horse Island**, once inhabited, now supports only a herd of wild goats, first recorded in 1937. To the south-south-west is **Carn nan Sgeir**, two islets joined by a shingle spit. Orange, grey and black lichens hide the cliffs, and the ledges are covered with thrift, sea campion, scurvygrass and lovage.

The most westerly of the group are **Priest Island** (or Eilean a Chleirich, 300 acres), and the much smaller **Glas-leac Beag** (34 acres). There is no proper landing place on Priest Island and its exposed position makes access difficult – in spite of this, it was at one time occupied by a crofting family, originally an outlaw banished from the mainland. The third generation of this family left in the mid-19thC. Sir Frank Fraser Darling, naturalist, wrote about his stay on this island in *Island Years*. On its summit are three stone circles and seven small lochs. It is now notable for its colonies of storm petrels and otters. It is presently owned by the RSPB, and there is no visiting.

All of these islands are rich in bird life – heron, shelduck, fulmar, snipe, and eider are among the species commonly seen – and many are still grazed by sheep. There are boat trips from Achiltibuie and Ullapool, but most of the islands are privately owned.

Isle Martin lies to the east of the Summer Isles, to the north of Loch Broom, and is composed of Torridonian sandstone, with an area of 390 acres and a maximum elevation of 393ft. In the late 18thC, at the start of the herring boom, the British Fisheries Society erected a curing station close by Ardmair Bay, the foundations of which still exist. In 1901 the population of the island was 33, but by the start of World War II the last resident had left. Mrs Monica Goldsmith bought the island in 1965, restoring the four houses and preserving it from development. She later gave it to the RSPB to manage as a reserve – of particular interest are the heronry, the tern colony, red-breasted merganisers, eiders, oystercatchers and ringed plovers. There is a legend about a cooper of Isle Martin who was miraculously transported to South Rona to cut brooms and then equally miraculously brought back – all, of course, arranged by the fairies. There are trips around the Summer Isles from both Achiltibuie and Ullapool. Ullapool is also the terminus for the Caledonian MacBrayne vehicle ferry *Isle of Lewis* to Stornoway, Isle of Lewis.

Gruinard Island

Highland. This island lies in the attractive Gruinard Bay, its name deriving from the Norse *grunna fjord* (shallow ford). During World War II it was used as a test site for biological weapons. The last inhabitants had left long before these experiments were carried out. During 1986 a cleaning up operation was undertaken, spraying the contaminated areas with formaldehyde and sea water, effectively surrounding any anthrax spores left in the soil in a chemical coffin, making the island safe, and the warning notices unnecessary.

A generally low-lying sandstone island in Loch Ewe, half a mile from Aultbea, the **Isle of Ewe** rises to 223ft at its northern tip, and 232ft in the west. Its population numbers 12, and a new pier, which will make the resident's lives a lot easier, is due to be built soon.

In Loch Gairloch, **Eilean Horrisdale** shelters the jetties of Aird and Badachro, and to the north of the loch is the sandstone **Longa Island**, sheltering the beach of Big Sand. To the south are Lochs Torridon and Shieldaig, the latter containing tiny **Shieldaig Island** which was purchased by the National Trust for Scotland in 1970, and adopted in 1974 by Mr and Mrs Armistead Peter III of Washington, D.C., who contributed a sum equivalent to the full purchase price. The name Shieldaig is of Norse origin, meaning 'herring bay'. In the 19thC this island had been planted with Scots pine, which, now with a lush growth of birch, rowan, dog-rose, holly and heather make a welcome contrast to the surrounding barren hills, and demonstrate what the landscape would be like (indeed once was like) without the devastating effects of deforestation and sheep farming.

The mainland coast to Applecross is bare and mountainous – splendid walking country. To the south of this village, **Eilean nan Naomh** shelters Camusterrach harbour. Little more than a rocky outcrop, this is the Holy Isle where St Maolrubha is said to have landed in AD 671; he founded a monastery at Applecross, which was later destroyed by the Vikings. To the south there are a few islets and rocks. About a mile south-west of Loch Toscaig, the **Crowlin Islands** are reached, a volcanic outcrop with a north-south split giving a sheltered central channel 50-yds wide. The largest of the three islands, **Eilean Mór,** rises to a summit of 374ft, and has some ruined cottages in the north-east corner. A lighthouse stands on the smallest island, **Eilean Beag**, and its shoreline, rocky and with caves, is inhabited by both common and Atlantic seals. Regular summer boat-trips are made from the Kyle of Lochalsh. The waters of the Inner Sound, to the north, are the deepest off the immediate coast of Britain; Royal Navy torpedo tests are conducted here.

Eilean na Creige Duibhe is a Scottish Wildlife Trust conservation area where herons nest by fine Scots pines. Visits can be made by boat from Plockton.

Eilean Bàn

Highland. **Eilean Bàn** (white island) lies off Kyle of Lochalsh, with a pretty white lighthouse (now automatic) at its western end. The white painted cottages were built for the keepers and their families who once tended the light. The late Gavin Maxwell, author of *Ring of Bright Water,* bought the island in 1963 intending to turn it into a private zoo for Scottish wildlife. He converted the two cottages into one, and moved to the island in 1968 after his house at Sandaig on the mainland burned down. Ill-health prevented him realising this plan and, after living for a while at Kyle House on Skye, he died in Broadford Hospital on 7 September 1969. His otter, Teko, the last survivor from the *Ring,* is buried beneath a boulder on Eilean Bàn.

The island's special character has been largely overwhelmed by the new road bridge to Skye, one of it's support pylons towering above and making a grotesque intrusion. Eilean Bàn is, however, now to be preserved as an otter sanctuary, and Gavin Maxwell's house will be restored. In March 1997 there were two pairs of otters recorded living on the island, and it is hoped to attract more.

Island of Skye

Highland. The name Skye derives from the Norse *skuy,* meaning cloud; in Gaelic it is *Eilean a Cheo*, isle of mist. Easy access, breath-taking scenery and romantic associations with Bonnie Prince Charlie have made Skye popular since Victorian times, when the new railway to Stromeferry opened up the island. Now it is a favourite venue for tourists from all over the world, who come in droves over the new bridge during the summer months.

The island, which has a population of 7000, is 48 miles long and 24 miles wide as far as its shape allows determination, and has an area of 430,000 acres. Near the centre are the magnificent Cuillin Hills, the most dramatic manifestation of the volcanic activity which shaped the bulk of the island, formed from the solidified reservoir from which the lavas flowed some 40 million years ago during the Tertiary period. These granite mountains culminate in extremely sharp ridges of pointed rock, an edge like broken china above the dark grey slopes. This rock is extremely hard and owes its present form to its (relatively) young age and the abrasive effect of ice. The Red Cuillins were formed much earlier during the Lewisian period and as a consequence have been subjected to prolonged weathering –

The Cuillin Hills, viewed from Portnalong

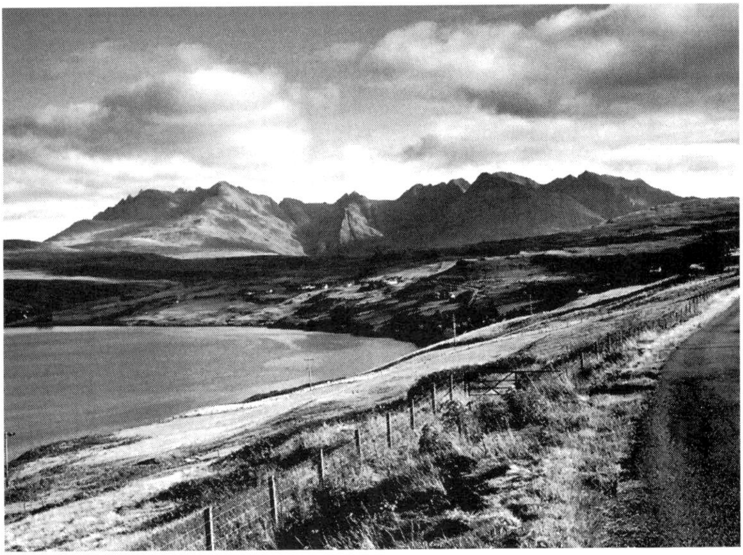

hence their more rounded appearance.

The north of the island, including Duirinish, Waternish and half of Trotternish, was formed from a succession of lava flows, giving the land a stepped appearance, seen clearly on Macleod's Tables – Healabhal Bheag and Healabhal Mhor – where softer outpourings have been eroded leaving the characteristic flat tops and tiered slopes. The oldest rock on Skye, gneiss, is found in Sleat (pronounced slate), south of Isleornsay, with old red sandstone forming the rest of the peninsula.

In Trotternish, the Quiraing and the Old Man of Storr are the remains of volcanic rock which was left stranded on top of soft clays when the glaciers melted – the softer material giving way, leaving the blocks to slip down, creating cliffs and ravines.

Underlying sandstones, limestones and clays surface around the volcanic rock to give the best soils on the island, and this has generally determined human settlement. Northern Trotternish, Broadford and the west of Loch Slapin are typical of these areas, with many farms and crofts. Areas of lush green vegetation behind Broadford mark the limestone outcrops. Where this limestone was baked by volcanic activity, marble was produced, and this is still quarried near Torrin.

There are coral beaches at Claigan on Loch Dunvegan, formed by the seaweed *Lithothamnion*, and to the south of Duntulm Castle in Trotternish the sand has a green tint due to the sea eroding the mineral, olivine, from the cliffs. Gold has been found on the island.

There are 20 peaks in the Cuillins, 15 over 3000ft high with the highest, Sgurr Alasdair, being 3257ft. The first to be recorded as being climbed, in 1836, was Sgurr nan Gillean (3167ft), by a geologist named Forbes. Sgurr a'Ghreadaidh, at 3190ft, is ascended from the Loch Coruisk side, one of the longest rock climbs in Britain.

Much of the island landscape is empty, with small crofting townships of scattered cottages only where the soil is workable. There are many ruined houses and empty glens, evidence of the Jacobites who were forced to leave after the unsuccessful rising of 1745, the bad harvests of 1881-85 and the Clearances.

A croft is a small farm usually of five to ten acres. The original crofters were self-sufficient, occupying arable land, divided into small areas, on a rotation basis, and sharing hill grazing.

This way of life ended for many with the introduction of large-scale sheep farming, often by absentee landlords, and the clearance of the crofters from the land. Whole townships were evicted and forced to emigrate to the New World; between 1840 and 1888 over 30,000 people left. By 1882 over 365,000 acres of Skye were owned by absentee landlords, and it was then that things came to a head when crofters at The Braes were denied grazing rights they considered theirs. A force of 50 Glasgow policemen was dispatched to quell the riot that had developed and they fought a battle with the crofters.

Later gunboats were sent and marines landed at Uig.

The result of this was a Royal Commission, set up by Gladstone, to investigate the crofters' grievances, and in 1886 the Crofters Act was passed, giving security of tenure at a fair rent. The present-day crofter usually has a full-time job or a pension, using his land to supplement his livelihood.

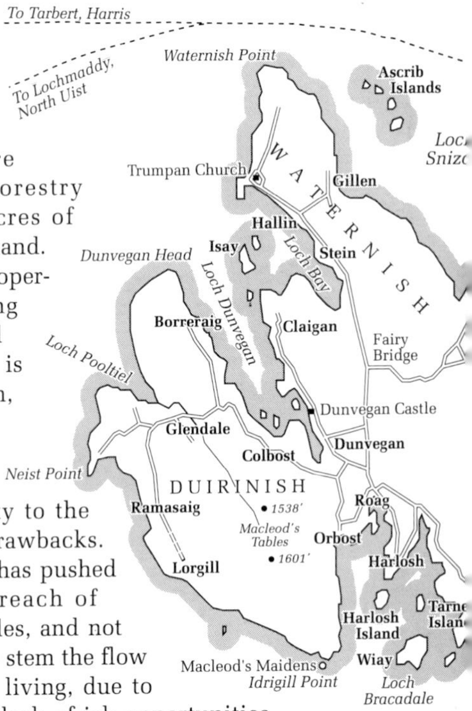

The sheep kept on the island are mainly Scottish blackface, an exceptionally hardy breed, and Cheviots. Cattle are also kept, mainly for beef, and many of these are exported each year. The Forestry Commission has over 8000 acres of trees; there is little natural woodland.

A small inshore fishing fleet operates around the island catching prawns for export to France and Italy and some white fish, which is sent to Aberdeen. Other shellfish, including scallops, are also taken.

It is tourism that has brought a measure of prosperity to the island, but even this has its drawbacks. The demand for holiday homes has pushed property prices beyond the reach of indigenous young married couples, and not enough jobs have been created to stem the flow of emigration. The high cost of living, due to transport costs, coupled with a lack of job opportunities, provides little incentive to stay.

In AD 585 St Columba visited Skye, and later Maolrubha became the patron saint of the central and southern areas – in the past, 25 August was celebrated in Broadford as his feast day. In the 8thC, Norsemen began raiding, and finally settled; their domination of Skye, under the Kingdom of Man and the Isles, lasted until three years after the Battle of Largs in 1263, when King Haakon of Norway was defeated. A legacy of Norse blood and place-names remains strong on the island.

John MacDonald of Islay, a descendant of Somerled (who split the Kingdom of Man and the Isles in 1158), first adopted the title Lord of the Isles, with Skye as an administrative centre; the title lasted until 1748. The land was divided between the MacDonalds and the MacLeods, and the sites of their battles on the island are a reminder of constant feuding. The inhabitants professed Catholicism until the Reformation in 1561; Evangelism spread from 1805, followed by the

Fladda-Chùain
Lord MacDonald's Table
Eilean Trodday
Duntulm
Eilean Flodigarry
Flodigarry
Kilmuir
Quiraing
Staffin Island
Monkstadt
Staffin
Kilt Rock
TROTTERNISH
Elishader
Uig
Beinn Edra 2003'
Longfearn
Lealt
Loch Snizort Beag
Eaglais Bhreagach
RONA
Caisteal Uisdein
Kingsburgh
Romesdale
The Storr 2358'
Old Man of Storr
The Hydro
Kensaleyre
Suladale
Edinbane
Lochs Fada & Leathan
Tote
Skeabost
Sound of Raasay
Inner Sound
Loch Torridon
SKYE
Applecross
PORTREE
RAASAY
Camastianavaig
Bracadale
Glen Varragill
Eilean nan Naomh
Loch Kishorn
The Braes
Portnalong
Crowlin Islands
Carbost
Sconser
SCALPAY
Longay
Sligachan Hotel
Glamaig 2542'
Glen Sligachan
Pabay
Kyle of Lochalsh
Eilean Bàn
Caisteal Maol
Luib
Strollamus
Airport
Kyleakin
Eynort
Sgurr nan Gillean 3167'
Marsco 2414'
Beinn na Caillich 2400'
Sgurr na Coinnich 2424'
THE CUILLINS
Breakish
BROADFORD
Glen Arroch
Loch Eynort
Glen Brittle
Sgurr Dearg 3234'
Loch Coruisk
Blà Bheinn 3044'
Torrin
Cill Chriosd
Kylerhea
Sgurr Alisdair 3257'
STRATHAIRD
Kilmarie
Drumfearn
Camasunary
Loch Brittle
Soay Sound
Loch Scavaig
Loch Slapin
Loch Eishort
SLEAT
Sandaig
Elgol
Ord
SOAY
Dunscaith Castle
Spar Cave
Tokavaig
Isleornsay
Loch Hourn
SOUND OF SLEAT
Knock Castle
Tarskavaig
Ostaig
Knock Bay
0 Miles 10
Armadale Castle
Ardvasar
Armadale Bay
To Mallaig
Aird of Sleat
Loch Nevis

Free Church from 1843, with its dour teachings. In common with other Protestant western islands, Sunday is observed as the Lord's Day. Most shops, pubs and restaurants close, and little work, unless absolutely essential, is done. There are those who will not listen to the radio, watch television, read a newspaper or even light a fire on a Sunday – but the influence of hundreds of thousands of visitors to the island has generally made for a more relaxed approach here than on, say, Lewis in the Outer Hebrides. The Gaelic language is spoken, but most young people now use English.

Skye people once had a reputation for second sight: seeing a person in a shroud prophesied death; seeing a fire spark fall on someone's arm signified they would soon carry a dead child. The other people on the island were the fairies, or *sithche* (pronounced sheeche) – from *sithchean* (the noiseless people) – who lived in any rounded grassy mound (a *sithein,* pronounced shi-en) and performed miraculous or mischievous deeds. If you wanted protection from these small people, you carried iron, steel or oatmeal.

The story of one of Scotland's most popular and heroic partnerships unfolded on Skye. Bonnie Prince Charlie, came to Scotland to attempt to depose George II and regain the crown of England for the Stuarts. After gathering together a small army, the Young Pretender enjoyed some initial success, but was finally routed at Culloden and his Jacobite army dispersed. Pursued by the King's forces, with a price of £30,000 on his head, he fled to the islands from whence he hoped to escape to Scandinavia or France. Disguised as Betty Burke, a maid, he was brought from Benbecula to Kilbride Bay in Trotternish by Flora MacDonald, a 24-year-old Edinburgh-educated Skye girl. After some close escapes, hiding in caves and cattle byres, he left Flora and went to Raasay the night after it had been sacked by troops from the Royal Navy ship *Furnace* as retribution against the men of the island who had supported the Jacobites. After a short stay, waiting for a French ship which never appeared, he went back to Skye, then on to Knoydart on the mainland. Finally, on 19 September 1746 a French ship took him from Loch nam Uamh. He died in Rome in 1778. Flora was arrested after his escape and held prisoner in a private house in London, but she was freed after the passing of the Indemnity Act in 1747, when she became the heroine

The museum at Luib

of London society. Her grave and monument are in a simple burial ground in Kilmuir.

The bare rocks and peaks of the Cuillins and Trotternish and the sea cliffs around Dunvegan Head and Loch Harport are the habitat of the island's golden eagles. Sea birds and waterfowl inhabit the lochs, and many of these are fished for brown trout; the rivers run with sea trout and salmon, although these have declined due to over-fishing at sea.

The richness of the island's flora was shown in a detailed study which revealed 589 species of flowering plants and ferns, 370 mosses, 181 liverworts and 154 lichens. Many alpines are to be found on the eastern side of the Trotternish ridge, including the tiny Iceland-purslane (*Koenigia islandica*), a relative of the sorrels, first discovered here in 1934. In the limestone crossing Strath Suardal behind Broadford, there is a birchwood where mountain avens, guelder-rose and helleborine grow. The rare red broomrape is found on grassy slopes above the sea, and rock whitebeam occurs on some of the low cliffs.

The largest wild mammal in Britain, the red deer, is found mostly round Loch Coruisk and in Sleat. Minke and pilot whales are regularly spotted off the coast, and killer whales have also been seen.

PORTREE AND TROTTERNISH

The only town on Skye is Portree, and its name is probably anglicised from *Port-righe,* the port at the bottom of the hill. It is attractively sited with a fine sheltered anchorage, but apart from the usual services of a town – shops, hotels, library, schools, police station and lifeboat station – there is little of architectural or historic interest, although the Aros centre for traditional Gaelic culture is a popular venue. McNab's Inn, once the Royal Hotel, does have associations with Bonnie Prince Charlie and Flora MacDonald (the room in which he bade her farewell is here). The Tourist Information Centre is situated in the building that was once both courthouse and jail for the whole island. Two murderers were held here in 1742, one being hanged out the back in front of a crowd of 5000 onlookers, the other being taken to Inverness to suffer a similar fate. The present courthouse in Somerled Square was built in 1867. In the cliffs to the north of Loch Portree is Mac Coitir's Cave, said to run beneath the island to Bracadale. Portree is the natural centre for touring the Trotternish, Waternish and Duirinish peninsulas, and the centre of the island.

The coast road north of Portree to Trotternish is dominated by The Storr (2358ft) and the Old Man of Storr, a rock needle 165ft tall, balanced amongst sheer cliffs and many smaller pinnacles. Take the new footpath from Storr Wood Car Park between Portree and Staffin for a closer look. It was first recorded as being climbed in 1955. The name Storr is from *fiacaill storach*, meaning buck tooth. Here the ground is loose and treacherous and should be treated with caution. Below are Lochs Fada and Leathan, the reservoir for the Hydro which has supplied the island's electricity since 1952 (there is also an electric cable across the Kyle of Lochalsh). Before 1949 the only electricity was generated by a diesel engine belonging to the Portree Hotel.

In the cliffs east of Loch Fada is the cave where Bonnie Prince Charlie landed on his return from Raasay, and at Lealt there are spectacular waterfalls which can be seen by taking a not too difficult climb down the ravine. Three-quarters of a mile south, on the shore, is Eaglais Bhreagach, a church-shaped rock where the Clan MacQueen is said to have raised the devil, using an ancient ceremony called *Taghairm,* involving the roasting of live cats.

At Lonfearn the remains of beehive dwellings (early Christian circular stone cells) were discovered – in Gaelic they are called *tighean nan druineach*, druids' houses. To the west, on the Trotternish ridge, can be seen the summit of Beinn Edra (2003ft); in the spring of 1945 a Flying Fortress bomber hit it in the midday mist – all on board were killed. Up the coast again there is a simple black-house museum at Elishader, and in the cliffs nearby can be seen the kil rock, black basalt so called because of the folds and pattern of its strata.

A galleon of the Spanish Armada was reputed to have been wrecked near Staffin, some coins having been found, and there are people here said to be of Spanish descent. The crofting townships here are overlooked by the fantastic Quiraing (round fold) – awesome rock formations where whole herds of cattle could be hidden. The Table, the 120-ft-tall Needle and the Prison can all be explored by walking north from the Staffin-to-Uig road near its highest point.

In the bay below, a road signposted Staffin Slip leads to some areas of dark sand among boulders, facing the low-lying **Staffin Island**, with its grazing sheep and bothy used by fishermen. **Eilean Flodigarry**, rising to a steep point at its eastern tip, once (according to legend) had its corn reaped in two nights by seven score and ten fairies. When they had finished, they asked for more work, so the owner set them to empty the sea! Behind the bay, the crofting land can be seen clearly divided into regular strips.

To the north of the Quiraing is the Flodigarry Hotel, a turreted building, once the home of Flora MacDonald after her escapades with the Prince. North of The Aird lies the grassy **Eilean Trodday**, the trolls isle, which once supported a herd of dairy cattle. This northern end of Trotternish was known as the granary of Skye due to its fertile basaltic soil.

As the road reaches the west coast the few craggy remains of Duntulm Castle can be seen at the top of a steep cliff, above the hotel. The main part of the castle is 15thC (it was occupied up to 1732), and a footpath from the road leads to the ruin. In the bay lies **Tulm**

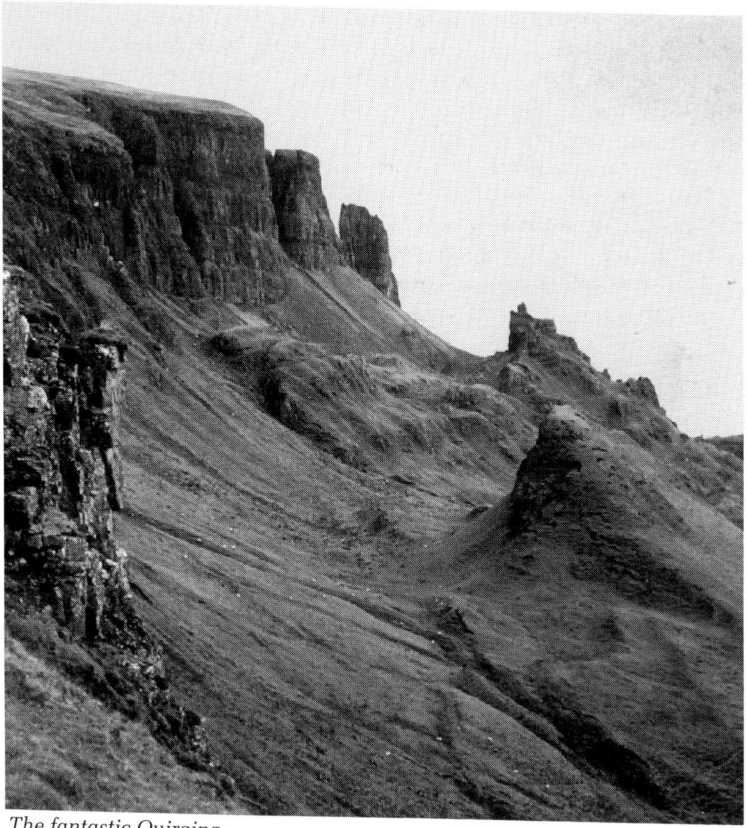

The fantastic Quiraing

Island, a narrow green hump, and about three miles north-west are the flat-topped **Lord Macdonald's Table, Gearran Island, Gaeilavore Island** and the largest of the group, **Fladda-chùain** with its ruined chapel dedicated to St Columba, the blue altar stone said to bring fair winds to becalmed fishermen. Sir Donald MacDonald of the Isles is supposed to have hidden title deeds here before taking part in the Rising of 1715.

The Skye Cottage Museum at Kilmuir consists of four restored black houses on an exposed site overlooking the sea, with typical room settings and a peat fire, Bonnie Prince Charlie and Flora MacDonald relics and a particularly interesting collection of historical documents relating to life on the islands. Nearby in a small graveyard is the new memorial to Flora MacDonald; the original MacDonald mausoleum was gradually taken, piece by piece, by tourists. Close to this is a well-preserved crusader slab.

Between Balgown and the coast lies an area of marshy ground, which was once Loch Chaluim Chille. Drained in 1824, on what were once islands are the remains of beehive dwellings. From the main road at Linicro a very rough track leads to the ruins of Sir Alexander MacDonald's once-fine house, Monkstadt. Flora and the Prince landed at Kilbride Bay and came to the house only to find it occupied by the King's officers; the pair then fled through Kingsburgh to Portree.

The road descends steeply to the very pretty township of Uig (bay or nook), sheltered by steep basaltic cliffs, its scattered crofts stretching back to the hills where there is, along Glen Uig to Balnacnock, a Quiraing in miniature. The round tower opposite the Uig pier is a folly built by Captain Fraser. There is a youth hostel at Uig.

At the head of Loch Snizort Beag, on the eastern side, stands Caisteal Uisdein (Hugh's Castle) built around 1580 by Hugh MacDonald of Sleat, who schemed against his chief and died entombed in Duntulm Castle with a piece of salt beef and an empty water jug. A farm track north of Hinnisdal Bridge leads towards the ruin. Further south, at Kensaleyre, the fine church was built in 1805 by James Gillespie Graham, one of the best known Scottish architects of his time. It has recently been restored

The central region of the Trotternish peninsula is wild, inhospitable, heather-clad country with steep cliffs and peat bogs.

LOCH SNIZORT BEAG AND WATERNISH

The route from Portree to the Waternish peninsula goes through a broad valley at the head of Loch Snizort Beag. On an islet in the River Snizort are the scant ruins of a chapel associated with St Columba, best seen from the old bridge by Skeabost post office (a path and stepping stones lead to the ruin), and the Skeabost Hotel, an imposing white castellated building. The village itself is notable as the birthplace of the poet, Mary MacPherson. On a hill above Clachamish stand the remains of Dun Suladale, one of the best preserved of the 20 brochs on the island.

The road then passes Edinbane, where there is a pottery, and on through peaty moorland to the Fairy Bridge with its legendary associations with the MacLeods of Dunvegan. As you head north along the Waternish peninsula, the village of Stein is reached, which was established by the British Fisheries Society in 1790, and was designed by Thomas Telford. It looks out towards the cliffs of Beinn Bhreac, where eagles soar, and the low-lying islands of **Isay, Mingay** and **Clett**, once inhabited, but cleared in 1860. Isay was offered to Dr Johnson by the MacLeods, on condition that he built a house on it but, needless to say, such a comfort-lover did not accept the offer. Stein has a fine inn, re-opened after a 14-year closure, an attractive terrace, a handsome stone house and a small jetty by a stony beach. In 1787 a fishing industry was started here, but the project was abandoned in 1837. Above Hallin the remains of a broch can be seen, the walls standing about seven-feet high in places. To the east is Gillen, where there is a knitting workshop, and fine views of the **Ascrib Islands,** where a colony of puffins have burrowed into the basalt. Stone for Caisteal Uisdein is said to have been quarried there. The single house on the islands has been renovated.

At the end of the road, above Ardmore Bay, stands the lonely and windswept ruin of Trumpan Church. It was here in 1578 that the MacDonalds of Uist barred the door on a congregation of MacLeods, and set fire to the church, to avenge the Eigg massacre (*see* Eigg). The only survivor in 1578, a girl, escaped by a window, severing one of her breasts as she squeezed through to raise the alarm. Other MacLeods arrived, carrying their legendary Fairy Flag, and captured the MacDonald galleys, slaughtering all on board. The bodies were buried in a dyke – so the battle is known as the spoiling of the dyke.

In the churchyard are some ancient graves, including that of Lady Grange, who was exiled on St Kilda for eight years by her husband, and died three years after her return in 1742. A track near the church leads north towards Waternish Point.

DUNVEGAN AND DUIRINISH

One mile north of the Fairy Bridge is Annait where there are remains of some early Christian cells. From the bridge the road continues south to Dunvegan, with its hotels, shops, boat trips to see the seals, and Dunvegan Castle, seat of the Clan MacLeod since 1200 – no other Scottish castle has been continuously occupied as long. The first building on the site is said to date from the 9thC, but the major part of the present one is 19thC, beautifully situated at the head of Loch Dunvegan and backed by mixed woodland planted since 1890. The castle contains many MacLeod relics including the 15thC Dunvegan Cup, Rory Mor's drinking horn and the legendary Fairy Flag (*Bratach shith MhicLeoid*), made of yellow silk from the Near East. Its miraculous saving powers can only be used three times, when the survival of the clan is threatened; there is now only one more opportunity left. Pregnant women should also take into consideration the myth that, upon seeing the flag, they may go into premature labour. The castle is closed from mid-October to March.

To the north is Claigan, where a signposted track leads down to the coral beaches – the first a small rocky bay, then on to a more dramatic sweep. Up a track behind Claigan Farm, the entrance to a souterrain (an Iron Age or earlier earth house or food store) can be found. There is another example near Loch Duagrich, to the east of Bracadale.

Duirnish is dominated by the twin flat peaks of Healabhal Bheag (1601ft) and Healabhal Mhor (1538ft) – MacLeod's Tables. It is an area of wild moorland, with the few roads keeping to the coast – the southern part is accessible only on foot. The main road rounds the head of Loch Dunvegan; a narrow track leads south to Orbost where a small art gallery has been established. From here, another track leads down to a small sheltered beach.

By heading north-west along the side of Loch Dunvegan, containing low-lying islands grazed by sheep, the tiny village of Colbost, with its Black House Museum and Three Chimneys restaurant, is reached. Behind the museum, which depicts life around 100 years ago, is a replica of an illicit whisky still.

To the north, past Husabost, is Borreraig, where the legendary MacCrimmons, hereditary pipers to the MacLeod chiefs from 1500 to 1800, are said to have established their piping college. They were the first composers, players and teachers of *pibroch* (a tune with variations), and their history and folklore is recorded in the museum, founded in 1975 in the unimposing cream house to the west of the road. On the promontory opposite, above the supposed remains of the original college, stands the beehive-shaped MacCrimmon Memorial Cairn, the focal point of an annual pilgrimage of MacCrimmons, and in the cliffs below is the Piper's Cave. The first piping school on Skye was established by the MacArthurs, who later went to Islay as hereditary pipers to the Lords of the Isles.

The main road from Colbost to Glendale passes the memorial to the Glendale Land Leaguers, 600 crofters who challenged Government forces and now own the Glendale Estate. The township of Glendale stretches back along the river valley behind Loch Pooltiel, where the hills to the west slope gently away and the scattered crofts are well tended and productive. Below the low cliffs at the water's edge is the Glendale Water Mill, a 200-year-old dry-stone grain mill with a thatched roof. It ceased operation in 1914, but was restored in 1971-72 to virtually its original working condition, the project being carried out on local initiative using local skills. Unfortunately the mill burned down in 1973, on the day the Skeabost mill stones were brought here: in legend, whenever these stones are moved, there is a disaster. The second restoration started immediately, and the mill now sells hand-made oiled woollen knitwear and tweed. Close by stands a dry-stone kiln, where peat was burned to dry grain before milling. There is a spectacular waterfall tumbling down the cliffs opposite.

The most westerly point on Skye is the sheer-sided and narrow Neist peninsula, where the well-made but steep path to the lighthouse makes a good walk. There are some accessible small bays, towering cliffs with sea birds, and superb views of Waterstein Head, 967-ft high. On a clear day, North and South Uist and Benbecula can be seen, low on the horizon.

A narrow and bumpy road across rugged moorland and peat bogs leads to Ramasaig, an isolated settlement, from which a track goes to Lorgill, the glen of the deer's cry. In 1830 all ten crofting families there were ordered to Loch Snizort to either board the *Midlothian* bound for Nova Scotia, or go to prison, and those over 70 years of age were to be sent to the county poorhouse. On 4 August that year, they all left. Idrigill Point can be reached on foot, but it is stiff walking.

BRACADALE AND MINGINISH

The south of Duirinish shelters Loch Bracadale, with its calm inlets and small islands, tiered cliffs and irregular hills. It is a magical part of the island, especially at sunset on a fine day, when the Cuillins are etched with deep shadows, and the sea glows between the head-lands.

Above the township of Struan is Dun Beag, the best-preserved broch on Skye – parts of the galleries may still be seen. Struan is notable for being the home of John Campbell, an elder of the Free Presbyterian church whose offspring numbered twenty when his wife was still only 44 years old. Since she would therefore still be of child bearing age, the tally may yet have increased. This, Scotland's largest family, has an entry in the Guinness Book of Records. Bracadale, established in 1772 by Thomas Pennant, stands at the head of Loch Beag, scattered crofts above a small beach. The view towards the lighthouse at Ardtreck Point and Portnalong is splendid.

Loch Bracadale, with MacLeod's Maidens and the Outer Hebrides in the distance.

The main road to Sligachan passes through Glen Drynoch. At the head of Loch Harport a minor road crosses the River Drynoch and continues along the west side of the loch, passing the Talisker Malt Whisky Distillery at Carbost. Originally founded by Kenneth MacAskill of Talisker House at Snizort, it was first moved to Fiskavaig, then to Carbost in 1830. There are conducted tours in the summer and a dram to taste. The road behind the distillery leads to Talisker Bay, reached through a steep-sided glen, where cattle and sheep graze, and crops grow on the fertile plain. In the cliffs to the north a fine waterfall spills to the sea, and a footpath leads to a secluded beach with views of the Outer Hebrides.

To the south, at the head of the loch, is Eynort, with its wooden houses among conifer plantations, behind a sheltered beach. Further north along Loch Harport, the road finishes by the pier and sheltered small boat anchorage of Portnalong, a township of crofters from Lewis and Harris who came here in 1921. To the west is Fiskavaig, a crofting township above a stony bay, and to the north-west, across the mouth of Loch Bracadale, the three basaltic stacks of MacLeod's Maidens can be seen just off Idrigill Point, named after a MacLeod chief's wife and daughters who drowned near here. The views of the Cuillins from Loch Harport are dramatic, the stark black gabbro contrasting with the softer crofting land at the head of the loch.

From Carbost, a narrow road leads south between the Cuillins and the Glen Brittle Forest, ending by the sandy beach at Loch Brittle where, in summer, the campsite with its handy shop is full of the brightly-coloured tents of the climbers tackling the sharp peaks, the surfaces of which appear barren and lunar – land stripped to the bone, beautiful and cruel. The rock is hard, making for some of the best climbing in the country. Those who do not climb can stare in wonder at the tiny figures traversing and ascending the steep slopes. Those who climb (or walk up) are rewarded, in clear weather, with a staggering panorama of the Hebrides, as distant as St Kilda. There *are* paths to the top (the summit with the best access for walkers is Sgurr Alasdair via Coire Lagan, also Bruach na Frithe via the north-west ridge from Sligachan – guide books are available at the campsite shop), but it must be remembered that this is no place to get stranded in mist or a squall without proper equipment and experience. The mountains *do not* forgive your mistakes. A Forestry Commission picnic site halfway along the glen overlooks Coire na Creiche, the scene of the last battle between the MacDonalds and the MacLeods.

CENTRAL SKYE

South of Portree the road to Sligachan passes through Glen Verragill – unremarkable apart from good views of the Cuillins at the southern end. To the east lie The Braes, scene of a fight on 19 April 1882

Evening at Broadford

between crofters denied grazing rights and an expeditionary force of Glasgow policemen. This melee is sometimes referred to as the last battle on British soil. A small cairn by the roadside commemorates this battle fought on behalf of the crofters of Gaeldom. The road finishes at Peinchorran: along its length are a few crofts where once there were many, and ruined black houses now stand beside modern chalet bungalows, yet the feeling is of peace, and the views of Raasay are worthwhile.

The Sligachan Hotel, beautifully situated at the head of the loch with a mountain backdrop, is a popular and comfortable centre for the Cuillins. From the bridge, as you look south along Glen Sligachan, the difference between the young mountains to the west, spiky and angular, and the older mountains to the east, smoothed by erosion, can be clearly seen. A track through the glen leads to the isolated and dramatic glacial basin of Loch Coruisk (*coire uish,* the cauldron of water) at the head of Loch Scavaig. Loch Coruisk remains little changed since the thawing of the ice that scooped it out 100-ft deeper than the water of Loch Scavaig – a primeval, lonely place. At the seaward end of Loch Sligachan is Sconser, the ferry terminal for Raasay and site of the island's main nine-hole golf course. Of the two routes to Loch Ainort, the minor road by the coast is more pleasant.

On the southern shore of the loch is Luib, with its folk museum, a black house restored in 1978 by the energetic Peter MacAskill, who has been responsible for saving other similar buildings on the island. There are room settings, showing interiors of about 50 years ago, a peat fire burning in the stove and some farm implements. During restoration two guns, dating from the 1745 rising, were found hidden under the roof. Outside roam a small flock of blackface tups, sheep noted for their longevity.

Beyond the forestry plantations is Broadford, a formless village that serves as the main centre for the south of the island. There is little of interest, but all main services – shops, hotels, bed-and-breakfasts, bank, post office, garage, youth hostel and Tourist Information Centre - are available. The beach is untidy stone and shingle, and at one time the steamer used to call here on the way to Portree. The village is dominated by Bienn na Callich (2403ft), on the top of which is a large and conspicuous cairn with, reputedly, a Norwegian princess buried beneath. The walk to the summit is not difficult and the views of Skye and Wester Ross are just reward.

Across Broadford Bay can be seen **Pabay** (priest or monk island – 350 acres) noted for its limestone fossils and past associations with pirates. Licensed to produce postage stamps, it has a ruined chapel, a burial ground and two houses. It was described in the 1500s as being 'full of woods, good for fishing, and a main shelter for thieves and cut-throats'. To the north east is **Scalpay,** rough and heather-clad, rising to 1298ft at the summit of Mullach na Carn, although the area around Scalpay House, in the south-east corner behind a small tidal harbour, is cultivated. There are several lochs and many streams, and large areas of conifers have been planted. 4000 acres on the north-west side are fenced for deer farming.

The island was first developed in the 19thC by Sir Donald Currie who made roads and planted trees; it is now owned by a merchant banker and worked by his sons.

To the west of Scalpay House are the remains of a chapel, built on the site of a Celtic cell. At low tide the island seems almost to join Skye at Caolas Scalpay. To the east is **Longay,** rising to 221ft at the southern end of a reef running parallel to Scalpay; to the south is the small low-lying **Guillamon Island.**

Waterloo is the eastward continuation of Broadford; in 1815, over 1500 Skye men fought at the Battle of Waterloo and, on return, many veterans made their home here. Behind Broadford the road to Elgol passes along Strath Suardal, a wide valley to the south of Bienn na Caillich. Below here, at Coire-chatachan, are the ruins of the house where Mackinnon entertained Boswell and Johnson during their tour of the Hebrides in 1773. By the road on a small rise is the ancient graveyard and crumbling walls of Cill Chriosd, where St Maolrubha founded a church in the 7thC – the last service was held in the mid-19thC. As you approach Torrin, by Loch Slapin, there is a marble quarry, its spoil heaps gleaming white, and nearby a track leads to a

small beach. To the south, a few ruined walls are all that remain of Suisnish, a once thriving crofting community that was cleared to Canada. Over the loch the bare rock, deep crevices and scree of Bla Bheinn (3044ft) contrast dramatically with the gentle shoreline. Kilmarie, on the east of Strathiard, was once the home of the Mackinnon chiefs. From the main road, a well-signposted track leads west to the fine isolated beach at Camasunary and on over the bridge to Loch Coruisk, this gruelling walk made even more difficult by The Bad Step, a rock obstacle.

The main road ends at Elgol, passing a thriving area of crofts before descending steeply to the stone and shingle beach and jetty. Virtually on the beach is the school – a marvellous, if somewhat exposed, position, where the view across Loch Scavaig to the Cuillins is particularly good. At Suidhe Biorach, half a mile to the south, is the cave where Bonnie Prince Charlie was hidden before leaving Skye – childless women were supposed to become fertile after sitting on this promontory.

A narrow and winding road crosses the peninsula to Glasnakille, a village of crofts along a steep and mainly inaccessible shore; the Spar Cave, best explored at low tide with a torch, contains stalactites. A track leads down to a deep gash in the cliffs; the path along the top affords fine views of Sleat.

SLEAT

The road from Broadford to Sleat passes a low-lying area. A smaller road west of the main one leads to Drumfearn, a pretty crofting township where a track leads down to the sheltered rocky head of Loch Eishort, with small fishing boats, and cattle and sheep grazing by the shore.

The main road and the main centres of population are on the fertile eastern side of the peninsula, the garden of Skye, with woodland, forest plantations, crofts and farms, and a mainly rocky shore. At the southern end of Loch na Dal is Isleornsay, a very pretty village with a welcoming hotel, an art gallery, a pier with sculptures, rusting anchors and chains, and small moored boats. The small tidal island of **Ornsay**, to which you can cross at low tide, has a ruined chapel and an unmanned lighthouse, built in 1857. There is an attractive beach at Camascross to the south. The road rejoins the coast at Teangue, where the ivy-clad ruins of Knock Castle, built in the 14thC, stand at the edge of a small bay. Many of its stones were taken to build Knock House.

A Gaelic college has been established in the restored farm at Ostaig, part of a large estate owned by an Edinburgh merchant banker who has successfully revitalised this part of the island. Gaelic language courses are held in the summer, with piping courses in the spring and autumn. There is a bookshop selling Gaelic books and souvenirs.

The island of Ornsay

Armadale Castle, designed by Gillespie Graham and built 1815-19 for the second Lord MacDonald, stands above the road in fine grounds planted with North American hardwoods, conifers and Australasian and European trees. The castle is now the Clan Donald Centre (there are estimated to be three million MacDonalds, dispersed throughout the world), with a display of relics, crafts and books, and a restaurant. The pier to the south is the terminal for the Mallaig ferry, and provides limited shelter for the Skye Yacht Club moorings. South of Ardvasar the road narrows and becomes quite dramatic, with fine views of Knoydart, Morar and Moidart and ending at the crofting township of Aird of Sleat where a track, impassable for cars, continues to the lighthouse at the Point of Sleat. This is the extreme southern tip of Skye, looking out towards Rum, Eigg and Ardnamurchan.

On the west of Sleat there are three settlements reached by a narrow scenic road through low irregular hills, in a loop from Knock to Ostaig. The most northerly of these habitations is Ord, where there is a hotel above a small bay of pebbles and a little sand. Further south is Tokavaig, with crofts, and the remains of Dunscaith Castle built into the rock and overlooking the bay, a stronghold of the MacDonalds during the 15th and 16thC, and in legend occupied by the Queen of Skye, who taught the art of war to Cuchulainn, an Irish hero. It is one of the oldest fortified headlands in the Hebrides and was last occupied around 1570; access to it is difficult. The largest of the three communities is Tarskavaig, with crofts to the north of a small beach with sand at low tide, and rocks and skerries out to sea. This isolated area of western Sleat is well worth visiting. It has great intrinsic beauty, and a superb view of the jagged peaks of the Cuillins, cloud-topped in a sweep above Coruisk.

EASTERN SKYE AND THE KYLES

Skye's most ancient ferry terminal is at Kylerhea, a small township overlooking Kyle Rhea. As recently as 1906, cattle were swum across the narrows to the mainland at slack water, tied nose to tail in strings of six or eight behind a boat – up to 8000 head a year were once taken off the island in this way. It is presently the terminal for the Glenelg ferry, linked to the main Broadford to Kyleakin road by the narrow pass through Glen Arroch, with its summit at 911ft.

Kyleakin was once a fishing village and the main ferry terminal for Skye, with a continuous seven-day-a-week service until the new bridge opened. A Sunday ferry service was started here in 1965 against a background of strong protest, led by Rev. Angus Smith, Free Church minister for Skeabost, who also instigated the narrowly defeated anti-alcohol poll two years later. The village overlooks the swift-flowing waters of Kyle Akin, now overlooked by the new road bridge, where King Haakon moored in 1263 on his way to defeat at the Battle of Largs. The entrance to the harbour is guarded by the ruins of Caisteal Maol, used by the Mackinnons from the 12th to the 15thC. Apparently a Norwegian princess, resident in an earlier building on this site, stretched a chain across the Kyle to extract tolls from passing ships – an imaginative legend and an equally imaginative piece of engineering! The village has shops, hotels, restaurants and other services, and there are boat trips from here during the summer.

Four miles to the west of Kyleakin is the Skye airstrip. Close by, where a stream crosses the shore, is the spot where St Maolrubha preached – keeping his scriptures in the rocks and hanging a bell from the branches of a tree. A graveyard at the end of the runway overlooks many small islands and skerries where cattle are sometimes stranded by the tide. A neat row of graves stands as a reminder of the sinking of the cruiser, *HMS Curacao,* cut in two by the liner, *Queen Mary,* while acting as her escort on 2 October 1942. The scattered crofts of Upper and Lower Breakish (the name is said to derive from *a'bhreac,* smallpox, that swept through the island in the 17th and 18thC) are of little interest, but the old schoolhouse on the main road is the office of the *West Highland Free Press,* a controversial campaigning newspaper which started in 1972, and is distributed throughout the islands.

Skye's link with the mainland via the new bridge, and good rail connections, make for very easy access, which has resulted in the island becoming extremely busy during the main holiday months. To enjoy it at its best and with much less traffic around, you might consider visiting during May, June or September, when the weather is often better. A toll is charged for crossing the new bridge. A passenger-only ferry, carrying up to 50 people, has started in competition with the bridge, offering very reasonable rates for those who would still wish to go 'over the sea' to Skye.

A Monday to Saturday ferry service is operated in the summer between Glenelg and Kylerhea, carrying vehicles up to four tons; this is a five-minute passage. Another seasonal ferry service is operated by Caledonian MacBrayne's *Lord of the Isles* between Mallaig (which is a railhead) and Armadale: a 30 minute passage. During the winter this service is for passengers only, and is provided by Caledonian MacBrayne's *Lochmor.*

Caledonian MacBrayne's ferry *Loch Striven* operates between Sconser and Raasay, and the *Hebridean Isles* links Uig with Tarbert and Lochmaddy in the Outer Hebrides. The main Tourist Information Centre is in Portree, with smaller offices in Uig, Broadford and the Kyle of Lochalsh.

Raasay

Highland. With a population of 150, Raasay is 13 miles long by 3 miles wide, rising to a height of 1456ft at the distinctive flat-topped summit of Dun Caan, upon which the ebullient Dr Johnson danced a reel after consuming an alcoholic open air breakfast.

The north of the island is composed of Archaean gneiss, the south being Torridonian sandstone with two large areas of granite. Some of the Torridonian shales contain the oldest plant remains yet discovered. A feature almost unique in the Highlands is the strong loam present between 600 and 900 ft at The Glam. The presence of this soil suggests that Raasay probably escaped glaciation leaving much ancient and rare flora on the east coast. The disused mine-workings in the south are evidence of ironstone deposits, no longer of economic use.

The present ferry service between Sconser and Suisnish, started by Caledonian MacBrayne in July 1976 after a long campaign by the islanders, helped to stem the island's declining fortunes. Although there is full employment many of the people are elderly, and the boarding out in Portree of children over 11 years of age during the school term does little to encourage them to stay in later years. Raasay was once the centre of a breakaway section of the Free Church, formed in 1893 by a Mr MacFarlane, with an even more uncompromising doctrine than the original. All pleasure was suspect: music, dancing and poetry, once strong on the island, were banned. Today the original Free Church on the island has a few supporters, but most people belong to the church of the breakaway group, and this plays an important part in the island's life. The Sabbath is therefore strictly observed – no work, no play, and people going out only to church. The community is a caring one, sharing fortune and misfortune alike, and the people are happy to receive visitors – as long as their lifestyle is respected.

Inverarish is the main village, with a fine general store, a post office, and terraced houses built by Baird & Co. for their mine-workers. Above the village are the remains of Dun Borodale, a broch with parts of the walls and galleries remaining.

Raasay House

Behind Inverarish the road passes through the forest and the disused

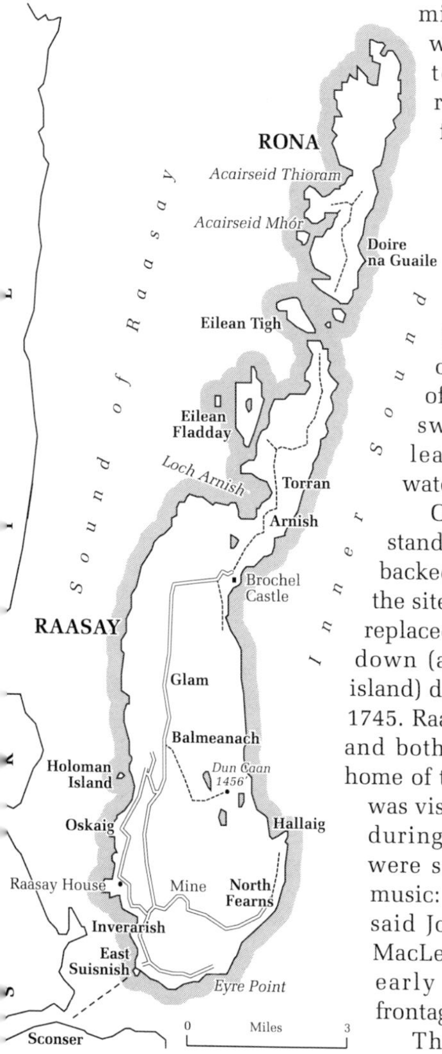

mine-workings where German POWs worked during World War I, and on to North and South Fearns, four restored cottages where, in 1919, families from Rona (the Rona Raiders) seized the land from Baird's. The men were put on trial amid a public outcry, but were subsequently released and piped triumphantly home. The view from here towards the Kyle is of immense beauty – layer upon layer of mountains in receding colours, often set against vast cloud formations swept in from the Atlantic. A path leads north from the Fearns to the waterfall by the shore at Hallaig.

On the north side of Churchton Bay stands Raasay House, a once-fine building backed by mixed woodland. It stands on the site of a tower built in 1549, which was replaced with a house subsequently burned down (along with all the cottages on the island) during the reprisals after the Rising of 1745. Raasay and Rona supported the Prince, and both paid dearly for it. This ancestral home of the MacLeods was again rebuilt, and was visited by Johnson and Boswell in 1773 during their tour of the Hebrides. They were suitably entertained with food and music: 'I know not how we shall get away' said Johnson, in his contentment. James MacLeod improved the estate during the early 1800s and added the Regency frontage to the house.

The population on the island grew rapidly, poverty became widespread, and emigration began. In 1843, due to heavy debt, John MacLeod was forced to sell the island. The purchaser was George Rainy of Edinburgh, who paid 35,000 guineas (£36,750), taking possession in 1846 after the last of the MacLeods had emigrated to Australia. Rainy genuinely tried to improve conditions on Raasay, but without success – so he turned to sheep farming and evicted over 100 families. On his death in 1863, ownership passed to his son, who before his premature death in 1872, aged 27, used the island as a holiday retreat.

Raasay then had several owners, each with little sympathy for the crofters, until Baird's bought it in 1912 to extract the iron-ore; the mine was worked from 1913 to 1919. The present owners of the island, the Scottish Department of Agriculture and Fisheries, bought it for £37,000 in 1922, following the exploits of the Rona Raiders.

Raasay House was run as a hotel from 1937 to 1960, after which a doctor from Sussex bought it, together with the Home Farm and various other buildings. He allowed the house, its contents, and the garden to fall into decay, as well as refusing to sell the more suitable pier at Clachan for use as a terminal for the much-needed ferry. All this echoed the attitudes of the absentee landlords of the last century. After years of uncertainty, Raasay House was finally sold, in a sorry and dilapidated state, and part of it is now used as an outdoor pursuits centre. Borodale House is run as a hotel.

The narrow road north passes by the stable and beneath the clocktower where 36 men of Raasay assembled in 1914 to go to war. The clock stopped as they left and, despite many attempts at repair, has never been restarted: it was an ill omen – only 14 men returned and they found the island in a very poor state. Behind the house stand the ruins of the 13thC chapel dedicated to St Moluag, on an ancient burial ground with two other buildings, the smaller of which possibly dates from the 11thC. One of the gravestones records the drowning off Rona in 1880 of Murdoch and Roderich MacLeod, brothers aged 26 and 24.

Beyond here, at the start of the signposted Temptation Hill, by a fuchsia hedge, stands an incised Pictish symbol stone, perhaps dating from the 7thC; another similar design is carved into a rock near the Battery, a small defensive structure built in 1807 in front of Raasay House, armed with cannon and two less-than-beautiful mermaids. These incised stones may have been part of a series marking an area of sanctuary.

The road winds around Balmeanach, with its crofts and a loch nestling in a sheltered valley. A path south-east to the summit of Dun Caan leaves the road near here; the view from the flat top is magnificent. To the south of the mountains is Loch na Mna, the woman's loch, so named because a water-horse haunting it abducted a woman; the local smithy killed the monster, finding it to be made of jelly. To the west is Loch Storab, taking its name from the nearby grave of a Norwegian prince.

The tarmac road ends at the scant remains of Brochel Castle, probably built by the MacLeods of Lewis in the 15thC, from which they raided ships in the Inner Sound, attracting many lawless men into the Clan. Iain Garbh was the last MacLeod chief to live here, dying in 1671. One-and-a half miles south, on the coast, are the remains of the township of South Screapadal, nestling in a steep valley. It is a good two-and-a-half hour walk from here through broken, rocky, heather-clad ground to Caol Rona. The first two miles of road were built single-handed with pick, shovel and wheelbarrow by Calum MacLeod, one of the island's most northerly inhabitants, to

Eyre Point, Raasay

his home at Arnish. Through Torran, where the post office and school closed in 1960, **Eilean Fladday** is reached, where there were once four families with their own school, but now all the cottages are holiday homes. The island can be reached on foot at low tide. Off the north tip of Raasay is **Eilean Tigh**; at low tide , a rock ledge, joining it to Raasay and wide enough to walk across, is uncovered. The rough, rocky country here is the haunt of golden eagles.

The plant life on the island is particularly rich, with many ancient and rare plants making the island a venue for botanists. You can expect to find many alpines, saxifrages, ferns and mosses; also orchids, sea aster and bog asphodel. Mammals include red deer, otter, alpine hare, water shrew and a species of bank vole with a skull slightly larger than normal, and unique to Raasay.

The only means of public transport to the island is the Caledonian MacBrayne vehicle ferry *Loch Striven* from Sconser on Skye. There are up to five daily return journeys, Monday to Saturday, a 15-minute crossing. There is no petrol for sale on the island.

Island of Rona

Highland. Often known as South Rona, this is the northerly continuation of Raasay, separated from it by the half-mile channel of Caol Rona. Five miles long by about one-and-a-half miles wide, rising to 404 ft at the centre, Rona is composed of Archaean gneiss. Its only inhabitants, apart from the seals and birds, are the caretakers, who live at Rona Lodge, and the Royal Navy personnel who man the NATO signal station at the far northern tip. Please let the caretakers know if you are intending to visit (see below), so they can advise you where the cattle and bull are likely to be! There are now toilets, showers and a washing machine at Big Harbour, so if you arrive by boat you can take advantage of these facilities. The lighthouse is automatic.

At one time there were three settlements, two schools and a church. During the 16thC, the island, then thickly wooded, was the retreat of robbers and pirates who raided shipping from the fine natural harbour of Acairseid Mhor – known at the time as *Port nan Robaireann*, the Port of Robbers.

The island belonged to the MacLeods of Raasay until the time of the Clearances, when crofters evicted from Raasay settled at Doire na Guaile, Acairseid Mhor (Big Harbour) and Acairseid Thioram (Dry Harbour), breaking the barren ground with picks and fertilising it with seaweed. In the mid-19thC there were 150 head of cattle kept on Rona in spite of the poor soil, and now once again cattle graze here.

By the end of World War I, Rona, like Raasay, was in a poor economic state and no Government help was made available to the crofters. In 1919 a group of seven families seized fertile land at Eyre and North and South Fearns on Raasay, rowing across Caol Rona with their sheep and 20 cattle; soon there was only one family on Rona who also subsequently left. The overgrown remains of the three settlements can still be seen.

Those who land on the island should try to visit the Church Cave on the east coast. A vast cavern with seats and an altar of natural rock, the last service was held here in the 19thC. There are trips from Portree to view Rona. If you wish to land, write to J. R Dixon or Donald MacCalman, Rona Lodge, Island of Rona, c/o The Post Office, Portree, Isle of Skye IV51 9RA to let them know.

Soay

Highland. Three miles due west of Elgol, rising to 455 ft at the summit of Beinn Bhreac, Soay (pronounced *soy*) is pinched into a central isthmus by the narrow cut of the harbour on the north-west coast, and by the bay of Camas nan Gall on the south-east, where the islanders live. Composed of Torridonian sandstone, it has many sea cliffs but is not very fertile.

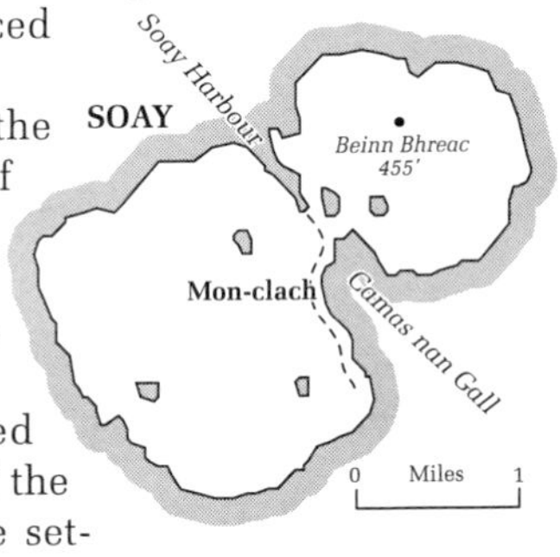

Before 1823 only one family lived here, tending stock, but, as a result of the Clearances, crofters evicted from Skye settled on Soay and by 1861 the population had risen to 129.

In 1946 the author Gavin Maxwell bought the island and started a basking shark fishery, building a slip and a small factory. Lack of demand for shark oil brought it to an end three years later; the project was revived briefly by Maxwell's harpooner Tex Geddes in 1950, although the fishing was no longer based on Soay. By 19 June 1953, all except Geddes and his family had left the island, the final evacuation being made, in a blaze of publicity, aboard the *SS Hebrides,* the crofters re-settling on Mull. A succession of people seeking the quiet life then came and went until the situation stabilised, and now there is a thriving small community of 17 people, whose telephones are powered by solar panels. A boat from the mainland calls monthly; boats to bring you here may be hired from Arisaig or Elgol.

Eilean Donnan

This is a tidal islet at the entrance to Loch Duich, upon which stands a beautifully reconstructed medieval fortress, among splendid and dramatic scenery. The original fortress was built in 1230 on the site of earlier defensive structures, but this was destroyed in 1719 after 45 Spanish allies of the Old Pretender surrendered to a squadron of British frigates commanded by Captain Boyle. After centuries of neglect, restoration – faithful to the original plans which had been kept in Edinburgh – began in 1912 and was completed in 1932 at a cost of £250,000. Access is gained by a stone bridge, and the castle is open to visitors.

To the west, in Loch Alsh, are the low-lying **Eilean Tioram** and **Glas Eilean**.

The many small islands in and around Loch Hourn are dwarfed by the grandeur of the surrounding mountains. **Eilean à Phiobair**, the Piper's Island, is one of them – perhaps his playing was not all it could be, and he was sent there to practise. **Sandaig Islands**, to the north of the Loch, shelter the bay which was called Camusfearna by Gavin Maxwell, who wrote *Ring of Bright Water* here in 1960. The cottage he occupied was destroyed by fire, and the ruin has been cleared. Boat trips run to here from the Kyle of Lochalsh.

The Small Isles Parish

Highland. Canna, Rum, Eigg and Muck lie as a group to the south-west of Skye and to the west of Mallaig, and they are all inhabited. Their history is that of the surrounding isles – early conversion to Christianity, Viking raids then settlement under the suzerainty of Norway, finally becoming part of the Kingdom of Scotland in 1266. Then followed the rule of the Lords of the Isles until the end of the 15thC, feuding by the clans vying for power, the '45 rebellion, the famines and the Clearances. Today Canna, Eigg and Muck are working islands, with small communities proving that island life is viable and valuable. Rum, owned by Scottish Natural Heritage and, in spite of its size never really habitable, is now functioning as a unique open-air laboratory.

Canna

Canna's population numbers about 20. Its name comes from the Gaelic, either *Canna* (porpoise) or *Kanin* (isle of rabbits). It extends about five miles by one mile north-west of Rum and halfway between Mallaig and Lochboisdale, South Uist. A steep-sided island, it is made up of terraced Tertiary basalt which breaks down into extremely fertile soil, on which some of the earliest crops in the West Highlands are grown. Rainfall is about 60 inches each year. At the eastern end is the harbour, with the only deep-water pier in the Small Isles Parish, sheltered by the tidal island of **Sanday,** which is linked to Canna by a footbridge. A walk around Sanday will reveal this island's almost irresistible attraction to flotsam. The catholic church here has, quite extraordinarily, suffered vandalism.

At the eastern tip of Canna is Compass Hill (458ft), so called due to the high metal content of the rock and the effect this has on a ship's compass. A mile to the west is Carn a Ghaill, the island's summit, 690ft high, and three miles south-west is the isolated basalt rock of **Humla.**

The island of Sanday is crofted; and Canna itself is run as a single farm. John Lorne Campbell bought the island in 1938 from the widow of Robert Thorn, a Glasgow ship owner. Thorn had purchased the island from Donald MacNeil in 1881, after 60 years of drastic clearances during which the population fell to 48. Thorn was a benevolent and responsible man and Canna remained in good hands

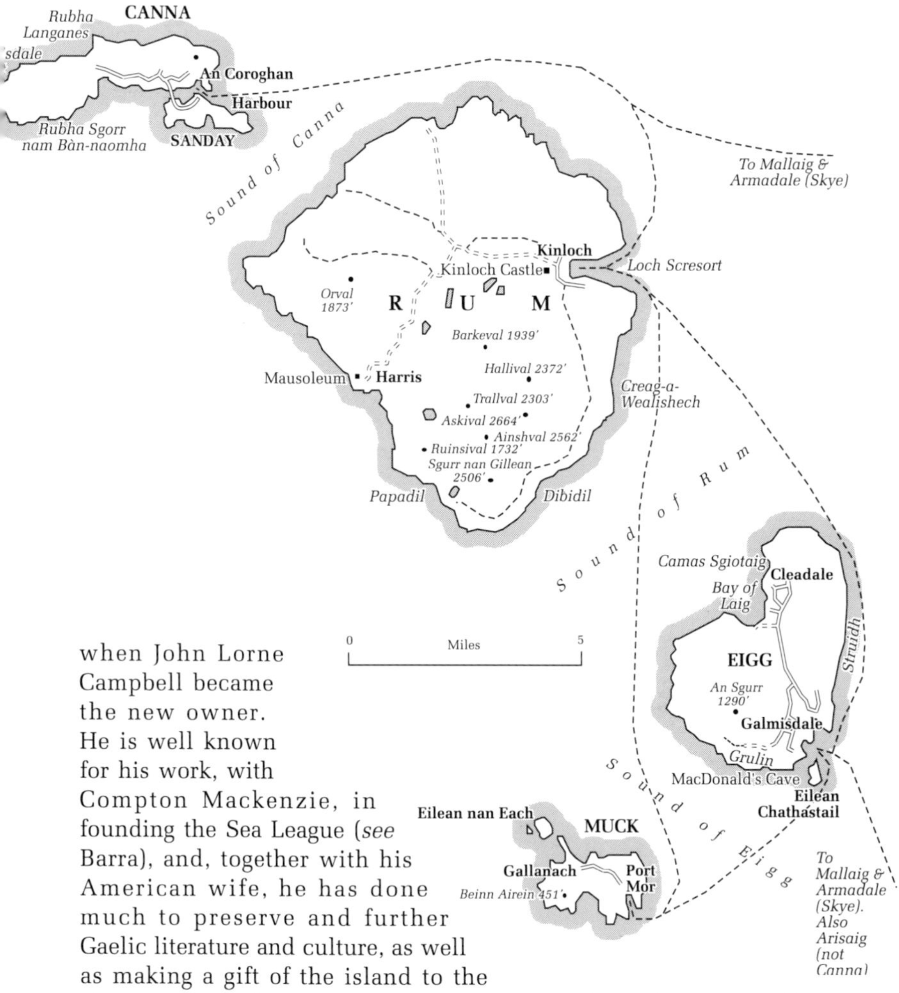

when John Lorne Campbell became the new owner. He is well known for his work, with Compton Mackenzie, in founding the Sea League (*see* Barra), and, together with his American wife, he has done much to preserve and further Gaelic literature and culture, as well as making a gift of the island to the National Trust for Scotland. The people are Catholic, and Gaelic speaking; the island is viable and happy. There is a valuable stock of Highland cattle and Cheviot sheep, and early potatoes are grown on the farm.

Evidence of Viking occupation can be seen at Rubha Langanes on the north coast, where one of the finest examples of a ship burial was uncovered. The original township before the Clearances was A'Chill, to the north of the harbour, near the site of the 7thC St Columba's Chapel. Only a Celtic cross, a column and the faint patterns of lazybeds remain. A geo-physical survey has been conducted on the buried remnants of St Columba's settlement, which lays claim to being Na In Ba, the saint's favourite retreat. Eileach an Naoimh, one of the Isles of the Sea, has also long been thought to have been this place.

To the east of the harbour is An Goroghan, a ruined tower on top of an isolated stack, where a Clanranald chief imprisoned his wife to frustrate the attentions of her lover, a MacLeod from Skye. On the south coast is a ruined convent at Rubha Sgorr nam Ban-naomha – the headland of holy women – which has associations with Columba.

Sea eagles, released on Rum, can now be seen over the cliffs of Canna. There is no holiday accommodation but those who wish to camp may do so, with permission.

Rum

Rum's population is about 20 – all, apart from the schoolmistress, employed by Scottish Natural Heritage. The name is pronounced Room, possibly from the Norse *Rom oe* – wide island. Once commonly, and incorrectly, written as Rhum, this spelling was introduced by the Bulloughs, the English owners between 1886 and 1957. It is the largest island in the Parish, diamond-shaped (eight by eight-and-a-half miles), nearly 26,400 acres in extent and rising to a maxi-mum height of 2664ft at the summit of Askival in the south. It is situated nine miles south-west of Skye. Being able to support only a small population relative to its area resulted in its being described as a wet desert. Now over 10,000 visitors come each year.

It is of great interest to geologists, having certain formations that are quite unique. The northern and least mountainous part is Torridonian sandstone sloping gently to the sea, with a beautiful beach at Kilmory. The central high ground is Tertiary Peridotite related closely to the Cuillins of Skye, with here and there a patch of gabbro or gneiss. The western point is composed of steep-sided granite, with dramatic sheer cliffs where huge blocks have tumbled pell-mell to the shore. A half a mile to the north-east of Harris is the spot which has the strongest gravitational pull in the British Isles.

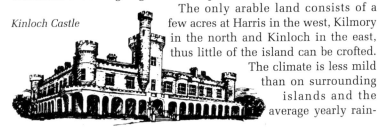

Kinloch Castle

The only arable land consists of a few acres at Harris in the west, Kilmory in the north and Kinloch in the east, thus little of the island can be crofted. The climate is less mild than on surrounding islands and the average yearly rain-

Eigg and Rum

fall is 93 inches, although this varies, being as low as 56 inches at Harris and as high as 122 inches in the mountains. The topography of Rum results in prolonged periods of cloud cover when surrounding areas may be clear, and gusty winds.

In 1346 Rum was owned by John of Islay, passing to McKenabrey of Coll in 1549, then to the MacLeans of Coll in 1695. By the early 19thC it was vastly overcrowded, and the islanders were poor and unable to pay their rent. A clearance was arranged, and on the 11th July 1826 over 300 crofters left, bound for Canada and America to face a hard winter. Two years later a further 50 souls left, leaving only one native family of Macleans on the island. 8000 sheep were then brought in. Crofters came to the island from Mull and Skye and, by 1831, the population had risen to 134. But the sheep proved unprofitable, and the island was sold in 1845 to the Marquis of Salisbury, who stocked the streams with trout and the hills with deer. After being sold and re-sold, and with another attempt at sheep farming proving unsuccessful, Rum was finally bought for £35,000 in 1886 by the remarkable John Bullough of Oswaldtwistle, who had made his fortune designing milling machinery. It became his holiday retreat and sporting estate, with deer partly replacing the sheep.

John Bullough's son, Sir George, became the owner in 1891, and spared no expense in building Kinloch Castle, an extravagant monument to the Edwardian opulence which ended with the outbreak of war. Turtles and alligators were kept in heated tanks, a pure white Arab stallion was imported to improve the stock of the native Rum ponies (said to descend from Spanish ponies which swam ashore from a wrecked Armada galleon, but it is more likely they came from Eriskay), and two exotic Albion cars were used to transport guests. Muscatel grapes, figs, peaches and nectarines were grown under glass, and dances were held to the music of an electric organ in the sumptuous ballroom.

The island population stabilised at about 90 people until the outbreak of the war, and all regarded the Bullough family as kindly and courteous people, although the press labelled Rum 'The Forbidden Island' – a strange but predictable media response to an estate kept no more private than those on the mainland. In 1957 the island was purchased from Sir George's widow, Monica Lady Bullough, by the Nature Conservancy Council (now Scottish Natural Heritage), to be used as a natural outdoor laboratory. Kinloch Castle has been preserved, and part is now run as a hotel.

Red deer, wild goats, domestic Highland cattle and ponies are maintained and studied. Sheltered glens are being replanted with native trees and shrubs, and open heathland is managed in order to preserve natural flora and fauna. Geology, ecology and conservation can all be studied in a unique environment, with little disturbance.

The earliest signs of human habitation, flint and bloodstone flakes dating from 6000BC, have been uncovered near Kinloch, which is now the main area of occupation with a shop and post office. There is no pier, and all cargo and passengers have to be transshipped to the jetty. Tarmac roads are also non-existent, but a good track leads due west to the centre of the island, where it forks – north to Kilmory with its fine beach and cemetery with a gravestone bearing the names of six children of the Matheson family, five of whom died in the space of a week, and south to Harris and the Bullough mausoleum, built in the style of a Greek temple and not a little incongruous. A rugged track leads south from Kinloch to the east of Hallival and Askival to Dibidil and Papadil, passing near Creag-a-Wealishech – the Welshman's cliff, in memory of a gang of Welsh slate quarriers who widened a precipitous path.

The sea cliffs attract kittiwake, puffin, guillemot and razorbill and the mountain tops Manx shearwater (over 60,000 pairs). In all, over 150 species of birds have been recorded, and the sea eagle has been re-introduced using chicks taken from nests on the Norwegian coast.

Plant life is prolific and varied, little disturbed on the cliffs and mountain summits since the last ice age. There are many alpines, including the rare arctic sandwort and penny-cress; roseroot, thrift, sea campion and Scots lovage on the cliffs; bog asphodel, heath spotted-orchid, sundew, butterwort and black bog-rush on the moors.

Day visitors are welcome. Those who wish to stay longer must

Red deer stags feeding on seaweed at Kilmory, Rum.

make *prior* arrangements with the SNH Warden at White House, Kinloch. Accommodation is limited and priority is given to those engaged in research work. Climbers require a permit and must be in organised parties. There is also accommodation at the hotel.

About nine miles west of Rum lie **Oigh-sgeir** and **Garbh Sgeir** the (maiden rock), hexagonal basalt columns with an area of about 10 acres, rising 33 ft above sea level. The channel between the two outcrops has often provided welcome shelter for small boats caught by storms, the spray passing overhead as the craft lie in calm water. During the 19thC, Canna cattle were grazed on the islets' lush grass. The lighthouse was built in 1902 by D A Stevenson. Lighthouse keepers once grew vegetables and flowers here in what must have been the country's most remote walled garden. They also fished lobsters and built a miniature golf course.

Eigg

Pronounced egg, the name is probably derived from the Gaelic eige (a notch) and was once known as *Eilean Nimban-More* (island of the big women). It has an area of over 5000 acres, a population which numbers just 68, and is dominated by An Sgurr at the southern end, the largest mass of columnar pitchstone lava in Britain, rising a sheer 290ft above the 1000ft contour, best seen from the south. The view from the top is superb. A large colony of Manx shearwater has established itself on An Sgurr, burrowing into the soil.

The northern plateau and southern moor are basalt and have weathered into excellent soil. Cliffs around the northern point are sandstone, eroded into fantastic shapes at Camas Sgiotaig, where the beach is composed of grains of quartz, white with black flecks, which creak underfoot – Eigg's famous singing sands (but only when they are dry). To the north of the pretty Bay of Laig there are limestone blocks and nodules, some trapped in rock cages and rattled by the waves. The crofting township of Cleadale lies behind the bay.

Eigg's main village is Galmisdale, on the south-east corner, its small pier partially sheltered by the columnar basalt **Eilean Chathastail** (castle island) with its lighthouse. The harbour is not deep but can be used by launches. There is a shop and post office situated here.

Half a mile south-west of the pier is MacDonalds Cave or Uamh Fhraing (St Francis Cave), where, in the winter of 1577 and after an exchange of minor atrocities the MacLeods of Skye suffocated 395 MacDonalds by burning brushwood at the narrow entrance. The MacDonalds were undiscovered until one of their scouts was spotted by the MacLeods who then traced his footprints in the snow leading to the cave. The feuding continued at Trumpan in Skye. A little further to the west is Cathedral Cave, used by Roman Catholics during the time of their persecution; a stone wall in the cave may have served as an altar. In the 7thC, a monastery was founded by St Donnan, who, with his brothers, was killed by the islanders. The building was later destroyed by Norsemen, and the ruins of the 14thC Kildonnan Church stand on the site of this earlier building.

MacDonald of Clanranald was given the island by Robert the Bruce in 1309. The Clan supported the Prince during the unsuccessful '45 rebellion. Captain John Ferguson of the King's ship, *Furnace,* later visited Eigg to arrest John MacDonald, who surrendered to avoid bloodshed. Ferguson gave an undertaking that, if the MacDonalds gave up their weapons, there would be no reprisals. After agreeing to this, those who were suspected of supporting the rebellion were taken, the island was sacked and the young men transported.

The MacDonalds sold Eigg in 1827 for £15,000 to Dr Hugh MacPherson, and several clearances took place. Upon his death the island passed to his children and became relatively prosperous during the 1870s, the population at this time being over 300. In the 1890s it was bought by Robert Thompson, and again the island prospered, but he died a sick and lonely man. He was buried beneath a marble slab at the summit of Eilean Cathastail on Christmas Day, 1913.

The Sgurr of Eigg

In the 1920s the island was bought by the Runciman family, who developed the land, ploughed back profits, and made a self-sufficient and mechanised 2000-acre farm. In 1966 it was sold to Robert Evans, a Welsh Border farmer, who in turn sold it in 1971 to a Christian charity, which succeeded in upsetting and demoralising the whole population with grandiose schemes that took no account of the islander's needs.

In 1975 it was purchased by Keith Schellenburg, who actively promoted Eigg as a holiday island, but once again seemed only to alienate the islanders. It was then bought by a German artist known as *Maruma,* and matters went from bad to worse. Now The Isle of Eigg Heritage Trust, which consists of the Scottish Wildlife Trust, the Highland Council and *the islanders themselves* have at last bought Eigg, and its future is now secure. Their first major development project consists of a Visitor Centre next to the pier, consisting of a tea room, post office, craft shop, display area and toilets and showers. There is guest-house, caravan and cottage accommodation available, but demand usually exceeds supply.

Muck

The name comes from the Gaelic, *eilean a muic* (isle of the sow), and was referred to by Buchanan in 1582 as *insula porcorum* (pigs' island). With an area of 1586 acres, rising to a maximum height of 451ft at the summit of Beinn Airein, it lies about two-and-a-half miles south-west of Eigg and eight miles north of Ardnamurchan. A fertile island of Tertiary basalt, which receives beneficial dressings of wind-blown shell sand, it is a pretty and peaceful place with pleasant beaches, even if somewhat exposed to the weather. At the south-east corner is Port Mor, a small harbour with a difficult rocky entrance. Off the north-west tip, **Eilean nan Each** (horse island), where ponies were kept, and **Eilean Aird nan Uan** (the lambs' lofty isle) can be reached at low tide.

Muck is run as a single unit by Lawrence MacEwan, a caring and tenacious laird who keeps cattle, sheep and a small dairy herd, and grows potatoes, oats and root crops – quite an achievement on what is truly an oceanic island. The laird's house is at Gallanach.

In 1828, 150 kelp collectors were cleared and in 1854 Captain Thomas Swinburne, RN, the new owner, began a fishing industry, renting the land out for sheep. By 1861 the population was 58; today it is about 25.

There are a few acres of woodland, and in spring and early summer the fields are coloured by cornflower, harebell, marigold and iris. Above Port Mór there is a ruined chapel by the graveyard, and at the entrance to the harbour are the few remains of a defensive structure, the Castle of the White Fort. There is a limited amount of holiday accommodation at the guest house or holiday cottage. Tents may be used.

The Small Isles Parish is served by Caledonian MacBrayne's passenger ferry *Lochmor* from Mallaig via Armadale on Skye, which does a round trip three times each week. There are also boats from Mallaig and Arisaig during the summer serving Eigg and Rum, and a ferry from Glenuig and Lochailort, to Eigg, also during the summer only.

Mallaig to Loch Linnhe

On **Eilean a'Ghaill**, to the south-east of Rubh'Arisaig, are the remains of a fort; there are others on Rubh'Aird Ghamhsgail, on the northern shore of Loch nan Uamh, and on **Eilean nan Gobhar** (goat island) at the entrance to Loch Ailort. Loch nan Uamh (loch of the caves) was the scene of the end of the '45 Rising, where Prince Charlie, after his adventures in the Outer Hebrides and on Skye with Flora MacDonald, finally left Scotland for the last time aboard the *Heureux*. A cairn has been erected to mark this historic event. On the southern shore of the Sound of Arisaig is the tidal **Samalaman Island,** which has a fine sandy beach and picnic area.

Eilean Shona (island of the ford) splits the entrance to Loch Moidart, and is extensively forested on the eastern side; composed mainly of rugged igneous rock, it rises to a height of 870ft. The *New Statistical Account of Scotland* of 1845 says that it was 'the only island worth noticing' in Ardnamurchan and that 'the dwelling house and surrounding scenery of the residence of a respectable family are very beautiful.' It has a population of about 10. The private estate has a deer herd, oyster fisheries, plantations and reports at one time of a wild cat estimated to be 4ft long. The dramatist James Barrie wrote *Mary Rose* while staying here.

To the south is the wooded **Riska Island**, and Castle Tioram (or *Tirrin*, the dry castle) standing on a rocky tidal islet off Cul Doirlinn in the beautiful Loch Moidart. Built in the 13thC, it was the seat of the MacDonalds of Clanranald, and around 1600 some domestic buildings were added to the original massive curtain walls. This area was the centre of both Jacobite risings in 1715 and 1745. The castle was partly destroyed, at the orders of Clanranald, after the failure of the '45, although parts remained habitable. The unfortunate Lady Grange spent some time here *en route* to her exile on St Kilda.

In Loch Sunart are the islands of **Risga**, **Carna** and **Oronsay**; their position in the entrance to the loch causes the tide to flow swiftly around them. Oronsay, low-lying, barren and rocky, deeply indented with sea lochs, was once inhabited. Carna, recorded in 1845 as being a more fertile island has been continuously inhabited for the past 300 years, and is presently occupied by resident caretakers, and a flock of sheep. Seals breed around **Eilean nan Eildean** to the west, and can also be seen in Glenmore Bay, sheltered by the tidal **Eilean Mór**.

The island of Risga has cup-marked rocks which may have been part of some kind of moon and sun calendar. It is the breeding ground of oystercatcher, merganser, eider duck and tern.

Mull

Strathclyde. The name means mass of hill, an apt description for this volcanic island, the third largest in the Hebrides. With an area of nearly 225,000 acres, it lies to the west of Oban, its east coast roughly parallel to the Morven shore. In the south, the Ross of Mull extends as a long peninsula, with the island of Iona off the tip. The west is deeply indented with sea lochs leaving only a narrow neck of land between Loch na Keal and Salen.

The highest point, at the summit of Ben More, is 3170ft and there are several other peaks well over 2000ft. Most characteristic of the landscape are the terraced hills known as trap – Tertiary basalt plateau lavas, the volcanic out-pourings of 40–50 million years ago, now much eroded. These stepped hillsides are best seen around Loch Scridain. The mountain of Ben More is the highest Tertiary basalt in Britain – the trap layers beneath the summit end in dramatic sea cliffs at Ardnamurchan. Later eruptions, centred on Beinn Chasgidle and Loch Ba, formed circular granitic dykes some five miles in diameter and 300-ft thick – the collapsed cores of the vents.

Northern Mull is plateau basalt, flat wet moorland rising to the trap layers, never higher than 1500 ft. 'S Airde Beinn is a volcanic plug. On the headland south of Treshnish Point there is a pre-glacial raised beach, 125-ft high and fertile, and in the south-east, Loch Spelve and Loch Buie are the end of the Great Glen fault. Glen More has many glacial features, including a terminal moraine above Graig Cottage.

Westward along the Ross of Mull the trap country gives way first to crystalline gneiss and then to a boss of pink granite, four miles square. Beneath the basalt lavas is a thin layer of chalk, exposed at Carsaig where lime-laden water washes over lias on a south-facing coast, giving extremely favourable growing conditions. Here, as in the chalk streams of southern England, watercress grows.

Columnar basalt, which perhaps reaches its apogee on Staffa, is also to be found on Ulva and Gometra, near Tavool on Ardmeanach and near Bunessan and at Carsaig. The east coast, sheltered from the erosive forces of the prevailing weather, consists of raised beaches above shallow bays.

Mull's climate is mild Atlantic, with very high rainfall in the mountains, making the growing season long. Wind is funnelled to the island's centre by the sea lochs.

The largest landowner and main source of employment is the Forestry Commission, who have vast plantations of Sitka spruce and

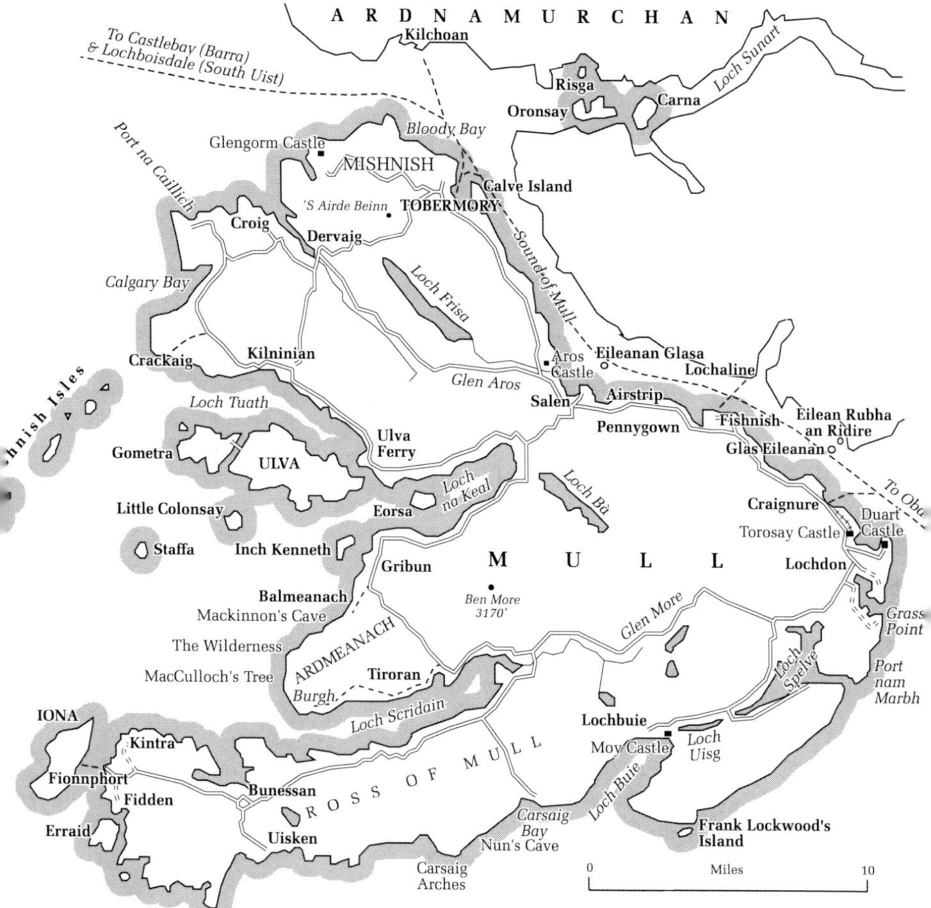

larch in the north-east, at Ardmeanach and on the Ross of Mull. There are a few large farms, a little crofting centred on the Ross and large areas of deer forest. Since the introduction of large-scale sheep farming in the 19thC and the consequent despoilation of cultivated land, Mull's considerable agricultural potential has never been fully realised – a fact reflected by the modest population of 1500. The lobster fishing industry thrives (in the 1920s a 12-pounder was taken in Calgary Bay) and there are, of course, tourists coming in ever-increasing numbers.

The first inhabitants of Mull left stones, circles and cairns scattered over the island. Crannogs (lake dwellings) were built on stilts in Lochs Ba, Assapol, Frisa, Sguabain, Poit na h-I and na Keal. The Irish Celts came in the 2ndC, a turbulent period when many forts and duns were built; there are fine examples at Dun Aisgain to the north of Loch Tuath; Dun Urgadul (vitrified) one mile north of Tobermory;

The trap country of Mull, viewed from Bunessan

Dun nan Gall (fort of the stranger) on Loch Tuath; and An Sean Dun (the bewitched fort), south-west of Glengorm – the last two being brochs.

Christianity came to Iona with the arrival of St Columba in AD 563. The Norsemen raided then settled, and Mull came under Norwegian suzerainty until 1266 when, along with the other islands, it was controlled by Scotland under the Lordship of the Isles. Following this period, the MacLeans became the dominant clan on Mull until the clan system was forcibly broken after the '45 rebellion.

During the 18thC the population increased rapidly, peaking at 10,600 in 1821. There was enormous pressure on the land, although the kelp industry alone sustained many people until it collapsed in 1852. Emigration began even before the lairds and newcomers began clearing the land for sheep, and many evictions were made by owners with little regard for the hardships caused. An exception was the Duke of Argyll, who tried to find employment for his tenants. However, by 1881 the population had been halved, and the Crofters' Act of 1886 did little to help matters, many of the remaining crofts being amalgamated into larger farming units. When the grazings were ruined, the Victorians turned to the sporting potential of the island, stocking it with red deer, which are now to be seen around Torosay, Laggan and Ben More.

CRAIGNURE TO TOBERMORY

The main ferry terminal on Mull is at Craignure, where the pier was built in 1964 for the vehicle & passenger ferry from Oban. Here you will find Scotland's only island railway, which links the terminal

Tobermory harbour

with Torosay castle, about a mile away. To the north, beyond Scalastle Bay, is the terminal from where the smaller car & passenger ferry *Loch Fyne* sails to Lochaline. The airstrip at Glenforsa was built in 54 days in 1966 by the 38th Engineer Regiment, as an exercise.

At Pennygown only the walls remain of a medieval chapel; inside is the shaft of a Celtic cross, probably brought from Iona, showing the Virgin and Child. It is said that there were once benevolent fairies here who would complete any task that was left on their mound – spinning, weaving or the like – until someone left a short piece of wood, asking them to make a ship's mast. After that, no more favours were done.

Salen village sits in a wide bay at the mid-point of the Sound of Mull, and is a convenient touring centre for the island. At the north of the bay are the ruins of Aros Castle, built in the 14thC by the Lord of the Isles, and last occupied in 1608, beneath which treasure from the Tobermory galleon is said to lie buried.

There are several small islands in the Sound of Mull. At the southern entrance close to the mainland, beyond the lighthouse on **Glas Eileanan**, is **Eilean Rubha an Ridire**. In 1973 divers discovered the wreck of the 17thC Royal Navy frigate *Dartmouth* off the north-west shore: she was torn from her moorings in the Sound during a storm and was wrecked on 19 October 1690. Off Salen is **Eileanan Glasa** where, on 25 January 1935, the cargo ship *Rondo* was wrecked, totally demolishing the original lighthouse.

At the northern end of the Sound is the beautiful harbour of Tobermory (*Tobar Mhoire,* Mary's well), full of visiting yachts in the summer and sheltered by **Calve Island** (used as a summer residence) and the steep hills behind. This colourful town is one of the smallest to have had burgh status (from 1875 to 1975), with a population of about 700. The port was developed by the British Fisheries Society in 1788, who built the fine stone houses in the main street, now brightly painted and giving the town a Continental atmosphere. The courthouse, built in 1862, serves as the police station and council offices. There are hotels, a museum, boarding houses, a tourist information office, a youth hostel, shops, bank, library, petrol stations, good junior and senior schools, and a fine public park – the Aros House Policies – given to the town by the Forestry Commission in 1969. There is also a nine-hole golf course.

Buried in the mud at the bottom of the bay lies the remains of a galleon from the routed Spanish Armada, which went down while undergoing repairs in 1588. Long thought to be the *Almirante de Florencia* carrying 30 million ducats, it attracted many salvage attempts, none of which retrieved anything of great monetary value but destroyed a historical site potentially as valuable as that of the *Mary Rose* in Solent. Research by Alison McLeay, documented in her excellent book 'The Tobermory Treasure', has shown beyond reasonable doubt that it was the *San Juan de Sicilia*, a Ragusan ship from what is now Dubrovnik, which foundered here after a fierce fire on board. Stories that it was sabotaged by Donald MacLean, imprisoned on board, are without foundation. To the north is Bloody Bay, scene of a battle between John, last Lord of the Isles, and his son Angus.

A minor road west from Tobermory passes Dun Urgadul, a vitrified fort, before ending at the private Glengorm Castle (built 1860), well situated near the windswept Mishnish headland. Glengorm means blue glen, a name suggested to the unwitting owner and which referred to the blue smoke of the burning crofts when the area was cleared. The main road to Dervaig passes the three Mishnish lochs, set in wild open moorland and well stocked with trout.

DERVAIG TO ARDMEANACH

The pretty village of Dervaig (the little grove), sitting at the head of Loch a'Chumhainn, was built by the MacLeans of Coll in 1799. By the road is the Kilmore Parish Church which has a pencil steeple, more commonly seen in Ireland, and an attractive interior. The Mull Little Theatre was founded in the village, and to the south is The Old Byre, with its unusual tableaux of crofting life. The road south-east to Aros passes Loch Frisa (a trout fishery) and, just before its summit Druimtigh-macgillechattan, Mull's longest place-name and site of an ancient market which was held at the ridge of the house of the Cattenach fellow.

At the mouth of Loch a'Chumhainn is Croig, a little rocky inlet where cattle from the outer isles were once landed on their way to the mainland. At Calgary there is a fine sweep of pale sand backed by machair and, on the northern side, by the old pier, is a prominent basalt dyke which may have given the bay its name – *Calagharaidh*,

The deserted village of Crackaig, Mull

the haven by the wall. The city of Calgary in Canada was *not* so named by emigrants from Mull, contrary to popular belief.

The road south passes the gaunt ruin of Reudle schoolhouse, standing alone on the moor. About a mile south-west along the valley are the substantial remains of Crackaig and Clac Gugairdh, the hollow of the dark grazings, overlooking the Treshnish Isles; 200 people lived in these two villages until the end of the last century. The ash tree where a villager hanged himself still grows in the walled garden by the burn, and below in the cliffs is the Still Cave, where illicit whisky was made.

At Kilninian there is a small area of fine natural woodland and beyond this, near Ulva Ferry, a waterfall. The view across Loch Tuath to the trap hills of **Ulva** and **Gometra** is excellent. These islands, with **Little Colonsay**, were the scene of an almost total clearance of 600 inhabitants by F.W. Clark between 1846 and 1851. **Ulva** (wolf island) was held by the MacQuarries for 800 years until the 18thC; there was once a piping college founded by a MacArthur, a pupil of the famed McCrimmons of Skye, and Ulva House stands in fine woodland on the site of an earlier house once visited by Sir Walter Scott. A museum and tea-room has been opened on Ulva, and many of the recipes on offer feature seaweed, mainly carragheen. This is a reminder of a time around 1800 when the kelp industry on the island supported 600 inhabitants. Evidence gathered from a cave nearby suggests Mesolithic inhabitants some 9000 years ago may also have been eating seaweed. Ulva and Gometra are joined by a bridge. The latter was once the home of Himalayan explorer Hugh Ruttledge. Little Colonsay was at one time farmed by a single family, living in a large Victorian farmhouse, until forced to leave by a plague of rats.

Near Ulva Ferry, Mull

The island of **Eorsa**, in Loch na Keal (the loch of the cliffs), once belonged to the Priory of Iona – it is grazed by a few sheep and has a ruined bothy at the eastern end. The southern shore of the loch is dramatic, the slopes of Ben More (which is most easily climbed from Dhiseig) falling steeply to the water. At Gribun there are huge boulders which have fallen from the cliffs – one of these, now lying by a stone wall, flattened a small cottage in which two newlyweds lay. For them, the earth really did move.

Off the Gribun shore is **Inch Kenneth** – flat, fertile and farmed it was once the granary of Iona. There is a ruined chapel but no remains of the accompanying monastery. Sir Alan MacLean's grave in the burial ground is covered by an intricately carved slab showing the Chief in armour with his dog at his feet. The island is private.

One mile south of Balmeanach is Mackinnon's Cave, about 100-ft high and 600-ft deep, with stalactites in the deepest part. It can only be entered at low tide, and a torch is essential. At Rubha na h-Uamha, which is the most westerly point of the boulder-strewn cliffs of the wild Ardmeanach peninsula, is MacCulloch's Tree, a fossil 40-ft high, engulfed by lava 50 million years ago. It was first described by Dr MacCulloch in 1819, and can be reached either from Balmeanach or Tiroran on Loch Scridain, where there is a National Trust for Scotland office. The walk along the shore is difficult but fascinating; try to arrive at half tide on the ebb.

The south-west end of Ardmeanach, known as the Burgh, was given to the National Trust for Scotland in 1932 by A. Campbell Blair of Dolgellau. It is a natural reserve for red deer, wild goat, otter, golden eagle, hen harrier, peregrine, sparrow-hawk, buzzard and numerous smaller birds.

To the east of Tiroran the road skirts Loch Scridain to join the main Craignure-Fionnphort road. To the south of Craignure is Torosay Castle, designed in the Scottish baronial style by David Bryce and built in 1856. The name means a hill covered with shrubs. Beautiful gardens, designed in 1899 by Sir Robert Lorimer around formal Italianate terraces slope down to the shore. These now include statues by Antonio Bonazza, and a Japanese garden. Run by its present owner, the house is a fascinating tribute to his father, the explorer David Guthrie-James who, amongst other adventures, managed to escape from Colditz. The house and gardens are open to the public, and a miniature railway links with Craignure.

DUART CASTLE AND THE ROSS

Duart Castle stands on a dark headland, the imposing ancestral home of the MacLeans since about 1250. Overrun and put to fire by the Duke of Argyll in 1691, it was only returned to MacLean hands in 1912, and is now the residence of the 27th Chief and his wife, having been lovingly restored from ruins. It is open to the public who can explore the keep, battlements, and cells, examine MacLean relics, and see a scouting exhibition. On the coast to the south, at the entrance to Loch Don, is Grass Point, terminal for the old Oban-Kerrera-Mull ferry, and start of the pilgrim's path to Iona. Further south, at the entrance to Loch Spelve, is Port nam Marbh, the port of the dead, where corpses were landed from the mainland for burial on Iona. A minor road west passes along the northern shores of Lochs Spelve and Uisg, through attractive scenery and mixed woodlands with masses of rhododendrons to Lochbuie. Moy Castle, built in the 15thC by the MacLeans of Lochbuie, is a sturdy tower with a spring in the natural rock floor. Unfortunately there is no public access. Two miles to the east of the mouth of Loch Buie is the interestingly-named **Frank Lockwood's Island** – he was Solicitor General in Lord Rosebery's administration 1894-5 and brother-in-law of the 21st MacLean of Lochbuie.

Duart Castle

The main road passes through the bare, glaciated Glen More, above the Lussa River. The Glen once separated the kingdoms of the Picts and the Scots (Dalriada). A cairn at Pedlars Pool marks the spot where a pedlar, who took care of two households with smallpox, died of the disease himself, and another cairn at Pennyghael commemorates the Beatons, hereditary doctors to the Lords of the Isles. A minor road south across the moor finishes at the fertile valley and farm at Carsaig. Along the shore to the west is the Nun's Cave, which contains early Christian carvings. Sandstone was quarried nearby until 1873, and was used in Iona Cathedral. Two miles beyond the cave at Malcolm's Point, beneath 700ft cliffs, are the dark red basaltic Carsaig Arches.

The coast of the Ross is broken with many small bays and some fine beaches, such as that at Uisken; Bunessan is the touring centre for this area. Inland is windswept, undulating moorland. The road finishes at Fionnphort, where the ferry leaves for Iona. Half a mile to the north granite was quarried until the late 19thC; stone from here was used to build Holborn Viaduct, Blackfriars Bridge and the Albert Memorial in London, and the Skerryvore and Dubh Artach lighthouses. Further north is the pretty harbour of Kintra. To the south, beyond the fine beach at Fidden, is the tidal island of **Erraid**, remembered in Robert Louis Stevenson's *Memoirs of an Islet,* and also in *Kidnapped*, which he is said to have written in one of the houses behind the row of granite cottages used as the shore station for the Dubh Artach and Skerryvore lighthouses (*see* Tiree) until 1952. In the book, David Balfour thought himself stranded on Erraid after the brig *Covenant* was wrecked on the seaward side – not realising that he could cross the sand at low tide. At the summit of Crioc Mor is the iron observatory once used to signal to the lighthouses. The island is now occupied by members of the Findhorn Community for eleven months of the year on behalf of two Dutch brothers who bought it in 1977. They wanted their children to experience wilderness for the one remaining month. The Findhorn population numbers up to 20 adults and children, who care for the island, and maintain its natural state.

The Dubh Artach lighthouse marks the end of a reef running south from Mull, which manifests itself as the Torran Rocks (*torunn* means a loud murmuring noise). The lighthouse, which became operational in 1872, was designed by Thomas and David Stevenson, R.L.S.'s father and uncle respectively. From base of the tower to the base of the lantern measures 106ft, and it is built on a rock 35ft above mean high water.

Although Mull's proximity to the mainland is making it increasingly popular with tourists, it is still easy to find vast open spaces with no one else around.

Caledonian MacBrayne operate the ferry *Isle of Mull* between Oban and Craignure, the voyage taking 40 minutes; and they also operate a smaller ferry, the *Loch Fyne,* between Lochaline and Fishnish, with a journey time of 15 minutes. The *Loch Linnhe* sails between Kilchoan and Tobermory during the summer. There are flights to Glenforsa from Glasgow.

Excursions are run from Oban via Mull to Iona. There is a bus service on Mull, and Tourist Information Centres in Tobermory and Craignure. The Saint Columba Exhibition at Fionnphort provides an excellent introduction to any trip to Iona.

Treshnish Isles

These are a string of volcanic islands lying on a south-west/north-east axis, about three-and-a-half miles west of Gometra, off Mull and designated since 1974 as a Site of Special Scientific Interest. At the southern end, and separated from the rest of the group, is **Bac Mór**, the Dutchman's Cap, its old lava cone encircled by a lava rim – a distinctive landmark. The central and largest island is **Lunga**, rising to 338ft at the summit of Cruachan, below which are the remains of some black houses, last occupied in 1857 as summer sheilings: permanent occupation ended in 1824 when Donald Campbell and his family finally left. On the west coast are the sea-bird cliffs and pinnacle of Dun Cruit. 25 species of sea birds breed on the islands, and barnacle geese winter here. Sheep still graze the larger islands, and grey seals breed among the rocks by the shore.

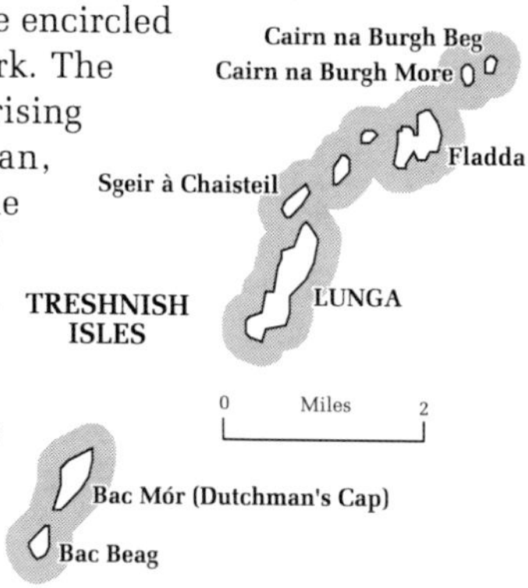

To the north-east of Lunga, across a profusion of rocks and skerries, is **Fladda**, once occupied each summer by a lobster fisherman. On the island of **Cairn na Burgh More** are the remains of a fort believed to have belonged to the Chief of Clan MacDougall, Lord of Lorn, on the site of an older Norse building. It once marked the division between the Nordreys (Northern isles) and the Sudreys (southern isles), and was given up to the Lord of the Isles in 1354. Religious books and records from Iona were said to have been hidden here at the time of the Reformation; when Cromwell took the fort in 1650, the books were lost – although recent research has called the whole story into question. In 1715 it was held by the MacLeans of Duart.

There are the remains of a small chapel, and the Well of the Half Gallon. On **Cairn na Burgh Beg** are the ruins of a smaller fort occupied during the 1715 Jacobite rising. The islands were bought by the late Colonel Niall Rankin, explorer and naturalist, in 1938. The islands were offered for sale in 1994. They look quite spectacular when viewed from the ruined village of Crackaig on Mull.

Cruises around the Treshnish Isles are arranged from Ulva Ferry and Fionnphort, on Mull.

Staffa

This is a tiny island that is known worldwide. It covers 71 acres, rising to a maximum height of 135ft, and the name derives from the Norse *stafr-ey* (pillar or post island), after the wooden posts the Norsemen set vertically to build their houses. Staffa resulted from the same volcanic activity which formed the Giant's Causeway in Ireland and the Ardmeanach promontory on Mull, six miles to the south-east, and consists of grey-black fine-grained Tertiary basalt surmounted by amorphous lava, the basalt lavas having cooled slowly, resulting in patterns of three breaks radiating from single points equidistant over the surface, relieving the tension evenly. The results are the spectacular hexagonal columns which gave Staffa its name.

Perhaps more famous than the island itself is Fingal's Cave, a cavern among the pillars at the southern tip, 65ft high, 50ft wide and 123ft deep. Although flooded by the sea, it is possible to walk inside along natural causeways. It may be named after Fionn MacCaul, a legendary Celtic giant who is supposed to have built the Giant's Causeway, and in Gaelic it is known as *An Uamh Binn*, the melodious cave – the sea makes strange noises among the pillars. A musical tribute was made to the cavern by Felix Mendelssohn in his *Hebrides Overture* after he visited Staffa in 1829. From inside the cave, the view south is of Iona, and to the west of the cave is the Great Face or Colonnade, an expanse of columns about 55ft tall, below which is Boat Cave. The cliff near Fingal's Cave

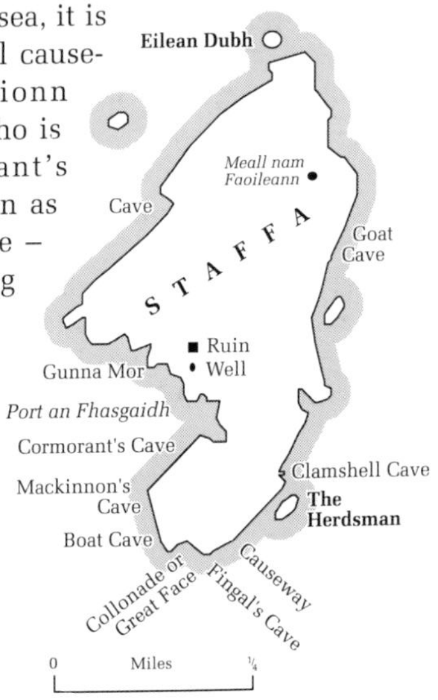

The entrance to Fingal's Cave, Staffa

was marked by a mine which exploded in May 1945.

On the west side of Staffa is Port an Fhasgaidh (shelter bay), a strange name considering its exposure to the prevailing weather. To the south is MacKinnon's Cave, nearly as grand as Fingal's and connected to Cormorant's Cave by a narrow tunnel. It is traditionally thought to be named after Abbot MacKinnon (died c. 1500), Abbot of Iona.

Off the south-east shore is **Am Buachaille** (the herdsman), a columnar rock separated from Staffa by 15ft of water. Opposite the southern end is a peculiar formation known as the Wishing Chair. A little to the north is the landing place, with a jetty accessible at all states of the tide, by Clamshell Cave. Its strikingly curved columns give it its name. A path from here leads to Fingal's Cave. Little of all this can be seen from the island's grassy summit; a boat affords the best view.

Staffa was, of course, known to the local people, and to the Norsemen, long before it was discovered by the President of the Royal Society, Sir Joseph Banks, on 13 August 1772, while on his way to Iceland. After him followed a stream of visitors, and soon paddle-steamers were bringing hundreds of tourists. Among those who made the trip were: Sir Walter Scott in 1810, John Keats in 1818, Mendelssohn in 1829, J.M.W. Turner in 1830, William Wordsworth, Queen Victoria and Prince Albert in 1833, Jules Verne in 1859 (he featured Staffa in his book, *The Green Ray,* in 1885), Dr David Livingstone in 1864 and Robert Louis Stevenson in 1870. In August 1884 two tourists off the paddle steamer *Chevalier* were drowned in Fingal's Cave. When Banks first came, the island had only one inhabitant, a herdsman living in a rough hut; by 1784 there were 16 people and livestock and in 1788 it was recorded that barley, oats, flax and potatoes were grown near the island's centre. Permanent habitation ceased at the end of the 18thC, although a herdsman continued to come for the summer grazing. In 1800 there were three red deer. Now there is a resident herd of black cattle.

Boat trips to the island are run from Iona and Ulva Ferry. Staffa is owned by the National Trust for Scotland.

Iona

Strathclyde. An island of great Christian importance, Iona is three-and-a-half miles by one-and-a-half miles, lying three-quarters of a mile off the Ross of Mull. It consists of low-lying Torridonian sandstone, with Archaean gneiss on the western side – it is not related geologically to Mull. The highest point is Dùn-I (pronounced doon-ee) in the north, rising to 332ft; there is another small hill in the south, and the valley between these two points is farmed, more so to the east. In the west, Camas Cuil an t-Saimh (the bay at the back of the ocean) is backed by machair, and Iona marble was quarried near Cul Bhurig. The southern coast comprises cliffs and bays; the north has sandy beaches and machair. The main area of settlement and ferry terminal is Baile Mór facing Fionnphort, where there are hotels, shops, restaurants and a post office.

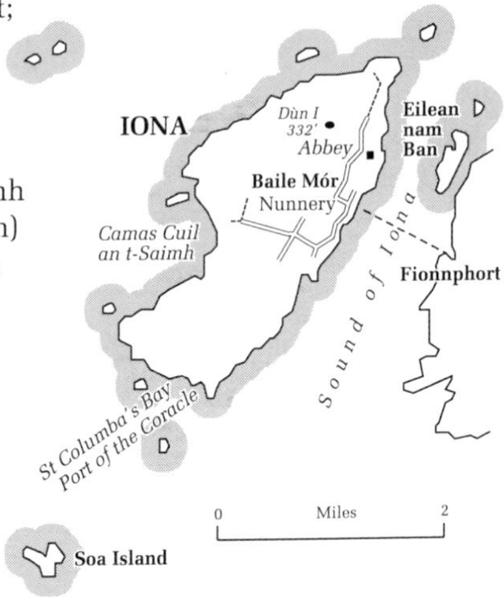

The island was used by Druids before the birth of Christ, and was known in Gaelic as *Innis nan Druinich* (isle of the Druidic hermits). It was also called *Ioua*, later, *I-Chaluim-cille,* island of St Columba); during the 1500s it was once again known as Ioua, finally to become Iona. St Columba landed here from Ireland in AD 563 to found a monastery, a centre from which the mainland Picts could be converted. St Columba lived on the island for 34 years until his death in AD 597. Under his influence, Iona became the Christian centre of Europe (the *Book of Kells*, now in Dublin, was begun here), but was later destroyed by the Norsemen who raided in the years 795, 801, 806 (killing 68 monks at Martyrs Bay near the jetty), 825 and 986 (when the abbot and 15 monks were massacred at the White Strand).

In 1074 the monastery was rebuilt by St Margaret, Queen of Scotland, for the Roman Catholic order of St Augustine, and it was again rebuilt in 1203 by Reginald of Islay, King of the Isles and Somerled's son, for the Benedictine order. He also built the convent; much of this fine pink granite building remains, covered with grass and wild flowers. In 1430 the Bishopric of the Isles was created, with a seat in Iona, and in 1500 Iona achieved cathedral status. During the Reformation, all the ecclesiastical buildings were dismantled and nearly all the island's 350 crosses were destroyed. Taken by MacLean of Duart in 1574, the island was re-taken by Argyll in 1688. Excavations conducted in 1992 now suggest that the community on Iona may have been much larger than was originally thought, being more like a small university town founded some 300 years before Oxford or Cambridge. This would suggest that the community was not entirely male at that time. The ruins of the abbey church were gifted to the Church of Scotland in 1899, and were restored by 1910.

The monastic buildings were restored by the Iona Community between 1938 and 1965. Recently the island, excluding the cathedral area, was bought on behalf of the Scottish nation from the Duke of Argyll by the Fraser Foundation, and recently gifted to the National Trust for Scotland.

The Cathedral Church of St Mary is a simple cruciform building with a short tower, built in scale with its surroundings. The 10thC crosses of St Martin and St John (a replica), both standing near the west door, are beautiful, but no equal to the Kildalton High Cross on Islay; behind them is the tiny St Columba's shrine. The infirmary museum houses a collection of carved slabs, and along the marble causeway known as the Street of the Dead is St Oran's Chapel. It was recorded in 1549 that 60 kings – 48 Scottish, 4 Irish and 8 Norwegian – were buried in the graveyard, Reilig Odhrain, including Duncan who was murdered by Macbeth. The tombs have long since vanished.

The Iona Community was founded in the 1930s by George MacLeod (to become the Very Rev. Lord MacLeod of Fuinary, died 27th June 1991), and was known as the Rome Express by the

The Abbey, Iona

Baile Mór, Iona

Scottish Presbyterians. Their work in rebuilding Iona was to make possible an experiment in full Christian living. Today the Community numbers 150, with many more associate members worldwide. It is especially concerned with what it calls industrial evangelism, its members working in industry, depressed city areas and new towns. The MacLeod Centre, opened in August 1988, accommodates 50 guests each week who come to share the life of the community, still finding Iona a place of retreat, regeneration and inspiration. One such visitor was the late leader of the British Labour Party, John Smith, who spent many summers on Iona, and chose to be buried there.

Each year 500,000 visitors, mainly day-trippers, come to the island. Most day trippers stray no further than the village and the cathedral and, with such an influx to cope with, it is inevitable that this area has a touristy feel. But wander further, and peace and natural beauty can be found.

On the south coast are St Columba's Bay and the Port of the Coracle, where St Columba landed. Along here are beautifully coloured pebbles of green serpentine, and one-and-a-half miles offshore is the low-lying **Soa Island.** South of the village are two fine white shell-sand bays, backed by heather and wild flowers. From the modest summit of Dun-I may be seen a panorama of the Inner Hebrides and, to the south of this hill below a hillock called Tor Abb in the Secluded Hollow, are the foundations of a hermit's cell, traditionally considered to be a spot frequented by St Columba. **Eilean nam Ban**, in the Sound of Iona, is said to be where St Columba sent all the women from Iona during his lifetime.

The island's main income is derived from visitors, but the primary source of employment is crofting. On the fine west-coast farmlands, with sandy beaches backed by machair and secluded bays with semi-precious stones, Iona's other, more typically Hebridean, life goes on untouched by the thousands of visitors. The permanent population (excluding the Community) now numbers about 90.

Iona is reached by the Caledonian MacBrayne passenger ferry *Loch Buie* from Fionnphort, Mull. There are trips from Oban during the summer by the ferry *Isle of Mull, with* special coaches across Mull to connect with the ferry at Fionnphort, where you will be able to see the Saint Columba Exhibition, which contains exhibits commemorating the 1400th anniversary of Saint Columba's death using light and sound, and including contemporary artefacts.

Cruises to Staffa leave from Iona.

John's Cross, Iona

Lismore

Strathclyde. Covering 10,000 acres, Lismore measures nine-and-a-half miles by one-and-three-quarter miles, and lies in Loch Linnhe to the north of Oban. Its Gaelic name is *Ieis Mor* (the great garden). It is composed of Dalradian limestone, with shallow longitudinal valleys that provide shelter for livestock, and good farming conditions on extremely fertile soil. The highest point is Barr Mor (416ft). There is now little natural woodland although, in 1596, the island was reported to have been thickly forested with oak; however, some splendid trees have now been planted around the well cared for 19thC farmhouses. An influx of younger people into the farming community has revitalised the island, which has probably never reached its full potential as a rearing ground for cattle and sheep.

Until half a century ago limestone was quarried at An Sailean and shipped to the surrounding islands and mainland, and two

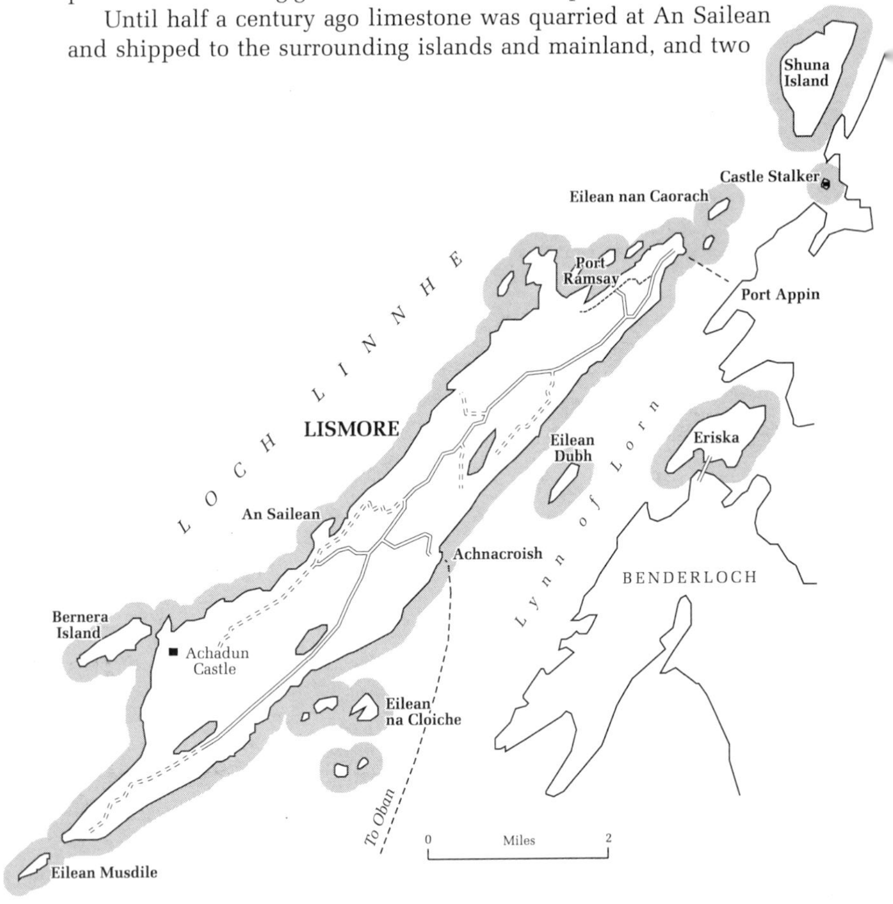

Lismore

quarrymen's cottages and some lime kilns can still be seen on the tiny **Eilean nan Caorach** off the northern tip. Many lime-carrying boats operated from Port Ramsay close by, where there is a sheltered anchorage and two attractive rows of neat cottages, now used mainly as holiday homes. The view from here along Loch Linnhe, towards Ben Nevis, is superb.

Lismore was the seat of the diocese of Argyll from the 13thC until 1507, the bishops receiving the title *Episcopi Lismorenses*. Incorporated into the tiny parish church are parts of the choir of the original medieval cathedral, and on the west coast, facing Bernera Island, are the ruins of the Bishop's Castle, Achadun. **Bernera Island** is also known as Berneray an Iubhar Uasail, Berneray of the Noble Yew. Dean Munro wrote in the 16thC that it was a holy place associated with St Columba, who preached under the yew, which is said to have been felled in 1850 to build a staircase in Lochnell Castle on the mainland. There are no remains of the small chapel which once existed.

In the 6thC a legendary race for possession of Lismore took place between St Moluag and St Mulhac: whoever made the first landfall would take possession. It is said that St Moluag, on seeing that his boat would not be first, cut off his finger and threw it ashore, thus securing the title. St Moluag did, however, found a monastery on Lismore between AD 561 and 564. Some 30 years ago the *buchull mor* (pastoral staff) of St Moluag was brought back to the island.

There is one main road running almost the length of the island, and most of the dwellings are sited by it, with the majority in the north; near the centre there is a post office, general store, and a junior

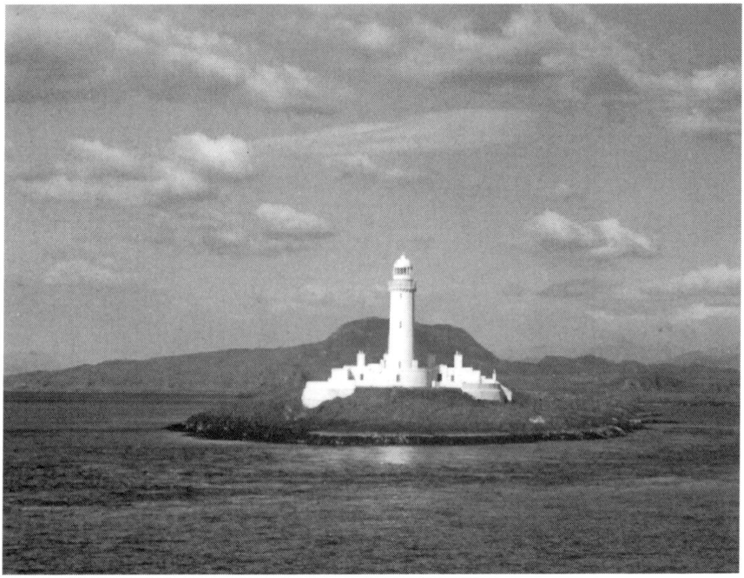

The lighthouse on Eilean Musdile, off the south west tip of Lismore

school. Much of Lismore is owned by the Duke of Argyll, and is farmed by tenants, the present population numbering around 100. There is no mains water, the houses being supplied by springs which are vulnerable should there be a long dry spell. Much of the shoreline is low sea cliffs, with some pleasant shingle beaches, and on the east side, and off the northern tip, there are some small islands, rocks and skerries. Between **Eilean Musdile**, off Lismore's south west tip, and Duart Point, can be seen Lady's Rock. It is said that here, in 1523, Lachlan Cattenach of Duart Castle left his wife Elisabeth naked to drown on the rising tide, because she did not bear him a son. Although assumed to have drowned, she was rescued by a passing boat, and confronted Lachlan some time later in Inverary. On the 10th September 1524 Lachlan was killed in Edinburgh by Campbell of Calder, one of Elisabeth's relatives.

The island of Lismore, as a platform from which to view the surrounding sea and landscape, is unequalled. On the mainland to the north are the mountains of Kingairloch, to the north-east Ben Nevis, to the east Port Appin, Loch Creran and Benderloch, and to the south and west the islands of the Firth of Lorn, and Mull – surely one of the most stunning settings in the west Highlands.

The Caledonian MacBrayne ferry *Eigg* operates between Oban and Achnacroish, taking 50 minutes. A passenger ferry makes a much shorter crossing to the northern tip from Port Appin, where the ferryman lives.

Castle Stalker

Shuna Island, one-and-a-half miles north-east of Lismore, is owned by a Glasgow industrialist and run as a farm; to the south of the fine white farmhouse is the substantial ruin of Castle Shuna. To the north-east of Shuna is the small **Eilean Balnagowan**. At the entrance of Loch Creran is the island of **Eriska**, reached via a narrow bridge. The turreted Eriska House is now a luxurious hotel.

In Loch Laich, on the tidal isle of the falconer, stands the beautiful rectangular **Castle Stalker**, ancient seat of the Stewarts of Appin, built in the 15thC and used by James IV as a hunting lodge. Once a ruin, it has now been restored. It is private.

Kerrera

Strathclyde. Four-and-a-half miles long by two miles wide, Kerrera lies to the west of Oban – a natural breakwater for one of the best harbours on the west coast of Scotland. The island is green and hilly, composed of a mixture of secondary basalt, graphitic schists and old red sandstone. The name derives possibly from the Norse *Kjarbarey,* copse isle.

The island has belonged to the MacDougalls since the founding of the Clan by Somerled in the 12thC. In 1249 King Alexander II of Scotland, with his fleet, anchored in The Horse Shoe bay, determined to wrest the Hebrides from King Haakon of Norway. But Alexander died quite suddenly, his army dispersed and his body was taken to Melrose. His visit is commemorated in the name of the land behind the bay – *Dalrigh,* the field of the King. Later, in 1263, King Haakon rallied his fleet in the bay, *en route* to the Battle of Largs where he was defeated, and the remains of his force once again anchored off Kerrera before travelling home to Norway. King Haakon never completed the journey, being taken ill and dying in Orkney.

Gylen Castle, the ruins of which now stand at the southern end of Kerrera, was built on the site of an earlier fortification in 1587 by Duncan MacDougall of Dunollie, the 16th Chief. The building, a handsomely detailed tower standing above the cliffs, was besieged in 1647 by General Leslie during the Covenanting Wars and subsequently burned. It has never been restored.

Kerrera was used for many years as a stepping stone between Mull and the mainland. Cattle were swum to the mainland from Ardantrive Bay at the north-east tip of Kerrera, where there are a jetty and moorings. The prominent memorial at the north end above the bay commemorates

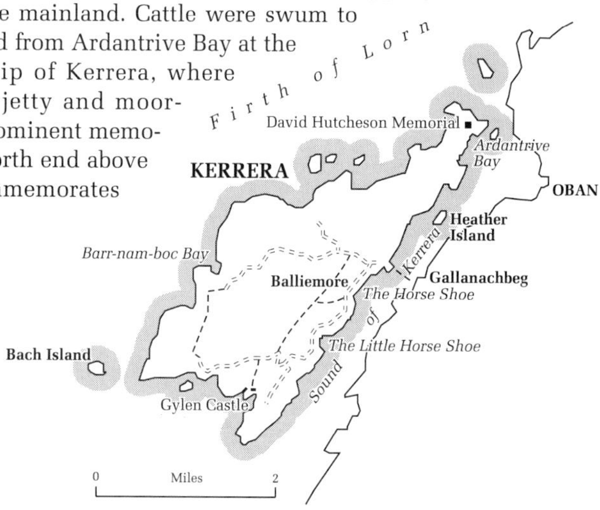

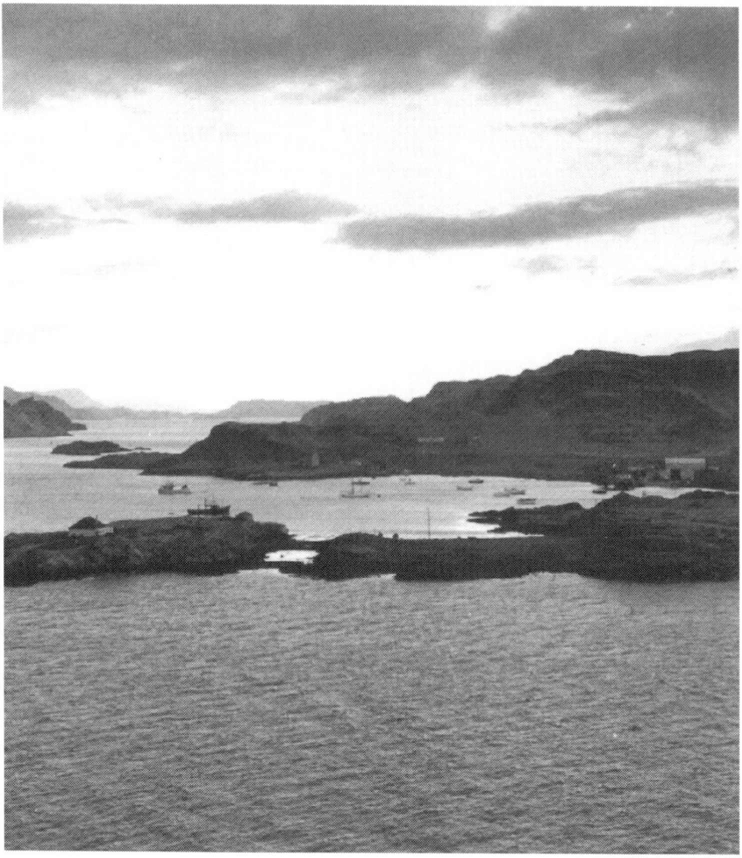

Ardantrive Bay, Kerrera

David Hutcheson, one of the founders of what is now Caledonian MacBrayne.

By 1861 the population of the island was 105, in 1879 a post office was established. The present schoolhouse and church overlooking the Sound of Kerrera, were built in 1872. The population is now about 50. This compact and attractive island is ideal for gentle walks in attractive scenery, having fine views of Mull and Lismore to the west and north. It is easily reached by the small passenger ferry which operates from Gallanach-beg, to the south of Oban.

Tiree and Coll

As far west as Harris in the Outer Hebrides, Tiree and Coll have little in common apart from their outstanding. sunshine record. Both have great charm, and are well worth visiting.

Tiree

Strathclyde. The north-east corner of Tiree is 15 miles from Treshnish Point, Mull, and is separated from its island partner, Coll, to the north-east, by the two-mile wide Gunna Sound. It lies as far west as Harris in the Outer Hebrides, and measures a little over ten miles long by about six miles at the widest point, with an area of 19,000 acres. It was called *Tir-Iodh* (the land of corn), and was once known as the granary of the isles for, although the bedrock is Archaean gneiss, a poor infertile rock, over two-thirds of it has been deeply covered with wind-blown shell sand, which has blessed the island with fertile, well-drained machair, deep enough for the plough.

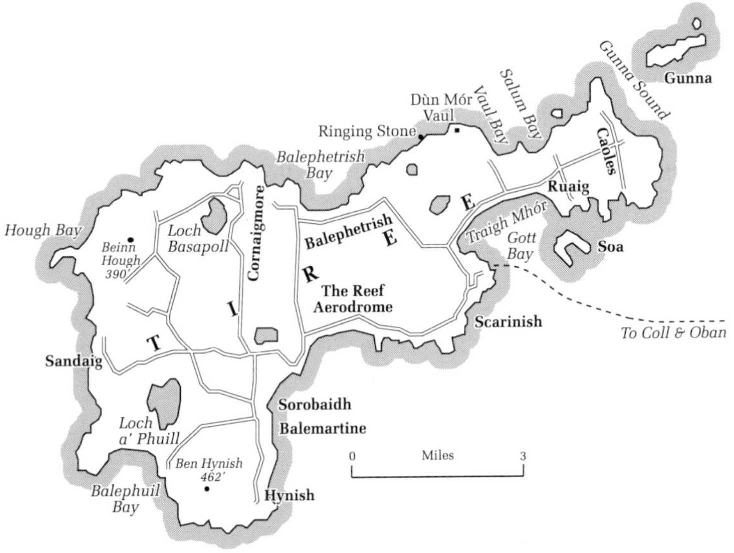

Tiree

The landscape of Tiree is unique among the larger Hebridean islands, being one of houses and not hills. It is flat, for the most part a hairline on the horizon with only two high points: Ben Hynish in the south rising to 462ft, and Ben Hough in the north-west rising to 390ft. Average rainfall is low, about 45-50 inches, and there are more hours of sun in the spring than anywhere else in Scotland, with an average of 223 hours in May. But Tiree's fertile soil was brought by the wind, and there is no shelter from it – in February 1961 it gusted at 116 mph, a record at the time. Living on Tiree has been likened to living on the deck of an aircraft carrier.

The population peaked at 4450 in 1831; 50 years later it was 2700, following the potato famines and forced evictions. In 1885 there was a revolt against the landowners, when landless families took over a vacated farm and demanded it be turned into crofts. The government sent two ships, the *Ajax* and the *Assistance*, and marines to deal with this disturbance; five men were arrested and imprisoned for a short while, but there was no fighting, and the marines became great friends with the islanders. With the passing of the Crofters' Act in 1886 (*see* Skye) the farms were split into the present 270 or so small crofts, maintaining a higher population (now 870) on the island than if amalgamated. Cattle and sheep are grazed on the fertile machair, and crops provide winter fodder. There is a lobster-fishing industry, which has benefited from the building of a pier at Caoles. Trawling ceased due to over-exploitation.

Evidence of occupation on Tiree dates back to 800 BC – pottery and tools uncovered at Dùn Mor Vaul date from this period. A broch

Towards Balemartine from Hynish, Tiree

was built on the site of this earlier settlement. In AD 565 Batheine, a follower of St Columba, founded a monastery at Sorobaidh. St Columba also visited Tiree; in legend he cursed a rock in Gott Bay to remain weed-less after his boat struck it and nearly sank.

The Vikings raided Tiree – burning Sorobaidh in AD 672 – then later settled; Norse burials have been found at Cornaig-beg. Control then passed to the Kingdom of Man and the Isles, and, in 1123, Reginald, son of King Godfrey, ruled the area which included Tiree.

In 1164, upon the death of Somerled, his son Dougall inherited the island (along with Coll and Mull) which he in turn passed on to his son Duncan. After the defeat of the Norwegian force under King Haakon at the Battle of Largs in 1263, control of the isles passed to Alexander III of Scotland who confirmed ownership upon the MacDougalls. The Scottish Wars of Independence brought changes in ownership, with the MacDonalds acquiring Tiree (and Coll), only to

Balephuil Bay

return it to the MacDougalls in 1354. Their influence was negligible and, by 1390, Lachlan MacLean was Baillie of Tiree and Coll, his descendants disputing ownership until the 16thC. In 1562 and again in 1578, Tiree was invaded by the MacDonalds of Islay; in the latter part of the 17thC the present owners, the Argylls, took control.

The traditional homes on Tiree were of the black house type (*tigh dubh*), with dry-stone walls up to nine-feet thick, rounded corners and a thatched roof resting on inner walls – all designed so that the gales would sweep over them. These have now been converted into white houses (*tigh geal*) with cemented stones, tar and felt roofs and a fireplace at one end, and the outside painted white.

The main pier and ferry terminal, sheltered in most conditions, is in Gott Bay, to the west of Traigh Mhor, a fine beach and the longest on Tiree. Scarinish, the main village, lies behind the old harbour, and has a post office, shops and hotel. To the east, at Ruiag, The Hebridean Trust is developing a museum of Tiree's religious history in the old Congregational church. There is a golf course, notable for the local ravens which steal golf balls – as many as three or four per round have been lost.

At Tiree's flat centre is The Reef, an airfield built by the RAF in 1941 on the site of a grass landing-strip, from where 518 Squadron flew Halifax and 218 Squadron flew Warwicks. With the airfield came good roads and electricity, and it is now used for civil aviation, with a regular daily service from Glasgow. The weather station here, which reports regularly for the BBC shipping forecasts, is a legacy of the early work done by D.O. MacLean, head of Cornaigmore School, who started keeping records in 1926.

To the south of Sorobaidh Bay is Balemartine, the largest village, with many *tigh geal*. At the end of the road to the south is Hynish, with granite houses built for the workers on the Skerryvore lighthouse. Standing ten miles south-west of here, it is 138 ft from the base of the lantern, on a rock only ten feet above mean high water, and was built in 1838-43 by Alan Stevenson, another uncle of Robert Louis Stevenson. The 4308 tons of granite used in its construction was quarried on the Ross of Mull. First lit in 1844, it was extensively damaged by fire in 1954, following which new diesel generators were installed. It is now automatic. The sea area between the rocks and reefs of the Skerryvore and Tiree can be extremely rough during north-westerly gales. Above Hynish is a granite tower, once used to signal to the lighthouse and now housing the Skerryvore Museum. The harbour at Hynish has also been restored. This involved clearing a unique scouring system designed by Alan Stevenson to ensure the harbour was always clear for the supply ships. Other buildings and store-rooms have been converted into an activity centre managed by a local warden. All of these restorations have been initiated by The Hebridean Trust.

The pretty white houses of Balephuil stand to the east of a mile of beach backed by flat machair, in the midst of which Loch a'Phuill glistens. Above the village is Ben Hynish, from the summit of which there is a fine view of Skerryvore. On the west coast there are extensive areas of dunes grazed by cattle and sheep, and behind these grow crops of barley and corn. At Sandaig, on the west coast, three traditional thatched houses now comprise a museum displaying a late 19thC interior, with local artifacts and furniture.

Off the north-west corner of Tiree there are numerous rocks and skerries. Behind the shell-sand bay of Cornaigmore is Loch Bhasapoll, surrounded by machair, and known for its duck population. On its north side it is said that there was once a township called Baile nan Craganach (the town of the clumsy ones); five men each with 12 fingers lived there. The next bay east, Balephetrish Bay, takes its name from *Baile Pheadairich* (the township of the storm petrel), and is where Tiree marble, pink flecked with green, was quarried between 1791 and 1794 and again briefly in 1910. On the coast is Clacha Choire, the ringing stone, a glacial erratic which originated on Rum. It is said to contain a crock of gold – but if ever split, Tiree will disappear beneath the waves. Such legends were collected by John Gregorson Campbell, minister of Tiree from 1861 to 1891, and published in his *Superstitions of the Scottish Highlands* in 1900.

On the rocky coast to the west of Vaul Bay is Dùn Mór Vaul (fort of the big wall), built in the 1stC. On the east of the island, at Caoles, there are attractive outcrops of pink orthogneiss. Across Gunna Sound lies the island of **Gunna**, once inhabited, now grazed by cattle.

Tiree can fairly lay claim to being Scotland's sunshine island, and in the spring and early summer the extensive machair is thick with blossom and heady with perfume. The island's large and robust population imparts a feeling of activity rare in the Western Isles, and the recent influx of windsurfers, following the 1987 Tiree Wave Classic, in which 50 top British exponents of the sport competed, make a colourful contribution.

The Caledonian MacBrayne ferry *Clansman* operates between Oban and Gott Bay – a four-and-a-quarter hour journey via Coll. It is the only ferry between these two islands. British Airways make a daily flight (not Sundays) from Glasgow to The Reef airfield and then on to Barra. There is a post bus service on the island.

Clacha Choire, the 'Ringing Stone', Tiree

Coll

Strathclyde. With an area 18,300 acres, Coll measures thirteen-and-a-half by four miles, lying two miles to the west of Caillich Point, Mull.

The northern two-thirds of the island are Lewisian gneiss, showing itself everywhere, its low hummocks infilled with peat bogs and lochans. The remaining third of Coll, apart from the extreme south-west tip which is also gneiss, consists of very ancient metamorphosised sandstones containing quartz and marble, particularly beautiful by the shore at Gorton. The west coast has a covering of wind-blown shell sand, forming dunes over 100-ft high and machair suitable for grazing. The summit of Ben Hogh (341ft) is the highest point; on its northern side are two glacial erratics, boulders of gabbro, probably from Mull. There are raised beaches at Arinagour and Arnabost.

The climate, like that of Tiree, is favourable, with many hours of sunshine early in the summer, mild winters and rainfall that is less than 50 inches each year. It is, of course, windy.

The early history of Coll is closely linked to that of Tiree – Norse settlement followed by the rule of Somerled and then Clan Donald. By 1841, the population had risen to 1440 and the laird, MacLean, given the island by Clan Donald, was unable to support such numbers and, during the next 15 or so years, half the

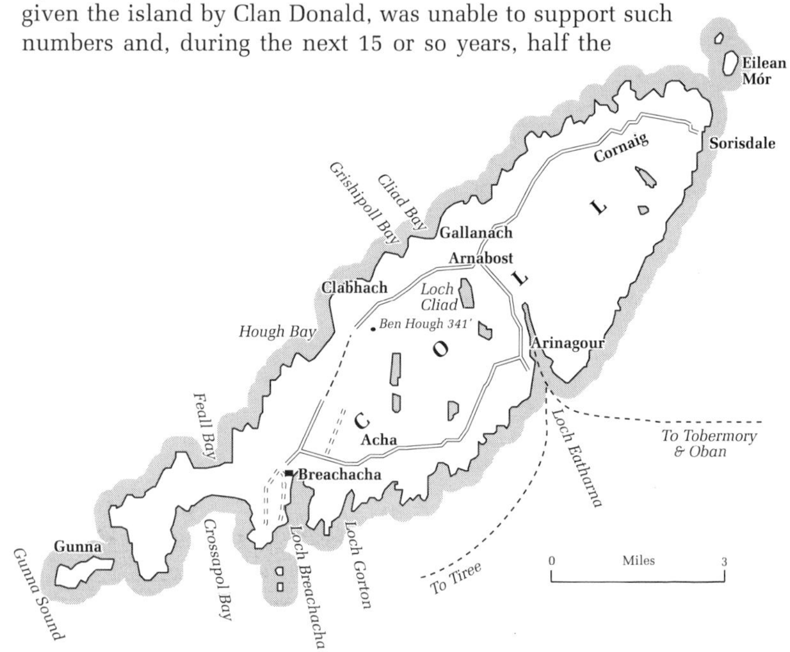

Breachacha Castle, Coll

population was cleared to Australia and Canada. In 1856 MacLean sold the island to the Stewarts, and now two-thirds are owned by a Dutch millionaire.

The shock waves of such a drastic solution as clearance continued for many years with further clearances and continued depopulation. The emphasis of agriculture turned to dairy cattle and the production of the famous Coll cheese, with farmers from Kintyre being brought to the island. With this came the virtual demise of Gaelic culture and language on Coll. At the turn of the century the market for dairy produce collapsed, and a gradual shift to stock-raising began. Today there are about 1000 beef cattle, a few dairy cattle, and 7000 sheep. The current population is about 150. There is a lobster-fishing industry, the numerous rocks and skerries off the north-east tip providing breeding grounds. At one time ling were caught and salted, but this industry died due to over-fishing.

Arinagour, Coll's only village, lies on the west side of Loch Eatharna, and about half the population lives here. There are shops, a church, post office, hotel, school and bicycles for hire. The pier, built in 1967, is a stopping point for the Oban and Tiree ferry. The coast to the north-east, and the land behind, is empty.

The road to Breachacha lies a little less than a mile inland from the south-east coast, which is deeply bayed and attractive. The

Arinagour, Coll

ancient Breachacha Castle, standing by the shore of the loch, was thought to have been the 14thC home of the MacLeans, part of the defenses of the Lords of the Isles, but recent excavations now suggest 15thC construction. It is a good example of such a medieval fortress, little altered and now the headquarters of The Project Trust, run by Major Maclean-Bristol, which trains young volunteers for aid work overseas.

The newer castle close by was built in 1750 by Hector MacLean and visited by Boswell and Johnson on their tour of the Hebrides in October 1773. They were entertained there by Coll's last hereditary piper. Confined to the building by a series of gales, they condemned it as a mere tradesman's box.

After the battle in 1593 between the MacLeans of Coll and the invading Duarts, the burn that flows into Loch Breachacha was choked with Duart heads, and ducks swam in the blood – it is now called *Struthan nan Ceann*, the stream of the heads.

To the west a neck of marram dunes separates Crossapol Bay from the very beautiful Feall Bay to the north. Two miles away, beyond Gunna, lies Tiree – close, but unreachable from here. The west coast is broken into sandy dune-backed bays by low rocky headlands, the valleys between these headlands sheltering the farms. The golden sands of Hogh Bay are fringed with rose- and ochre-coloured gneiss glistening with mica. The tiny Clabhach Bay has white sand, Grishipoll Bay is rocky, Cliad Bay has shell sand. At Arnabost the school, now in ruins, was built over an earth house where the

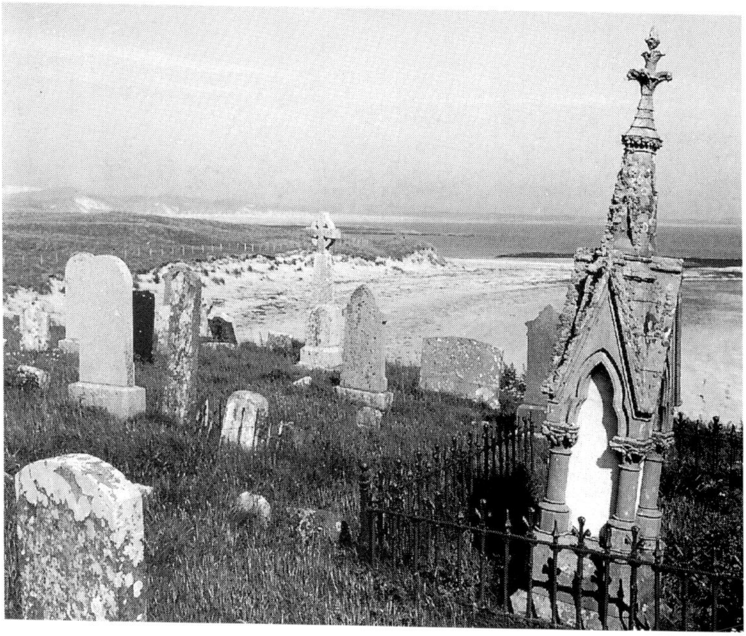

Coll

islanders hid during Viking raids. The entrance was beneath the school porch.

The coast north of Coll's largest farm, Gallanach, is one of pretty and secluded coves, the haunt of many seabirds. Cornaig was once the centre of the ling fisheries; it is now an area of prosperous farms intersected with trout streams. Off the north-east tip are rocks and skerries which are fished for lobsters.

To the east a lonely dwelling is all that remains of the community of Sorisdale, and between here and Arinagour there is little but wet and rocky moorland, lochs and streams.

Coll is reached by the Caledonian MacBrayne ferry *Clansman* from Oban, which also provides the link with its green and populous neighbour, Tiree.

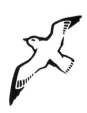

The islands of Nether Lorn

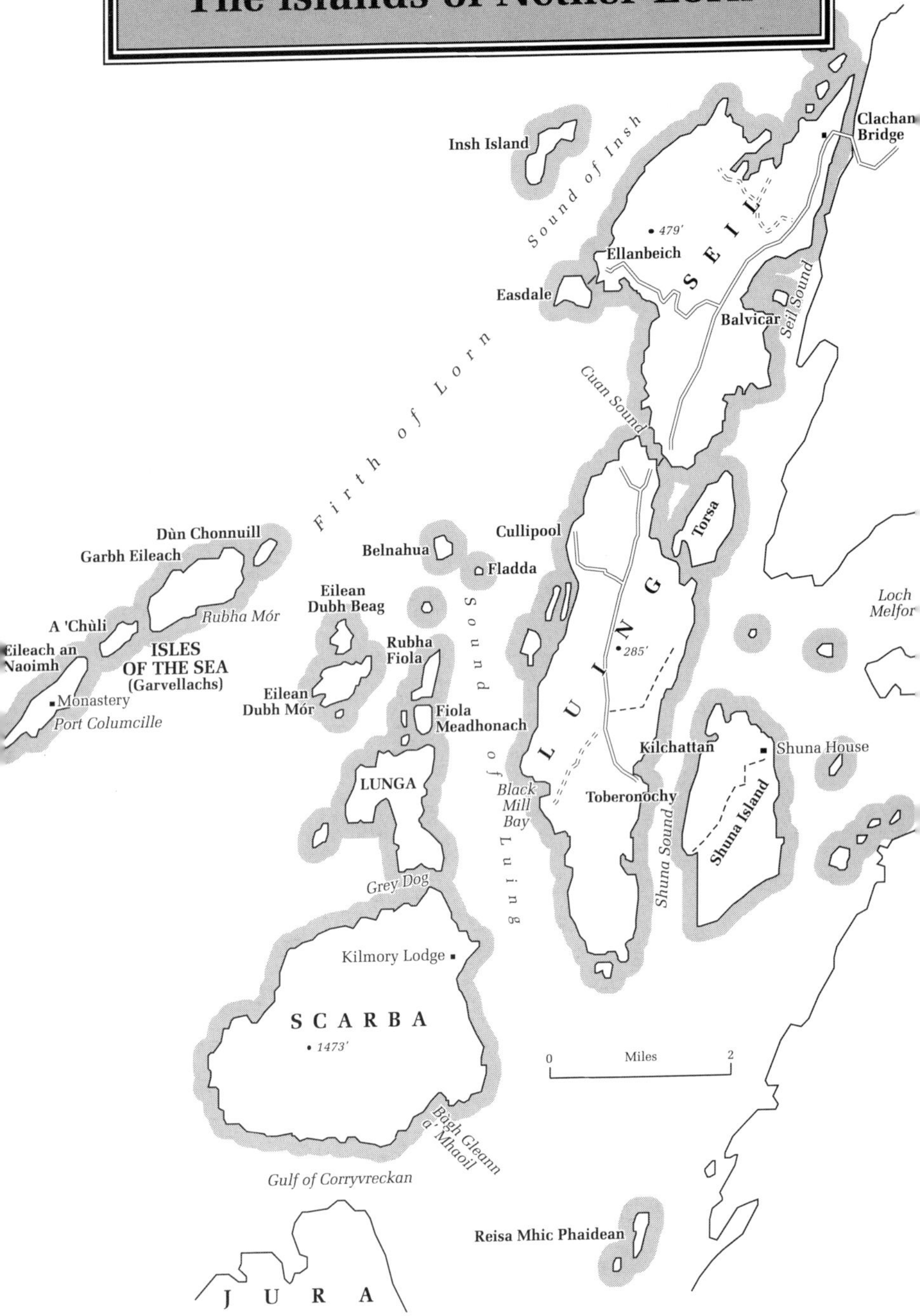
Insh Island
Sound of Insh
Clachan Bridge
479'
Ellanbeich
SEIL
Easdale
Balvicar
Seil Sound
Firth of Lorn
Cuan Sound
Torsa
Cullipool
Dùn Chonnuill
Garbh Eileach
Belnahua
Fladda
Eilean Dubh Beag
Rubha Mór
A 'Chùli
Eileach an Naoimh
ISLES OF THE SEA (Garvellachs)
Monastery
Port Columcille
Rubha Fiola
Sound of Luing
Eilean Dubh Mór
Fiola Meadhonach
LUING
285'
Loch Melfor
Kilchattan
Shuna House
LUNGA
Black Mill Bay
Toberonochy
Shuna Island
Shuna Sound
Grey Dog
Kilmory Lodge
SCARBA
1473'
0 Miles 2
Bàgh Gleann a' Mhaoil
Gulf of Corryvreckan
Reisa Mhic Phaidean
JURA

Seil

Strathclyde. A 'slate island', Seil has been joined to the mainland since 1792 by Robert Mylne's Clachan Bridge, upon which grows the fairy foxglove, *Erinus alpinus.* The ancient and very hospitable inn by the bridge was used by the Highlanders after the '45 rebellion to change from trousers into the forbidden kilt, which could be legally worn only 'overseas'. At Easdale, where the sea flooded the quarries in November 1881, 240 men lost their livelihoods overnight. The remains of disused slate workings, which closed down in 1965, can also be seen at Balvicar. It is all in many ways reminiscent of North Wales. The island is farmed, lobsters are fished, and there is now a population of 425. The An Cala Gardens at Ellanbeich, *open Apr-Oct*, are well worth visiting. They have been owned since 1986 by Sheila and Thomas Downie, and are at their best in late spring. An Cala house was once a whisky distillery, and was converted in the 1930s by the Hon. Arthur Murray, later Lord Elibank. His wife was Faith Celli, the 'original' Peter Pan, and it was she who devised the planting schemes. In 1873 a herd of 192 pilot whales were left stranded by the tide in Clachan Sound, which separates Seil from the mainland.

The island of **Easdale,** with a population of about 30, is reached by a small passenger ferry from Ellanbeich, and has workers' cottages around an attractive little harbour. There is an excellent folk museum. To the south-west is the tiny island of **Belnahua**, itself once a slate quarry, where drinking water was brought to the workers by boat from Lunga in times of drought. Their ruined cottages can still be seen. To the west is the cliff-bound and grassy **Insh Island,** with caves at the northern end.

Clachan Bridge

Luing

Strathclyde. Pronounced ling, this is, like Seil, a slate island. The main village is Cullipool on the west coast, where the quarries which closed down in 1965 once employed 150 men and produced 700,000 slates each year. Slates from here were used to re-roof Iona Cathedral. It is now a lobster-fishing centre, with the lobster pond at Fraoch Eilean being one of Scotland's largest. Luing is also well known for the prize beef cattle bred by the island's owner. The island's popula-

Alex Campbell's gravestone, Luing

Easdale

tion is now 130. On a ridge to the south of Torsa are the remains of two Iron Age forts, Dun Ballycastle and Dun Leccamore, which has some rooms and a stairway remaining.

A road runs from the ferry at Cuan Sound to Toberonochy on the east coast. Above the village is the ruined chapel of Kilchattan, surrounded by some magnificent slate gravestones including that of the Covenanter Alex Campbell, who 'digged my grave before I died' (sic), and a memorial to 15 Latvian seamen who drowned when their ship *SS Helena Faulbaums* was wrecked on Belnahua during a hurricane on 26th October 1936. Four survivors were rescued from Belnahua by the Islay lifeboat. At the island's centre is a school, a new church, and a ruined water mill, with the Fairy Knoll not far away, a favourite resting place for travellers who should place a hair or thread on top to gain favour with the spirits of the glen. The view from the west side of the island's modest summit (285ft), towards the Isles of the Sea and the Ross of Mull, is ample reward for the easy climb. To the east of Toberonochy lies **Shuna**, wooded and grazed by sheep, on which is the castellated Shuna House at the north-west corner. To the east of Cuan Sound is the green island of **Torsa**, reached from Luing at low tide, with a farmhouse in the south and the ruined 16thC fortress of Caisteal nan Con, Castle of the Dogs, once a hunting lodge of the Lords of the Isles. At one time there was a thriving crofting community on the island.

Luing is served by both passenger and vehicle ferries which operate from the south of Seil across the swift-flowing waters of Cuan Sound.

The Isles of the Sea

Strathclyde. These islands are commonly known as the Garvellachs, deriving from *Garbh Eileach* (rough isles). Lying about three miles west of Luing, their remoteness is made greater by the rocks and reefs of the surrounding seas. The north coasts comprise steep cliffs with sea caves, sloping to the more sheltered south sides, where landings can, with caution, be made.

Eileach an Naoimh (pronounced ellan nave) is the most southerly. It has some substantial remains of beehive cells from the original monastery founded by St Brendan in AD 542, 21 years before Iona. Landings are made at Port Columcille, where there is a small shingle beach and a freshwater spring. Nearby are a ruined chapel and burial ground – a stone slab is supposed to mark the grave of Eithne, St Columba's mother, although this is unlikely. This island is thought to have been St Columba's secret retreat, as close to his heart as Iona; it was referred to as Hinba from the Gaelic *Na In Ba* (isle of the sea), although Canna, in the Small Isles Parish, might also have been the saint's chosen hideaway.

The small island of **A'Chuli** is reputed to have been St Brendan's resting place. Landings can also be made at Rubha Mor on **Garbh Eileach**, where there is a small burial ground. The northern-most island is **Dùn Chonnuill**, where the ruined 13thC castle is said to stand on the site of an earlier fortress built in the 1stC by Conal Cearnach, an Irish king. There are trips around the island from Cuan on Luing.

Lunga

Strathclyde. Lunga (Isle of the Longships) is situated to the north of Scarba, separated by the Grey Dog tide-race. The grassy top of the island rises to a height of 321ft and is grazed by sheep, and the northern extremity breaks into several smaller tidal islands; the most northerly, Rubha Fiola, is run as an adventure centre for young people, who stay in the timber chalet, by the remains of an old blackhouse. The graves of some of Lunga's past inhabitants can be found in the burial ground of Kilchattan on Luing. At the northern end of

Lunga is St Columba's Well, which has never run dry and was used by quarry workers on Belnahua in time of drought.

To the west are the low-lying islands of **Eilean Dubh Beag** and **Eilean Dubh Mór,** beyond which rise the mysterious Isles of the Sea.

To the north is the tiny lighthouse island of **Fladda**. To the east is Luing, across the swift-flowing waters of the sound.

Scarba

Strathclyde. The name derives from the Norse *Skarpoe* (rough isle). Three miles long by two-and-a-half miles wide it lies to the north of Jura across the Corryvreckan tide-race, separated from Lunga, to the north, by another tide-race, the Grey Dog. Although it is grazed by cattle and sheep, the island is basically rough and craggy – graphite schist in the east, and quartzite in the west where it rises to a height of 1473ft. At one time it supported 14 families. The coast is rocky, with many caves.

On the east side, above woodland, is the refurbished Kilmory Lodge. Bagh Cleanh a'Mhaoil in the south has a good beach, and further round to the west are the whirlpools of the Gulf of Corryvreckan. Above Port nan Urrachan, on the west coast, are the remains of early Christian beehive cells.

The Isles of the Sea, the lighthouse island of Fladda, and Belnahua

Colonsay and Oronsay

Strathclyde. With a joint population of 120, these two islands, joined by sand passable at low tide, cover 11,075 acres, and are 10½ miles long by 3½ miles wide, lying a little over eight miles to the west of Jura. They have been inhabited for 7000 years: neolithic flint tools and the bones of domesticated animals were found in Uamh Uir (the cave of the grave) on the south side of Kiloran Bay. In the dunes a Viking ship burial was uncovered, the warrior having been buried along with his weapons, his horse and coins dated AD 831–854.

The name Colonsay probably derives from *Chaileiney* (Colin's island). The land is lower mudstone strata of Torridonian sandstone containing lime, and breaks down into good soil. There are some basalt dykes, and much of the higher ground is broken moorland and scrub inhabited by shaggy wild goats. There are raised beaches on the west coast (fine examples are seen to the north of Kiloran Bay behind Port Sgibinis), evidence of a time when the sea level was higher, and Colonsay was in

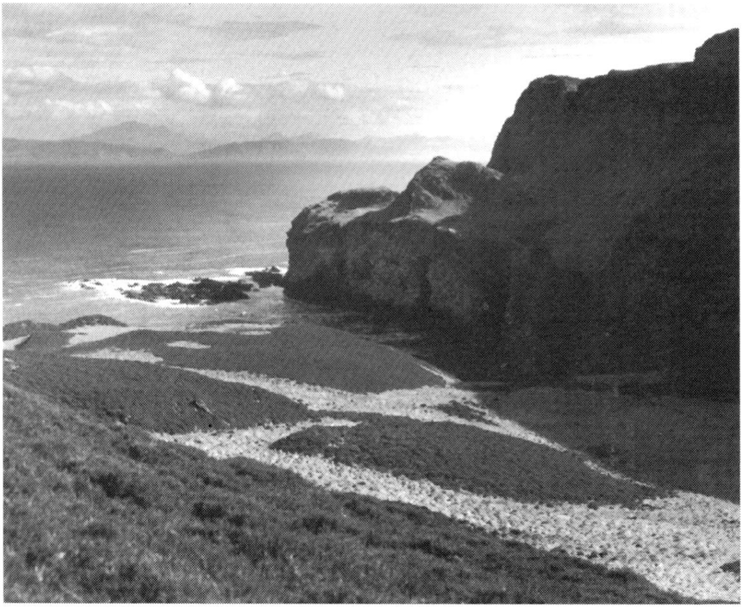

Near Pig's Paradise, Colonsay

fact four islands. There are also beaches backed by machair on the west – the Traigh Ban, Kiloran, and Plaide Mhór are particularly notable. The valley by Rubh' a'Geodha in the north is dune-filled – a rabbit warren culminating in a beautiful beach facing east.

To the west of Kiloran village, the coast around Pig's Paradise (where pigs *were* once kept) is all craggy high cliffs cut by deep ravines – a superb place from which to view Mull, Iona, the Torran Rocks and Dubh Artach lighthouse. The highest point is Carnan Eoin (the hill of the birds), rising to 470ft to the north-east of Kiloran Bay. The Piper's Cave, on the coast beneath Beinn Bhreac, is the cavern where, in legend, a piper went in search of hell. He was never seen again, but his dog appeared from another cave four miles south, with all his hair singed off.

The first known owners of Colonsay were the MacPhees, followed by the Campbells of Argyll, and in 1701 it was purchased by Malcolm McNeil of Knapdale. In legend the McNeils of Colonsay are descended from a family that, with their cattle, came across from Barra in an open boat. McNeil's wife gave birth on the trip, one of the beasts being slaughtered and the mother and child placed inside the carcass for warmth and shelter. Malcolm McNeil built Colonsay House in 1722, using stones taken from Kiloran Abbey.

In the 19thC the McNeils planted many trees in Kiloran Valley, which provided shelter for the fine gardens developed by Lord Strathcona, who bought the islands in 1904 with part of his fortune made building the Canadian Pacific Railway. He planted rhododendrons, azalea, eucalyptus, acacia, maple and magnolia. The woods have elm, ash, beech, sycamore, spruce, larch, silver fir and pine. Palm trees and bamboo grow in the open, sheltered by the gentle valley which creates a mild micro-climate. Lord Strathcona took a great interest in the island and its people, stemming depopulation and giving stable management that ensured long-term prosperity.

Colonsay House is now converted, for the most part, into holiday flats, and the gardens are rather a shadow of their former glory.

The economy of Colonsay is based on crofting and farming with a little fishing, supplemented by tourism. Milk and butter are produced for home consumption. There is a hotel, some summer cottages and bed-and-breakfast accommodation. For the peak holiday period, it is usually all fully booked.

The ferry terminal is at Scalasaig, the main village, where the pier was built in 1965 at a cost of £1½ million. There is a post office/store, petrol pump and resident doctor here, as well as the hotel. The other areas of population are Kilchattan in the west, and Kiloran. The island has its own junior school, and there is a minister, but no police. Gaelic is the predominant language.

To the east of the bays of Tobar Fuar (cold well) and Port Lobh (apparently Port Stink, from the rotting seaweed, but definitely not always so), there is a simple 18-hole golf course. The large central Loch Fada and many coastal locations provide excellent birdwatching, and there is much fine walking. Off the west coast of the grassy Ardskenish peninsula, there is a small colony of seals among the skerries.

The island of **Oronsay**, now under separate ownership, is reached across The Strand, a wide expanse of dull shell sand which dries out about three hours either side of low water – it is advisable, however, to seek local advice before making the crossing. Halfway, in the sand, can be found the sanctuary cross – a fugitive fleeing from Colonsay was rendered immune from punishment when he reached the cross, provided he remained on Oronsay for a year and a day.

The name Oronsay derives from that of St Oran, a disciple of St Columba, who came here from Ireland in AD 563 and founded a monastery. The present ruined Augustinian priory is thought to have been built on the same site in 1380. The buildings are very fine, rivalling those on Iona, although on Oronsay farm buildings are quite close. There is also a new house. In the chapel there is a high altar, in which are kept human remains which have surfaced in the graveyard nearby. Outside stands a Celtic cross, 12ft high and of considerable beauty, and in the Prior's House alongside the chapel are slab-shaped tombstones, carved with knights and various other figures. Oronsay Farm was built by the McNeils using stones taken from the priory.

The highest point is Beinn Oronsay (305ft), from which there are excellent views. There are two good beaches on the west coast, and

Oronsay Priory and Farm, photographed in 1980

rocks and skerries to the south. On **Eilean nan Ron** (seal island) there was once a kelp-gatherer's cottage, and there is still a colony of grey seals.

The Colonsay community is well balanced, and the island appears well tended. Those who wish to find peace in beautiful and unspoiled surroundings should seriously consider visiting, although it is now necessary to book accommodation a year in advance.

The Caledonian MacBrayne ferry *Isle of Mull* operates from Oban on Mondays, Wednesdays and Fridays. *Isle of Arran* operates a seasonal service from Kennacraig via Port Askaig (Islay) on Wednesdays. There is a post bus on the island.

Islay and Jura

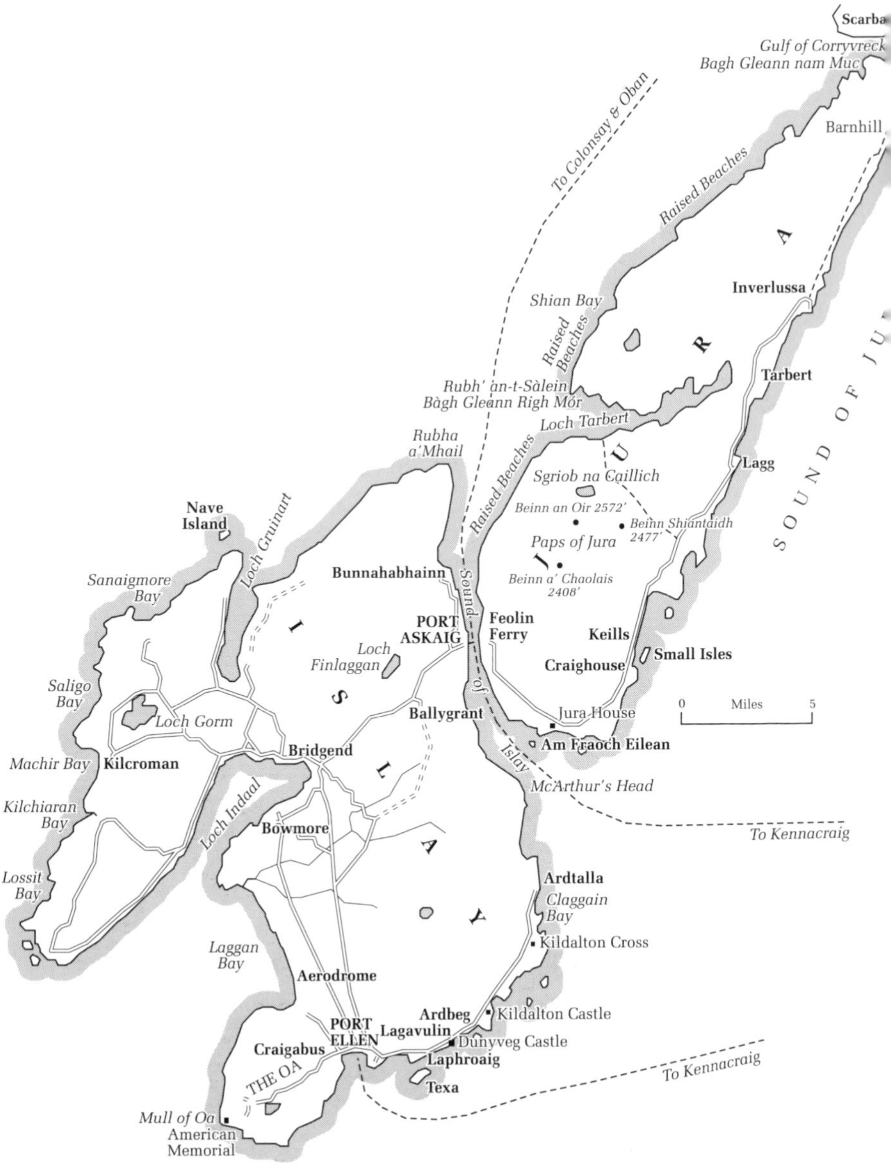

Islay

Strathclyde. Islay (pronounced eye-la), the green isle, measures 25 miles north to south and 20 miles east to west, and has an area of 150,500 acres. It lies 14 miles west of Kintyre, a mile south-west of its close neighbour, Jura, and is the most southerly of the Hebridean islands.

The geology of Islay is quite complex and, as a consequence, the landscape is varied. The southern end of the Rinns of Islay peninsula is Archaean gneiss with patches of hornblende, typically rough tree-less grassland with rock outcrops. The northern part of the Rinns, around the head of Loch Indaal to Bowmore, is calcareous Torridonian sandstone with deposits of good loam; this is the agricultural heart of the island. The Northern tip is Cambrian quartzite with belts of Dalradian limestone running through it, and from Port Askaig to the Mull of Oa (pronounced o) there is a strip of mica schist intersected with limestone. To the south-east of this is the mountainous belt of Dalradian quartzite – a continuation of the rocks of Jura also containing similarly barren sporting estates. On the extreme south-east coast, between Port Ellen and Ardtalla, there is a

The Lagavulin Distillery, Islay

Port Ellen, Islay

fringe of mica schist and hornblende, giving a beautifully broken coastline of bays and islands, backed by areas of woodland and scrub.

Coasts exposed to the west have benefited from deposits of wind-blown shell sand and the machair this promotes. There are also extensive deposits of peat, used both as domestic fuel and for preparing malt in the island's whisky distilleries. It is also worth noting that Islay has some mineral potential; indeed, lead and silver were mined in the 19thC to the west of Port Askaig, and copper and manganese are both known to be present.

The tidal range on the east coasts of Islay and Jura is less than anywhere else in the British Isles. The spring range rarely exceeds five feet and may be as little as two. At neap tides the sea level seems to remain constant for days. The climate of Islay is typically oceanic. There is little shelter from the weather, and Loch Indaal tends to funnel the prevailing winds right to the centre.

There are prehistoric remains scattered all over the island, and written records are available for Islay from an earlier time than any other Hebridean island. The Irish came in the 3rdC, and St Columba is said to have founded a chapel at Kilchiaran, on the west of the Rinns.

On two islets in Loch Finlaggan, to the south-west of Port Askaig, there once stood castles from which the Lord of the Isles ruled the Hebrides. Excavations are now revealing the importance of this site, from which the whole of the west coast islands of Scotland were administered from the 12th to 15thC. Remains of thirty or more buildings have been discovered, together with medieval grave slabs on Eilean More, not far from the ruined chapel. The smaller of the two islands is Eilean na Comhairle, meaning the council isle. Here the Lords of the Isles and their councillors administered their

Bowmore, Islay, dominated by the church of Kilarrow

domain. There is also a theory that the *genuine* and revered Stone of Scone, the 'rock of Scottish royalty', lies hidden here, brought to Islay in the 14thC by Angus Og. This stone is said to contain a footprint to fit the new Lord of the Isles, and may have disappeared in the 17thC. A visitor centre is open, and there is restricted access to the islands.

John, first Lord of the Isles, erected the beautiful 14thC Celtic cross in the churchyard at Kilchoman (the cell of Comman, long since vanished) in the west, in memory of his second wife, Margaret. It is eight-feet high, slim and elegant. At the base is a wishing stone, to be turned by expectant mothers who wish to have a son; the hollow in which it rests has been worn deep. To the north-west the foundations of the summer palace of the Lord of the Isles has been discovered. It is said that the legendary Skye piping family, the McCrimmons, derived their art from the magic black chanter (part of a bagpipe) obtained on Islay.

The main industries are farming, distilling, tourism and fishing. There are about 500 farms, and nearly all the farmers are the tenants of large estates. Sheep and beef and dairy cattle are kept – a mellow cheese is produced from surplus milk at the Port Charlotte Creamery, established in 1939. Barley was once grown for the distillers, but this raw material is now imported. The island's modest fishing fleet takes mostly shellfish, processed on the island.

On Islay, and throughout the Highlands, whisky was once distilled illicitly. Legitimate distilling began about 180 years ago, with many distilleries being built on the sites of old stills. For a period there was no duty payable on whisky produced and consumed on Islay, and drunkenness was rife, the standard of husbandry went into a decline and the ministers complained. The Islay distilleries each employ about 20 people and until recently produced a combined total of some four million proof gallons each year, of which 75 per cent was exported. The remaining 25 per cent, consumed on the British home market, resulted in the Exchequer receiving almost £7000 duty each year for every man, woman and child on the island. The distilleries currently in production are: Ardbeg, established on a

The Mull of Oa, Islay

site used by smugglers in 1815, producing an exclusive malt varying in age from 17 to 24 years; Bowmore, established in 1799 and the oldest legal distillery on Islay, producing malt; Bunnahabhainn, established in 1881, used in blends; Caol Ila, established in 1846, mostly blended; Lagavulin, built in early 19thC on the site of an illegal still and producing a splendidly smooth, aromatic peaty malt; Laphroaig, established in 1820, producing a renowned peaty malt, which is also used to blend Islay Mist, a milder flavour.

The main village of Islay is Bowmore, near the head of Loch Indaal, with a population of about 900. It is dominated by the unusual round church of Kilarrow, built that way in 1769 by the Campbells of Shawfield so there would be no corners in which the devil could hide. A pleasant wide street of shops and bars leads downhill to the small harbour. Islay's administrative centre Bowmore, has a school for over 500 children, a police station, hospital, hotels, swimming pool and Tourist Information Centre.

To the north, at the head of the loch, is Bridgend, where a private road to Islay House crosses the main road. There are woods, and the area is covered with flowers in the spring and summer – daffodil, bluebell, celandine, primrose and wild hyacinth. On a hill nearby stands a memorial to John F. Campbell, collector of Islay folklore.

The main road passes some pleasant beaches, a distillery and a small lighthouse before reaching Port Charlotte, a pretty village of neat pastel-painted houses, known as the Queen of the Rinns, where there is also a museum housed in an old church (opposite the creamery) and a small pier.

Claggain Bay, Islay

At the exposed western tip of the Rinns of Islay are Port Wemyss and Portnahaven, separated by a burn and sheltered by two islands, the larger of which, **Orsay,** has a ruined chapel and a lighthouse. The west coast of the Rinns is rocky with some fine sandy bays, namely Lossit (look out for the experimental wave powered generator), Machir and Saligo. To the north of Saligo there are dramatic steep cliffs, and behind the bay is Loch Gorm, with the stump of a ruined castle on an islet, the largest expanse of water on Islay. Every winter there are enormous numbers of geese here – barnacle (as many as 8000), greylag and the rare Greenland white-fronted.

To the west of Loch Gruinart the land undulates towards the sand and machair of Ardnave Point, with low-lying **Nave Island** off the tip. Many fine stone farmhouses around here have been allowed to fall into ruin. At the head of the long sandy Loch Gruinart, a bloody battle was fought on 5 August 1598 between Sir Lochlan Mor MacLean of Duart and Sir James MacDonald of Islay, due to a dispute over the ownership of land. It is said that the MacDonalds of Islay won with the magical help of *Du-sith*, the black elf. The remains of Kilnave Chapel with its 8thC cross, lying on the shore of the loch about two miles south of Ardnave Point, is where, after the battle, the MacDonalds burned to death 30 of the MacLeans of Duart, mistakenly believing they had killed their leader, Sir James. To the south of Loch Gruinart are extensive deposits of peat.

The area to the north of Ballygrant (on the road to Port Askaig), where limestone is quarried, is a hilly wilderness, the haunt of sportsmen: there are herds of deer, many pheasants, and lochs well stocked with trout. On either side of Rubha a'Mhail, the northernmost tip of Islay, there are raised beaches.

Port Askaig is one of the terminals used by the Caledonian MacBrayne ferry from Kennacraig. A small landing craft-type ferry plies across the swift-flowing Sound of Islay to Jura. There are a few houses, a store, an attractive hotel (dating from the 16thC) and a lifeboat station, all overlooked by Dunlossit House. To the north are two distilleries, to the south the coast is rocky with small bays, a haven for sea birds and seals. There is no road until Ardtalla. The lighthouse at McArthur's Head marks the southern entrance to the Sound of Islay.

To the west of the trackless mountains of Islay is the six-mile shell-sand beach of Laggan, backed by dunes and machair, with a golf course at the southern end. To the south-east is Port Ellen, a simple workman-like village and Islay's other ferry terminal, the largest centre of population, built 100 years ago, with shops, a bank and hotels. To the west of Port Ellen, Kilnaughton Bay has a fine beach. The point of Carraig Fhada is guarded by a curious white light tower built in 1832 and dedicated to Lady Eleanor Campbell. The Oa peninsula, the most southerly part of Islay, has a rock and cliff coastline with many caves, once the scene of illicit distilling and smuggling. At the Mull of Oa, above sheer cliffs with views of Antrim and Rathlin Island, stands the American Memorial, built by the American Red Cross to commemorate U.S. servicemen lost when the *Tuscania* was torpedoed in February 1918 and the *Otranto* was wrecked in a gale in October 1918. Many bodies were washed ashore here.

To the east of Port Ellen the road heads north-east to Ardtalla, through one of the most attractive and interesting parts of the island, with white-painted and tidily kept distilleries of Laphroaig, Lagavulin and Ardbeg standing by the shore. To the south of Laphroaig is the small island of **Texa**, a rocky hump with a ruined chapel, a ruined cottage and two wells. Somerled anchored his fleet in Lagavulin Bay in the 12thC. To the east stands the fine ruin of Dunyveg Castle, built into the rock in the 13thC by Donald I and at one time a stronghold of the Lord of the Isles and their main naval base. The magical Loch a'Chnuic is overlooked by Kildalton Castle, standing in woodland, once owned by John Ramsay MP, who carried out forced evictions in the 19thC, and for his trouble received a curse from an old woman bound for America. Whether or not as a result of this, he and his wife both died prematurely, and his estate attracted bad fortune.

Two miles further north, by a ruined chapel, stands Kildalton High Cross, possibly the finest in the Hebrides. It dates from about AD 800 and was carved in local blue stone by a sculptor from Iona. On one side is the Virgin and Child, and David and his Lion; on the other are carved animals and bosses.

Between Aros Bay and the superb sand and shingle Claggain Bay is Trudernish Point, upon which stands a vitrified *dun* (fort). Inland, and to the north-west of Ardtalla, a scrubby woodland gives way to barren private sporting estates, where herds of deer roam and where there are many pheasants and lochs full of trout. With such a variety of habitat, and so much land left wild, it is not surprising that Islay has the richest bird life in the Hebrides, with over 180 different species having been recorded – an ornithologist's paradise.

Islay's population peaked at nearly 15,000 in 1831; it is now 4000. There are few job opportunities and many young men go to sea – Islay has been called a nursery of sea captains. Many of the farms have been taken over by Lowlanders and Gaelic culture has declined; although Gaelic is taught in the schools and spoken by the older folk, English still predominates. Islay has great agricultural potential, never fully realised, but *Ileachs* still believe that their island is the Queen of the Hebrides.

The island is served by the Caledonian MacBrayne ferry *Isle of Arran* which provides a service from Kennacraig to Port Askaig and Port Ellen, and in summer links once a week with Oban and twice a week with Colonsay. There is a regular flight to Islay from Glasgow, and a bus service on Islay.

The magnificent Kildalton High Cross, Islay

Jura

Strathclyde. Jura's name comes from the Norse *Dyr Oe* (deer island). It has an area of 93,700 acres (including Scarba), and is 28 miles long by eight miles wide, lying just half a mile from Islay. As well as a narrow strip of schist along the east coast, Jura has the largest area of metamorphic quartzite – a poor, infertile rock – in the Highlands.

Loch Tarbert almost bisects the island. In the southern half are the Paps of Jura, prominent landmarks for miles around: Beinn a'Chaolais (mountain of the sound) rises to 2408ft, Beinn an Oir (mountain of the boundary, often called the mountain of gold) to 2572ft, and Beinn Shiantaidh (holy mountain) to 2477ft. The slopes are barren and scree-covered, but the views from the top are splendid – on a clear day Ireland and the Isle of Man are visible. To the north-west of Beinn an Oir is a large rock scar called Sgriob na Caillich, the witches scrape. The majority of the island is trackless blanket bog, with about 5000 red deer, some wild goats and, of course, birds. It is extremely difficult country to cross.

Along the west coast are raised beaches, long stretches of white stones among the grass and heather, formed when the sea level was higher. Notable are those at Bagh Gleann Righ Mor, Rubh' an t-Sailen

Jura's east coast

The Paps of Jura

and Shian. There are many caves, used for shelter by both the deer and their hunters, as sheep folds and, in the past, by the islanders transporting their dead to Iona and Oronsay. Rudimentary altars were built in some.

A large cave about 180ft deep, at the northern end of Jura in Bagh Gleann nam Muc, overlooking the Gulf of Corryvreckan, is said to be the burial place of a Norwegian prince named Breacan, whose galley was consumed by the treacherous waters between here and Scarba. This tide-race runs west on the flood and east on the ebb at speeds of up to 10 knots (11½ mph). A pinnacle of rock rising from the sea bed causes violent overfalls and breakers, with whirlpools on the Scarba side. Spring tides, and a westerly blowing against the flood, results in the maelstrom that can be heard many miles away. There is only a short period of slack water. The gulf is presided over by the legendary Caillich, an old woman who decides which ships shall sink and which shall survive, and indeed there have been some terrible disasters and some remarkable escapes. St Columba is said to have navigated it in full flood calming the waters with words alone.

The island of Jura was owned by the Clan Donald before being sold to the Campbells of Argyll in 1607, who later sold it in 1938. During the 18thC and early 19thC it was a centre for breeding Highland cattle, and the population rose to over 1300 in the 1840s. The glens were, at this time, green with grass. There then followed the widespread introduction of sheep, the despoilation of good land and mass emigration. Farming and crofting are now the main means of employment, with beef cattle and sheep being kept, but the major part of the island is used for sporting activities and is owned by five landlords.

All Jura's 200 or so inhabitants live on the east coast, and the main centre of population is at Craighouse, in the south of Small Isles Bay. There is a post office, shop, hotel, school, doctor and distillery – a new building, replacing the original built in the mid-19thC by the Campbells, which opened in 1963, with the product, a malt whisky, first being bottled in 1974. One of the two piers was built in 1814 by Thomas Telford, and in Craighouse churchyard a stone commemorating Gillouir MacCrain, who saw 180 Christmasses before dying in 1645. To the north of Craighouse, Loch na Mile has a fine beach, and two-and-a-half miles off-shore is the Skervuile Lighthouse. At the southern end of the island, Jura House stands among woods and rhododendrons. On the small island of **Am Fraoch Eilean** (heather isle), lying to the southwest, are the ruins of Caisteal Claidh (castle of the trench) built on the square Norman plan about 1154 by Somerled, to defend the Sound of Islay.

Jura's only road finishes at Inverlussa, passing through areas of moorland and patches of attractive woodland above the mainly rocky shoreline, although at Tarbert there is a fine sheltered beach.

Six miles to the south east is the remote **Eilean Mór,** the retreat of St Abban mac ui Charmaig (died AD 640) who founded a monastery at Keills on the mainland. On the island is a medieval chapel, once used as an ale house, built around an older building; it was visited by John Paul Jones during the American War of Independence. There is a standing cross close by, and a replica of another to the south on higher ground, and there is also a small sanctuary cave.

In the graveyard at Inverlussa lies Mary MacCrain, another member of a family noted for its longevity; she died in 1856, aged 126. A track continues towards the north of the island, passing close to Barnhill, the stone farmhouse where George Orwell wrote *Nineteen Eighty-Four* each summer from 1946-49.

Jura stands in complete contrast to the fertile land of its well-endowed neighbour, Islay, but it is blessed with a sheltered position and a mild climate – palm trees and fuschias grow in the open. It will never be more than trackless moor and mountain, but its rugged beauty will continue to tempt visitors on to the small vehicle ferry which plies between Port Askaig and Feolin.

Gigha

Strathclyde. Gigha is pronounced gee-ah, with a hard g. Although it has been suggested the name may derive from the Norse *Gjedoe* (goat island), a more apt and descriptive alternative is *Gud-ey* – good island or God's island – for what appears barren and rocky at a distance is a fertile and productive island with much good grazing (900 acres of arable land out of a total of 3600 acres) and a mild climate.

A ridge of epidiorite runs the length of Gigha, and the surrounding land is lime-free sandy loam, which is best on the east. The highest point is 331ft, at the summit of Creag Bhan, and there are some fine sandy beaches.

The island is divided into about a dozen farms and half a dozen crofts. A large stock of Ayrshires produce over 250,000 gallons of milk a year, once processed in the island's own creamery, but now shipped daily to Campbeltown for pasteurisation. There are also some beef cattle and sheep, with fish farming replacing the traditional fishing industry.

The island was purchased in 1944 by the late Sir James Horlick (maker of the well-known beverage), who modernised the farms and converted 50 acres of woodland into the supremely beautiful and well-tended Achamore Gardens, transplanting many specimens from his garden near Ascot. Rare plants from Achamore are now being propagated and planted at Brodick, Arran.

The pastoral island of Gigha

There are, among varied deciduous woodland, laburnum, *Primula candelabra,* azalea, hybrid rhododendron and various sub-tropical plants including palms and palm lilies (*Cordyline australis).* The gardens were gifted to the National Trust for Scotland in 1962 and are open during the summer. Gigha was next owned by the Landale family, Dumfriesshire farmers who husbanded the island's resources well, and then by businessman Malcolm Potir, who invested quite heavily to keep Gigha viable. It was then purchased in 1992 by Holt Leisure Parks, owners of Kip Marina on the Clyde.

The main area of population (which totals 160), the only village and the ferry terminal is Ardminish. Here there is a shop, the renowned post office run by the McSporrans (where bicycles can be hired) and an attractive hotel frequented by passing yachts-persons. A nine-hole golf course and an airstrip have been built. The church has a stained-glass window dedicated to Kenneth MacLeod (born on Eigg in 1872), translator and composer of songs, including 'The Road to the Isles'. South of the village is the ancient chapel of Kilchattan, with an ogham stone nearby.

Over 70 species of birds have been recorded on Gigha; **Eun Eilean,** off the west coast, is noted for its sea birds and there is a gullery on Eilean Garbh, to the north. None of the usual mammals exists on Gigha – deer, stoat, weasel, mole, fox and hare have never established themselves, and the rabbits were almost completely killed off by myxomatosis. Grey seals play off the rocky shores and around the numerous outlying reefs and skerries, and wild flowers bloom everywhere. Gigha should not be missed.

The Caledonian MacBrayne ferry *Loch Ranza* operates between the island and Tayinloan, on Kintyre.

To the south of Gigha is the barren island of **Cara** (from the Norse *Karoe,* coffin island), uninhabited for over 30 years. On it are a holiday house and a ruined 15thC chapel; it is grazed by sheep and goats, and there are also otters.

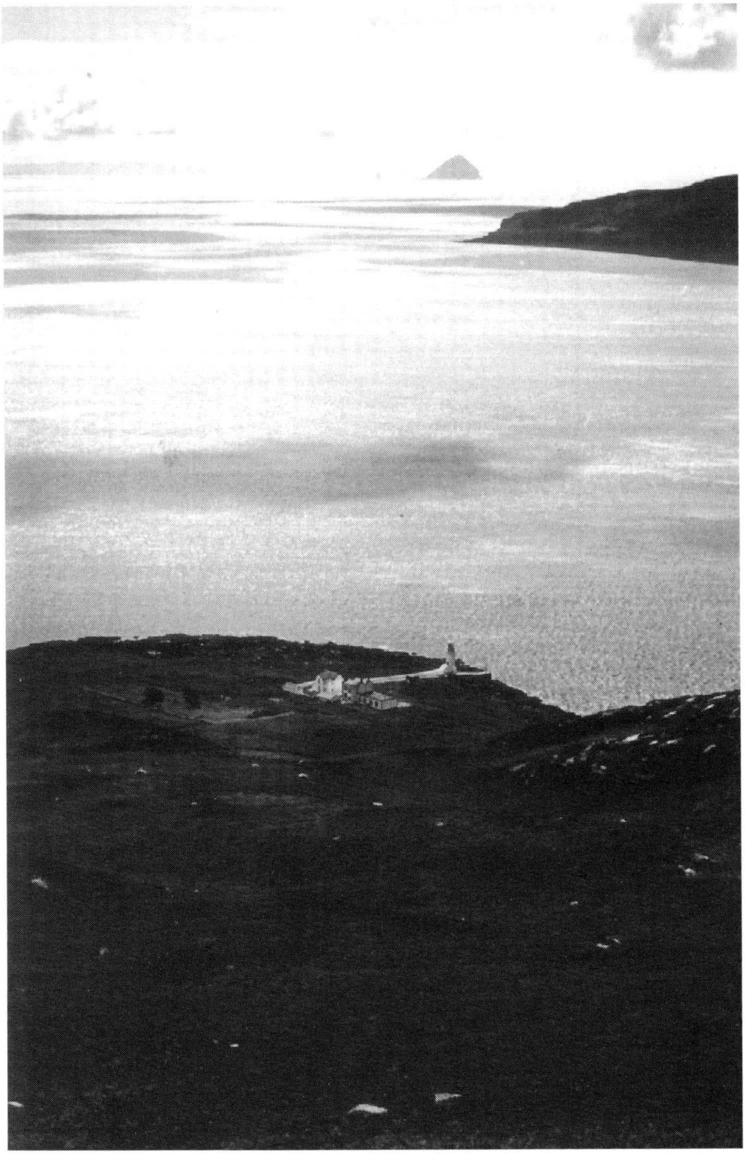

Looking south from the summit of Holy Island, Arran, towards Ailsa Craig

The Clyde Islands

Tucked in behind Kintyre, these splendid islands are well worth a visit in their own right, and will whet your appetite for futher island exploration, with only a modest commitment.

Bute

Argyll & Bute. Bute measures 16 miles by 4 miles, with an area of 31,000 acres. Its northern half is enclosed by the Cowal peninsula which seems, in places, to be only a stone's throw away across the Kyles of Bute. The Highland Boundary Fault, a geological feature, splits the island along the line of Loch Fad – to the north is Dalradian schistose grit, to the south more recent old red sandstone with some basaltic lavas. To the north of Ettrick Bay the island is quite hilly, rising to 911 ft at the summit of Windy Hill.

Apart from the southern tip, the rest of the land undulates gently, and much is green and fertile. There are some areas of mixed woodland; Torr Wood, north of Kingarth, is particularly pleasant. As Bute is highly cultivated the bird life is not outstanding, but the island's long-tailed field-mouse is a sub-species of the mainland species, with a shorter tail and smaller ears.

Prior to local council reorganisation in the early 1970s, Rothesay was capital of the County of Bute, which included Arran and the Cumbraes. Rothesay attained the status of a Royal Burgh in 1403, and the charter was extended by James VI of Scotland in 1584. The Bute family have for a long time taken an active interest in the affairs of the Burgh, often occupying the position of Provost. The history of the island is centred on the massive, circular, moated Rothesay Castle, first recorded in 1230 when it was besieged by Norsemen, a portion of the eastern wall still showing signs of the breach made when they eventually captured the fortress, and in 1263 it fell to

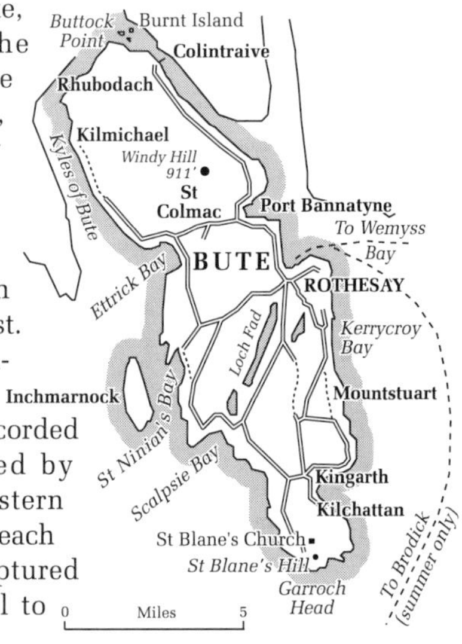

The west coast of Bute, towards Garroch Head.

King Haakon of Norway. The wars of independence touched the castle little, although it was taken from the English by Sir Colin Campbell in about 1334. During the 15thC it was attacked by the Lord of the Isles.

During the reigns of James IV and James V it became an important base during their campaigns to subdue the Hebrides, a lawless part of the realm, and improvements were made to the fabric of the building, including the construction of the great tower, completed in 1541. In 1498 the Bute family were appointed hereditary keepers of the castle (an office still held by the present Marquess, although the Department of the Environment now maintains the building). The castle was successfully defended in 1527 against the rebel Master of Ruthven; however the surrounding burgh was destroyed, a common occurrence each time the castle was attacked and a hindrance to continuing development of the town. In 1544 the Earl of Lennox took it for the English. When Cromwell withdrew his garrison in 1659 much of the building was dismantled; what was left was burned during the Duke of Monmouth's rebellion in 1685. The second Marquess of Bute began restoration in 1816, and further work was done by the third Marquess in 1872 and 1900.

Inside the massive sandstone curtain walls stands the chapel of St Michael; to the north-east of this is a well. The great hall, renovated in 1970 by the sixth Marquess, has a fine fireplace along one side, and a tapestry of the Prayer for Victory at Prestonpans on the wall. The castle is open to the public daily, and is well worth visiting, as is the museum to the south. At the top of the High Street is the ancient chapel of St Mary's, once part of the Bishopric of (the Isle of) Man.

Rothesay's population accounts for three-quarters of the island's total of 8100. It is a pleasant holiday place with a fine winter garden and all the facilities a million visitors each year would expect, including visits from the *Waverley*, the last sea-going paddle steamer on the Clyde during July and August.

In 1882 the Rothesay Tramways Company began a horse-drawn tram service between Guildford Square in Rothesay and Port

Bannatyne and, after considerable success, the line was electrified in 1902 and extended to Ettrick Bay in 1905. The company's eventual demise began with competition from motor coaches in the 1920s, and it eventually became a summer only service in 1931 before the last tram ran on 30 September 1936. It was unique in being the only such service on a Scottish island, comparable with that which still exists on the Isle of Man.

Rothesay harbour, an important ferry terminal, was built during the 17thC for the fishing fleet, and subsequently rebuilt and enlarged during the heyday of the Clyde steamers. Now it provides shelter for a small marina. From 1940 to 1957 the bay was a naval anchorage.

Prior to the advent of tourism as its main industry Bute was a major supplier of agricultural produce to the surrounding mainland, and it is still very productive, concentrating on dairy farming. The first cotton mill was built in Rothesay in 1779 and this industry flourished in the early 19thC. Slate was mined on the island during medieval times, but the material produced here is too soft for present day use. Along with the rest of the west coast of Scotland, there was a great deal of prosperity during the herring fishing boom. Present industries, as well as tourism and agriculture include weaving and shellfish processing.

To the south of the capital is Kerrycroy Bay, with very pretty houses among tall trees at the back of a green, a sand and pebble beach and a small stone jetty. This village was planned by the Marquis of Bute, and built in 1803, complete with a pub. The pier here provided a link with the mainland which preceded Rothesay.

Mount Stuart, to the south, has been the home of successive earls and marquesses of Bute for over 250 years. The present building replaced an earlier house built by the second Earl of Bute in 1719, and which was destroyed by fire in 1877. The family is directly descended from King Robert the Bruce, whose daughter Majorie married Walter, 'Steward of Bute', in 1315. Indeed their name derives from this hereditary office, held by the family since 1157. The interior of the house is a splendid Victorian Gothic fantasy, designed by the 3rd Marquess of Bute (1847-1900) and architect Robert Rowand Anderson. Colonnaded halls, richly painted ceilings and fine murals, featuring astrological designs, and paintings create a breathtaking and rewarding experience. The splendid gardens contains a Victorian Pinetum and a large octagonal glass pavilion. Limetree Avenue leads down to a beautiful unspoiled stretch of seashore. Mount Stuart is open May to mid-Oct (not Tue or Thur). At Kilchattan (the cell of St Cattan), red sandstone houses match the sand and stones of the beach, and a track from the end of the road leads to the lighthouse at Rubha'n Eun, with fine views of the Cumbraes.

The southern tip of Bute is marked by the steep St Blane's Hill, rising to 403 ft above a rocky shoreline. A path from the road's end leads to St Blane's Chapel, among the ruins of a 6thC Celtic monastery in a beautiful and secluded wooded glade. Established by St Catan, the monastery took the name of his nephew, St Blane. Remains of the cells are still visible, and the medieval church shows fine 12thC craftsmanship. It is well worth visiting. Dunagoil, a vitrified Iron Age fort, stands on a promontory nearby.

Kerrycroy, Bute

The west-coast bays of Scalpsie, St Ninian's and Ettrick all have sand, if only at low tide. Inland Lochs Quien and Fad almost split the island – the latter is a popular trout fishery. The low-lying island of **Inchmarnock** (675 acres) lies three-quarters of a mile west of St Ninian's Point, where there are the remains of a chapel, built in the 6th or 7thC. Inchmarnock is divided into two farms with two farmhouses. Remains of the monastery founded by St Marnoc in the 7thC can be seen, and cross fragments have been uncovered around the ancient chapel. A Bronze Age cairn containing three burial cists has been excavated; in one was the skeleton of a young woman and a fine lignite (old wood) collar. Except for a short period during World War II when it was used for commando training, the island has remained a haven of peace, with prolific bird life and the largest herring-gull colony on the Clyde.

The main road skirts the low land behind Ettrick Bay, where there is a friendly tearoom. At St Colmac, near the chapel, is the Cross of Kilmachalmaig, possibly an old preaching cross. To the north-west of the bay, the road ends at Clate Point; inland, the hills are empty and unpopulated. At the north-west corner are the remains of Kilmichael Chapel, destroyed by the Norsemen, and higher up the hillside is the burial cairn of Glenroidean.

Port Bannatyne is a northerly extension of Rothesay. The pier is in ruins, but the houses are pretty and there are nice pubs, and a boatyard. Kames Bay has a little sand, but beyond here the shore is stony. The road ends at Rhubodach, where a vehicle ferry across the Kyles to Colintrave was established in 1950. The **Burnt Islands** to the north are a natural haven for birds.

Bute is easily reached by the Caledonian MacBrayne vehicle and passenger ferries *Juno, Jupiter, Saturn and Pioneer* sailing between Wemyss Bay and Rothesay (half hour crossing) and by the *Loch Dunvegan* between Colintrave and Rhubodach (five minute crossing). A summer-only ferry, *Pioneer*, connects with Brodick, Arran on Monday, Wednesday & Friday. There is a bus service on the island, and the Tourist Information Centre is in Rothesay.

The Cumbraes

North Ayrshire. Great Cumbrae, part of the Bute estate, lies one mile west of Largs and just over two miles east of Bute. Little Cumbrae is half a mile to the south across The Tan; between Rubha'n Eun on Bute and Little Cumbrae is the route taken by all the Clyde shipping.

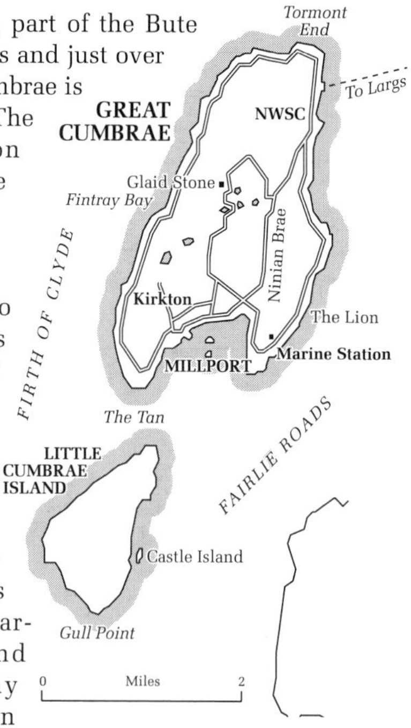

Great Cumbrae Island measures just four miles by two miles, has an area of 5120 acres and attains a maximum height of 416 ft, the summit of the hills being marked by the Glaid Stone. Views from the top extend as far as the Paps of Jura and Ben Lomond. The coast is rocky and broken, with low cliffs. Central and northern areas are old red sandstone, with carboniferous limestone around Millport, and there are many igneous dykes, the outcrop known as The Lion on the south-east coast being particularly notable.

Millport wraps itself around the back of the bay, facing south towards Ailsa Craig and giving a spectacular view of Arran to the south-west. It offers all you would expect of a small resort, including golf, bowling, riding, boating, sea fishing, a cinema and an attractive museum of local history, and has sandy beaches and pleasant gardens. A popular way of seeing the island is to cycle its 12-mile circumference, with bicycles being available for hire in the town. The total population is about 1200.

During the late 19thC and early 20thC the harbour was a regular port of call for the many Clyde steamers. In 1906 the steamer companies, who objected to excessive pier dues, refused to call during the holiday season, and Great Cumbrae became a deserted island until Lloyd George arranged a compromise, just before the annual Glasgow holidays. The Episcopal church was consecrated as the Cathedral of Argyll and the Isles in 1876, and is the smallest cathedral in Britain.

It was in Millport Bay in 1812 that Dr MacDougal first identified the roseate tern (*Sterna dougalii*) as a separate species. The

University Marine Biological Station is situated to the east of the town, at Keppel pier. The rich marine life around the islands has been studied since the 1840s, when David Robertson, the Cumbrae naturalist, made frequent visits, eventually establishing a floating laboratory in Kames bay. The present building dates from 1896, and was the headquarters of the Scottish Marine Biological Association until 1970, when it was transferred to Dunstaffnage, near Oban. The marine station is now controlled by the Universities of London and Glasgow. There are research vessels and diving facilities, including a decompression chamber. Undergraduate and post-graduate courses are run, and independent research projects can be accommodated. For visitors there is an interesting aquarium and the Robertson Museum to be seen.

Close to the ferry terminal on the east side is the Scottish Sports Council's National Water Sports Training Centre where sailing, sub-aqua and canoeing are taught. At the north-east tip – Tormont End – there are thought to be graves of Norsemen killed at the battle of Largs in 1263. A monument here commemorates two young seamen from HMS Shearwater who drowned nearby in 1844. The rocky west coast is punctuated by the pleasant sand and shingle crescent of Fintray Bay. Kirkton, in the south-west, was the first village on Great Cumbrae. There has been a chapel there since at least the 13thC; the present church dates from 1802. The inner road traverses the island's backbone, and the views from the road of Bute, Arran and the mainland are superb.

Little Cumbrae Island has an area of 700 acres and is privately owned. A disused lighthouse (the first light signal was erected here in 1750) marks the western tip. The house and farm buildings on the east, used as a holiday retreat, look out towards the remains of a tower on **Castle Island**. In the 14thC, Robert II and Robert III maintained the island as a deer forest. The Hunters of Hunterston were the castle's hereditary keepers until 1515, and in 1653 it was sacked by Cromwell. In 1845 Little Cumbrae supported four families, and over 5000 rabbits were taken each year. In 1880 John Blain, a local historian, wrote: 'The islands of Larger and Lesser Cumbray (sic) intervene between Bute and the Continent'. A local minister, thought to have been the Rev James Adam (1748-1831), also considered the islands of no little importance, praying for the inhabitants of Cumbrae and *the adjacent islands* of Great Britain and Ireland.

Caledonian MacBrayne operate the ferries *Loch Alainn* and *Loch Riddon* from Largs to Cumbrae Slip (a 10 minute crossing), where buses connect with Millport.

There are Tourist Information Centres in Millport (summer only) and Largs.

The Lion

Arran

North Ayrshire. The island of Arran covers 105,600 acres, and is 20 miles long by 11 miles wide, lying three miles east of Kintyre in the Firth of Clyde. The name may derive from the Gaelic 'ara', meaning kidney, or kidney shaped.

Arran was described by Sir Archibald Geike, the eminent geologist, as a complete synopsis of Scottish geology. James Hutton, during the 18thC, confirmed his theories of igneous geology on this island, when he discovered 'unconformity', finding rocks of different ages meeting at a discordant angle, just north of Lochranza near where Allt Beithe enters the sea. This remains one of the world's most important geological locations. Today Arran is regularly visited by scores of students who come to study the various rock formations. The island's most striking features are the high peaks and corries of Goat Fell (2867 ft), an igneous intrusion into the Devonian sandstones and schists. This has resulted in a ring of upturned strata around the granite.

The south of Arran is composed of new red sandstone, and in the north-east there is an area of carboniferous limestone. Throughout there are basaltic dykes which form ridges where the surrounding rock is softer (in the south) and fissures where the surrounding rock is harder (in the granite). Ice Age glaciers deposited many erratics and spread boulders of northern granite all over the south. A raised beach at the 25 ft level is easily recognised, virtually encircling the island.

Climate is mild Atlantic, with the low hills of Kintyre providing little shelter. Average rainfall varies from 50 inches each year in the west to 100 inches in the mountains, with the east receiving 70 inches. Snow generally lies only on the mountains, and frosts are rarely severe. Palm lilies, a sub-tropical native of New Zealand, grow in the open in the south and west.

Beef and dairy cattle, and blackface and Cheviot sheep are kept, and potatoes are grown. Amazingly a special type of sand found on the island is exported to Arab countries, but the main industry is now tourism. There is plenty of accommodation, and much to see and do in a relatively small area.

The history of Arran has much in common with the Hebrides. There are cairns, standing stones are to be found all around the coast and in the glens, and Bronze Age cists (burial chambers) have been found inside a stone circle on Machrie Moor. By 200 BC the island was populated by Celts. Kilpatrick is thought by some to be one of

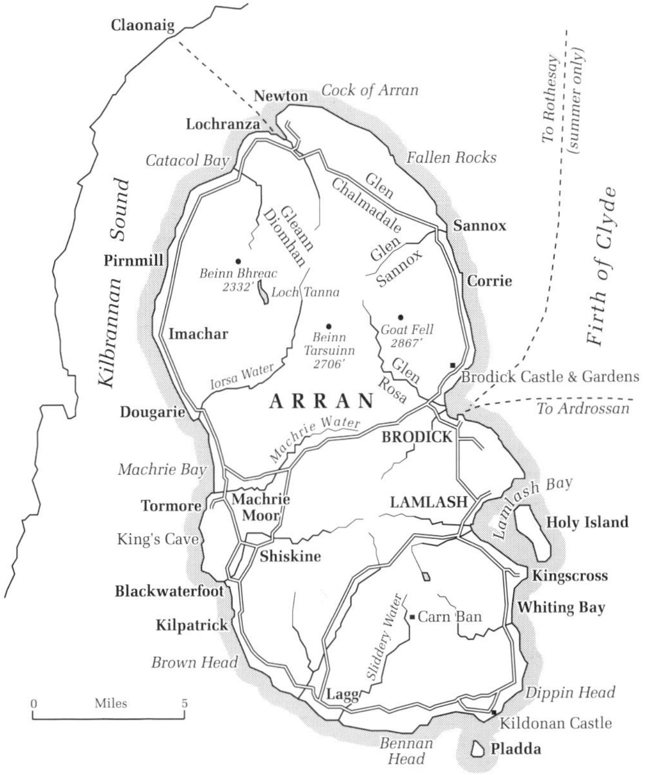

the earliest Celtic Christian sites in Scotland, visited in AD 545 by St Brendan; it was probably sacked by the Vikings in 797. St Mo Las (born AD 566) came to nearby Holy Island during the 7thC; it was later called Eilean Molaise after him, then becoming Lamlash, its name until 1830 and now the name of the village on Arran facing Holy Island.

Viking raids were followed by settlement. The Norsemen separated the island from the Kingdom of Dalriada and held it until Somerled took it in 1156. After the Battle of Largs in 1263 the islands became part of the Kingdom of Scotland, under the Lord of the Isles.

In 1503 the island was awarded to the Hamiltons by Royal Charter. The Jacobite rebellion of 1745 hardly touched Arran at all, but the Highland clearances which followed caused massive emigration and the desertion of villages and crofts. The introduction of large-scale sheep farming which brought quick profits to the landlords eventually laid waste to large areas. As land was enclosed for sheep, the people moved to small coastal holdings; when these were exhausted, they left for the industrial centres of the New World. Gaelic life and culture on Arran suffered a blow from which it was never to recover. Between 1821 and 1881 the population fell from

Brodick Castle, Arran

6600 to 4750; it currently stands at about 3450. Arran is now owned by the family of the Duchess of Montrose, jointly with the National Trust for Scotland and the Forestry Commission, who hold between them 22,500 acres.

There are presently about 2000 red deer roaming wild, although by the end of the 18thC the herds had been hunted almost to extinction. Wild goats, once common, are now found only on Holy Island. There are no foxes, grey squirrels, stoats, weasels or moles. Badgers are rare and adders are no longer as common as once they were. All characteristic moorland birds are represented, and golden eagles are seen in the high peaks.

Most types of deciduous trees are present and there are two protected species unique to the island, rare whitebeams: *sorbus arrenensis* and *sorbus pseudo-fennica*. Among the expected species of plants to be seen are some less common varieties – alpine ladies mantle grows in Glen Sannox, and alpine enchanter's-nightshade is occasionally found in areas of deep shade.

The great majority of Arran's thousands of visitors arrive at Brodick, which has all main services and a Tourist Information Centre near the pier. The village is unremarkable, but its central position makes it an ideal touring centre. To the north of the bay is Brodick Castle and grounds, with Goat Fell behind, the summit of which can be reached by a pleasurable stiff walk from the car park at Cladach (allow about five hours for the walk up and back). The view from the top extends from Ireland to Mull on a clear day. The castle and the mountain are both owned by the National Trust for Scotland. Although the Round Tower, a part of the castle, dates from the early 15thC, the vast majority of the building owes its existence to the Hamiltons, who began adding to the earlier structure in 1558. In 1652 Cromwell's forces, later massacred by the islanders at Corrie,

Looking towards Goat Fell from Holy Island, Lamlash Bay

built the Battery and an additional wing. The final additions, including the Great West Tower, were started in 1844 by the architect Gillespie Graham, who was commissioned by William, son of the tenth Duke and his new wife, Princess Mary of Baden, a great-niece of the Empress Josephine. When the direct line of the Hamiltons finished in 1895 Brodick passed to the Duchess of Montrose.

The castle has an elegant simplicity, a fine example of the indigenous Scottish baronial style which belies the richness of its interiors. The drawing room is furnished with Italian marquetry and french gilt and ormolu pieces, and has a rich plaster ceiling. Other rooms contain Hamilton treasures, paintings by Watteau and Turner, and the Hamilton collection of sporting pictures, including works by Rowlandson, Pollard and Reinagle. The Victorian kitchen has been restored. The informal woodland garden of 60 acres, rich with rhododendrons, was started in 1923; the walled garden dates from 1710, and now contains an area devoted to specimens from the late Sir James Horlick's garden at Achamore, Gigha. Brodick Castle is open April to October, with the gardens open all year. Seals can often be seen off the shore below the castle.

The Isle of Arran Heritage Museum is to be found at Rosaburn, housed in what was once an 18thC croft, with a smithy, coach house, cottage, stables and bothy. There is also an excellent tea room and garden, and demonstrations of lace making, spinning and weaving are given. Nearby, Arran Aromatics make natural body care products,

The Drawing Room, Brodick Castle, Arran

and you can 'stamp' your own soap here. Next door is the Island Cheese Company.

To the north of Brodick is Corrie, a village of gaily painted cottages around two tiny harbours. Stone used in the construction of the Crinan Canal was quarried in the hills behind. There is a 2-mile path to Goat fell from here. The road follows the coast to Sannox Bay, then turns north-west through North Glen Sannox and Glen Chalmadale to Lochranza. At the mouth of Glen Sannox are the remains of the old barytes (barium sulphate, used in some white paints) mines, last worked in 1938, and there is a fine walk up the Glen, beneath Cir Mhór, to the high peaks.

At the northern end of Arran is an area of wild moorland, the haunt of red deer, and a dramatic stretch of coastline, with great rockfalls dating from the Mesozoic and Palaeozoic periods. The large sandstone outcrop at the northern-most point is the Cock of Arran.

Lochranza has Arran's other ferry terminal, connecting with Claonaig, Kintyre. The village and youth hostel sit comfortably to the south of the loch, dominated by the ruined tower of Lochranza Castle, standing on a shingle spit. The existing building dates from the 16thC, and incorporates fragments of an earlier fortification, first recorded by Fordun in the late 14thC. In the early 15thC it was held by John de Mentieth; by 1450 it had been granted to Alexander Lord Montgomery by James II of Scotland. A key is available for those who wish to enter the castle from the post office, from April to September. The village was once a herring port, the anchorage being well shel-

Whitefarland, Arran, where palm lilies grow in the open

tered by the enveloping hills. Newly built, the Isle of Arran Distillers Visitor Centre has fascinating exhibits demonstrating the art of whisky making, including stills, and an 18thC crofters inn. Samples will become available during 1998, although the finished product will be allowed to mature for a few years longer.

The west coast offers fine views of Kintyre across Kilbrannen Sound, and the shoreline is also extremely attractive – bright pebbles with the occasional sandy beach. At Catacol (either from the Norse 'ravine of the wild cat' or the Gaelic 'cat or ship's glen') are the Twelve Apostles, a terrace of pretty and almost identical cottages overlooking the bay at the mouth of a steep sided glen and built in the mid-1860s. They were intended for those displaced by the clearances (for sheep), but remained empty for two years, being known at that time as 'hungry row'. At the summit of Glen Catacol, beneath the wild hills around Beinn Bhreac (2332 ft), is Loch Tanna, the largest loch on the island. On the coast to the west of the mountains is Pirnmill, where pirns (bobbins) were made between 1780 and 1840; there is a fine beach here. The Arran Pottery is situated 200 yards off the road between Catacol and Pirnmill, at Thunderguy. Past the palms of Whitefarland and Imachar, Iorsa Water empties into the sea by Dougarie Lodge, built by the Hamiltons and where Arran's first telephone was installed in 1891. The terraces of glacial material below the lodge are of great geological interest. Iorsa and Machrie Waters both contain salmon and trout, the island's most expensive fishing.

At Machrie Moor the hills retreat and evidence of the distant past is profuse. A stone circle above the road at Auchagallon, standing stones and circles on the moor, and remains of burial chambers, can all be clearly seen. A large cairn at Blackwaterfoot, spoiled during the 19thC, contained relics, including a dagger, which suggest a connection with the culture of southern England which conceived Stonehenge. From Tormore there is a fine walk above the stony shore to the King's Caves, eroded into the sandstone on the level of the 25 ft raised beach, on the wall of which early Christian or Viking carvings can be discerned. Traditionally the caves are associated with Robert Bruce, who came to Arran to try to oust the English, but it is unlikely that Bruce ever stayed in any of them. In the 18thC the Kirk session met there, and in the 19thC they were used as a school. In legend they were occupied by Fingal, Fionn MacCaul.

The village of Shiskine, on the south of Machrie Moor, is said to be the burial place of St Mo Las. The String, the road across the island to Brodick, was built in 1817 by Thomas Telford, passing through bare moorland and rough grazing.

The village of Blackwaterfoot stands in the centre of Drumadoon Bay, around a minuscule harbour. Towards the south the scenery becomes gentler and more pastoral. A minor road follows Sliddery water through the green glen to Lamlash – about a mile up is the Balmichael Motor Museum and quad bike centre. At Lagg, a supposedly haunted inn stands among trees by Kilmory Water. The rocky coast, once the haunt of smugglers from Ireland, lies a short walk to the south.

Three miles north-east of Lagg, in the valley of Allt an t-Sluice, a tributary of Kilmory Water, is Carn Ban, 950 ft above sea level. This chambered cairn, 100 ft long by 60 ft wide, dates from the neolithic period and has been little disturbed. Torrylinn, Kilmory, is the home of the Arran Creamery, where fine Cheddar cheese is made, and sold. Between Kilmory and Kildonan is South Bank Farm, where rare breeds, heavy horses and Highland cattle can be seen.

Kildonan overlooks the low-lying lighthouse island of **Pladda**, beyond which the triangular hump of Ailsa Craig looks deceptively close. To the south-west the Mull of Kintyre can be seen. There are some good areas of sand below the remains of Kildonan Castle, a mysterious 14thC ruin.

At Dippin Head the road rises high above the basaltic rocks of the shoreline, then descends to Whiting Bay, a sprawling village of cafés and craft shops, with a mainly stony beach. A mile up Glenashdale Burn, which enters the sea by the youth hostel, there are dramatic waterfalls, tumbling 100 ft down a lava sill. To the north-east are the remains of a fort. A track leads from the village of Kingscross to Kingscross Point, where there are the substantial remains of a Viking fort and burial mound.

Lamlash is a sea angling and sailing centre, spread along the north-east shore of Lamlash Bay facing towards Holy Island. The line of houses, hotels and shops are backed by trees and high moorland.

By the beach there is a green. It is a delightful, relaxing place, where the hospital, council offices and a high school are intermingled with craft shops and cafés. Donald McKelvie cultivated over 30 varieties of seed potatoes here, all with the prefix 'Arran'. He also bred Highland ponies, and blended tea. Large mooring buoys in the bay remain from the time when this was a fleet anchorage. In 1263 King Haakon moored here, *en route* to the Battle of Largs.

During the summer there are boat trips across Lamlash Bay to Holy Island, a brooding hump rising to 1030 ft at the summit of Mullach Mòr. Above the island's pier stands the farmhouse. There is a story that a farmer murdered his wife here, driven to it by her bearing him 15 daughters, but no sons; she is supposedly buried under the kitchen floor. On the west side is the cave used by St Mo Las in the 7thC, with early Christian and Viking carvings on the walls. Below, near the shore, is the Judgement Stone, a flat sandstone table, with St Mo Las' Well nearby. Beyond the cave, at the south-west tip, is the larger of the island's two lighthouses. There are traces of a 12thC fortress built by Somerled, and in the early 14thC a monastery was established; the remaining small chapel was used for burials on Holy Island until 1790. The seaward side of the island falls steeply to the sea, and a small lighthouse stands on the south-east coast. Eriskay ponies, Soay sheep, Highland cattle and Saanen goats roam freely, while on the rocky cliffs peregrines breed. The island is now under the stewardship of the Samye Ling Buddhist Community, who have planted 27,000 trees and are establishing a Tibetan Buddhist retreat, dedicated to the preservation of the natural environment, peace and spirituality. The island's population numbers 14 at present, but this swells during the summer months with visitors on retreat, and day trippers from Lamlash.

The Caledonian MacBrayne ferry *Caledonian Isles* (which has a Tourist Information Centre on board) operates regularly from Ardrossan to Brodick, a 55 minute crossing. The smaller ferry *Loch Tarbert* provides a summer-only service between Claonaig (Kintyre) and Lochranza, taking 30 minutes. Another summer-only ferry, *Pioneer*, connects with Rothesay, Bute on Monday, Wednesday & Friday. There is a bus service on Arran, and cars and bicycles can be easily hired. The Tourist Information Centre is in Brodick.

The 'haunted' Lagg Inn

Ailsa Craig

South Ayrshire. This is a volcanic hump in the Firth of Clyde, ten miles west of Girvan. It is no longer inhabited: the last lighthouse keepers left in 1990, when it became automatic. It is two miles in circumference, and rises to a height of 1114 ft. Its name, in Gaelic, means 'fairy rock', although it is more affectionately known as 'Paddy's Milestone'. It has been mentioned in poems by both Keats and Wordsworth.

It is composed of microgranite, acid-igneous rock with fine-grained crystals of quartz, felspar and mica, which was quarried until quite recently. The quarrymen's cottages and the old trans-shipment pier, to the north, remain. The granite was famous for its use in the manufacture of curling stones.

Landings are made around high tide at the jetty by the lighthouse at Foreland Point, in the north-east. A narrow-gauge tramway ran from here to the quarry. Other man-made relics include a forge, disused foghorns and the castle, a square tower about 300 ft up the slope behind the lighthouse. Little has been recorded about this building, but it is said to have been used by the monks of Crossraguel Abbey, near Maybole in Strathclyde. It was once held by Catholics on behalf of Philip II of Spain. Half-way up the eastern side of the hill is a lochan, and from the top the view takes in the hills from Renfrewshire to Galloway, and Kintyre, Jura, Arran, Cowal, the Isle of Man and Ireland.

In the south-west corner is the Water Cave, approachable only at low tide, when it is possible to walk right round the base of the island. There has been a colony of gannets on Ailsa Craig since at least 1526; during the 1970s their numbers were estimated at 9500 breeding pairs, about 5 per cent of the world population of gannets at that time. They are to be seen mainly on the southern side.

There are boat trips from Girvan, weather permitting.

Sanda Island

Argyll & Bute. Two miles off the south-east tip of Kintyre, this is a group of islands and skerries, including the demure Sheep Island. Sanda consists of old red sandstone rising to a height of 405 ft, and was farmed until 1946. On it are the remains of the Bloody Castle and a chapel dedicated to St Ninian. It was much visited by the Vikings; in the burial ground is an old Norse grave. On the most southerly point is a lighthouse. **Sheep Island** and the tiny **Glunimore Island** are the most important breeding stations in the Clyde area for puffin.

In 1946 the lifeboatmen of Campbeltown made a remarkable res-

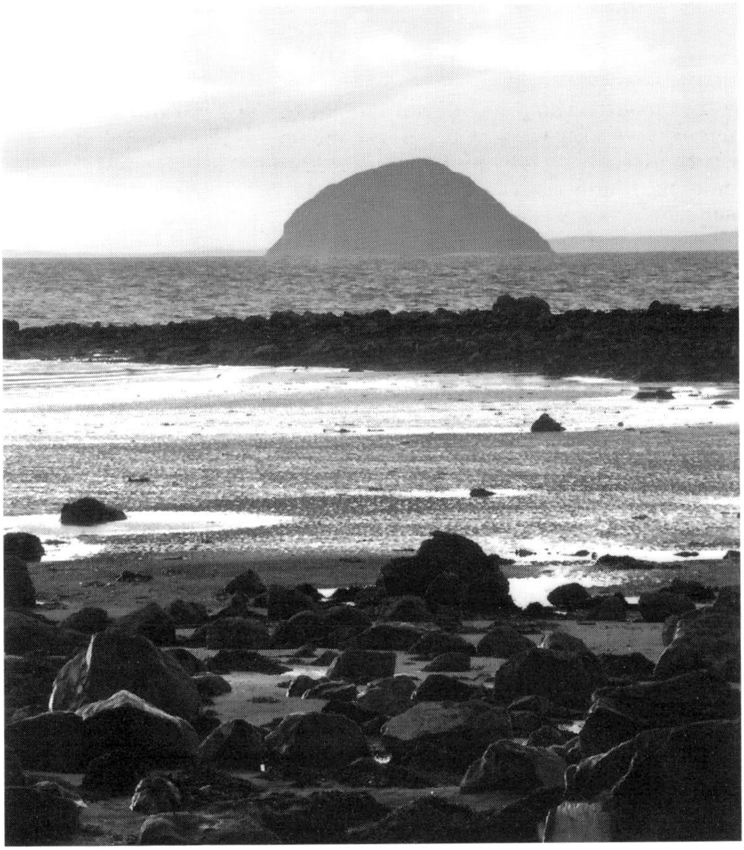

Ailsa Craig

cue off Sanda, using the reserve boat *The Duke of Connaught*. Over a period of 18 hours, in terrible storm conditions, 54 passengers and crew, and a dog, were rescued from the 7000-ton *Byron Darnton*. The lifeboat pulled clear as the ship broke in two and, despite suffering engine trouble, returned safely.

Island Davaar

Argyll & Bute. Sheltering Campbeltown Loch, this tidal island is linked to the mainland by a shingle causeway, treacherous when covered by the tide. On the northern tip of the island is a lighthouse, and on the southern side, in the fifth of the seven caves, is a wall painting of Christ crucified, secretly executed in 1887 by the local artist Alexander MacKinnon, which caused a sensation when first 'discovered'.

Tourist Information

MAINLAND

Lochinver – 01571 844330

Ullapool – 01854 612135

Gairloch – 01445 712130

Kyle of Lochalsh – 01599 534276

Mallaig – 01687 462170

Kilchoan – 01972 510222

Oban – 01631 563122

Tarbert (Kintyre) – 01880 820429

Largs – 01475 673765

Campbeltown – 01586 552056

Girvan – 01465 714950

THE OUTER HEBRIDES

Stornoway, Lewis – 01851 703088

Tarbert, Harris – 01859 502011

Lochmaddy, North Uist – 01876 500321

Lochboisdale, South Uist – 01878 700286

Castlebay, Barra – 01871 810336

SKYE

Portree – 01478 612137

Uig – 01470 542404

Broadford – 01471 822361

MULL

Tobermory – 01688 302182

Craignure – 01680 812377

ISLAY

Bowmore – 01496 810254

THE CLYDE ISLANDS

Rothesay, Bute – 01700 502151

Millport, Cumbrae – 01475 530753

Largs (for Cumbrae) – 01475 673765

Brodick, Arran – 01770 302140/302401

CALEDONIAN MACBRAYNE FERRIES

Vehicle reservations – 0990 650000

Service information – 01475 650100

Web site: http//www.calmac.co.uk.

Index

Photo left: Gilpin Lake House, Cumbria, entry 50
Photo right: Elvey Farm, Kent, entry 131

England

Photo: Hell Bay,
Isles of Sclly, entry 16

SACO Bath - St James's Place

Bath is one of England's loveliest cities, Georgian to its bone. It's built of mellow golden stone, so wander its streets for elegant squares, beautiful gardens, pavement cafés, delicious delis and the imperious Roman Baths (there's a spa if you want to take a dip). Close to the river, bang in the middle of town, these serviced apartments bask behind a beautifully restored Regency façade – look out for the pillared entrances. Inside you find a collection of airy studios and apartments, all of which come with sparkling kitchens fully stocked with ovens, dishwashers, washer/dryers, microwaves, fridges and freezers. Some are small, some are big. If you need a bolthole for a night, a base for a fun-filled weekend or a cool pad for a week, you'll find one here. You get white walls, Italian designer furniture, flat-screen TVs, CD players and good-sized bathrooms. There's a lift to whisk you up and away, 24-hour reception, and high-speed broadband connection throughout. Supermarkets are close, but there are masses of great restaurants on your doorstep.

Rooms	43: 9 studios, 34 apartments.
Price	Studios £106-£120. Apartments £125-£192.
Meals	Self-catered. Restaurants within 0.5 miles.
Closed	Never.
Directions	In centre of town, 5-minute walk from station. Full directions on booking.

Karen Sheppard
SACO Bath - St James's Place,
37 St James's Parade, Bath BA1 1UH

Tel +44 (0)1225 486540
Email bath@sacoapartments.com
Web www.sacoapartments.com/serviced-apartments/uk/bath/saco-bath

Brooks Guesthouse Bath

Owners and staff go out of their way to make your stay here special. Add to this comfy rooms, excellent breakfasts and a central position and you have a great base from which to explore Bath. The house is close to Victoria Park (hot-air balloon rides, children's playground, botanical gardens) and just below the stupendous Royal Crescent, a three-minute walk. Inside, an easy style flows. There's a sitting room in vibrant yellow, an honesty bar if you fancy a drink and a breakfast room for smoked salmon and scrambled eggs or the full cooked works; there are daily specials, free-range eggs, while the meat is reared in Somerset. Bedrooms are split between two Victorian townhouses. A couple are small, a couple are big, most are somewhere in between. All have a similar style: big colours, good beds, crisp white linen, excellent shower rooms; two have baths. A map of town, compiled by guests, shows the top ten sights: don't miss the Roman Baths or the Thermae Spa. One of the best pubs in Bath is around the corner and serves great food. Expect a little noise from the road.

Rooms	21: 10 twins/doubles, 7 doubles, 2 singles, 2 family rooms.
Price	£75-£150. Family rooms £120-£160. Singles from £70.
Meals	Restaurants close by.
Closed	Christmas Day.
Directions	Head west on A4 from centre of town. On right before Victoria Park, below Royal Avenue.

Carla & Andrew Brooks
Brooks Guesthouse Bath,
1 Crescent Gardens, Bath BA1 2NA

Tel +44 (0)1225 425543
Email info@brooksguesthouse.com
Web www.brooksguesthouse.com

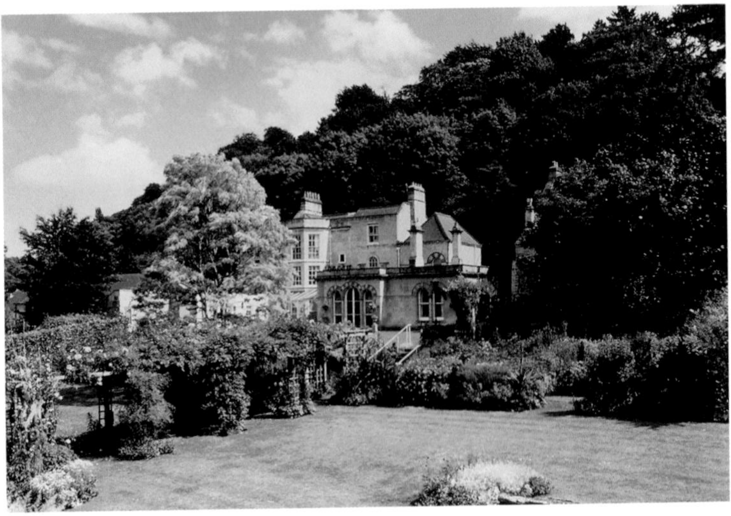

Bath Paradise House Hotel

You'll be hard pressed to find better views in Bath. They draw you out as soon as you enter these cosy, intimate, Georgian interiors, while the 180-degree panorama from the garden is a dazzling advertisement for this World Heritage city. The Royal Crescent and the Abbey are floodlit at night; in summer, hot-air balloons float by low enough to hear the roar of the burners. Nearly all the rooms make full use of the view – the best have bay windows – and all have a soft, luxurious, country feel with contemporary fabrics and white waffle robes in fabulous bathrooms. Two garden rooms in a smart extension took years to approve; it's quite an achievement, and in keeping with the original Bath stone house. The whole place has glass in all the right places, especially the sitting room, with its lovely stone-arched French windows that pull in the light. Don't miss afternoon tea in summer in the half-acre garden, a perfect place to lose yourself in the view. The occasional peal of bells comes for a nearby church. The Thermae Spa with its rooftop pool is a must. *7-minute walk down to centre.*

Rooms	11: 3 doubles, 3 twins, 4 four-posters, 1 family room.
Price	£120-£175. Family room £120-£175. Singles from £75.
Meals	Restaurants in Bath 0.5 miles.
Closed	24 & 25 December.
Directions	From train station one-way system to Churchill Bridge. A367 exit from r'bout up hill; 0.75 miles, left at Andrews estate agents. Left down hill into cul-de-sac; on left.

David & Annie Lanz
Bath Paradise House Hotel,
86-88 Holloway, Bath BA2 4PX

Tel	+44 (0)1225 317723
Email	info@paradise-house.co.uk
Web	www.paradise-house.co.uk

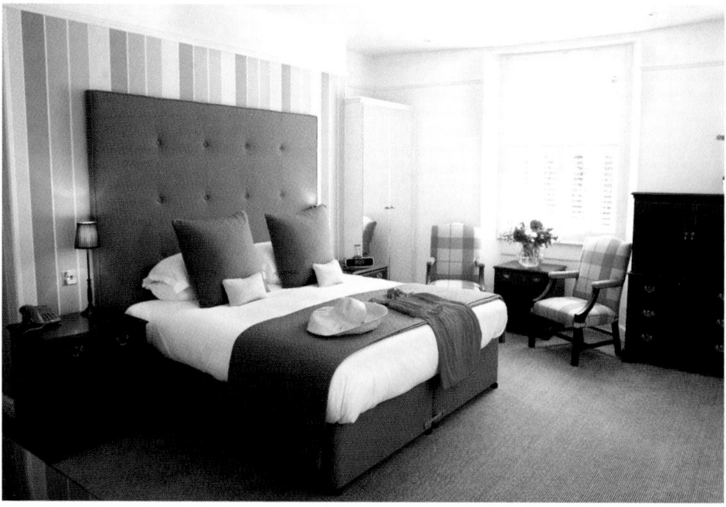

Villa Magdala

Villa Magdala is one of those lovely places that scores top marks across the board. You're pretty much in the middle of town, but nicely hidden away on a side street opposite a park. Then, there's a batch of lovely bedrooms, all recently refurbished in great style. Add to this staff on hand to book restaurants, balloon flights or day trips to Stonehenge and you have a perfect base. You're a five-minute stroll from magnificent Pulteney Bridge; the station isn't much further, so leave your car at home and come by train; you can hire bikes in town, then follow a towpath along the river and into the country. Back home, there's tea and cake on arrival, buck's fizz for breakfast, even bats and balls for children who want to go to the park. Breakfast is served in an airy dining room: smoked salmon and free-range scrambled eggs, buttermilk pancakes, the full cooked works. Smart rooms have big beds, pretty wallpaper, small armchairs and lovely sparkling bathrooms. Excellent restaurants wait close by. Don't miss the Christmas market or the magnificent Thermae Spa. *Minimum stay two nights at weekends.*

Rooms	20: 9 doubles, 11 twins/doubles.
Price	£120-£180. Singles from £110.
Meals	Restaurant within 500m.
Closed	24-29 December.
Directions	West into Bath on A4. Left into Cleveland Place (signed 'Through Traffic & University'). Over bridge, 2nd right and on right opposite park.

Amanda & John Willmott
Villa Magdala,
Henrietta Street, Bath BA2 6LX

Tel +44 (0)1225 466329
Email enquiries@villamagdala.co.uk
Web www.villamagdala.co.uk

Drakes

Drakes has the lot: cool rooms, a funky bar, big sea views, the best restaurant in town. It stands across the road from the beach, with the famous pier a three-minute walk and the big wheel even closer. Inside, a chic style has conquered every corner. Bedrooms are exemplary. Eleven have free-standing baths in the room, all have waffle bathrobes and White Company lotions, but what impresses most is the detail and workmanship. Handmade beds rest on carpets that are changed every year, contemporary plaster mouldings curl around ceilings like mountain terraces, Vi-Spring mattresses, wrapped in the crispest linen, are piled high with pillows. Don't worry if you can't afford the best rooms; others may be smaller and those at the back have city views, but all are fantastic and the attic rooms are as cute as could be (Kylie loved hers). As for the food, it's the best in town, perhaps cauliflower soup with a smoked quail egg, honey-glazed duck with cassis sauce, pears poached in sweet wine with a chocolate and hazelnut mousse. The Lanes are close and packed with hip shops. Don't miss the Royal Pavilion. *Minimum stay two nights at weekends. Off-street parking available.*

Rooms	20: 16 doubles, 1 twin/double, 2 singles, 1 suite.
Price	£115-£275. Suite £295-£345.
Meals	Breakfast £5-£12.50. Lunch from £20. Dinner from £39.95
Closed	Never.
Directions	M23 & A23 into Brighton. At seafront, with pier in front, turn left up the hill. Drakes on left after 300m.

Richard Hayes
Drakes,
43-44 Marine Parade,
Brighton BN2 1PE

Tel +44 (0)1273 696934
Email info@drakesofbrighton.com
Web www.drakesofbrighton.com

Kemp Townhouse

The sun rises over the sea – just at the end of the street. A big wheel spins on the beach, Brighton Pier is a breezy stroll and the cool restaurants and bars of Kemptown are around the corner; the rest of Brighton's colourful cornucopia is not much further away. This is a beautifully renovated Regency townhouse. Suave, spotless interiors come as standard, filling the place with cool comfort. Walls shine in period colours, charcoal carpets run throughout, an Art Deco-style chandelier hangs in the dining room/bar. Bedrooms come in different shapes and sizes but all have the same graceful restraint: gorgeous bijou wet rooms, lovely linen, padded headboards, incredibly comfortable beds. You glimpse the sea from front-facing rooms (one has a free-standing bath). Spin down to the dining room for an excellent breakfast (proper orange juice, baskets of pâtisserie, American pancakes, the full cooked works) or drop in for a glass of wine 'on the house' before heading out for the evening. Impeccable service, stylish comfort, great breakfasts – and Brighton; all to be relished. *Minimum two nights at weekends.*

Rooms	9: 6 doubles, 2 four-posters, 1 single.
Price	£95-£215. Singles from £75.
Meals	Pubs/restaurants nearby.
Closed	Never.
Directions	South to seafront, then left at r'bout in front of pier. Uphill, past New Steine, then left at lights into Lower Rock Gardens. Right at lights; 1st right into Atlingworth. On left.

Paul Lantsbury & Robert Philpot
Kemp Townhouse,
21 Atlingworth Street,
Brighton BN2 1PL

Tel +44 (0)1273 681400
Email reservations@kemptownhouse.com
Web www.kemptownhouse.com

brightonwave

A small, friendly, boutique B&B hotel in the epicentre of trendy Brighton. The beach and the pier are a two-minute walk, the bars and restaurants of St James Street are around the corner. An open-plan sitting room/dining room comes in cool colours with big suede sofas, fairy lights in the fireplace and ever-changing art on the walls. Bedrooms at the front are big and fancy, with huge padded headboards that fill the wall, and deluge showers in sandstone bathrooms. Those at the back have been recently renovated in great style; they may be smaller, but so is their price and they come with spotless compact showers; if you're out more than in, why worry? All rooms have fat duvets, lush linen, flat-screen TVs and DVD/CD players; the lower-ground king-size has its own whirlpool bath and garden. Richard and Simon are easy-going and happy for guests to chill drinks in the kitchen (there are corkscrews in all the rooms). Breakfast, served late at weekends, offers pancakes, the full English or sautéed tarragon mushrooms on toast. Fabulous Brighton waits. *Minimum two nights at weekends.*

Rooms	8: 4 twins/doubles, 3 doubles, 1 four-poster.
Price	£95-£185. Singles from £65.
Meals	Restaurants nearby.
Closed	Rarely.
Directions	A23 to Brighton Pier roundabout at seafront; left towards Marina; 5th street on left. On-street parking vouchers £9 for 24 hours.

Richard Adams & Simon Throp
brightonwave,
10 Madeira Place,
Brighton BN2 1TN

Tel +44 (0)1273 676794
Email info@brightonwave.co.uk
Web www.brightonwave.co.uk

Brooks Guesthouse Bristol

Super rooms, irresistible prices and a great position in the middle of the old town make this funky hotel a great launch pad for one of England's loveliest cities. You're close to the floating harbour, St Nicholas market stands directly outside, and there's a fabulous sun-trapping courtyard for inner-city peace. Inside: airy interiors, leather sofas, and walls of glass that open onto the courtyard. Free WiFi runs throughout, a computer is on hand for guests to use, and you can help yourself to drinks at the honesty bar. Breakfast is served leisurely – though if you're in a hurry you can take it with you – and you eat at pretty tables while watching the chef whisk up your scrambled eggs. Stylish bedrooms aren't huge, but nor is their price. You get super comfy beds, crisp white linen, Cole & Son wallpaper and iPod docks. Excellent travertine shower rooms have underfloor heating and White Company oils. Rooms at the back get noise from nearby bars, so ask for a room at the front if that matters. Bristol waits: the water, the Downs, Clifton's 'camera obscura', Brunel's spectacular suspension bridge.

Rooms	23: 17 doubles, 4 twins, 2 triples.
Price	£79-£99. Triples £99-£129. Singles from £69.
Meals	Restaurants on your doorstep.
Closed	24-27 December.
Directions	Hotel entrance on St Nicholas Court, an alleyway marking the western flank of the covered market; it runs between St Nicholas St & Corn St.

Carla & Andrew Brooks
Brooks Guesthouse Bristol,
St Nicholas Court, Exchange Avenue,
Bristol BS1 1UB

Tel +44 (0)117 930 0066
Email info@brooksguesthousebristol.com
Web www.brooksguesthousebristol.com

SACO Bristol - Broad Quay

SACO and their wonderful serviced apartments are going from strength to strength and here's the evidence: a fantastic new property down by the water in the middle of Bristol. So what do you get? Think cool hotel suites with sparkly kitchens thrown in for good measure. Walls of glass bring in the view, those at the front overlook the water, several have balconies that make the most of good weather. Prices are attractive too – good for business in the week (WiFi and parking) and great for weekends away (you breakfast whenever you want). You're in one of Britain's loveliest cities: stroll around the floating harbour, spin up the hill to Clifton, check out St Nicholas market, or head off to the posh shops at Cabot Circus. Come back to stylish interiors: smartly tiled bathrooms, fully loaded kitchens, chic sofas in front of flat-screen TVs, comfy beds for a good night's sleep; studios are smaller, but nice and snug, perfect for weekends. There are local shops if you want to cook, and restaurants everywhere if you don't. Don't miss Brunel's magnificent suspension bridge. The train from London is fast.

Rooms	70: 12 studios, 58 apartments.
Price	Studios £86-£107. Apartments £101-£231.
Meals	Self-catered. Restaurants within 0.5 miles.
Closed	Never.
Directions	Sent on booking.

Emma Granado
SACO Bristol - Broad Quay,
Central Quay South, Broad Quay,
Bristol BS1 4AW

Tel +44 (0)117 927 6722
Email bristol@sacoapartments.com
Web www.sacoapartments.com

Five Arrows Hotel

Baron Ferdinand de Rothschild began building Waddesdon Manor in 1874. Modelled on the grand châteaux of the Dordogne, it was built in Renaissance style, then filled with the baron's enormous art collection. As for the Five Arrows (the Rothschild coat of arms), it stands by the main gate and was built to accommodate the architects and artisans who worked on the house. It's not as vast as you might expect, but few inns have mullioned windows and gilded ironwork, or a lawned garden tended by gardeners from the manor. You enter through a cobbled courtyard to the rear, where wicker chairs sprout in summer, then step into the house for high ceilings, comfy armchairs, pictures from the big house, warm reds and yellows. Bedrooms upstairs have period colours, one has a half tester, others are simpler with padded headboards, perhaps a chandelier; ask for one away from the road. The bridal suite, in the old stables, has high ceilings and a four-poster bed. Delicious dinner is an English affair: crispy free-range Hampshire pork belly, treacle tart with clotted cream. The inn is owned by the National Trust.

Rooms	11: 8 twins/doubles, 1 single, 2 suites.
Price	£105-£135. Suites £185. Singles from £75.
Meals	Lunch & dinner £5-£30.
Closed	Never.
Directions	In village on A41, 6 miles west of Aylesbury.

Alex McEwen
Five Arrows Hotel,
High Street, Waddesdon,
Aylesbury HP18 0JE
Tel +44 (0)1296 651727
Email five.arrows@nationaltrust.org.uk
Web www.thefivearrows.co.uk

The Old Bridge Hotel

A smart hotel, the best in town, one which inspired the founders of Hotel du Vin. A battalion of devoted locals come for the food (delicious), the wines (exceptional) and the hugely comfortable interiors. Ladies lunch, businessmen chatter, kind staff weave through the throng. You can eat wherever you want: in the muralled restaurant; from a sofa in the lounge; or sitting in a winged armchair in front of the fire in the bar. You feast on anything from homemade soups to rack of lamb (starters are available all day), while breakfast is served in a panelled morning room with Buddha in the fireplace. Beautiful bedrooms are scattered about. Expect warm colours, fine fabrics, padded bedheads, crisp linen. One has a mirrored four-poster, several have vast bathrooms, others overlook the river Ouse, all have spoiling extras: Bose iPod docks, Bang & Olufsen TVs, power showers and bathrobes. John, a Master of Wine, has an irresistible wine shop opposite reception, so expect to take something home with you. The A14 may pass to the back, but it doesn't matter a jot.

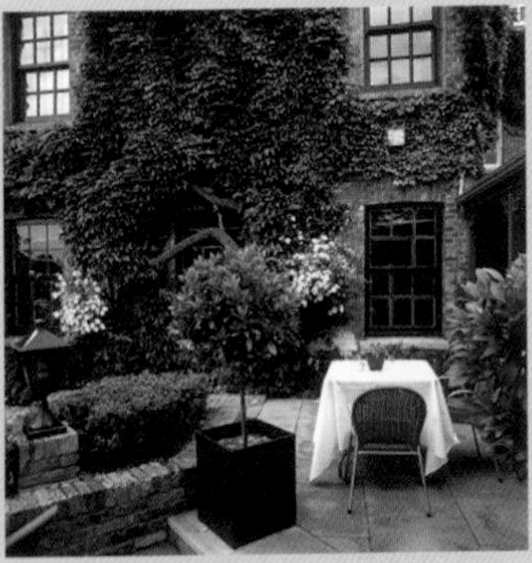

Rooms	24: 13 doubles, 1 twin, 3 four-posters, 7 singles.
Price	£160-£230. Singles from £89. Dinner, B&B from £99.50 p.p.
Meals	Lunch & dinner £5-£35.
Closed	Never.
Directions	A1, then A14 into Huntingdon. Hotel on southwest flank of one-way system that circles town.

Nina Rhodes
The Old Bridge Hotel,
1 High Street, Huntingdon PE29 3TQ

Tel	+44 (0)1480 424300
Email	oldbridge@huntsbridge.co.uk
Web	www.huntsbridge.com

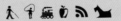

Hotel Felix

Propel your punt along the Cam, duck your head to avoid stone bridges, stop to explore riverside colleges or head to King's for evensong. Beautiful Cambridge is a great place to while away a weekend. If you prefer to escape the city at night, then potter up to Hotel Felix. It stands in peaceful gardens two miles north, a metaphor for this resurgent city – a grand old villa reborn in contemporary style. Two new wings run off at right angles, creating a courtyard with parterre garden. Bedrooms have a smart simplicity and mix corporate necessities (this is Silicon Fen, after all) with comfort and style: dark wood furniture, crisp white linen, silky curtains, a sofa if there's room. Some are big, others smaller, all have excellent bathrooms with robes and White Company lotions. There's a peaceful sitting room for the daily papers, an attractive terrace for afternoon tea, an airy bar for pre-dinner drinks. As for the restaurant, you eat surrounded by contemporary art, perhaps seared scallops, Gressingham duck, pineapple tarte tatin; a bar menu runs at night, too. Very dog-friendly.

Rooms	52: 28 doubles, 19 twins/doubles, 5 suites.
Price	£205-£255. Suites £300-£320. Singles from £165.
Meals	Continental breakfast included; cooked breakfast £7.95. Lunch & dinner £5-£45.
Closed	Never.
Directions	M11, junc. 13, then A1303 into Cambridge. Left at T-junction, 2nd left into Castle Street/Huntingdon Road, signed right after a mile.

Shara Ross
Hotel Felix,
Huntingdon Road, Girton,
Cambridge CB3 OLX
Tel +44 (0)1223 277977
Email help@hotelfelix.co.uk
Web www.hotelfelix.co.uk

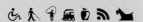

The Anchor Inn

A 1650 ale house on Chatteris Fen. The New Bedford river streams past outside. It was cut from the soil by the pub's first residents, Scottish prisoners of war brought in by Cromwell to dig the dykes that drain the fens. These days, cosy comforts infuse every corner. Inside, you find low ceilings, timber-framed walls, dark panelling and terracotta-tiled floors. A wood-burner warms the bar, so stop for a pint of cask ale, then feast on fresh local produce served by charming staff, perhaps king scallops with chorizo jam, Denham venison with red cabbage, chocolate fondant with beetroot sorbet and marshmallow sauce. Four rooms above the shop fit the mood nicely – very comfy, not too posh. Expect trim carpets, wicker chairs, crisp white duvets and Indian cotton throws. One room gets a little noise from the restaurant below. The suites have sofabeds, three rooms have river views. Footpaths flank the water; stroll down and you might see mallards or Hooper swans, even a seal (the river is tidal to the Wash). Don't miss Ely (the bishop comes to eat), Cambridge, or the nesting swans at Welney.

Rooms	4: 1 double, 1 twin/double, 2 suites.
Price	£80-£99. Suites £115-£155. Singles from £59.50. Extra bed £20.
Meals	Lunch, 2 courses, £13.95. Dinner, 3 courses, £25-£30. Sunday lunch from £12.95.
Closed	Never.
Directions	From Ely A142 west. In Sutton left on B1381 for Earith. Right in southern Sutton, signed Sutton Gault. 1 mile north on left at bridge.

Jeanene Flack & Mike Connolly
The Anchor Inn,
Bury Lane,
Sutton Gault, Ely CB6 2BD

Tel	+44 (0)1353 778537
Email	anchorinn@popmail.bta.com
Web	www.anchorsuttongault.co.uk

The Crown Inn

A dreamy inn built of mellow stone that stands on the green in this gorgeous village. Paths lead out into open country, so follow the river up to Fotheringhay, where Mary Queen of Scots lost her head. Back at the pub, warm interiors mix style and tradition to great effect. You can eat wherever you want – in the flagged bar where a fire roars, in the airy snug with views of the green, or in the circular conservatory that opens onto a terrace. Chef/patron Marcus Lamb guarantees you dine deliciously, on classic beef, mushroom and ale pie, or Shetland mussels in white wine; there's a kids' menu, too. In summer life spills outside; on May Day there's a hog roast for the village fête. Six hand pumps (including their own Golden Crown) bring in the locals, as do quiz nights, live music and the odd game of rugby on the telly. Bedrooms are excellent. The two quiet courtyard rooms come with padded bedheads, pretty art, lovely fabrics; one has a magnificent bathroom. Those in the main house overlook the green, the small room has a four-poster, the big room is perfect for families. All are spoiling. *Seasonal price variations on website.*

Rooms	8 doubles.
Price	£95-£180. Singles from £55. Sofabed for 2, £30 per child.
Meals	Lunch & dinner £5-£25 (not Sun night or Mon lunch). Restaurant closed first week January.
Closed	Rarely.
Directions	A1(M), junc. 17, then A605 west for 3 miles. Right on B671 for Elton. In village left, signed Nassington.

Marcus Lamb
The Crown Inn,
8 Duck Street, Elton,
Peterborough PE8 6RQ

Tel +44 (0)1832 280232
Email inncrown@googlemail.com
Web www.thecrowninn.org

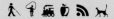

Judges Country House Hotel

This fine old country house is English to its core. It stands in 26 acres of attractive gardens with lawns that sweep down to a small river and paths that weave through private woods. Inside, wonderful interiors carry you back to grander days. There's an elegant entrance hall that floods with light, a sitting room bar in racing green, and a golden drawing room where doors open to a pretty terrace for lunch in summer. Wander about and find fires primed for combustion, the daily papers laid out in reception, a elegant staircase that rises towards a glass dome. Country-house bedrooms are full of colour. You get bowls of fruit, beautiful beds, gorgeous linen, garden flowers. Bigger rooms have sofas, all have robes in super bathrooms. Back downstairs, there's serious food in the restaurant, perhaps Whitby crab with mango and lemongrass, local venison with chicory and orange, macadamia nut parfait with pears and Earl Grey jelly. If that's not enough, then bring a party and dine in style in the Dom Perignon room surrounded by an irresistible supply of champagne. The Moors are close.

Rooms	21: 14 twins/doubles, 3 four-posters, 2 singles, 2 suites.
Price	£130-£220. Suites £160-£220. Singles from £99. Dinner, B&B from £102.50 p.p.
Meals	Lunch from £16.95. Dinner, 3 courses, £37.50.
Closed	Never.
Directions	A1(M), then A19 for Middlesbrough. Left onto A67, through Kirklevington, hotel signed left.

Tim Howard
Judges Country House Hotel,
Kirklevington Hall, Kirklevington,
Yarm TS15 9LW

Tel	+44 (0)1642 789000
Email	enquiries@judgeshotel.co.uk
Web	www.judgeshotel.co.uk

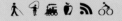

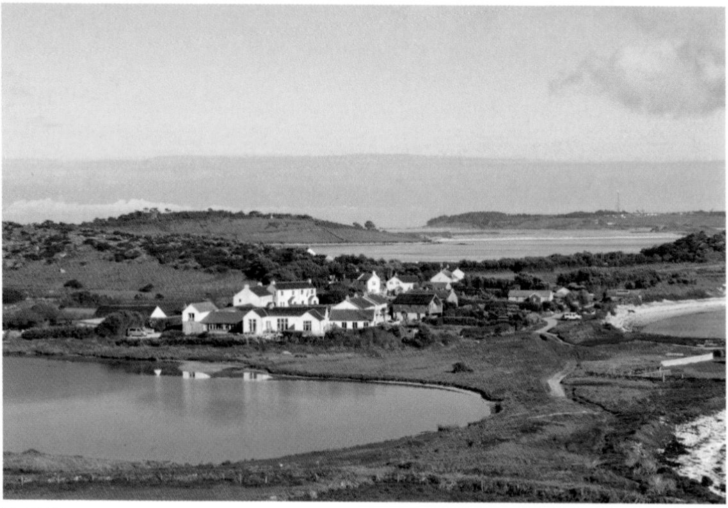

Hell Bay

This must be one of the most inaccurately named hotels in Britain – Hell Bay is heaven! It sits on Bryher, one of the smaller islands on the Scillies. You can walk around it in a couple of hours, one sandy beach after another. As for the hotel, it's lovely from top to toe. Bedrooms have a smart beach-house feel with airy colours, wicker sofas and robes in excellent bathrooms, but best of all is your terrace or balcony for fabulous watery views. Elsewhere, there's a heated swimming pool flanked by sun loungers and a treatment room that looks the right way. It's very family friendly, too; children can gather eggs from the coop and have them cooked for breakfast, and there's a playroom with games galore. The hotel lazes on the west coast. There's nothing between you and America, so grab a drink and wander onto the terrace for sunset. Back inside, there's great local food – scallops with chilli and honey, lamb with a rosemary jus, chocolate fondant with pistachio ice-cream. Also, boat trips, babysitters, lovely staff and islands to explore. Honeymooners love it. Dogs are very welcome, too. *Child in parents' room £55 (incl. high tea). Under twos free. Dogs £12 a night.*

Rooms	25 suites.
Price	£270-£640. Price includes dinner for two.
Meals	Lunch from £6.95. Dinner included; non-residents £39.
Closed	November to mid-March.
Directions	Ship from Penzance, or fly to St Mary's from Exeter, Newquay or Land's End; boat transfer to Bryher.

Philip Callan
Hell Bay,
Bryher, Isles of Scilly TR23 0PR
Tel +44 (0)1720 422947
Email contactus@hellbay.co.uk
Web www.hellbay.co.uk

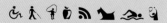

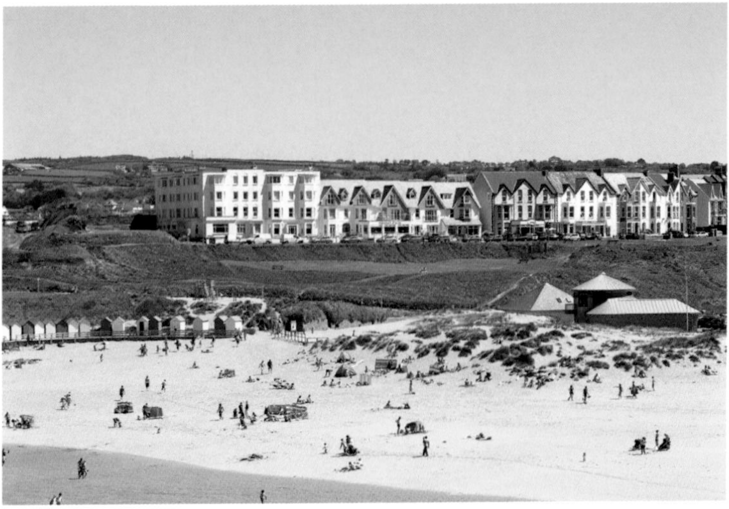

The Beach at Bude

In a fine position above the beach with huge Atlantic views, a fabulous base with beautiful rooms from which to explore this magical stretch of coast. It's just what Bude has been crying out for and it stands in a row of smart Victorian villas that look out over the town, the harbour, the canal, Compass Point and the ocean. You breakfast heartily in the large, airy dining room/lounge with a New England, uncluttered feel. Bedrooms (two on the ground floor, some right up in the loft) are all a good size: find lime-washed, solid oak furniture, Lloyd Loom chairs and fabulous bathrooms. Some have a private terrace or Juliet balcony, most come with sea views, all have thick Vi-Spring mattresses and lovely white cotton. It's all new, pristine and modern. Sandy surf beaches wait, there's a tidal swimming pool, safe bathing for children, the coastal path to stroll, and plenty of space to store gear. Beach bunnies have Bude – the 'Bondi of Britain'; hikers have the coastal path. Come back to a safe small garden with raised beds and slate-chip pathways, and a view of the fields. *Children over eight welcome.*

Rooms	17: 15 doubles, 1 twin/double, 1 twin.
Price	£125-£175. Singles from £105.
Meals	Pubs/restaurants within walking distance. Tea/coffee and cake served 11am-5pm.
Closed	Rarely.
Directions	In Bude, north of bay, overlooking sea.

Sara Whiteman
The Beach at Bude,
Summerleaze Crescent,
Bude EX23 8HN

Tel	+44 (0)1288 389800
Email	enquiries@thebeachatbude.co.uk
Web	www.thebeachatbude.co.uk

The Seafood Restaurant

In 1975 a young chef called Rick Stein opened a restaurant in Padstow. These days he has four more as well as a deli, a pâtisserie, a seafood cookery school and 40 beautiful bedrooms. Despite this success, his homespun philosophy has never wavered: buy the freshest seafood from fisherman on the quay, then cook it simply and eat it with friends. It is a viewpoint half the country seems to share – the Seafood Restaurant is now a place of pilgrimage – so come to discover the Cornish coast, walk on the cliffs, paddle in the estuary, then drop into this lively restaurant for a fabulous meal, perhaps hot shellfish with garlic and lemon juice, Dover sole with sea salt and lime, apple and quince tartlet with vanilla ice-cream. Book in for the night and a table in the restaurant is yours, though flawless bedrooms are so seductive you may find them hard to leave. They are scattered about town, some above the restaurant, others at the bistro or just around the corner. All are immaculate. Expect the best fabrics, stunning bathrooms, the odd terrace with estuary views. *Minimum stay two nights at weekends.*

Rooms	40: 32 doubles, 8 twins/doubles.
Price	£100-£290.
Meals	Lunch £38.50. Dinner £58.50.
Closed	25-26 December.
Directions	A39, then A389 to Padstow. Follow signs to centre; restaurant on left opposite harbour car park.

Jill & Rick Stein
The Seafood Restaurant,
Riverside, Padstow PL28 8BY

Tel	+44 (0)1841 532700
Email	reservations@rickstein.com
Web	www.rickstein.com

Woodlands Country House

A big house in the country, half a mile west of Padstow, with views across fields towards the sea. Pippa and Hugo are larger than life and run things informally with great panache. You get an honesty bar in the sitting room, a croquet lawn by the fountain and stripped floorboards in the Victorian breakfast room, where you gather for a legendary feast each morning (Hugo sells his own granola to local delis). Spotless bedrooms are smart and homely, some big, some smaller, all with a price to match. Expect lots of colour, comfy beds, pretty fabrics, Frette linen. One room has a four-poster, another a claw-foot bath. All have robes in good bathrooms, flat-screen TVs and DVD players, then a library of films downstairs. WiFi runs throughout, there's a computer guests can use, and Hugo will order taxis or book tables in restaurants (book in advance for Rick Stein, Nathan Outlaw and Jamie Oliver). Hire bikes in town and follow the Camel trail, take the ferry over to Rock, head down to the beach. Dogs are very welcome, electricity is solar powered. Don't miss Padstow's Christmas festival.

Rooms	8: 4 doubles, 3 twins/doubles, 1 four-poster.
Price	£98-£138. Singles from £74.
Meals	Picnics £18. Restaurants in Padstow, 0.5 miles. Breakfast for non-residents £15.
Closed	20 December-1 February.
Directions	On A389, just before Padstow, left for Newquay, then west on B3276. House signed on right in village.

Hugo & Pippa Woolley
Woodlands Country House,
Treator, Padstow PL28 8RU

Tel	+44 (0)1841 532426
Email	info@woodlands-padstow.co.uk
Web	www.woodlands-padstow.co.uk

The Scarlet

A super-cool design hotel which overlooks the sea; a vast wall of glass in reception frames the view perfectly. The Scarlet does nothing by halves – this is a serious contender for Britain's funkiest bolthole – but it also offers a guilt-free destination as it's green to its core. Cutting-edge technology includes a biomass boiler, solar panels and state-of-the-art insulation. You'll find a couple of swimming pools to insure against the weather, then hot tubs in a garden from which you can stargaze at night. There's a cool bar, a pool table in the library, a restaurant that opens onto a decked terrace, where you eat fabulous Cornish food while gazing out to sea. Exceptional bedrooms come with huge views: all have balconies or terraces, private gardens or viewing pods. Expect oak floors from sustainable forests, organic cotton, perhaps a free-standing bath in your room. Some are enormous, one has a dual-aspect balcony, another comes with a rooftop lounge. If that's not enough, there's an ayurvedic-inspired spa, where tented treatment rooms are lit by lanterns. Amazing. *Minimum two nights at weekends.*

Rooms	37: 21 doubles, 8 twins/doubles, 8 suites.
Price	£195-£405. Suites £270-£460. Singles from £175.
Meals	Lunch, 2 courses £18. Afternoon tea £16.50. Dinner, 3 courses, £42.50.
Closed	2-30 January.
Directions	North from Newquay on B3276 to Mawgan Porth. Signed left in village halfway up hill.

Nikki Broom
The Scarlet,
Tredragon Road,
Mawgan Porth TR8 4DQ

Tel	+44 (0)1637 861800
Email	stay@scarlethotel.co.uk
Web	www.scarlethotel.co.uk

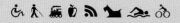

Bedruthan Hotel & Spa

A family friendly hotel that delights parents and children alike. It has beautiful interiors, delicious food, sea views and an inexhaustible supply of distractions. There's a football pitch, surf school, a zip wire, then a cool spa with a couple of pools. If you can think of it, it's probably here, and younger children can be supervised by lovely, qualified staff. There's lots for adults, too, who get the run of the place during school time: a sitting room that hogs the view, a wood-burner to keep things cosy and colourful art on every wall. There are three restaurants (one for children's parties). Younger children have early suppers, adults return later for a slap-up meal, perhaps hand-picked crab, chargrilled steak, hazelnut tart with pistachio ice-cream. There's a beach below, but you may spurn it for the indoor pool or a game of tennis. Lovely bedrooms have warm retro colours, blond wood, sparkling bathrooms, then separate rooms for children. Some open onto private terraces, lots have sea views, a few overlook the car park. Impeccable eco credentials and fantastic staff, too.

Rooms	101: 38 twins/doubles, 6 singles, 27 suites, 30 family rooms.
Price	£135-£270. Suites £205-£490. Family rooms £175-£305. Singles from £75. Dinner, B&B from £95 p.p.
Meals	Lunch from £7. Dinner £30-£35. Sunday lunch from £15.
Closed	Christmas & 3 weeks in January.
Directions	On B3276 in Mawgan Porth.

Matthew Burns
Bedruthan Hotel & Spa,
Mawgan Porth TR8 4BU

Tel	+44 (0)1637 860860
Email	stay@bedruthan.com
Web	www.bedruthan.com

Headland House

A super-cool B&B hotel that stands above Cabris Bay with big views across the water to St Ives. Mark and Fenella refurbished from top to toe, turning their home into a small-scale pleasure dome. Outside, you find sunloungers and a hammock in the lawned garden; inside, there's a snug bar with leather sofas, then a gorgeous breakfast room that floods with light. Here you feast on lavender-scented yogurt, freshly pressed smoothies, perhaps smoked salmon and scrambled eggs or the full Cornish works. In summer, doors open onto a deck for breakfast in the sun. Back inside, seven gorgeous rooms wait. All have the same seaside chic: white walls to soak up the light, pretty fabrics, lovely beds, fabulous bathrooms. Most have sea views, a couple have claw-foot baths, one has its own small garden. There's tea and cake 'on the house' in the afternoon, then a glass of sherry before heading out to St Ives for dinner overlooking the harbour. You can walk down to the beach (glorious), follow the coastal path, or call for a taxi. Leave your car at home and take the sleeper from Paddington. Brilliant.

Rooms	7 doubles.
Price	£89–£145.
Meals	Pubs/restaurants 5-minute walk.
Closed	November to March.
Directions	Sent on booking.

Mark & Fenella Thomas
Headland House,
Headland Road, Carbis Bay,
St Ives TR26 2NS
Tel +44 (0)1736 796647
Email info@headlandhousehotel.co.uk
Web www.headlandhousehotel.co.uk

Boskerris Hotel

A lovely little hotel with big views of ocean and headland. In summer, sofas appear on the decked terrace so you can gaze out on the water in comfort. Godrevy lighthouse twinkles to the right, St Ives slips into the sea on the left, the wide sands of Carbis Bay and Lelant shimmer between. Back inside, white walls and big mirrors soak up the light. You get painted floorboards and smart sofas in the sitting room, fresh flowers and big views with your bacon and eggs in the dining room. Airy bedrooms are nicely uncluttered, with silky throws, padded headboards, seaside colours and crisp linen. Eleven rooms have the view, all have fancy bathrooms, some with deep baths and deluge showers. You'll find White Company lotions, Designers Guild fabrics; in one room you can soak in the bath whilst gazing out to sea. Staff are kind, nothing is too much trouble, breakfasts are exceptional. A coastal path leads down to St Ives (20 mins), mazy streets snake up to the Tate. There's good food on your return, perhaps Newlyn crab salad, Trevaskis Farm steak, pear and almond tarte tatin with vanilla ice-cream. *Children over seven welcome.*

Rooms	15: 10 doubles, 3 twins, 1 triple,1 family room.
Price	£125-£255. Triple £165-£200. Family room £190-£240. Singles from £93.50.
Meals	Dinner, 3 courses, about £30.
Closed	Mid-November to late February.
Directions	A30 past Hayle, then A3074 for St Ives. After 3 miles pass sign for Carbis Bay, then third right into Boskerris Road. Down hill, on left.

Jonathan & Marianne Bassett
Boskerris Hotel,
Boskerris Road, Carbis Bay,
St Ives TR26 2NQ

Tel	+44 (0)1736 795295
Email	reservations@boskerrishotel.co.uk
Web	www.boskerrishotel.co.uk

Blue Hayes Private Hotel

The view from the terrace is hard to beat, a clean sweep across the bay to St Ives. You breakfast here in good weather in the shade of a Monterey pine, as if transported back to the French Riviera of the fifties. As for the rest of the hotel, it's an unadulterated treat, mostly due to Malcolm, whose infectious generosity is stamped over every square inch. Few hoteliers close for four months to redecorate over winter, but that's the way things are done here and the house shines as a result. It comes in ivory white, with the occasional dash of colour from carpet and curtain. The bar has a vaulted ceiling and a wall of glass that runs along the front to weatherproof the view. Big bedrooms are gorgeous, two with balconies, one with a terrace, all with sparkling bathrooms. Light suppers are on hand, though a short stroll into town leads to dozens of restaurants; Alfresco on the harbour is excellent, torches are provided for the journey back. Penzance, Zennor, the New Tate and a host of beaches are all close. There's folk and jazz for the September festival, a great time to visit.

Rooms	6: 4 doubles, 1 triple, 1 suite.
Price	£170-£200. Suite £230-£240. Singles from £110.
Meals	Packed lunch by arrangement. Light suppers from £12. Restaurants within walking distance.
Closed	November-February.
Directions	A30, then A3074 to St Ives. Through Lelant & Carbis Bay, over mini-r'bout (Tesco on left) and down hill. On right immed. after garage on right.

Malcolm Herring
Blue Hayes Private Hotel,
Trelyon Avenue,
St Ives TR26 2AD

Tel +44 (0)1736 797129
Email info@bluehayes.co.uk
Web www.bluehayes.co.uk

Primrose Valley Hotel

Roll out of bed, drop down for breakfast, spin off to the beach, stroll into town. If you want St Ives bang on your doorstep, this is the hotel for you; the sands are a 30-second stroll. Half the rooms have views across the bay, two have balconies for lazy afternoons. Inside, open-plan interiors revel in an earthy contemporary chic, with leather sofas, varnished floors, fresh flowers and glossy magazines. Bedrooms aren't huge, but have lots of style, so come for Hypnos beds, bespoke furniture and good bathrooms; the suite comes with a red leather sofa, hi-tech gadgetry and a fancy bathroom. Andrew and Sue are environmentally aware, committed to sustainable tourism and community projects. Their popular breakfast is mostly sourced within the county, and food provenance is listed on the menu. There's a bar that's stocked with potions from far and wide, but St Ives waits at the front door – the old town and beach, the Tate and Barbara Hepworth's sculpture garden, Alba and Alfresco, a couple of lovely restaurants overlooking the harbour. Penzance, a cool little town, is a short drive. *Minimum two nights at weekends.*

Rooms	10: 7 doubles, 2 twins, 1 suite.
Price	£75-£170. Suite £175-£240. Singles from £65.
Meals	Platters £8. Restaurant 200m.
Closed	Christmas. 3 weeks in January. Open for New Year.
Directions	From A3074 Trelyon Avenue; before hospital sign slow down, indicate right & turn down Primrose Valley; under bridge, left, then back under bridge; signs for hotel parking.

Andrew & Sue Biss
Primrose Valley Hotel,
Primrose Valley, St Ives TR26 2ED

Tel	+44 (0)1736 794939
Email	info@primroseonline.co.uk
Web	www.primroseonline.co.uk

The Tide House

Suzy's eye for beautiful design has turned this medieval building into one of the loveliest small hotels you are ever likely to bump into. It sits on what was the main road into town, a tiny lane that weaves gently downhill towards the harbour. Step inside – the walls are three-foot thick – to discover a small-scale pleasure dome: golden stone walls, padded window seats, an honesty bar in the snug drawing room, fabulous art on the walls. Beautiful simplicity abounds, there isn't an ounce of clutter to be seen. Instead, you find a mirrored sitting room with a wood-burner and the daily papers; a shiny white breakfast room with a wall of glass that opens onto a courtyard; then a kids' room with a PlayStation. Bedrooms are divine: chalk whites, driftwood lamps, beautifully dressed beds, fabulous bathrooms. The big room at the top has views over rooftops to the harbour. Outside: engaging St Ives, the special coastal light, the higgledy-piggledy lanes, the arty vibe. There's a treatment room, too, and great restaurants waiting on your doorstep. Take the whole place and bring your friends. *Minimum stay two nights at weekends (for 2014).*

Rooms	6: 3 doubles, 2 family rooms, 1 suite.
Price	£115-£190. Family rooms £140-£180. Suite £195-£240. Child in parents' room £25.
Meals	Restaurants nearby.
Closed	23-26 December.
Directions	A30 west, then A3074 for St Ives. Pass beach, into town, then right at church. On right after 200m.

David & Suzy Fairfield
The Tide House,
Skidden Hill, St Ives TR26 2DU

Tel +44 (0)1736 791803
Email enquiries@thetidehouse.co.uk
Web www.thetidehouse.co.uk

The Gurnard's Head

The coastline here is utterly magical and the walk to St Ives hard to beat. Secret beaches appear at low tide, cliffs tumble down to the water and wild flowers streak the land pink in summer. As for this inn, you couldn't hope for a better base. It's earthy, warm, stylish and friendly, with airy interiors, colour-washed walls, stripped wooden floors and fires at both ends of the bar. Logs are piled up in an alcove, maps and art hang on the walls, books fill every shelf; if you pick one up and don't finish it, take it home and post it back. Rooms are warm, cosy and spotless, with Vi-Spring mattresses, crisp white linen, throws over armchairs, Roberts radios. Downstairs, super food, all homemade, can be eaten wherever you want: in the bar, in the restaurant or out in the garden in good weather. Snack on rustic delights – pork pies, crab claws, half a pint of Atlantic prawns – or tuck into more substantial treats, maybe salt and pepper squid, braised shoulder of lamb, pineapple tarte tatin. Picnics are easily arranged, there's bluegrass folk music in the bar most weeks. Dogs are very welcome. *Ask about seasonal offers.*

Rooms	7: 4 doubles, 3 twins/doubles.
Price	£100-£170. Dinner, B&B from £75 p.p.
Meals	Lunch from £12. Dinner, 3 courses, from £26.50. Sunday lunch, 3 courses, £21.
Closed	24-25 December; 4 days in mid-January.
Directions	On B3306 between St Ives & St Just, 2 miles west of Zennor, at head of village of Treen.

Charles & Edmund Inkin
The Gurnard's Head,
Zennor, St Ives TR26 3DE

Tel +44 (0)1736 796928
Email enquiries@gurnardshead.co.uk
Web www.gurnardshead.co.uk

The Summer House

A glittering find, a small enclave of Mediterranean goodness a hundred yards up from the sea. Stylish and informal, colourful and welcoming; what's more, it's super value for money. Linda and Ciro, English and Italian respectively, run the place with great affection. Linda, bubbling away out front, is the designer, her breezy interiors warm and elegant with stripped floors, Ciro's art, panelled windows and murals in the dining room (the breakfast chef is a sculptress). Ciro worked in some of London's best restaurants before heading west to go it alone and will whisk up culinary delights for dinner. In good weather you can eat his ambrosial food in a small, lush courtyard garden, perhaps langoustine with mango and chives, rack of lamb with herbes de Provence, warm apple tart with armagnac sorbet. Breakfast – also served in the courtyard when the sun shines – is a feast. Stylish rooms are the final delight: seaside colours, well-dressed beds, freshly cut flowers, flat-screen TVs, super little bathrooms. *Possible minimum two nights at weekends & bank holidays.*

Rooms	5: 4 doubles, 1 twin/double.
Price	£95-£150. Singles from £90.
Meals	Simple suppers £20 (Mon to Fri). Dinner, 3 courses, £29.50 (Sat & Sun).
Closed	November-March.
Directions	With sea on left, along harbourside, past open-air pool, then immediate right after Queens Hotel. House 30m up on left. Private car park.

Linda & Ciro Zaino
The Summer House,
Cornwall Terrace, Penzance TR18 4HL
Tel +44 (0)1736 363744
Email reception@summerhouse-cornwall.com
Web www.summerhouse-cornwall.com

The Abbey Hotel & Restaurant

Jean Shrimpton's Penzance bolthole sits in the old town above the harbour with views from the front across to St Michael's Mount. Outside, a tangle of lanes lead down to the water. Inside, beautiful interiors come in country-house style – a bust of Lafayette in the drawing room, an open fire in the panelled breakfast room, beautiful art everywhere you go. In summer, you decant into a peaceful walled garden for afternoon tea, a perfect spot to escape the crowds. Bedrooms are grand, quirky and laden with comfort. There are chandeliers, quilted bedspreads, French armoires and plump-cushioned armchairs. Those at the front have the view (in one you open a cupboard to find an en suite shower), the suite is perfect for families. As for the food, nip next door to the hotel's restaurant for exciting cooking. Street food waits at lunch – Thai pad noodles, Moroccan cous cous, even a mini rump steak burger; then at night it gets fancier, perhaps cucumber soup with curried scallops, wild sea bream with Bombay potatoes, Earl Grey panna cotta with orange jelly. St Ives and the coastal path wait.

Rooms	7 + 1: 4 doubles, 1 twin, 1 family room, 1 suite. Self-catering flat for 4.
Price	£105-£200. Family room & suite £150-£210. Flat £115-£170. Singles from £75.
Meals	Lunch from £3.50. Dinner, 3 courses, about £30.
Closed	Rarely.
Directions	Follow signs to town centre. Up hill (Market Jew St). Left at top, then fork left & 3rd on the left.

Thaddeus Cox
The Abbey Hotel & Restaurant,
Abbey Street, Penzance TR18 4AR

Tel	+44 (0)1736 366906
Email	hotel@theabbeyonline.co.uk
Web	www.theabbeyonline.co.uk

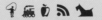

Artist Residence Penzance

Distinctly hip, deliciously quirky and overflowing with colour, this groovy little bolthole is hard to resist. The house dates to 1600 and stands on the ley line that connects St Michael's Mount to Stonehenge. You're in the old quarter of town, a stone's throw from the harbour. Inside, Charlie and her staff potter about informally, stopping to chat and point you in the right direction. Downstairs, you find a cute dining room that doubles variously as a sitting room, a clothes shop, an art gallery and bar – a very sociable spot. Bedrooms are scattered about, each designed by a different artist; many have brightly coloured murals. One has a wall you can write on, another is pretty in pink, yet another shows a cartoon version of the street outside your window; in short, you sleep amid art. Most have compact shower rooms, one has a claw-foot bath. All have smart beds, white linen and toppers for a good night's sleep; the family room has a fridge, too. Back downstairs, lovely breakfasts offer honey-roast ham, local eggs, delicious smoothies. Good pubs and restaurants are very close, too.

Rooms	9: 6 doubles, 2 twins/doubles, 1 family room.
Price	£70-£140. Singles from £60.
Meals	Pub/restaurant across the road.
Closed	December and January.
Directions	A30 into Penzance. Follow signs to town centre; up main street; left at top; keep left and on right after 200m.

Charlie Newey
Artist Residence Penzance,
20 Chapel Street, Penzance TR18 4AW

Tel	+44 (0)1736 365664
Email	penzance@artistresidence.co.uk
Web	www.arthotelcornwall.co.uk

The Old Coastguard

The Old Coastguard stands bang on the water in one of Cornwall's loveliest coastal villages. It's a super spot and rather peaceful – little has happened here since 1595, when the Spanish sacked the place. Recently, the hotel fell into the benign hands of Edmund and Charles, past masters at reinvigorating lovely small hotels; warm colours, attractive prices, great food and a happy vibe are their hallmarks. Downstairs, the airy bar and the dining room come together as one, the informality of open plan creating a great space to hang out. There are smart rustic tables, earthy colours, local ales and local art, then a crackling fire in the restaurant. Drop down a few steps to find a bank of sofas and a wall of glass framing sea views; in summer, doors open onto a decked terrace, a lush lawn, then the coastal path weaving down to the small harbour. Bedrooms are lovely: sand-coloured walls, excellent beds, robes in fine bathrooms, books everywhere. Most have the view, eight have balconies. Don't miss dinner: crab rarebit, fish stew, chocolate fondant and marmalade ice-cream. Dogs are very welcome. *Ask about seasonal offers.*

Rooms	14: 9 doubles, 3 twins/doubles, 1 family room, 1 suite.
Price	£110-£185. Family room £170-£220. Suite £195. Dinner, B&B from £75 p.p.
Meals	Lunch from £6. Dinner, 3 courses, about £27. Sunday lunch from £12.50.
Closed	1 week in early January.
Directions	Take A30 to Penzance then Land's End. Signs to Newlyn & Mousehole. Hotel on left immed. as you enter Mousehole. Limited parking or public car park next door; £2 on departure.

Charles & Edmund Inkin
The Old Coastguard,
The Parade, Mousehole,
Penzance TR19 6PR

Tel +44 (0)1736 731222
Email enquiries@oldcoastguardhotel.co.uk
Web www.oldcoastguardhotel.co.uk

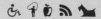

Mount Haven Hotel & Restaurant

A magical hotel with sublime views of St Michael's Mount, an ancient Cornish totem that's been pulling in the crowds for millennia. Most rooms look the right way and have a balcony to boot, but there's a decked terrace in case yours doesn't and the causeway leads over at low tide, so make sure you discover the ancient castle and church. Back at the hotel, sink in to comfy sofas in the bar where huge windows frame the view, making sunsets rather special. Elsewhere, Eastern deities jostle for space, local art hugs the walls, and there's a treatment room for a soothing massage, the profits of which fund an orphanage and medical camp in India. The restaurant comes with big mirrors and doors that open onto a terrace where you eat in good weather; try Newlyn crab cakes, duck breast with a ginger marmalade, then chocolate pavé with blood-orange sorbet. Bedrooms are lovely. Most aren't huge, but nearly all have balconies or terraces and those on the top floor have unblemished views. They come with fresh flowers, crisp linen, flat-screen TVs. Bathrooms tend to be small but sweet.

Rooms	18: 10 doubles, 4 twins/doubles, 1 family room, 2 four-posters, 1 suite.
Price	£130-£155. Four-posters £170-£200. Suite £200-£230. Singles from £90.
Meals	Lunch from £5. Dinner, 3 courses, about £30.
Closed	Mid-December to mid-February.
Directions	Leave A30 for Marazion 1 mile east of Penzance at middle roundabout on dual carriageway. Left at T-junction by sea, then through village and signed on right.

Orange & Mike Trevillion
Mount Haven Hotel & Restaurant,
Turnpike Road,
Marazion TR17 0DQ

Tel +44 (0)1736 710249
Email reception@mounthaven.co.uk
Web www.mounthaven.co.uk

Bay Hotel

The Bay Hotel sits beneath a vast Cornish sky with views to the front of nothing but sea – unless you count the beach at low tide, where buckets and spades are mandatory. Outside, the lawn rolls down to the water, sprinkled with deckchairs and loungers in summer, so grab a book, snooze in the sun or listen to the sounds of the English seaside. Stylish interiors are just the ticket, but you can't escape the view: dining room, conservatory and sitting room all look the right way, with big windows to keep your eyes glued to the horizon. Warm colours fit the mood, there are flowers everywhere, cavernous sofas, a small bar for pre-dinner drinks. Bedrooms vary in size, some smaller, suites bigger; one has its own balcony, all have sea views (some from the side). Expect a Cape Cod feel – tongue-and-groove, airy colours, super bathrooms. As for Ric's delicious food, fish comes straight from the sea, though his steak and kidney pie is every bit as good. Try potted brown shrimps, salmon en croute, poached pears with vanilla ice-cream. The coastal path passes directly outside. Don't miss afternoon tea.

Rooms	13: 5 doubles, 5 twins/doubles, 3 suites.
Price	£146-£260. Suites £230-£290. Price includes dinner for two.
Meals	Lunch from £6. Dinner, 3 courses with coffee, included; non-residents, £34.95.
Closed	December-March (open Christmas & New Year).
Directions	A3083 south from Helston, then left onto B3293 for St Keverne. Right for Coverack after 8 miles. Down hill, right at sea, second on right.

Ric, Gina & Zoe House
Bay Hotel,
North Corner, Coverack,
Helston TR12 6TF

Tel	+44 (0)1326 280464
Email	enquiries@thebayhotel.co.uk
Web	www.thebayhotel.co.uk

The Rosevine

A perfect family bolthole on the Roseland peninsular with views that tumble across trim lawns and splash into the sea. Tim and Hazel welcome children with open arms and have created a small oasis where guests of all ages can have great fun. There's a playroom for kids (Xbox, plasma screen, DVDs, toys), an indoor pool, and a beach at the bottom of the hill. High teas are on hand, there are cots and highchairs, babysitters can be arranged. Parents don't fare badly either: an elegant sitting room with sofas in front of the wood-burner; sea views and Lloyd Loom furniture in a light-filled restaurant; sun loungers scattered about a semi-tropical garden. Suites and apartments come with small kitchens (fridge, sink, dishwasher, microwave/oven); you can self-cater, eat in the restaurant or mix and match (there's deli menu for posh takeaways). Some rooms are open-plan while others have separate bedrooms. Expect airy, uncluttered interiors, flat-screen TVs, top-notch bed linen and robes in good bathrooms. Eight have a balcony or terrace. St Mawes is close.

Rooms	12: 4 studios, 4 family rooms, 4 apartments.
Price	Studios £155-£215. Family rooms £175-£385. Apartments £175-£385.
Meals	Breakfast £3-£12. Lunch from £8. Dinner, 3 courses, about £30.
Closed	January.
Directions	From A390 south for St Mawes on A3078. Signed left after 8 miles. Right at bottom of road; just above beach.

Hazel & Tim Brocklebank
The Rosevine,
Rosevine, Portscatho,
Truro TR2 5EW

Tel +44 (0)1872 580206
Email info@rosevine.co.uk
Web www.rosevine.co.uk

Driftwood Hotel

A faultless position, one of the best. Six acres of gardens drop down to a private beach, coastal paths lead off for cliff-top walks. At Driftwood, Cape Cod meets Cape Cornwall with smart, airy interiors at every turn. The sitting room is stuffed with beautiful things – fat armchairs, deep sofas, driftwood lamps, a smouldering fire. Best of all are walls of glass that pull in the view. In summer, doors open onto a decked terrace for breakfast and lunch in the sun. Bedrooms are gorgeous (all but one have sea views), some big, others smaller, one in a cabin halfway down the cliff with its own terrace. All have the same clipped elegance: warm colours, big beds, white linen, wicker chairs. There are Roberts radios on bedside tables, cotton robes in excellent bathrooms. Drop down to the dining room for your Michelin-starred dinner: cuttlefish consommé, loin of fallow venison, spiced pineapple with coconut meringue. There are high teas for children, hampers for beach picnics and rucksacks for walkers. On clear nights the sky is full of stars. Brilliant.
Minimum two nights at weekends.

Rooms	15: 13 doubles, 1 twin, 1 cabin.
Price	£180-£270. Cabin £225-£255. Dinner, B&B from £122.50 p.p.
Meals	Dinner £50 (inc. in room price in low season). Tasting menu £80.
Closed	Early December to early February.
Directions	From St Austell, A390 west. Left on B3287 for St Mawes; left at Tregony on A3078 for approx. 7 miles. Signed left down lane.

Paul & Fiona Robinson
Driftwood Hotel,
Rosevine,
Portscatho, Truro TR2 5EW

Tel +44 (0)1872 580644
Email info@driftwoodhotel.co.uk
Web www.driftwoodhotel.co.uk

Trevalsa Court Hotel

This Arts and Crafts house has a fine position at the top of the cliffs with sprawling lawns that run down to Cornwall's coastal path; either turn right and amble along to Mevagissey or drop down to the beach with your bucket and spade. Don't dally too long: Trevalsa is a seaside treat – friendly, stylish, seriously spoiling. In summer, you can decamp onto the terrace and lawns or fall asleep in a deckchair, but the view here is weatherproofed by an enormous mullioned window seat in the sitting room, a great place to watch the weather spin by. Elsewhere, you'll find a small bar packed with art, then a panelled dining room where you dig into bistro-style food – homemade fishcakes, coq au vin, chocolate fondant with basil ice-cream. Bedrooms are lovely, all recently refurbished. They come in seaside colours with designer fabrics, the odd wall of paper, padded headboards and super new wet rooms. There are TVs and DVD players and most have sea views, while bigger rooms have sofas and spoil you all the way. The Lost Gardens of Heligan are on your doorstep. *Minimum stay two nights in high season.*

Rooms	14: 9 doubles, 2 twins, 2 singles, 1 suite.
Price	£105-£185. Suite £195-£235. Singles from £75. Dinner, B&B from £75 p.p.
Meals	Dinner £30.
Closed	December & January.
Directions	B3273 from St Austell signed Mevagissey, through Pentewan to top of the hill, left at the x-roads, over mini r'bout. Hotel on left, signed.

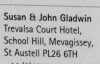

Susan & John Gladwin
Trevalsa Court Hotel,
School Hill, Mevagissey,
St Austell PL26 6TH

Tel +44 (0)1726 842468
Email stay@trevalsa-hotel.co.uk
Web www.trevalsa-hotel.co.uk

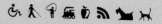

The Old Quay House Hotel

You drop down the hill, navigate the narrow lanes, then pull up at this boutique hotel which started life as a seaman's mission. It's a perfect spot, with the estuary lapping directly outside and a sun-trapping terrace for summer dining, a good spot to watch the boats zip past. Inside, stylish bedrooms treat you all the way with goose down duvets, beautiful fabrics and seriously spoiling bathrooms (replete with bathrobes, the odd claw-foot tub and maybe a separate shower). Most rooms look the right way, eight have balconies and the view from the penthouse suite is unbeatable. Downstairs great food waits, so trip to the terrace for a cocktail, then dig into excellent food prepared from a wealth of local ingredients: Fowey River oysters, Cornish scallops and West Country duck. Fowey is enchanting, bustles with life and fills with sailors for the August Regatta. If you want to escape, take the ferry across to Polruan where Daphne du Maurier lived and wrote. You can potter over to spectacular Lantic Bay for a picnic lunch on the beach. *Minimum two nights at weekends in high season.*

Rooms	11: 5 doubles, 5 twins/doubles, 1 suite.
Price	£180-£275. Suite £180-£325. Singles from £130.
Meals	Lunch (April-September) about £15. Dinner £30-£37.50.
Closed	Rarely.
Directions	Entering Fowey, follow one-way system past church. Hotel on right where road at narrowest point, next to Lloyds Bank. Nearest car park 800m.

Anthony Chapman
The Old Quay House Hotel,
28 Fore Street, Fowey PL23 1AQ

Tel +44 (0)1726 833302
Email info@theoldquayhouse.com
Web www.theoldquayhouse.com

Bishop's House

Fabulous Fowey. Drop off your luggage, forget the car and be spoilt at this 1802 townhouse, reputedly once the summer home of the Bishop of Truro. It's B&B but not as you know it: find a bursting library, a music room with a grand piano (yes, you can play it), big beds with the crispest white cotton, and charming Elizabeth and Nigel to look after you – impeccably. A cream tea in the terraced garden comes with breathtaking views over the estuary to Polruan, where bobbing boats, whirling gulls and ever-changing light will arrest you for hours; it's the best seat in town for Regatta week. Breakfast here at a time you choose: locally smoked haddock with poached eggs, Cornish bacon, homemade jams and marmalade; on cooler days retreat to the pretty orangery with its wall-to-wall windows. Sleep very peacefully in good-sized bedrooms (most have that view), with fresh flowers, restful colours, thick curtains in elegant fabrics and warm, sparkling bathrooms. And there are ferries, walks, great pubs, sailing, the Eden Centre and Rick Stein's on the doorstep. Delectable.

Rooms	4: 3 doubles, 1 twin/double.
Price	£150.
Meals	Restaurants nearby.
Closed	October-Easter.
Directions	Sent on booking.

Nigel & Elizabeth Wagstaff
Bishop's House,
Fowey PL23 1HY

Tel +44 (0)1726 833759
Email choices@foweyresidences.co.uk
Web www.foweyresidences.co.uk

The Cormorant Hotel

A sublime position on the side of a wooded hill, with the magical Fowey river curling past below. Oystercatchers swoop low across the water, sheep bleat in the fields, sail boats tug on their moorings. The hotel is one room deep, every window looks the right way, and most of the bedrooms have small balconies where you can doze in the sun. A terrace sweeps along the front of the house, a finger of lawn runs below, and the river follows wherever you go. Fresh flowers in the tiny bar, a wood-burner in the gorgeous sitting room, wooden floors in the airy dining room. Super bedrooms come without clutter: light colours, trim carpets, walls of glass, white linen. One has a slipper bath where you soak as you gaze down on the river. Swim in the pool, tan on its terrace, jump in the hot tub, then dine on fabulous Cornish food, perhaps seared scallops with cauliflower purée, grilled lemon sole with wild garlic, coconut marshmallow with a pineapple and chilli salsa. There are gardens to explore, and you may well linger.

Rooms	14: 10 doubles, 3 twins, 1 suite.
Price	£80-£200. Suite £140-£250.
Meals	Lunch from £12. Dinner, à la carte, from £30.
Closed	Rarely.
Directions	A390 west towards St Austell, then B3269 to Fowey. After 4 miles, left to Golant. Into village, along quay, hotel signed right up very steep hill.

Mary Tozer
The Cormorant Hotel,
Golant, Fowey PL23 1LL

Tel	+44 (0)1726 833426
Email	relax@cormoranthotel.co.uk
Web	www.cormoranthotel.co.uk

Talland Bay Hotel

The position here is magical. First you plunge down rollercoaster lanes, then you arrive at this lovely hotel. Directly in front, the sea sparkles through pine trees, an old church crowns the hill and two acres of lawns end in a ha-ha, then the land drops down to the bay. In summer, sun loungers and croquet hoops appear on the lawn and you can nip down to a beach café for lunch by the water. Back at the hotel there's a conservatory brasserie, a sitting room bar, and a roaring fire in the half-panelled dining room. Masses of art hangs on the walls, there are vast sofas, polished flagstones, a terrace for afternoon tea. Follow the coastal path over the hill, then return for a good dinner, perhaps John Dory and squid, Bodmin lamb with black olives, carrot cake with candied walnuts and cinnamon ice-cream. As for the bedrooms, they've been nicely refurbished and pamper you rotten. Expect rich colours, vast beds, beautiful linen, the odd panelled wall. One has a balcony, a couple open onto terraces, all have lovely bathrooms. Gardens, beaches, pretty villages and the coastal path all wait.

Rooms	22: 15 twins/doubles, 4 suites, 3 cottages.
Price	£120-£225. Suites £190-£245. Cottages £140-£210. Dinner, B&B from £95 p.p.
Meals	Lunch from £5.95. Dinner £32-£38.
Closed	Never.
Directions	From Looe A387 for Polperro. Ignore 1st sign to Talland. After 2 miles, left at x-roads; follow signs.

Vanessa Rees
Talland Bay Hotel,
Porthallow, Looe PL13 2JB
Tel +44 (0)1503 272667
Email info@tallandbayhotel.co.uk
Web www.tallandbayhotel.co.uk

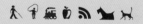

Augill Castle

Simon and Wendy's folly castle may look rather grand, but inside you find a wonderfully informal world – no uniforms, no rules, just a place to kick off your shoes and relax. It's extremely family-friendly with lots for children to do – dressing up boxes in one of the sitting rooms, five acres of gardens with a treehouse and a playground, even a cinema in the old potting shed. Adults don't fare badly either. Follow your nose and find sofas in front of the fire in the hall, a grand piano in the music room, an honesty bar that opens onto a terrace. Breakfast is served communally in a vast dining room under a wildly ornate ceiling – local bacon, eggs from resident hens, homemade breads and jams. Elsewhere, panelled walls, roaring fires, beautiful art, books and antiques. Bedrooms are deliciously different. A couple are enormous, one has a wardrobe in the turret, you'll find big bathrooms, bold colours and vintage luggage. Cottage suites have extra space for families. The Dales and the Lakes are close. *Weddings & house parties welcome by arrangement.*

Rooms	16: 8 doubles, 2 twins/doubles, 6 family suites for 4.
Price	£130-£180. Family suites £200-£280. Singles from £100.
Meals	Dinner, 3 courses, £30 (booking essential). Supper platter £15. Afternoon tea £18. Children's high tea £10.
Closed	Never.
Directions	M6 junc. 38; A685 thro' Kirkby Stephen. Before Brough right for South Stainmore; signed on left in 1 mile. Kirkby Stephen station 3 miles.

Simon & Wendy Bennett
Augill Castle,
South Stainmore,
Kirkby Stephen CA17 4DE

Tel	+44 (0)17683 41937
Email	enquiries@stayinacastle.com
Web	www.stayinacastle.com

The Black Swan

This fabulous small hotel is hard to fault. Bang in the middle of a pretty village, surrounded by blistering country, it's all things to all men: a smart restaurant, a lively bar, a village shop; they even hold a music festival here in September. A stream runs through an enormous garden where you can eat in good weather; free-range hens live in one corner. Inside, warm country interiors fit the mood perfectly. You get fresh flowers, tartan carpets, games on the piano, books galore. There's a bar for local ales and a sitting room bar with an open fire, but the hub of the hotel is the bar in the middle, where village life gathers. You can eat wherever you want, including the airy restaurant at the front where you dig into delicious country food (the meat is from the fields around you), perhaps smoked trout terrine, steak and venison casserole, lemon and ginger syllabub. Excellent bedrooms are fantastic for the money. Expect pretty colours, beautiful linen, smart furniture, super bathrooms. The Lakes and Dales are close, children and dogs are welcome. A very happy place.

Rooms	14: 11 twins/doubles, 2 suites, 1 single.
Price	£75-£115. Suites £110-£125. Singles from £55.
Meals	Lunch from £4.50. Dinner, 3 courses, £25-£30.
Closed	Never.
Directions	Off A685 between M6 junc. 38 & A66 at Brough.

Alan & Louise Dinnes
The Black Swan,
Ravenstonedale,
Kirkby Stephen CA17 4NG
Tel +44 (0)15396 23204
Email enquiries@blackswanhotel.com
Web www.blackswanhotel.com

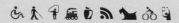

The Sun Inn

Extreme pleasure awaits those who book into The Sun. Not only is this ancient inn a delight to behold – thick stone walls, wood-burners, windows onto a cobbled passageway, beer pumps ready for action – but the town itself is a dreamy jewel of the north. The inn backs onto St Mary's churchyard, where wild flowers prosper and bumble bees ply their trade. Potter across and find 'one of the loveliest views in England, and therefore the world' to quote Ruskin. Herons fish the river, lambs graze the fields, hills soar into a vast sky. Turner painted it in 1825. Back at The Sun, all manner of good things: warm interiors, recently refurbished, come in elegant country style. You'll find old stone walls, boarded floors, cosy window seats, newspapers in a rack. Uncluttered bedrooms upstairs are just as good; expect trim carpets, comfy beds, crisp white linen, super bathrooms. Finally, the food – homemade soups, mussels in white wine, loin of local lamb, apple and chocolate pudding. Don't miss it. *Minimum stay two nights if booking Saturday night.*

Rooms	11: 8 doubles, 2 twins/doubles, 1 family room.
Price	£84-£164. Family room £99-£168. Singles from £76.
Meals	Lunch from £10.95. Dinner from £16.95. Not Monday lunch.
Closed	Never.
Directions	M6 junc. 36, then A65 for 5 miles following signs for Kirkby Lonsdale. In town centre.

Mark & Lucy Fuller
The Sun Inn,
6 Market Street, Kirkby Lonsdale,
Carnforth LA6 2AU

Tel +44 (0)15242 71965
Email email@sun-inn.info
Web www.sun-inn.info

Aynsome Manor Hotel

A small country house with a big heart. It may not be the grandest place in the book but the welcome is genuine, the peace is intoxicating and the value unmistakable. From the front, a long sweep across open meadows leads south to Cartmel and its priory, a view that has changed little in 800 years. The house, a mere pup by comparison, dates to 1512. Step in to find red armchairs, a grandfather clock and a coal fire in the hall. There's a small bar at the front and a cantilever staircase with cupola dome that sweeps you up to a first-floor drawing room where panelled windows frame the view. Downstairs, you eat under an ornate tongue-and-groove ceiling with Georgian colours and old portraits on the walls. You get good country cooking, too: French onion soup, roast leg of Cumbrian lamb, rich chocolate mousse served with white chocolate sauce. Bedrooms are simple, spotless, cosy and colourful. Some have views over the fields, one may be haunted, another has an avocado bathroom suite. Windermere and Coniston are close. Kippers with lemon at breakfast are a treat.

Rooms	12: 5 doubles, 4 twins, 1 four-poster, 2 family rooms.
Price	£80-£125. Family rooms £80-£250. Dinner, B&B from £73 p.p.
Meals	Packed lunches by arrangement £9.50. Dinner, 4 courses, £33.
Closed	25 & 26 December. January.
Directions	From M6 junc. 36 take A590 for Barrow. At top of Lindale Hill follow signs left to Cartmel. Hotel on right 3 miles from A590.

Christopher & Andrea Varley
Aynsome Manor Hotel,
Aynsome Lane, Cartmel,
Grange-over-Sands LA11 6HH

Tel +44 (0)15395 36653
Email aynsomemanor@btconnect.com
Web www.aynsomemanorhotel.co.uk

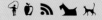

Masons Arms

A perfect Lakeland inn tucked away two miles inland from Windermere. You're on the side of a hill with huge views across ancient fields to Scout Scar in the distance. In summer, all pub life decants onto a spectacular terrace – a sitting room in the sun – where window boxes and flowerbeds tumble with colour. The inn dates from the 16th century and is impossibly pretty. The bar is wonderfully traditional with roaring fires, flagged floors, wavy beams and some good local ales to quench your thirst. Rustic elegance upstairs comes courtesy of stripped floors, country rugs and red walls in the first-floor dining room – so grab a window seat for fabulous views and dig into devilled crab cakes, Cartmel lamb shank, warm fudge sundae with Lakes ice-cream. Apartments (in the pub, nicely cosy) and cottages (off the courtyard, great for families) are a steal. All come with good kitchens to cook your own breakfast (hampers can be arranged). You get cool colours and comfy beds; several have private terraces. There's jazz on Sundays in summer and Cartmel priory is close. *Minimum two nights at weekends.*

Rooms	5 + 2: 5 apartments. 2 self-catering cottages: 1 for 2-4, 1 for 2-6.
Price	Apartments £75-£135. Cottages £110-£165.
Meals	Breakfast hampers £15-£25. Lunch from £4.95. Bar meals from £9.95. Dinner, 3 courses, £25-£30.
Closed	Never.
Directions	M6 junc. 36; A590 west, then A592 north. 1st right after Fell Foot Park. Straight ahead for 2.5 miles. On left after sharp right-hand turn.

John & Diane Taylor
Masons Arms,
Cartmel Fell,
Grange-over-Sands LA11 6NW

Tel +44 (0)15395 68486
Email info@masonsarmsstrawberrybank.co.uk
Web www.strawberrybank.com

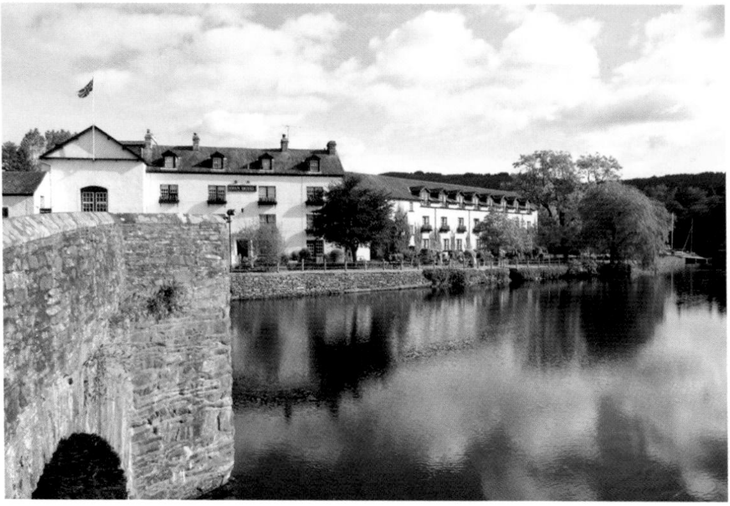

The Swan Hotel & Spa

This rather pretty hotel stands on the river Leven, a wide sweep of water that pours out of Windermere on its way south to Morecambe Bay. It's a fabulous spot and the Swan makes the most of it: a stone terrace runs along to an ancient packhorse bridge. The Swan was flooded in the great storm of 2009 and a recent refurbishment has breathed new life into old bones (this is a 17th-century monastic farmhouse). Inside, airy interiors have taken root. There are a couple of sitting rooms, open fires, the daily papers, a lively bar and a good restaurant to keep you going. There's also a spa: hard to miss as the swimming pool shimmers behind a wall of glass in reception. Treatment rooms, a sauna, steam room and gym all wait. Pretty bedrooms have the same crisp style: comfy beds, smart white linen, a wall of paper, a sofa if there's room. Those at the front have watery views, the family suites have dolls' houses and PlayStations. Back downstairs, dig into tasty food in the bar or brasserie, perhaps tiger prawn and chickpea broth, Chateaubriand steak with chunky chips, honeycomb cheesecake.

Rooms	51: 13 doubles, 30 twins/doubles, 8 suites.
Price	£99-£220. Suites £189-£320.
Meals	Lunch from £5.95. Bar meals from £9.95. Dinner from £13.95. Sunday lunch from £20.
Closed	Never.
Directions	M6 junc. 36, then A590 west. Into Newby Bridge. Over roundabout, then 1st right for hotel.

Sarah Gibbs
The Swan Hotel & Spa,
Newby Bridge LA12 8NB

Tel +44 (0)15395 31681
Email reservations@swanhotel.com
Web www.swanhotel.com

The Punch Bowl Inn

You're away from Windermere in a pretty village encircled by a tangle of lanes that defeat most tourists. This is a great spot, with views sweeping across a quilt of lush fields and a church that stands next door; bell ringers practise on Friday mornings, the odd bride glides out in summer. Yet while the Punch Bowl sits in a sleepy village lost to the world, it is actually a seriously funky inn. Rescued from neglect and renovated in great style, it now sparkles with a brilliant mix of old and new. Outside, honeysuckle and roses ramble on stone walls; inside open fires keep you warm in winter. A clipped elegance runs throughout – Farrow & Ball colours, sofas in front of a wood-burner – while Chris Meredith's fabulous food waits in the airy restaurant, perhaps Lancashire cheese soufflé, pan-fried sea bass, bread and butter pudding. Super bedrooms come with beautiful linen, lovely fabrics, Roberts radios, gorgeous bathrooms. Four rooms have big valley views; the vast suite, with double baths, is matchless. There's a sun-trapping terrace, too, but don't miss the lakes and the hills.

Rooms	9: 7 doubles, 1 twin/double, 1 suite.
Price	£95-£235. Suite £180-£305. Singles from £80.
Meals	Lunch from £5. Dinner, 3 courses, £30-£35.
Closed	Never.
Directions	M6 junc. 36, then A590 for Newby Bridge. Right onto A5074, then right for Crosthwaite after 3 miles. Pub on southern flank of village, next to church.

Abigail Lloyd
The Punch Bowl Inn,
Crosthwaite, Kendal LA8 8HR
Tel +44 (0)15395 68237
Email info@the-punchbowl.co.uk
Web www.the-punchbowl.co.uk

Linthwaite House Hotel & Restaurant

It's not just the view that makes Linthwaite so special, though Windermere sparkling half a mile below with a chain of peaks rising beyond does grab your attention. There's loads to enjoy here – 15 acres of gardens and grounds, a fantastic terrace for sunny days and interiors that go out of their way to pamper your pleasure receptors. The house itself is beautiful, one of those grand Lakeland Arts & Crafts wonders, with original woodwork and windows in all the right places. Logs are piled high by the front door, fires smoulder, sofas wait in the conservatory sitting room, where big views loom. Gorgeous country-house bedrooms are coolly uncluttered with warm colours, chic fabrics, hi-tech gadgetry, fabulous bathrooms. Those at the front have lake views, a couple have hot tubs, you can stargaze from one of the suites. Downstairs, ambrosial food waits in the dining rooms (one is decorated with nothing but mirrors), perhaps seared tuna with pickled ginger, chargrilled pigeon with beetroot purée, caramelised banana tart with peanut butter. Sunbeds wait on the terrace. Fabulous. *Minimum two nights at weekends.*

Rooms	30: 22 doubles, 5 twins/doubles, 3 suites.
Price	£240-£430. Suites £402-£630. Price includes dinner for two.
Meals	Lunch from £6.95. Dinner included; non-residents £52.
Closed	Rarely.
Directions	M6 junc. 36. Take A590 north, then A591 for Windermere. Left at roundabout onto B5284. Past golf course and hotel signed left after 1 mile.

Mike Bevans
Linthwaite House Hotel & Restaurant,
Crook Road, Bowness-on-Windermere,
Windermere LA23 3JA

Tel +44 (0)15394 88600
Email stay@linthwaite.com
Web www.linthwaite.com

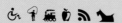

Gilpin Hotel

Gilpin is one of the loveliest places to stay in the country, simple as that. Run by two generations of the same family, it delivers at every turn, its staff delightful, its food divine – a treasure trove of beautiful things. It is a country house that has moved with the times, its sparkling interiors a beautiful fusion of contemporary and traditional styles. Cool elegance flows throughout – smouldering coals, Zoffany wallpaper, gilded mirrors, flowers everywhere. Afternoon tea is served every day, the wine cellar is on display in the bar, there's a beautiful sitting room in golden hues that overflows with art. Doors open onto a pretty terrace, perfect for Pimms in the sun; magnolia trees, cherry blossom and a copper beech wait in the garden. Bedrooms are divine: crisp white linen, exquisite fabrics, delicious art, fabulous bathrooms; garden suites have contemporary flair and hot tubs on private terraces. As for the food, it's marvellous stuff, perhaps poached pear with blue cheese mousse, Cartmel venison with liquorice and brambles, chocolate tart with orange sherbet and fennel ice. Unbeatable. *Minimum two nights at weekends. Special rates for three or more nights.*

Rooms	26: 8 doubles, 12 twins/doubles, 6 suites.
Price	£335-£385. Suites £385-£485. Price includes dinner for two.
Meals	Lunch £10-£35. Dinner included; non-residents £58.
Closed	Never.
Directions	M6 junc 36, A591 north, then B5284 west for Bowness. On right after 5 miles.

John, Christine, Barnaby & Zoe Cunliffe
Gilpin Hotel,
Crook Road, Windermere LA23 3NE

Tel +44 (0)15394 88818
Email hotel@thegilpin.co.uk
Web www.thegilpin.co.uk

Gilpin Lake House

Every now and then you bump into a hotel that knocks your socks off, and Gilpin Lake House does just that. This is an extraordinary little place – a tiny spa hotel with only six rooms, luxury and intimacy entwined. It sits away from the crowds, lost in the hills, surrounded by acres of peaceful woodland, with a private lake in front and a hot tub on the terrace. Sun loungers are sprinkled about, beautiful gardens and sun-dappled trees, a rowing boat for fun on the water. Best of all is the cabin above the lake that's a treatment room – pure heaven. There's an indoor pool and sauna, too, while the house itself is coolly elegant at every turn. You'll find sofas, a wood-burner and lake views in the sitting room, books galore and beautiful art. Bedrooms above are luxurious – sofas and armchairs, fabulous beds and fabrics, bathrooms that don't hold back. Breakfast is served wherever you want: in your room, on the terrace, in the conservatory. There's a chauffeur to take you to dinner, too. Come with friends and take the whole place. Out of this world.
Minimum two nights at weekends, three nights bank holidays & Easter. Children over seven welcome.

Rooms	6 twins/doubles.
Price	£495-£595. Price includes dinner for two at Gilpin Hotel, and chauffeur to and from the hotel.
Meals	Lunch from £10. Dinner included; non-residents £58.
Closed	Rarely.
Directions	B5284 west for Bowness. Left at Wild Boar pub, right through village and straight ahead for 2 miles. Keep right at fork and on left.

John, Christine, Barnaby & Zoe Cunliffe
Gilpin Lake House,
Crook, Windermere LA8 8LN

Tel	+44 (0)15394 88818
Email	hotel@thegilpin.co.uk
Web	www.thegilpin.co.uk/lake-house

Cedar Manor Hotel

A small country house on the edge of Windermere with good prices, pretty interiors and delicious food. Jonathan and Caroline love their world and can't stop spending money on it. Their most recent extravagance is the coach-house suite, a hedonist's dream; the bathroom is out of this world, the sitting room has a vast sofa, gadgets are sprinkled about (iPod dock, PlayStation, Nespresso coffee machine). The main house, originally a 17th-century cottage, was once home to a retired vicar, hence the ecclesiastic windows. Outside, an ancient cedar of Lebanon shades the lawn. Inside, cool colours and an easy style flourish. There's a beautiful sitting room in brown and cream with clumps of sofas and local art, then a sparkling dining room that overlooks the garden, where you dig into excellent food, perhaps crab cakes, rack of lamb, pear Charlotte with caramel mouse. Bedrooms – some warmly traditional, others nicely contemporary – have Zoffany fabrics, Lloyd Loom wicker and flat-screen TVs; most have fancy bathrooms, some have big views. All things Windermere wait. *Minimum two nights at weekends.*

Rooms	10: 7 doubles, 1 twin, 2 suites.
Price	£120-£170. Suites £220-£350. Singles from £100.
Meals	Dinner £32.95-£39.95.
Closed	12 December-23 January, but open for New Year.
Directions	From Windermere A591 east out of town for Kendal; hotel on right, next to church, before railway station.

Jonathan & Caroline Kaye
Cedar Manor Hotel,
Ambleside Road,
Windermere LA23 1AX

Tel	+44 (0)15394 43192
Email	info@cedarmanor.co.uk
Web	www.cedarmanor.co.uk

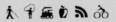

Jerichos

A super little B&B hotel with attractive prices in the middle of Windermere. Chris and Jo had a small restaurant in town, wanted something bigger, found this house, then spent a king's ransom doing it up. Step inside to find airy interiors with stripped wooden floors, Victorian windows and a splash of colour on the walls. There's a residents' sitting room with a couple of baby Chesterfields, then a pretty restaurant where you breakfast on homemade bread, local bacon and eggs, perhaps a grilled kipper. Spotless bedrooms are nicely priced. Those on the first floor have high ceilings, you get leather bedheads, comfy armchairs, fat white duvets and excellent bathrooms. Most have fancy showers, all come with iPod docks, a wall of paper, Lakeland art. There are good restaurants in town – Hooked for fish, Francine's for tasty bistro fare – but Chris cooks on Saturday and his food is exceptional, perhaps cauliflower, apple and blue cheese soup, silver hake with braised leeks, vanilla panna cotta with raspberry sorbet. The Lake is a short stroll, a good way to round off breakfast. *Minimum two nights at weekends and three nights on bank holiday weekends.*

Rooms	10: 8 doubles, 2 singles.
Price	£75-£125. Singles from £45.
Meals	Dinner, 3 courses, about £35 (Saturday only).
Closed	Last 3 weeks in January.
Directions	A591 from Kendal to Windermere. Pass train station, don't turn left into town, rather next left 200 yards on. First right and on right after 500m.

Chris & Jo Blaydes
Jerichos,
College Road,
Windermere LA23 1BX

Tel +44 (0)15394 42522
Email info@jerichos.co.uk
Web www.jerichos.co.uk

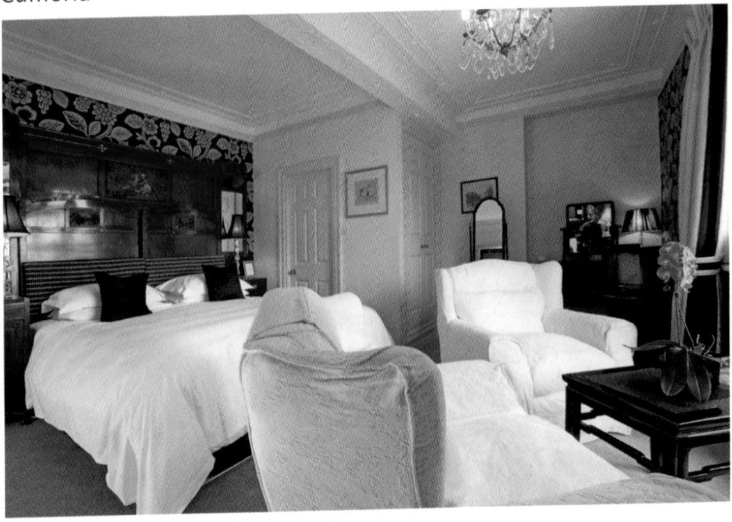

Miller Howe Hotel & Restaurant

The view is breathtaking, one of the best in the Lakes, a clean sweep over Windermere to the majestic Langdale Pikes. As for Miller Howe, it's just as good, an Edwardian country-house hotel made famous by TV chef John Tovey. These days a fine new look is emerging, all the result of a super refurbishment by passionate owners Helen and Martin Ainscough. Inside, new and old combine with ease. Contemporary art and beautiful fabrics blend seamlessly with period features, and the atmosphere is refreshingly relaxed. You can sink into a deep armchair by an open fire and soak up huge views of lake and mountain, then spin into the dining room where walls of glass open onto a dining terrace. Menus bristle with local food, perhaps Lancashire cheese soufflé, Cumbrian lamb, Yorkshire rhubarb crumble. Handsome bedrooms vary in size and style. All are individually designed with handmade fabrics, period furniture and posh TVs, some have balconies for fabulous lake views. Cottage suites in the glorious garden offer sublime peace. Perfect whatever the weather. *Minimum two nights at weekends. Pets allowed in two rooms.*

Rooms	15: 5 doubles, 7 twins/doubles, 3 suites.
Price	£210-£290. Suites £310. Price includes dinner for two.
Meals	Lunch from £6.50. Sunday lunch £27.50. Dinner included; non-residents £45.
Closed	Rarely.
Directions	From Kendal A591 to Windermere. Left at mini-r'bout onto A592 for Bowness; 0.25 miles on right.

Helen & Martin Ainscough
Miller Howe Hotel & Restaurant,
Rayrigg Road, Windermere LA23 1EY

Tel +44 (0)15394 42536
Email info@millerhowe.com
Web www.millerhowe.com

Nanny Brow

A beautiful Lakeland Arts & Crafts house which dates to 1903. It sits peacefully on the hill with views sweeping up the valley with the river Brathay pottering off towards Wrynose Pass. Interiors are no less beautiful. Sue and Peter rescued Nanny Brow from neglect, spent a small fortune doing it up and now it shines, a country house reborn. All the lovely old stuff has been restored, but the feel is fresh with airy rooms that bask in the light and an easy elegance flowing throughout. The half-panelled drawing room is gorgeous: smart sofas, original windows, an open fire, ornate ceiling friezes, vases of beautiful flowers. Bedrooms are lovely, too. Some have arched windows that frame the view, all have super-comfy beds, crisp colours, the odd wall of designer paper; gorgeous bathrooms have double-ended baths or walk-in power showers or both. Cumbrian breakfasts set you up for the day, paths through ancient woodlands lead onto the fells. There's a sitting-room bar, a drying room for walkers, secure storage for bikes and excellent restaurants in Ambleside, a mile up the road. *Minimum stay two nights at weekends.*

Rooms	10: 7 doubles, 3 suites.
Price	£120-£190. Suites £180-£300. Singles from £105.
Meals	Restaurants 1 mile.
Closed	Never.
Directions	West from Ambleside on A593. On right after a mile.

Peter & Susan Robinson
Nanny Brow,
Clappersgate, Ambleside LA22 9NF

Tel +44 (0)15394 33232
Email unwind@nannybrow.co.uk
Web www.nannybrow.co.uk

Drunken Duck Inn

The Duck is a Lakeland institution, blissfully hidden away from the crowds. You're up on the hill, cradled by woods and fells, with huge views from the terrace that shoot across to towering peaks. It's a great spot for a good pint – they brew their own ten yards from the front door – with roses rambling on the veranda and stone walls that double as flowerbeds. As for the Duck, she may be old, but she sure is pretty with airy interiors that drip with style. You'll find stripped floors in the beamed bar, timber-framed walls in the popular restaurant and a sitting room for guests, where afternoon tea is served 'on the house' every day. Wander at will and find open fires, grandfather clocks, the daily papers, exquisite art. Bedrooms come in different shapes and sizes with colours courtesy of Farrow & Ball. Rooms in the main house are snug; those in the courtyard are seriously indulging. Some have private terraces, one comes with a balcony, several have huge windows to frame the view. Lawns roll down to Black Tarn, where Greek gods gaze upon jumping fish. Fabulous.
Minimum two nights at weekends.

Rooms	17: 15 doubles, 2 twins/doubles.
Price	£105-£325. Singles from £76.25.
Meals	Lunch from £4.95. Dinner, 3 courses, about £35.
Closed	Christmas Day.
Directions	West from Ambleside on A593, then left at Clappersgate for Hawkshead on B5286. After 2 miles turn right, signed. Up hill to inn.

Stephanie Barton
Drunken Duck Inn,
Barngates, Ambleside LA22 0NG

Tel	+44 (0)15394 36347
Email	info@drunkenduckinn.co.uk
Web	www.drunkenduckinn.co.uk

The Eltermere Inn

This gorgeous Lakeland inn seems lost to the world, yet it's only a couple of miles from Grasmere. In summer you sit in the garden with local sheep for company and dig into afternoon tea; in winter you order a pint at the bar, then roast away in front of the fire. You're in an unblemished village that stands back from the water in the shade of forested hills. Inside, beautifully refurbished interiors are part country house, part village pub. There's a grand piano in the dining room, ancient slate floors in the bar, then big sofas and lovely art in the airy sitting rooms. Upstairs, stylish rooms have warm colours, local wool carpets, big beds and Mulberry fabrics. Some have padded window seats, others are open to the eaves, all have excellent bathrooms, those at the front have views of lake and mountain. Downstairs, you find the sort of food you crave after a day in the hills, perhaps mussels with white wine and garlic, rack of Cumbrian lamb, banana gingerbread with toffee sauce. Walks start from the front door, there's croquet on the lawn, they even grow their own vegetables. *Minimum stay two nights at weekends.*

Rooms	12 twins/doubles.
Price	£140-£225. Singles from £125.
Meals	Lunch from £6.95. Dinner, 3 courses, £30-£35.
Closed	Christmas.
Directions	West from Ambleside for 3 miles on A593, then right for Eltermere. On right in village.

Mark & Ruth Jones
The Eltermere Inn,
Elterwater, Ambleside LA22 9HY
Tel +44 (0)15394 37207
Email info@eltermere.co.uk
Web www.eltermere.co.uk

Borrowdale Gates

This super hotel sits peacefully in Borrowdale, 'the loveliest square mile in Lakeland' to quote Alfred Wainwright. High peaks encircle you, sheep grace the fields, the river Derwent potters past. The view from the top of High Seat is one of the best in the Lakes with Derwent Water sparkling under a vast sky, but the lowland walking is equally impressive: long or short, high or low, Borrowdale always delivers. At the end of the day, roll back to this deeply comfy hotel and recover in style. Downstairs, big windows follow you around and there are sofas and armchairs scattered about to make the most of the view. You get binoculars, the daily papers, afternoon tea in front of roaring fires. Bedrooms are immaculately traditional. Expect warm colours, super beds, smart bathrooms, armchairs or sofas if there's room. Some open onto terraces, several have small balconies, most have the view. As for the restaurant, a wall of glass looks out over the village and beyond, a perfect spot for a tasty meal, perhaps sweet potato soup, fell-bred lamb, sticky toffee pudding. *Minimum two nights at weekends. Pets welcome by arrangement.*

Rooms	25: 18 twins/doubles, 4 singles, 3 suites.
Price	£180-£210. Suites £216-£310. Singles £100-£123. All prices include dinner.
Meals	Light lunches from £4.50. Dinner £30-£39.
Closed	January.
Directions	M6 to Penrith, A66 to Keswick, then B5289 south for 4 miles. Right at humpback bridge, through Grange, hotel on right.

Colin Harrison
Borrowdale Gates,
Grange-in-Borrowdale,
Keswick CA12 5UQ

Tel +44 (0)17687 77204
Email hotel@borrowdale-gates.co.uk
Web www.borrowdale-gates.com

The Cottage in the Wood

A great little base for the northern Lakes with lots of style, super food and owners who go the extra mile. You're on the side of Whinlatter Pass with big views east to a chain of Lakeland peaks. Outside, the terrace looks the right way, a great spot for a drink in summer. Inside, chic interiors are just the ticket: an airy sitting room, a fire that burns on both sides, books and games to keep you amused, windows galore in the restaurant. Nicely priced bedrooms have white walls to soak up the light and sparkling bathrooms for a good wallow. One in the eaves has a claw-foot bath, four have mountains views, one has a fabulous bathroom and opens onto its own terrace. There's lots to do – lakes to visit, hills to climb, cycle trails to follow. Whatever you do, come home to some lovely local food, perhaps Curthwaite goats' curd with beetroot and rocket, Herdwick hoggat with garlic dumplings, passion fruit soufflé with mango ice-cream. There's a drying room for walkers, secure storage for bikes, a burn that tumbles down the hill. Starry skies on clear nights will amaze you. Brilliant. *Minimum two nights at weekends.*

Rooms	9: 6 doubles, 2 twins/doubles, 1 suite.
Price	£110-£150. Suite £180. Singles from £88.
Meals	Lunch from £14.95. Sunday lunch £25. Dinner £36-£55. Not Sunday night or Monday.
Closed	January.
Directions	M6 junc. 40, A66 west to Braithwaite, then B5292 for Lorton. On right after 2.5 miles (before visitor centre).

Kath & Liam Berney
The Cottage in the Wood,
Braithwaite, Keswick CA12 5TW

Tel +44 (0)17687 78409
Email relax@thecottageinthewood.co.uk
Web www.thecottageinthewood.co.uk

Swinside Lodge Hotel

Swinside is a dream – a small, intimate country house that sits in silence at the foot of Cat Bells. Fells rise, spirits soar, and Derwent Water, Queen of the Lakes, is a short stroll through the woods. Kath and Mike came back from France to take up the reins of this ever-popular hotel and they haven't stopped; sash windows have been replaced, bedrooms have been given a makeover, fancy bathrooms are now de rigueur. Downstairs, you'll find fresh flowers and comfy sofas in the yellow drawing room, shelves of books and a jukebox in the sitting room, red walls and gilt-framed mirrors in the dining room, where windows frame views of Skiddaw. Super food waits in the restaurant, exactly what you want after a day on the fells – tasty fishcakes, local lamb, chocolate mousse. Upstairs, a new regime is taking shape in the bedrooms with warm colours, golden throws and padded window seats spreading a cool country elegance. Outside, a host of characters visit the garden: a woodpecker, red squirrels, roe deer. Wonderful. *Children over 12 welcome.*

Rooms	7: 5 doubles, 2 twins.
Price	£172-£284. Singles from £116. All prices include dinner.
Meals	Dinner, 4 courses, included; non-residents £38. Packed lunches £9.
Closed	December & January.
Directions	M6 junc. 40. A66 west past Keswick, over r'bout, then 2nd left for Portinscale & Grange. Follow signs to Grange for 2 miles (not right hand turns). House signed on right.

Mike & Kathy Bilton
Swinside Lodge Hotel,
Newlands,
Keswick CA12 5UE

Tel +44 (0)17687 72948
Email info@swinsidelodge-hotel.co.uk
Web www.swinsidelodge-hotel.co.uk

The George

Charlotte Brontë set part of *Jane Eyre* here. She called the village Morton, referred to this hotel as The Feathers and stole the name of an old landlord for her heroine. A copy of her famous novel sits on the shelves of 'the smallest library in the world', which occupies a turret in the sitting room. The bigger turret, equally well employed, is now the bar. The George, a 500-year-old ale house, has grown in stature over time and a smart refurbishment recently propelled it into the 21st century. As a result, wood floors, stone walls and heavy beams mix with purple sofas, fancy wallpaper and Lloyd Loom furniture. It's an unexpected marriage that works rather well, making this small hotel quite a find in the northern Peak District. Airy bedrooms are good value for money, full of colour with spotless bathrooms. Excellent beds are dressed in crisp linen; those at the back are quietest. As for the food, a good meal waits in the dining room, so scale Arbor Low, then return to smoked salmon, chestnut and venison pudding, chocolate pavé with hazelnut macaroons.

Rooms	24: 17 doubles, 4 twins/doubles, 3 singles.
Price	£95-£198. Singles from £70.
Meals	Lunch from £4.75. Dinner, 3 courses, £36.50.
Closed	Never.
Directions	In village at junction of A6187 and B6001, 10 miles west of M1 at Sheffield.

Philip Joseph
The George,
Main Road, Hathersage,
Hope Valley S32 1BB

Tel	+44 (0)1433 650436
Email	info@george-hotel.net
Web	www.george-hotel.net

The Old Rectory Hotel Exmoor

A gorgeous small hotel in the hills above the Exmoor coast. The road from Lynton is a great way in, through woods that cling to a hill with the sea below. As for the Old Rectory, it's a mini Gidleigh Park, charming from top to toe. Three acres of spectacular gardens wrap around you, only birdsong disturbs you, though Exmoor deer occasionally come to drink from the pond. Inside, Huw and Sam continue to lavish love and money in all the right places. Their most recent addition is a beautiful orangery with smart sofas and warm colours, then doors onto the garden for afternoon tea in the sun. Interiors are lovely: Farrow & Ball colours, the odd stone wall, an open fire in the snug sitting room, fresh flowers and books everywhere. Bedrooms are just as good with big beds, crisp linen, cool colours and robes in beautiful bathrooms. You'll find digital radios, flat-screen TVs and the odd leather sofa, too. Spin into the restaurant for an excellent meal, perhaps Ilfracombe crab, Exmoor duck, Champagne strawberry trifle. Afternoon tea 'on the house' is served in the garden in good weather.

Rooms	11: 3 doubles, 4 twins/doubles, 4 suites.
Price	£185-£230. Suites £245-£260. Price includes dinner for two.
Meals	4-course dinner included in price; non-resident £35.
Closed	November to March.
Directions	M5 junc. 27, A361 to South Molton, then A399 north. Right at Blackmore Gate onto A39 for Lynton. Left after 3 miles, signed Martinhoe. In village, next to church.

Huw Rees & Sam Prosser
The Old Rectory Hotel Exmoor,
Martinhoe, Parracombe,
Barnstable EX31 4QT

Tel +44 (0)1598 763368
Email info@oldrectoryhotel.co.uk
Web www.oldrectoryhotel.co.uk

Heasley House

A beautiful house in a sleepy village lost in an Exmoor valley – the sort of place you return to again and again. It's a lovely spot, blissfully lost to the world. A river runs below, tree-clad hills rise above. As for this 1760 dower house, it stands in the middle of the village with a sun-trapping terrace at the front and big views from the garden behind. Inside, old and new mix stylishly. You find stripped boards, stone walls, timber frames, a rather lovely bar. Warm colours run throughout, fires burn in the sitting rooms, you get original art and fresh flowers everywhere. Airy bedrooms are more than comfy with big beds, good linen and lovely bathrooms. Those at the front have the view, those in the eaves have beams. All have flat-screen TVs, fluffy bathrobes and armchairs. Spin down to the restaurant for a feast of local produce, perhaps Brixham scallops with pea purée, pork stuffed with apricots, walnut and praline parfait with maple syrup. Paths lead out, so follow the river into the woods or head north for cliffs at the coast. House parties are very welcome, as are dogs. Brilliant.

Rooms	7: 6 twins/doubles, 1 suite.
Price	£150. Suite £170. Singles from £110. Dinner, B&B from £100 p.p.
Meals	Dinner £26-£32.
Closed	Christmas, New Year & February.
Directions	M5 junc. 27, A361 for Barnstaple. After South Molton right for North Molton, then left for Heasley Mill.

Paul & Jan Gambrill
Heasley House,
Heasley Mill,
South Molton EX36 3LE

Tel +44 (0)1598 740213
Email enquiries@heasley-house.co.uk
Web www.heasley-house.co.uk

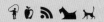

Northcote Manor

A small country-house hotel built on the site of a 15th-century monastery. Those who want peace in deep country will find it here. You wind up a one-mile drive, through a wood that bursts with colour in spring, then emerge onto a lush plateau of rolling hills; the view from the croquet lawn drifts east for ten miles. As for the house, wisteria wanders along old stone walls, while the odd open fire smoulders within. There's an airy hall that doubles as the bar, a country-house drawing room that floods with light, and a sitting room where you gather for pre-dinner drinks. Super food waits in a lovely dining room, steps lead down to a pretty conservatory, doors open onto a gravelled terrace for summer breakfasts with lovely views. Bedrooms are no less appealing – more traditional in the main house, more contemporary in the garden rooms. Expect padded bedheads, mahogany dressers, flat-screen TVs, silky throws. You can walk your socks off, then come home for a good meal, perhaps white Cornish crab, local lamb, strawberry soufflé with vanilla ice-cream. Exmoor and North Devon's coasts are close.

Rooms	16: 9 twins/doubles, 7 suites.
Price	£170-£225. Suites £280. Singles from £120. Dinner, B&B from £130 p.p.
Meals	Light dishes from £6.50. Lunch from £22.50. Dinner, 3 courses, £45. Tasting menu £80. Sunday lunch from £25.50.
Closed	Never.
Directions	M5 junc. 27, A361 to S. Molton. Fork left onto B3227; left on A377 for Exeter. Entrance 4.1 miles on right, signed.

Richie Herkes
Northcote Manor,
Burrington, Umberleigh EX37 9LZ

Tel +44 (0)1769 560501
Email rest@northcotemanor.co.uk
Web www.northcotemanor.co.uk

Lewtrenchard Manor

A magnificent Jacobean mansion, a wormhole back to the 16th century. Sue and James have returned to this fine country house, which they established 20 years ago as one of the loveliest hotels in the land. Inside, the full aristocratic monty: a spectacular hall with a cavernous fireplace, a dazzling ballroom with staggering plasterwork. There are priest holes, oak panelling, oils by the score. Best of all is the 1602 gallery with its majestic ceiling and grand piano; *Onward Christian Soldiers* could have been written in the library. Bedrooms are large. Most tend to be warmly traditional (the four-poster belonged to Queen Henrietta Maria, wife of Charles I), but some are contemporary with chic fabrics and fancy bathrooms. All have jugs of iced water, garden flowers and bathrobes. Delicious food waits – perhaps lemon sole, loin of venison, peanut parfait with banana sorbet – and there's a chef's table where you can watch the kitchen at work on a bank of TVs. Outside, a Gertrude Jekyll garden and an avenue of beech trees that make you feel you're in a Hardy novel. *Minimum stay two nights at weekends.*

Rooms	14: 4 doubles, 6 twins/doubles, 4 suites.
Price	£155-£220. Suites £220-£235. Singles from £120. Dinner, B&B from £122.50 p.p.
Meals	Lunch: bar meals from £5.25; restaurant from £19.50. Dinner, 3 courses, £49.50. Children over seven welcome in restaurant.
Closed	Rarely.
Directions	From Exeter, exit A30 for A386. At T-junc., right, then 1st left for Lewdown. After 6 miles, left for Lewtrenchard. Keep left; house on left after 0.5 miles.

Sue, James, Duncan & Joan Murray
Lewtrenchard Manor,
Lewdown, Okehampton EX20 4PN

Tel +44 (0)1566 783222
Email info@lewtrenchard.co.uk
Web www.lewtrenchard.co.uk

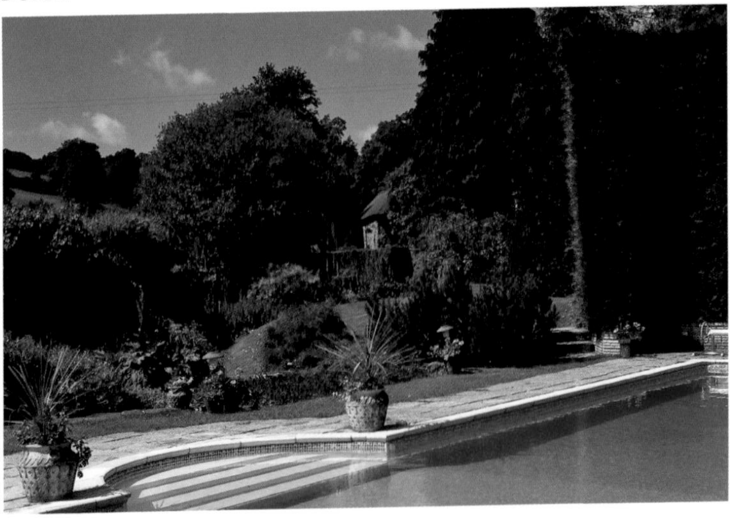

Tor Cottage

You're at the end of the track in a pretty valley lost to the world. It's a fabulous hideaway wrapped up in 28 acres of majestic country and those who like to be pampered in peace will love it here. Hills rise, cows sleep, streams run, birds sing. Bridle paths lead onto the hill and wild flowers carpet a hay meadow, but be warned – big rooms in converted outbuildings are the lap of rustic luxury and you may dawdle. Each comes with a wood-burner and private terrace: one is straight out of *House and Garden*, another has ceilings open to the rafters. Best of all is the cabin in its own valley – a wonderland in the woods – with a hammock in the trees, a stream passing below, the odd deer pottering past. Breakfast is served in the conservatory or on the terrace in good weather: homemade muesli, local sausages, farm-fresh eggs. You can have smoked salmon sandwiches by the pool for lunch or spark up the barbecue and cook your own dinner; all rooms have fridges and microwaves, so you don't have to go out. Maureen spoils you rotten, her staff couldn't be nicer. A wonderful place. *Minimum stay two nights.*

Rooms	5: 2 doubles, 1 twin/double, 1 suite. 1 woodland cabin for 2.
Price	£150. Cabin £115. Singles from £98.
Meals	Picnic platters £16. Pubs/restaurants 3 miles.
Closed	Mid-December to end of January.
Directions	In Chillaton keep pub & Post Office on left, up hill towards Tavistock. After 300m right down bridleway (ignore 'No Access' signs).

Maureen Rowlatt
Tor Cottage,
Chillaton, Lifton PL16 0JE

Tel	+44 (0)1822 860248
Email	info@torcottage.co.uk
Web	www.torcottage.co.uk

The Horn of Plenty

This country-house hotel has been thrilling guests for 40 years and it doesn't take long to work out why. The view, the food, the staff and the rooms: all deliver in spades. The house goes back to 1860 and was built for the captain of the mines, who could peer down the valley and check his men were at work; these days it's the Tamar snaking through the hills below that catches the eye. Inside you find the essence of graceful simplicity: stripped floors, gilt mirrors, exquisite art and flowers everywhere. Bedrooms are just as good. Some have terraces that look down to the river, others come in country-house style with vast beds, old armoires, shimmering throws and rugs on stripped floors; bathrooms are predictably divine. As for the food, it's the big draw, so expect to eat well, perhaps Falmouth Bay scallops with a carrot purée, Devonshire lamb with a Madeira sauce, then milk chocolate and hazelnut mousse with a passion fruit and banana parfait. Best of all are the staff, who couldn't be more helpful. Tavistock, Dartmoor and The Eden Project are all within striking distance.

Rooms	10 twins/doubles.
Price	£95-£225. Singles from £85.
Meals	Lunch £19.50-£24.50. Dinner £49.50.
Closed	Never.
Directions	West from Tavistock on A390 following signs to Callington. Right after 3 miles at Gulworthy Cross. Signed left after 0.75 miles.

Julie Leivers & Damien Pease
The Horn of Plenty,
Gulworthy, Tavistock PL19 8JD
Tel +44 (0)1822 832528
Email enquiries@thehornofplenty.co.uk
Web www.thehornofplenty.co.uk

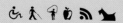

The Henley Hotel

A small house above the sea with fabulous views, super bedrooms and some of the loveliest food in Devon. Despite such credentials, it's Martyn and Petra who shine most brightly, and their kind, generous approach makes this a memorable place to stay. Warm Edwardian interiors come with stripped wood floors, seagrass matting, Lloyd Loom wicker chairs, the odd potted palm. Below, the Avon estuary slips gracefully out to sea: at high tide surfers ride the waves; at low tide you can walk on the sands. There's a pretty garden with a path tumbling down to the beach, binoculars in each room, a wood-burner in the snug and good books everywhere. Bedrooms are a steal (one is huge). Expect warm yellows, crisp linen, tongue-and-groove panelling and robes in super little bathrooms. As for Martyn's table d'hôte dinners, expect something special. Fish comes daily from Kingsbridge market, you might have warm crab and parmesan tart, roast monkfish with a lobster sauce, then hot chocolate soufflé with fresh raspberries. Gorgeous Devon is all around. Don't miss it. *Minimum two nights at weekends.*

Rooms	5: 2 doubles, 3 twins/doubles.
Price	£120-£145. Singles from £85. Dinner, B&B from £85 p.p. (min. 2 nights).
Meals	Dinner £36.
Closed	November-March.
Directions	From A38, A3121 to Modbury, then B3392 to Bigbury-on-Sea. Hotel on left as road slopes down to sea.

Martyn Scarterfield & Petra Lampe
The Henley Hotel,
Folly Hill, Bigbury-on-Sea,
Kingsbridge TQ7 4AR

Tel +44 (0)1548 810240
Email thehenleyhotel@btconnect.com
Web www.thehenleyhotel.co.uk

Burgh Island Hotel

Burgh is unique – grand English Art Deco trapped in aspic. Noel Coward loved it, Agatha Christie wrote here. It's much more than a hotel – you come to join a cast of players – so bring your pearls and come for cocktails under a stained-glass dome. By day you lie on steamer chairs in the garden, watch gulls wheeling above, dip your toes into Mermaid's pool or try your hand at a game of croquet. At night you dress for dinner, sip vermouth in a palm-fringed bar, then shuffle off to the ballroom and dine on delicious organic food while the sounds of swing and jazz fill the air. Follow your nose and find flowers in vases four-feet high, bronze ladies thrusting globes into the sky, walls clad in vitrolite, a 14th-century smugglers' inn. Art Deco bedrooms are the real thing: Bakelite telephones, ancient radios, bowls of fruit, panelled walls. Some have claw-foot baths, others have balconies, the Beach House suite juts out over rocks. There's snooker, tennis, massage, a sauna. You're on an island, so sweep across the sands at low tide or hitch a ride on the sea tractor. *Minimum two nights at weekends.*

Rooms	25: 10 doubles, 3 twins/doubles, 12 suites.
Price	£400-£430. Suites £485-£640. Price includes dinner for two.
Meals	Lunch from £13.50. Sunday lunch £48. Dinner included; non-residents £60. 24-hour residents' menu from £10.50.
Closed	Rarely.
Directions	Drive to Bigbury-on-Sea. At high tide you are transported by sea tractor, at low tide by Landrover. Walking over the beach takes 3 minutes. Eco-taxis can be arranged.

Deborah Clark & Tony Orchard
Burgh Island Hotel,
Burgh Island, Bigbury-on-Sea,
Kingsbridge TQ7 4BG

Tel +44 (0)1548 810514
Email reception@burghisland.com
Web www.burghisland.com

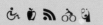

Seabreeze

A 16th-century teahouse with rooms on Slapton Sands: only in England. The sea laps ten paces from the front door, the hills of Devon soar behind, three miles of beach shoot off before your eyes. Seabreeze is a treat: cute, relaxed, a comforting dash of homespun magic. Step inside and the first thing you see is a mountain of irresistible cakes. Carol and Bonni bake the old-fashioned way. It's all utterly delicious: hot scones, Victoria sponge, banana and chocolate chip brownies. The tearoom itself – white walls, pretty art, tables topped with maps – is warmed by a wood-burner in winter. In summer you decamp onto the terrace, where sea and sky fuse. Both rooms have the view and come in seaside colours with jars of driftwood, padded bedheads and window seats. Outside, there's loads to do: buckets and spades on the beach, cliff walks to great pubs, kayaks for intrepid adventures. Epic breakfasts set you up for the day, while the Start Bay Inn for tasty seafood suppers is yards away. There's surf school at Bigbury or sailing at Salcombe. *Minimum two nights at weekends in high season.*

Rooms	2: 1 double, 1 twin/double.
Price	£100-£140.
Meals	Lunch from £4. Dinner by arrangement. Restaurants in village.
Closed	Never.
Directions	A379 south from Dartmouth to Torcross. House on seafront in village.

Carol Simmons & Bonni Lincoln
Seabreeze,
Torcross, Kingsbridge TQ7 2TQ

Tel	+44 (0)1548 580697
Email	info@seabreezebreaks.com
Web	www.seabreezebreaks.com

South Sands Hotel

Two coves west from the bustle of town, this super-smart hotel stands above the beach with views of water, hill and sky. Interiors have a New England feel – seaside colours, softly painted wood, walls of glass for views you can't escape. Doors in the restaurant open onto a decked terrace, where at high tide the beach disappears and the sea laps against the wall below. Pull yourself away to walk in the hills, sail on the water, hire a kayak or try your hand at paddle boarding. Alternatively, just drop down to the beach for family fun. Children are very welcome and you'll find beach towels, buckets and spades, even crabbing nets for excursions to rock pools. Back at the hotel, lovely food waits, perhaps duck liver brûlée, seafood spaghetti, chocolate sundae drenched in chocolate sauce. As for the rooms, those at the front have sublime views, a couple get terraces, all have fabulous bathrooms, cool colours and super-comfy beds. One has 'his and hers' claw-foot baths that look out to sea; the family suites have kitchens, dining tables and separate bedrooms for kids. Brilliant.
Minimum stay two nights at weekends. Dogs £12.50 per night.

Rooms	27: 16 doubles, 6 twins/doubles, 5 family suites.
Price	£150-£375. Suites £320-£435.
Meals	Lunch from £17.95. Dinner £15.95-£40.
Closed	Rarely.
Directions	A381 to Salcombe, then signed right to South Sands. Follow road down hill, then along water. On left.

Stephen Ball
South Sands Hotel,
Bolt Head, Salcombe TQ8 8LL
Tel +44 (0)1548 859000
Email enquiries@southsands.com
Web www.southsands.com

Plantation House

Plantation House is a small hotel where great food and cool interiors go hand in hand. To some this makes it a restaurant with rooms, but whatever it is, all who stay agree on one thing – it's an irresistible little place that shines from top to toe. Downstairs, a fire smoulders in the sitting room bar; upstairs, fine Georgian windows frame views of hill and forest; everywhere, vases of wild flowers. Bedrooms pamper you rotten: two are huge, the rest are merely big. They come with stunning bathrooms, lovely beds, crisp linen and warm colours. You get padded bedheads, sound systems, bowls of fruit. As for Richard's food, it bursts with flavour, perhaps turbot with crab and chardonnay bisque, crispy Devon duckling, cider and bramley apple jus, chocolate espresso tart and hazelnut ice-cream. Soft fruits, vegetables and potatoes come from the garden in summer, as do home-laid eggs at breakfast. The river Erme passes across the road, so follow it down to the sea and discover Wonwell Beach. Further afield you'll find Dartmoor and Dartmouth, Salcombe and Slapton Sands. Wonderful.

Rooms	8: 5 doubles, 1 twin, 1 single, 1 suite.
Price	£115-£180. Suite £240. Singles from £70.
Meals	Dinner, 5 courses, from £36.
Closed	Never.
Directions	A38, then A3121 for Ermington. In village on western fringe.

Richard Hendey
Plantation House,
Totnes Road, Ermington,
Ivybridge PL21 9NS

Tel +44 (0)1548 831100
Email info@plantationhousehotel.co.uk
Web www.plantationhousehotel.co.uk

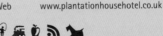

Bayards Cove Inn

In 1620 the Mayflower stopped in Bayards Cove before sailing for America. It docked just outside this gorgeous little inn, one of the oldest buildings in Dartmouth. But if its timber frames are ancient, then its jaunty interiors are the polar opposite with a warm contemporary feel that spreads itself far and wide. Once inside you realise you're really in a café/tapas bar that does a good line in world wines and local ales. You also realise you've landed in heaven and soon you're trying to muscle your way onto one of the sofas in the bay windows, from which you can survey life inside and out. Interiors have warm colours, low beams, white stone walls and ancient wood everywhere; there are fairy lights, too, a bar weighted down by freshly baked cakes, and cool tunes afloat in the air. Upstairs, lovely rooms have timber frames, padded bedheads, pretty fabrics, comfy beds. Most have compact shower rooms, but you won't mind for a minute; others have views of the water or wildly wonky floors. There's great food, too, and live flamenco on Sunday nights. Dartmouth waits at the front door. *Minimum stay two nights at weekends.*

Rooms	7: 4 doubles, 1 twin/double, 1 family room, 1 suite.
Price	£90-£135. Family room £110-£135. Suite £130-£150.
Meals	Lunch from £5.95. Dinner from £9.95 (not Monday-Wednesday off season).
Closed	6 January-1 February.
Directions	In Dartmouth south along sea front for lower ferry. Follow road right for 200m and on left at T-junction.

Charlie & Zuzana Deuchar
Bayards Cove Inn,
Lower Street,
Dartmouth TQ6 9AN

Tel +44 (0)1803 839278
Email bayardscove@gmail.com
Web www.bayardscoveinn.co.uk

Browns Hotel

Browns is all things to all men, a cool little wine bar bang in the middle of town. You can pop in for coffee, stay for lunch, come for a glass of excellent wine or book in for a good dinner. It's smart, but informal with chic interiors: leather banquettes in the restaurant, Philippe Starck chairs in the bar, comfy sofas scattered about. An open-plan feel runs throughout with big seaside oils on the walls and flames leaping from a pebbled fire. The bar buzzes at weekends, and there's some lovely food, too, nothing too fancy, just the sort of stuff you can't resist – grilled chorizo, a tasty pizza, Catalan fish stew with saffron and rosemary. As for the rooms, the stunning new suite has a huge bed and a magnificent bathroom (walk-in glass shower, contemporary double-ended bath). Other rooms are stylish, too, with warm colours, padded bedheads and small leather armchairs. Those at the back are quieter, all have radios, good bathrooms and a book that spills local secrets (the best walks and beaches, which ferries to use). If you like the wine, you can buy a bottle to take home. *Minimum two nights at weekends.*

Rooms	8: 7 doubles, 1 suite.
Price	£90-£185. Suite £130-£250.
Meals	Lunch from £6.95 (Tue-Sat). Dinner from £10.50 (Wed-Sat).
Closed	First 2 weeks in January.
Directions	Into Dartmouth on A3122. Left at 1st r'bout, straight over 2nd r'bout, then 3rd right (Townstal Road). Down into town. On right.

James & Clare Brown
Browns Hotel,
27-29 Victoria Road,
Dartmouth TQ6 9RT

Tel	+44 (0)1803 832572
Email	enquiries@brownshoteldartmouth.co.uk
Web	www.brownshoteldartmouth.co.uk

Fingals

People love the individualism of Fingals with the easy-going among us happiest there. Richard runs things in a rare laissez-faire style; Sheila is impossibly kind. Guests wander around as if at home, children and dogs potter about. Dinner (local and mostly organic) is served a couple of times a week in one of the panelled dining rooms and you can choose to eat with fellow guests. You may find yourself next to an earl, a comedian or an ambulance driver, all drawn by the charm of this place. Breakfast is served until 11am – a nice touch if you've stayed up late making friends in the honesty bar. The setting is a handsome Queen Anne farmhouse next to a stream with a small indoor pool, sauna and grass tennis court. With books and art everywhere, the rooms are full of personality in a mix of styles. Generous, engaging, occasionally chaotic... If you want to stay longer and look after yourselves, there are three lovely self-catering boltholes in the garden; the eco suite with its sunken bath overlooking the stream is impeccable. Don't miss Greenway by the Dart – Agatha Christie's atmospheric home. *Minimum two nights at weekends.*

Rooms	10 + 3: 8 doubles, 2 twins. Self-catering: 1 barn, 1 millhouse, 1 suite.
Price	£75-£220. Self-catering £300-£1,200 per week.
Meals	Dinner £36.
Closed	Mid-January to mid-March.
Directions	From Totnes A381 south; left for Cornworthy; right at x-roads for Cornworthy; right at ruined priory towards Dittisham. Down steep hill, over bridge. Sign on right.

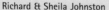

Richard & Sheila Johnston
Fingals,
Dittisham,
Dartmouth TQ6 0JA

Tel +44 (0)1803 722398
Email info@fingals.co.uk
Web www.fingals.co.uk

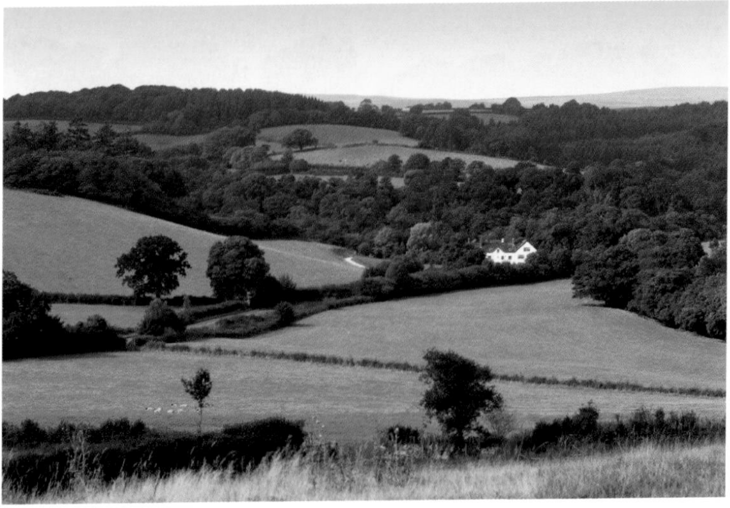

Mill End

Another Dartmoor gem, Mill End is flanked by the Two Moors Way, one of the loveliest walks in England. It leads along the river Teign, then up to Castle Drogo – not a bad way to follow your bacon and eggs. As for the hotel, inside is an elegant country retreat with timber frames, nooks and crannies, bowls of fruit, pretty art, vases of flowers on plinths in the sofa'd sitting room and smartly upholstered dining chairs in the airy restaurant. Bedrooms come in country-house style: white linen, big beds, moor views, the odd antique. You might find a chandelier, a large balcony or padded window seats. All come with flat-screen TVs, some have big baths stocked with lotions. Back down in the restaurant, where the mill wheel turns in the window, you find delicious food, perhaps mushroom and tarragon soup, Dartmoor lamb with fondant potato and rosemary jus, chocolate tart. Little ones have their own high tea at 6pm. In the morning there's porridge with cream and brown sugar, as well as the usual extravagance. Dogs are very welcome.

Rooms	15: 10 doubles, 2 twins, 1 family room, 2 suites.
Price	£90-£160. Suites £120-£210. Singles from £75.
Meals	Lunch from £5.50. Sunday lunch from £15.95. Dinner £21-£35.
Closed	2 weeks in January.
Directions	M5, then A30 to Whiddon Down. South on A382, through Sandy Park, over small bridge and on right.

Peter & Sue Davies
Mill End,
Chagford, Dartmoor TQ13 8JN

Tel +44 (0)1647 432282
Email info@millendhotel.com
Web www.millendhotel.com

The Lamb Inn

This 16th-century inn is nothing short of perfect, a proper local in the old tradition with gorgeous rooms and the odd touch of quirkiness to add authenticity to earthy bones. It stands on a cobbled walkway in a village lost down Devon's tiny lanes, and those lucky enough to chance upon it leave reluctantly. Outside, all manner of greenery covers its stone walls; inside there are beams, but they are not sandblasted, red carpets with a little swirl, sofas in front of an open fire and rough-hewn oak panels painted black. Boarded menus trumpet award-winning food – carrot and orange soup, whole baked trout with almond butter, an irresistible tarte tatin. There's a cobbled terrace, a walled garden, an occasional cinema, an open mic night, and a back bar where four ales are hand-pumped. Upstairs, seven marvellous bedrooms elate. One is large with a bath and a wood-burner in the room, but all are lovely with super-smart power showers, sash windows that give village views, hi-fis, flat-screen TVs, good linen and comfy beds. Dartmoor waits but you may well linger. There's Tiny, the guard dog, too.

Rooms	7: 5 doubles, 1 twin/double, 1 suite.
Price	£65-£120. Suite £170-£190.
Meals	Lunch from £9. Dinner, 3 courses, £20-£30. Sunday lunch from £8.90.
Closed	Rarely.
Directions	A377 north from Exeter. 1st right in Crediton, left, signed Sandford. 1 mile up & in village.

Mark Hildyard & Katharine Lightfoot
The Lamb Inn,
Sandford, Crediton EX17 4LW

Tel +44 (0)1363 773676
Email thelambinn@gmail.com
Web www.lambinnsandford.co.uk

The Lazy Toad Inn

This lovely little inn is humble and gracious and not like those fancy places that always want to blow their own trumpets. It's a way of life. Clive rears sheep and grows masses of food on their land behind, then Mo helps to cook it to keep the locals smiling. You're in a tiny Devon village, close to the church, where you'll find a river you can walk alongside. Back at the pub there's a cobbled courtyard, then a small lawn behind; in good weather both make a lovely spot for lunch. Inside, a warm cottage style runs throughout: painted settles, a wood-burner, the odd sofa, good art. Bedrooms above have irresistible prices and come in various shapes and sizes. You get pretty furniture, colourful throws, painted beams and Farrow & Ball colours; one has a funky bathroom. Back in the bar, find local ales, Devon wines, even homemade cordials. As for the food, some of which is foraged, well, we've left the best for last, perhaps goat cheese soufflé, shoulder of Devon lamb, home-grown rhubarb mousse. Exeter is five miles away, but it feels like a hundred. Fabulous.

Rooms	5 doubles.
Price	£80-£100. Singles from £58.
Meals	Lunch from £5.35. Bar meals from £11.50. Dinner from £14. Sunday lunch, 3 courses, £25. Not Sunday eves & Monday.
Closed	Last 3 weeks in January.
Directions	North from Exeter on A377 for Crediton. At roundabout at Cowley, take A377 for Brampford Speke. Right again after 1 mile & in village.

Mo & Clive Walker
The Lazy Toad Inn,
Brampford Speke, Exeter EX5 5DP

Tel +44 (0)1392 841591
Email thelazytoadinn@btinternet.com
Web www.thelazytoadinn.co.uk

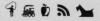

Southernhay House

A gorgeous small hotel on the loveliest square in town, a short stroll from the cathedral. The house dates to 1805 and was built for a major returning from the Raj. These days interiors sparkle, all the result of a wonderful refurbishment. It's proved hugely popular with locals – the restaurant was brimming the day we visited – and those clever enough to check in for the night find some deeply spoiling bedrooms. Downstairs, French windows at the back of the house draw you out to a small terrace. You can eat here when the sun shines, though the house is weatherproofed with a smart restaurant and a cool little bar should the rain dare to fall. Potter about and find electric blue sofas, 50s starlets framed on the wall, old style radiators and beautiful art. Delicious bedrooms wait upstairs – some are bigger, all are lovely. Expect grand colours, sumptuous fabrics, Indian art and hi-tech gadgetry. Fancy bathrooms come as standard, though bigger rooms have free-standing baths. Don't miss the food – Brown Windsor soup, Dover sole, damson gin jelly and cream. Exeter, Dartmoor and the south coast wait.

Rooms	10 doubles.
Price	£150-£240.
Meals	Lunch, 2 courses, £14.99. Dinner, 3 courses, about £30.
Closed	Never.
Directions	Sent on booking.

Deborah Clark & Tony Orchard
Southernhay House,
36 Southernhay East, Exeter EX1 1NX

Tel +44 (0)1392 439000
Email home@southernhayhouse.com
Web www.southernhayhouse.com

Magdalen Chapter

Where on earth do we start? It might be simpler to confine ourselves to a bald statement of facts to describe this contemporary wonderland. An open fire, terrazzo floors, big warm colours and the odd sofa greet you in the entrance hall. Contemporary art hangs on every wall. There's a curated library, where you can sit and flick through glossy pages; a sitting room bar with a funky fireplace and a Hugo Dalton mural; an interior courtyard with walls of glass that looks onto a gorgeous garden. The brasserie is magnificent, open to the rafters with white pods of light hanging on high and an open kitchen on display. In summer, glass doors fly open and you eat on the terrace, perhaps seafood spaghetti or a good steak. There are deckchairs on the lawn, a small kitchen garden, treatment rooms for stressed-out guests; there's even a small swimming pool that comes with a wood-burner. Bedrooms have an uncluttered, contemporary feel: iPads, flat-screen TVs, black-and-white photography, handmade furniture. Bathrooms are excellent; expect power showers, big vats of REN lotions and white bathrobes.

Rooms	59: 52 doubles, 5 singles, 2 twins/doubles.
Price	£120-£250. Singles from £105.
Meals	Lunch from £8. Dinner from £12.95; à la carte about £30.
Closed	Never.
Directions	Sent on booking.

Fiona Moores
Magdalen Chapter,
Magdalen Street,
Exeter EX2 4HY

Tel +44 (0)1392 281000
Email magdalen_ge@chapterhotels.com
Web www.chapterhotels.com

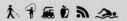

The Salutation Inn

You know you're in the right place when the best afternoon tea you've ever eaten is delivered by an opera singer who doubles as a waitress. Topsham has an arty crowd who love the river light and the reinvention of this cute old inn couldn't have come a day sooner. The front door is quite something, the biggest single-leaf wicket door in Britain. Inside, a gorgeous renovation has touched every square inch. You get the daily papers in a pretty sitting room, the Glasshouse Café for breakfast and lunch. Smart bedrooms have cool hues, snazzy bedheads, fancy bathrooms and hi-tech gadgets, but you're here for more than a bed. Tom cooks sublime stuff. He's worked with Michael Caines, Gordon Ramsay and Marcus Wareing; now he's going it alone, hoping to put Topsham on the culinary map. You eat off a tasting menu, five courses of bliss: perhaps wild mushroom soup, pan-fried brill, rump of Devon beef, a plate of local cheeses, rhubarb and custard soufflé. Take the ferry to the Turf for lunch, then walk along the estuary. Back at the hotel, there's a Graham Rich mural and lunch on Sunday is a treat.

Rooms	6: 4 doubles, 1 twin/double, 1 suite.
Price	£125-£165. Suite £180-£225. Singles from £112.50. Dinner, B&B from £75 p.p.
Meals	Lunch from £7.50. Afternoon tea from £12.50. Dinner: 5-course tasting menu £37.50; 7-course tasting menu £58. Sunday lunch from £13.50.
Closed	Never.
Directions	M5, junc. 30, then A376 south. Left for Topsham after 3 miles. Straight ahead, left for station, over level crossing and 2nd left into Fore Street. On right.

Tom Williams-Hawkes
The Salutation Inn,
68 Fore Street,
Topsham, Exeter EX3 0HL

Tel +44 (0)1392 873060
Email info@salutationtopsham.co.uk
Web www.salutationtopsham.co.uk

Combe House Devon

Combe is matchless, an ancient house on a huge estate, the full aristocratic monty. You spin up a long drive, pass the odd Arabian horse dawdling in the fields, then skip through the front door and enter a place of architectural wonder. A fire smoulders in the vast panelled hall, the muralled dining room gives huge country views, the sitting room bar in racing green opens onto the croquet lawn. Best of all is the way things are done: the feel is more home than hotel with a battalion of lovely staff on hand to attend to your every whim. Wander around and find medieval flagstones, William Morris wallpaper, Victorian kitchen gardens that provide much for the table; expect home-buzzed honey and fresh eggs from a roving band of exotic chickens. Rooms are stately with wonderful beds, stunning bathrooms and outstanding views, while the vast suite, once the laundry press, is the stuff of fashion shoots. There are 3,500 acres to explore, then ambrosial food waiting on your return, but it's Ruth and Ken who win the prize; they just know how to do it. Dogs are very welcome. *Minimum two nights at weekends.*

Rooms	15 + 2: 10 twins/doubles, 1 four-poster, 4 suites. Thatched cottage for 2 with walled garden. Thatched house for 8 with orchard.
Price	£215-£375. Suites £425-£450. Cottage £425-£450. House £720-£780.
Meals	Lunch from £9. Cream tea from £10. Dinner £54. Sunday lunch £39.
Closed	Rarely.
Directions	M5 junc. 29, then A30 to Honiton. Follow signs to Heathpark, then Gittisham. Hotel signed in village.

Ruth & Ken Hunt
Combe House Devon,
Gittisham, Honiton EX14 3AD
Tel +44 (0)1404 540400
Email stay@combehousedevon.com
Web www.combehousedevon.com

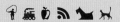

Alexandra Hotel & Restaurant

Everything here is lovely, but the view is hard to beat, a clean sweep up the Jurassic coast towards Portland Bill. The hotel overlooks Lyme Bay; the only thing between you and it is the lawn. Below, the Cobb curls into the sea, the very spot where Meryl Streep withstood the crashing waves in *The French Lieutenant's Woman*. In summer, steamer chairs pepper the garden and guests fall asleep, book in hand, under an English sun. As for the hotel, it's just as good. Kathryn, ex-Firmdale, bought it from her mother and has refurbished brilliantly. You get stripped wood floors, windows everywhere, an airy bar for pre-dinner drinks, an attractive sitting room with plenty of books. The dining room could double as a ballroom, the conservatory brasserie opens onto a terrace; both provide excellent sustenance, perhaps Lyme Bay scallops, roast rump of Devon lamb, gingerbread pudding with vanilla ice-cream. Beautiful rooms hit the spot, most have the view. Expect super beds, padded headboards, robes in lovely bathrooms. Lyme, the beach and the fossil-ridden coast all wait.

Rooms	25: 19 twins/doubles, 2 singles, 3 family rooms, 1 apartment.
Price	£177-£225. Apartment £320. Singles from £85. Dinner, B&B from £120 p.p.
Meals	Lunch from £9.90. Afternoon tea from £6.50. Dinner, 3 courses, about £35. Sunday lunch from £19.50.
Closed	Rarely.
Directions	In Lyme Regis up hill on high street; keep left at bend; on left after 200m.

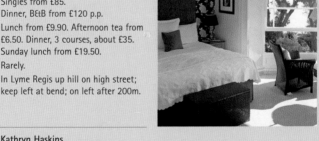

Kathryn Haskins
Alexandra Hotel & Restaurant,
Pound Street, Lyme Regis DT7 3HZ
Tel +44 (0)1297 442010
Email enquiries@hotelalexandra.co.uk
Web www.hotelalexandra.co.uk

The Abbot's House

Charmouth – epicentre of Dorset's Jurassic coast – was a model village built by the monks of Forde Abbey in medieval times. This was its principal house and Charles II slept here after his defeat at the Battle of Worcester in 1651. Inside, imperious panelling survives (along with 15th-century graffiti), as do ancient flagstones and a piece of plaster moulding now framed on a wall. Nick and Sheila have renovated in great style, their warm interiors a delightful mix of old and new. You find cross beams and regal reds in the cosy sitting room, then an airy breakfast room, where tables come with en suite sofas so you can sit with the papers after your bacon and eggs. Three lavish bedrooms are laden with luxury: period colours, beautiful fabrics, pressed linen, gorgeous bathrooms, technological excess, and freshly baked biscuits every day. Excellent local restaurants wait: Mark Hix in Lyme for the freshest fish and oysters, then the River Cottage Canteen at Axminster for lovely local fare. Back in Charmouth the beach backs onto rolling hills; it's rich with fossils, too.
Minimum two nights at weekends in high season.

Rooms	4 doubles.
Price	£120-£140.
Meals	Pub/restaurant within 200m.
Closed	Christmas & New Year.
Directions	Charmouth is 2 miles east of Lyme Regis, off A35. House on southern side of main street.

Nick & Sheila Gilbey
The Abbot's House,
The Street, Charmouth DT6 6QF
Tel +44 (0)1297 560339
Email info@abbotshouse.co.uk
Web www.abbotshouse.co.uk

The Bull Hotel

With Dorset's star firmly on the rise, it was only a matter of time before a funky hotel appeared on the radar. Step forward The Bull, a sparkling bolthole that comes in cool hues and stands on the high street in the middle of town. It's smart enough for a masked ball on New Year's Eve, and informal enough for ladies who lunch to pop in unannounced. It's a big hit with the locals and lively most days; at weekends the bar rocks. All of which makes it a lot of fun for guests passing through. Gorgeous rooms wait upstairs; French and English country elegance entwine with a touch of contemporary flair. Expect beautiful beds, pashmina throws, old radiators, perhaps an armoire. Most come in airy whites, some have striking wallpaper, maybe a claw-foot bath at the end of the bed. There are digital radios, flat-screen TVs, super little bathrooms. Back downstairs – stripped floorboards, Farrow & Ball walls, sofas in the bar, candles everywhere – dig into brasserie-style food; moules frites is on the menu every Wednesday night. Lyme Regis and Chesil Beach are close. *Minimum two nights at weekends.*

Rooms	20: 10 doubles, 1 twin, 3 four-posters, 1 single, 4 family rooms, 1 suite.
Price	£85-£200. Family rooms £170-£210. Suite £205-£265. Singles from £75.
Meals	Lunch, 2 courses, from £12. Dinner, 3 courses, around £35. Sunday lunch £19.
Closed	Never.
Directions	On main street in town. Car park at rear.

Nikki & Richard Cooper
The Bull Hotel,
34 East Street, Bridport DT6 3LF
Tel +44 (0)1308 422878
Email info@thebullhotel.co.uk
Web www.thebullhotel.co.uk

BridgeHouse Hotel

Beaminster – Emminster in Thomas Hardy's *Tess* – sits in a lush Dorset valley. From the hills above, rural England goes on show: quilted fields lead to a country town, the church tower soars towards heaven. At BridgeHouse stone flags, mullioned windows, old beams and huge inglenooks sweep you back to a graceful past. This is a comfortable hotel in a country town – intimate, friendly, quietly smart. There are rugs on parquet floors, a beamed bar in a turreted alcove, a sparkling dining room with Georgian panelling. Breakfast is served in the brasserie, where huge windows look onto the lawns, so watch the gardener potter about as you scoff your bacon and eggs. Delicious food – local and organic – is a big draw, perhaps seared scallops, Gressingham duck, champagne sorbet. And so to bed. Rooms in the main house are bigger and smarter, those in the coach house are simpler and less expensive; all are pretty with chic fabrics, crisp linen, flat-screen TVs and stylish bathrooms. There are river walks, antique shops and Dorset's Jurassic coast. *Minimum stay two nights at weekends.*

Rooms	13: 6 twins/doubles, 2 four-posters, 1 single. Coach House: 3 doubles, 1 family room.
Price	£125-£220. Singles from £95.
Meals	Lunch from £12.50. Dinner à la carte £15-£40.
Closed	Never.
Directions	From Yeovil A30 west; A3066 for Bridport to Beaminster. Hotel at far end of town as road bends to right.

Mark & Jo Donovan
BridgeHouse Hotel,
3 Prout Bridge,
Beaminster DT8 3AY

Tel	+44 (0)1308 862200
Email	enquiries@bridge-house.co.uk
Web	www.bridge-house.co.uk

The Greyhound Inn

It's hard to fault this fabulous inn. It sits in one of Dorset's loveliest villages, lost in a lush valley with big views that shoot uphill. Outside, roses, clematis and lavender add the colour; inside rustic interiors have a warm traditional feel. You find stone walls, old flagstones, gilt mirrors and a wood-burner to keep things cosy. There's a lively locals' bar where you can grab a pint of Butcombe and sink into a Chesterfield, then a lovely little restaurant with old beams and curios, where you dig into delicious food. The feel here is delightfully relaxed and you can eat wherever you want, so spin onto the terrace in good weather and feast on local food, perhaps clam chowder, venison Wellington, almond tart with vanilla ice-cream. Six lovely rooms wait in an old skittle alley. They're not huge, but nor is their price, and what they lack in space, they make up for in comfort and style with fluffy duvets, crisp white linen, iPod docks and painted beams. Not that you'll linger, you'll be too busy having fun in the pub. The Cerne Abbas giant is close, the walking exceptional.

Rooms	6 doubles.
Price	£90-£100. Singles from £80.
Meals	Lunch from £5.50. Dinner, 3 courses, about £30 (not Sunday evening).
Closed	Never.
Directions	South from Sherborne on A352. In Cerne Abbas right for Sydling. Left at ford for village.

Alex Bould
The Greyhound Inn,
26 High Street, Sydling St Nicholas,
Dorchester DT2 9PD

Tel +44 (0)1300 341303
Email info@dorsetgreyhound.co.uk
Web www.dorsetgreyhound.co.uk

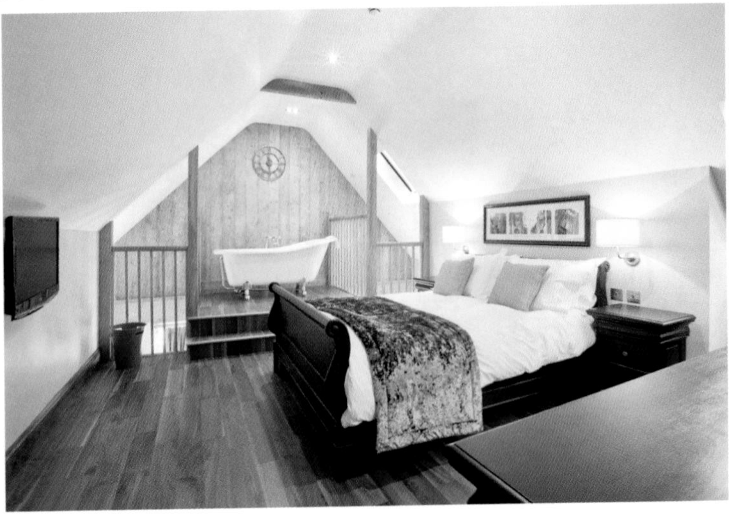

The New Inn Cerne Abbas

The New Inn is most certainly new; it may date to the 16th century, but Jeremy has recently spent the best part of a year refurbishing the place and now it shines. Gone are the swirly green carpets; local slate has been laid in the bar. Lots of lovely old stuff remains – timber frames, mullioned windows, the odd settle – but the feel is fresh with warm colours, engineered oak floors and a smart new bar where you can order a pint of Dorset Gold or a glass of good wine. An open-plan feel runs throughout and you dig into local food wherever you want, perhaps fish from Brixham, local game, sticky toffee pudding. Bedrooms – some in the main house, others in the old stables – are good value for money. You'll find Hypnos mattresses, blond wood furniture and super little bathrooms. Those in the converted stables feel more contemporary: ground-floor rooms open onto the terrace, where you eat in good weather; those above are built into the eaves. The suites come with double-ended baths in the room. Don't miss the Cerne Abbas Giant. *Minimum stay two nights at weekends.*

Rooms	12: 7 doubles, 2 suites, 3 twins/doubles.
Price	£95-£140. Suites £160-£170. Singles from £75.
Meals	Lunch & dinner £5-£35.
Closed	Christmas Day.
Directions	Village just off A352 between Dorchester & Sherborne.

Jeremy & Vanessa Lee
The New Inn Cerne Abbas,
14 Long Street,
Cerne Abbas DT2 7JF

Tel +44 (0)1300 341274
Email info@thenewinncerneabbas.co.uk
Web www.thenewinncerneabbas.co.uk

Plumber Manor

A grand old country house that sits in a couple of acres of green and pleasant land with the river Develish running through. It dates from 1650, with mullioned windows, huge stone flags and a fine terrace for afternoon tea. An avenue of horse chestnuts takes you to the front door. Inside, a pair of labradors rule the roost. Expect no designer trends – Plumber is old-school, defiantly so. Take the first-floor landing with its enormous sofa, gallery of family oils and grand piano thrown in for good measure. Bedrooms are split between the main house and converted barns. The latter tend to be bigger and are good for those with dogs. Décor is dated – 1980s florals – as are most bathrooms, though a couple now sparkle in travertine splendour. The family triumvirate of Brian (in the kitchen), Richard (behind the bar) and Alison (simply everywhere) excel in the art of old-fashioned hospitality. Delicious country food waits in the restaurant, try seared scallops with pea purée, rack of lamb with rosemary and garlic, lemon meringue pie. Bulbarrow Hill is close.

Rooms	17: 2 doubles, 14 twins/doubles, all en suite. 1 twin/double with separate bath.
Price	£150-£230. Singles from £115.
Meals	Sunday lunch £29.50. Dinner, 2 courses, £29; 3 courses, £36.
Closed	February.
Directions	West from Sturminster Newton on A357. Across traffic lights, up hill & left for Hazelbury Bryan. Follow brown tourism signs. Hotel signed left after 2 miles.

Richard, Alison & Brian Prideaux-Brune
Plumber Manor,
Plumber,
Sturminster Newton DT10 2AF

Tel	+44 (0)1258 472507
Email	book@plumbermanor.com
Web	www.plumbermanor.com

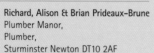

Stapleton Arms

A perfect village inn: loads of style, lovely staff, super food, excellent prices. The Stapleton started life as a Georgian home, becoming an inn after the war. These days, warm, hip interiors carry a streak of country glamour. Downstairs, amid the happy vibe, find sofas in front of the fire, a piano for live music, a restaurant with shuttered windows and candles in the fireplace. You can eat whatever you want, wherever you want; delicious pork pies wait at the bar, but it's hard to resist a three-course feast, perhaps Welsh rarebit with sautéed field mushrooms, Beef Wellington with horseradish mash, Mississippi mud pie. There's a beer menu to beat all others (ale matters here) and on Sundays groups can order their own joint of meat; there's always a menu for kids, too. Super rooms are soundproofed to ensure a good night's sleep. All have beautiful linen, fresh flowers, happy colours, fantastic showers. With maps and wellies if you want to walk, a DVD library for all ages, and a playground for kids in the garden. Wincanton is close for the races. One of the best.

Rooms	4 doubles.
Price	£80-£120. Singles from £72.
Meals	Lunch & bar meals from £7. Dinner, 3 courses, about £30.
Closed	Rarely.
Directions	A303 to Wincanton. Into town right after fire station, signed Buckhorn Weston. Left at T-junction after 3 miles. In village, pub on right.

Rupert & Victoria Reeves
Stapleton Arms,
Church Hill, Buckhorn Weston,
Gillingham SP8 5HS

Tel	+44 (0)1963 370396
Email	relax@thestapletonarms.com
Web	www.thestapletonarms.com

Castleman Hotel & Restaurant

It's a little like stepping into the pages of a Hardy novel: an untouched corner of idyllic Dorset, a 400-year-old bailiff's house, sheep grazing in lush fields and a rich cast of characters. The Castleman – a country-house, part restaurant with rooms – is a true one-off: quirky, intimate, defiantly English. It pays no heed to prevailing fashions, not least because the locals would revolt if it did. Barbara runs the place with relaxed informality, though touches of grandeur are hard to miss: a panelled hall, art from Chettle House, a magnificent Jacobean ceiling in one of the sitting rooms. Potter about and find a cosy bar, fresh flowers everywhere, books galore. The restaurant has garden views though your eyes will attend only to Barbara's deliciously old-fashioned English food, perhaps potted shrimp terrine, haunch of local venison, meringues with chocolate mousse and toasted almonds. Smart homely bedrooms fit the bill: eminently comfortable, delightfully priced; a couple have claw-foot baths. Magical Dorset will fill your days with splendour.

Rooms	8: 5 doubles, 1 twin, 1 twin/double, 1 family room.
Price	£90-£105.
Meals	Sunday lunch £24. Dinner, 3 courses, about £27.
Closed	February.
Directions	A354 north from Blandford Forum. 3rd left (about 4 miles up) and on left in village.

Barbara Garnsworthy
Castleman Hotel & Restaurant,
Chettle,
Blanford Forum DT11 8DB

Tel +44 (0)1258 830096
Email enquiry@castlemanhotel.co.uk
Web www.castlemanhotel.co.uk

The King John Inn

You're on the Dorset/Wiltshire border, lost in blissful country, with paths that lead up into glorious hills. Tumble back down to this super inn. Alex and Gretchen have refurbished every square inch and the place shines. Expect airy interiors, a smart country feel, a sun-trapping terrace and a fire that crackles in winter. Originally a foundry, it opened as a brewery in 1859, and, when beer proved more popular than horseshoes, the inn was born. You'll find three local ales on tap but great wines, too – Alex loves the stuff and has opened his own shop across the courtyard – take home a bottle if you like what you drink. As for the food, it's as local as can be with game straight off the Rushmore estate and meat from over the hill; the sausages are a thing of rare beauty. Country-house bedrooms are the final treat. Some are bigger than others, three are in the Coach House, all come with wonderful fabrics, padded headboards, crisp white linen and super bathrooms (one has a slipper bath). In summer, a terraced lawn gives views over a couple of rooftops onto the woods. A perfect spot.

Rooms	8: 6 doubles, 2 twins/doubles.
Price	£120-£170.
Meals	Lunch from £12.95. Bar meals from £8.95. Dinner from £13.95.
Closed	Rarely.
Directions	South from Salisbury on A354, then right onto B3081 at roundabout after 8 miles. In village on right.

Alex & Gretchen Boon
The King John Inn,
Tollard Royal,
Salisbury SP5 5PS

Tel	+44 (0)1725 516207
Email	info@kingjohninn.co.uk
Web	www.kingjohninn.co.uk

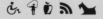

La Fosse at Cranborne

Cranborne was home to Robert Cecil, Earl of Salisbury, the Tudor spymaster who moved King James onto the throne when Elizabeth died in 1603. Under his patronage the village grew into a market town with a garrison to protect a plentiful supply of royal visitors; these days the village has returned to its sleepy roots and is all the better for it. Mark and Emmanuelle arrived three years ago, he to cook, she to polish and shine. It's a small affair, a restaurant with rooms that has resisted the urge for all-out contemporary design. Instead, you find something more homespun: a bar that doubles as reception; sofas in front of a wood-burner; travel books to sweep you away; maps galore for glorious walking. Bedrooms upstairs, recently refurbished, have a super style: warm yellows, pretty fabrics, comfy beds and crisp white linen, smart little bathrooms with underfloor heating. Best of all is the restaurant for Mark's rustic cooking: game terrine, roast shoulder of veal, Capricorn goat cheese with plum compote. Spin west a few miles to Hambledon Hill (a prehistoric hill fort) for huge country views. *Private house party hire and private lunch parties (8-25 persons) available.*

Rooms	6: 3 doubles, 2 twins/doubles, 1 suite.
Price	£65-£95. Suite £115. Singles from £56.
Meals	Dinner (not Sunday) £27.50.
Closed	Never.
Directions	A338 to Fordingbridge, then B3078 into Cranborne. Right at village shop and on right.

Emmanuelle & Mark Hartstone
La Fosse at Cranborne,
The Square, Cranborne,
Wimborne BH21 5PR
Tel +44 (0)1725 517604
Email lafossemail@gmail.com
Web www.la-fosse.com

Bishops Cottage

A homespun restaurant with rooms on the side of a hill above Lulworth Cove. The house was once home to the Bishop of Salisbury, Wordsworth's grandson. Outside: a swimming pool in the garden where you can soak up the sun while watching walkers pour off the hill. Inside: smart interiors have low beamed ceilings, painted wood floors, Farrow & Ball colours and a couple of sofas in front of the fire. Philip, larger than life, studied art at Goldsmiths and his work appears on a wall or two; he also made the bar from a hatch recovered from a military vessel sunk by a U-boat. Three lovely bedrooms wait upstairs: one has the view, the others have sofas in sitting rooms, then big comfy beds and lovely bathrooms. You get toppers, bathrobes, duck down duvets – Liesl's determination to pamper you rotten is unstinting. Outside, the coastal path weaves past one sandy cove after another, a rollercoaster ride through this magnificent World Heritage landscape. Come back for lovely food, perhaps seared scallops, wild sea bass, chocolate tart with vanilla ice-cream. *Minimum two nights at weekends.*

Rooms	3: 2 doubles, 1 twin/double.
Price	£120-£150. Singles from £110.
Meals	Lunch from £6.50. Dinner, 3 courses, £25-£30.
Closed	November to mid-March.
Directions	West from Wareham on A352, right for Lulworth on B3070. Last house on left before sea.

Liesl & Phillip Ashby Rudd
Bishops Cottage,
West Lulworth, Wareham BH20 5RQ

Tel	+44 (0)1929 400552
Email	bishopscottagelulworth@gmail.com
Web	www.bishopscottage.co.uk

The Priory Hotel

The lawns of this 16th-century priory run down to the river Frome. Boats float past, an old church rises behind, a gorgeous garden wraps around you filled with colour. As for this lovely country house, you'll find a grand piano in the drawing room, a first-floor sitting room with garden views, and a stone-vaulted dining room in the old cellar. Best of all is the terrace, where you can sit in the sun and watch the river pass – a perfect spot for lunch in summer. Bedrooms in the main house come in different sizes, some cosy in the eaves, others grandly adorned in reds and golds. You get Zoffany fabrics, padded window seats, bowls of fruit, the odd sofa. Eight have river views, others look onto the garden or church. Chic bathrooms – some dazzlingly contemporary – all come with white robes. Rooms in the boathouse, a 16th-century clay barn, are lavish, with oak panelling, stone walls and sublime views. Outside, climbing roses, a duck pond, then banks of daffs and snowdrops. Corfe Castle and Studland Bay are close. A slice of old England with delicious food to boot.
Minimum two nights at weekends. Over 14s welcome.

Rooms	18: 13 twins/doubles, 5 suites.
Price	£210-£305. Suites £340-£370. Dinner, B&B (obligatory at weekends) from £122.50 p.p. (min. two nights).
Meals	Lunch from £14.95. Dinner £45.
Closed	Never.
Directions	West from Poole on A35, then A351 for Wareham and B3075 into town. Through lights, 1st left, right out of square, then keep left. Entrance on left beyond church.

Jeremy Merchant
The Priory Hotel,
Church Green, Wareham BH20 4ND
Tel +44 (0)1929 551666
Email reservations@theprioryhotel.co.uk
Web www.theprioryhotel.co.uk

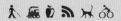

The Green House Hotel

Two streets up from the sea, a handsome Edwardian mansion that harks back to Bournemouth's Belle Epoque. Inside, zippy 21st-century interiors are as green as can be: pure lambswool carpets come from the Isle of Bute, eco beds were specially commissioned from Hypnos, solar panels provide all the hot water. Follow your nose and find cubist seats, a sitting room bar and delicate Farrow & Ball wallpapers. The restaurant, with its fine Art Deco bay window, serves great food from local farms, forests and waters, perhaps Dorset hedgerow garlic and pea soup, Poole Bay hake with tarragon gnocchi, apple soufflé with iced Granny Smith parfait, all of which you can wash down with English wines. Contemporary bedrooms in grey, plum and chocolate have goose down duvets, iPod docks and luxurious stone shower rooms; five rooms have roll top baths centre stage, and zany lime and charcoal wallpaper. Laid-back staff are non-preachy, the restaurant and bar are open every day, and the location couldn't be better – you're a short stroll from Bournemouth's sandy beach for swimming, sailing, golf and gardens. *Minimum two nights at weekends in high season.*

Rooms	32 doubles.
Price	£99-£240.
Meals	Lunch from £9.99. Dinner, 3 courses, about £30. Afternoon tea £18.50.
Closed	Never.
Directions	Sent on booking,

Olivia O'Sullivan
The Green House Hotel,
4 Grove Road,
Bournemouth BH1 3AX
Tel +44 (0)1202 498900
Email reservations@thegreenhousehotel.com
Web www.thegreenhousehotel.co.uk

Urban Beach Hotel

Urban Beach operates to different rules. The spirit here is infectious: very friendly with buckets of style – surfer chic in Bournemouth with seven miles of sandy beach waiting at the end of the road. When Mark and Fiona bought the place, they knocked down lots of walls to create one big room downstairs. The bar/restaurant is the now hub of the house. Surf movies play on the walls, you get the odd decorative surf board, big circular leather booths, driftwood lamps and a house guitar. In summer, doors open onto a decked terrace for cocktails, fresh fruit smoothies and barbecues in the sun. Lovely bedrooms, some big, some smaller, are all fitted to the same spec: flat-screen TVs, crushed velvet curtains, wonderful bathrooms. Drop down for a good breakfast: freshly-squeezed orange juice, warm croissants, the full cooked works. A brasserie-style menu runs all day – clam chowder, Dorset lamb, wine-poached pears; alternatively, decamp to Urban Reef (their other place) for big sea views. Follow the sea west into Bournemouth town centre. Brilliant. *Minimum two nights at weekends (three nights on bank holidays).*

Rooms	12: 9 doubles, 1 twin/double, 2 singles.
Price	£97-£180. Singles from £72.
Meals	Lunch & dinner £5-£25.
Closed	Never.
Directions	South from Ringwood on A338; left for Boscombe (east of centre). Over railway, right onto Centenary Way. Keep with the flow (left, then right) to join Christchurch Rd; 2nd left (St John's Rd); 2nd left.

Mark & Fiona Cribb
Urban Beach Hotel,
23 Argyll Road,
Bournemouth BH5 1EB

Tel +44 (0)1202 301509
Email reception@urbanbeach.co.uk
Web www.urbanbeach.co.uk

Captain's Club Hotel and Spa

A sparkling hotel on the banks on the Stour, where a tiny ferry potters along the river dodging swans and ducks. The hotel has its own launch and those who want to skim across to the Isle of Wight can do so in style. Back on dry land, locals love the big bar which hums with happy chatter, and they sink into sofas, sip cocktails or dig into a crab sandwich. There's live music on Sunday nights, newspapers at reception and doors that open onto a pretty terrace, perfect in good weather. Bedrooms all have river views and come in an uncluttered contemporary style, with low-slung beds, crisp white linen, neutral colours and excellent bathrooms. None are small, some are huge with separate sitting rooms, while apartments have more than one bedroom, thus perfect for families and friends. Residents have free access to the spa (hydrotherapy pool, sauna, four treatment rooms). Dinner is in an ultra-airy restaurant, where you dig into tasty brasserie-style food, perhaps goat cheese soufflé, Gressingham duck, pear mousse with Kir royale sorbet. Christchurch is a short walk upstream. *Minimum two nights at weekends.*

Rooms	29: 17 doubles, 12 apartments for 2-6.
Price	£199-£259. Apartments £289-£649.
Meals	Bar meals all day from £6. Lunch from £15. Dinner £30-£35.
Closed	Never.
Directions	M27/A31 west, then A338/B3073 south into Christchurch. At A35 (lights at big r'bout) follow one-way system left. Double back after 100m. Cross r'about heading west and 1st left into Sopers Lane. Signed left.

Timothy Lloyd & Robert Wilson
Captain's Club Hotel and Spa,
Wick Ferry, Wick Lane,
Christchurch BH23 1HU

Tel +44 (0)1202 475111
Email reservations@captainsclubhotel.com
Web www.captainsclubhotel.com

Rose & Crown

A charming northern refuge, beautiful inside and out. It stands in an idyllic village of mellow stone where little has changed in 200 years. The inn, on the green next to a Saxon church, dates to 1733. Roses ramble above the door in summer, so pick up a pint, sit in the sun and watch life pass by. In the tiny locals' bar, you can roast away in front of the fire while reading the *Teesdale Mercury*. Elsewhere, there's a panelled dining room, a peaceful sitting room and an informal brasserie if you don't want a three course feast. Bedrooms are split between the converted barn (large and colourful, but less character) and the main house (smarter altogether with the odd beam or wonky floor). All have Bose radios, good bathrooms, DVD players and free WiFi. A lovely cottage next door is available by the week, but also splits into two smart suites. Delicious food waits – fish pie or a good steak in the brasserie, smoked salmon, sea bream and chocolate tart in the restaurant. High Force waterfall and the Bowes Museum are close and there's a drying room for walkers. *Dinner, B&B only on Saturdays.*

Rooms	14 + 1: 7 doubles, 3 twins, 4 suites. Self-catering cottage for 6.
Price	£150-£190. Suites £210-£225. Singles from £95. Dinner, B&B from £79.50 p.p. Cottage £500-£800 p.w.
Meals	Lunch from £6.50. Dinner in bistro from £12; 4 courses in restaurant £35. Sunday lunch £19.50.
Closed	23-27 December; one week in January.
Directions	From Barnard Castle B6277 north for 6 miles. Right in village towards green. Inn on left.

Thomas & Cheryl Robinson
Rose & Crown,
Romaldkirk,
Barnard Castle DL12 9EB

Tel +44 (0)1833 650213
Email hotel@rose-and-crown.co.uk
Web www.rose-and-crown.co.uk

Maison Talbooth

An outdoor swimming pool that's heated to 29°C every day, a chauffeur on hand to whisk you down to the hotel's riverside restaurant, a grand piano in the golden sitting room where those in the know gather for a legendary afternoon tea. They don't do things by halves at Maison Talbooth, a small-scale pleasure dome with long views across Constable country. The house, an old rectory, stands in three acres of manicured grounds, the fabulous pool house a huge draw with its open fire, honesty bar, beautiful art and treatment rooms. Interiors are equally alluring. There are no rooms, only suites, each divine. Some on the ground floor have doors onto terraces where hot tubs wait, but all pamper you rotten with flawless bathrooms, fabulous beds, vintage wallpapers, hi-tech excess. At dinner you're chauffeured to the family's restaurants (both within half a mile): Milsoms for bistro food served informally, Le Talbooth for more serious fare, perhaps roasted scallops with a Sauternes velouté, fillet of halibut with walnuts and apple, banoffee soufflé with caramelised banana crumble. A great escape.

Rooms	12 suites.
Price	£210-£420. Singles from £170.
Meals	Dinner at Milsoms £25; at Le Talbooth £35-£50.
Closed	Never.
Directions	North on A12 past Colchester. Left to Dedham, right after S bend. Maison Talbooth is on right; follow brown signs.

Paul & Geraldine Milsom
Maison Talbooth,
Stratford Road, Dedham,
Colchester CO7 6HN

Tel	+44 (0)1255 241212
Email	maison@milsomhotels.com
Web	www.milsomhotels.com

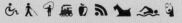

The Sun Inn

An idyllic village made rich by mills in the 16th century. These days you can hire boats on the river, so order a picnic at the inn, float down the glorious Stour, then tie up on the bank for lunch al fresco. You're in the epicentre of Constable country; the artist attended school in the village and often returned to paint St Mary's with its soaring tower; it stands directly opposite. As for The Sun, you couldn't hope to wash up in a better place. Step in to find open fires, boarded floors, timber frames and an easy elegance. A panelled lounge comes with sofas and armchairs, the bar is made from a slab of local elm and the dining room is beamed and airy, so come for fabulous food inspired by Italy: Calabrian salami, pheasant ravioli, spaghetti with chilli and lemon, venison stew with red wine and shallots. Rooms are gorgeous: creaking floorboards, timber-framed walls, a panelled four-poster. Those at the back (a recent addition) are bigger and come in grand style, but all are lovely with crisp linen and power showers in excellent bathrooms. There's afternoon tea on arrival if you book in advance.

Rooms	7: 6 doubles, 1 twin/double.
Price	£75-£150. Singles from £80.
Meals	Lunch & dinner from £12. Bar meals from £6.85. Sunday lunch £24.
Closed	25-26 December.
Directions	A12 north past Colchester. 2nd exit, signed Dedham. In village opposite church.

Piers Baker
The Sun Inn,
High Street, Dedham,
Colchester CO7 6DF

Tel +44 (0)1206 323351
Email office@thesuninndedham.com
Web www.thesuninndedham.com

The Mistley Thorn

This Georgian pub stands on the high street and dates back to 1746, but inside you find a fresh contemporary feel that will tickle your pleasure receptors. The mood is laid-back with a great little bar, an excellent restaurant and bedrooms that pack an understated punch. Downstairs, an open-plan feel sweeps you through high-ceilinged rooms that flood with light. Expect tongue-and-groove panelling, Farrow & Ball colours, blond wood furniture and smart wicker chairs. Climb up to excellent rooms for smartly dressed beds, flat-screen TVs, DVD players and iPod docks; you get power showers above double-ended baths too. Those at the front have fine views of the Stour estuary, all are exceptional value for money. Back down in the restaurant dig into delicious food; Sherri runs a cookery school next door and has a pizzeria in town. Try smoked haddock chowder, Debden duck with clementine sauce, chocolate mocha tart. Constable country is all around. There's history, too; the Witch-Finder General once lived here. Sunday nights are a steal: £100 for two with dinner included. Brilliant.

Rooms	9: 6 doubles, 3 twins/doubles.
Price	£90-£120. Singles from £75.
Meals	Lunch from £6.25. Set lunch £12.50 & £15. Dinner, 3 courses, about £25.
Closed	Rarely.
Directions	From A12 Hadleigh/East Bergholt exit north of Colchester. Thro' East Bergholt to A137; signed Manningtree; continue to Mistley High St. 50m from station.

David McKay & Sherri Singleton
The Mistley Thorn,
High Street, Mistley,
Manningtree CO11 1HE

Tel +44 (0)1206 392821
Email info@mistleythorn.co.uk
Web www.mistleythorn.co.uk

The Pier at Harwich

You're bang on the water, overlooking the historic Ha'penny Pier, with vast skies and watery views that shoot across to Felixstowe. The hotel was built in 1862 in the style of a Venetian palazzo and has remained in continuous service ever since. Inside are boarded floors, big arched windows, a granite bar and travel posters framed on the walls. Eat informally in the bistro downstairs (fish pie, grilled bream, beef stew and dumplings) or grab a window seat in the first-floor dining room and tuck into lobster bisque while huge ferries glide past outside. The owners took over the adjoining pub several years ago and have carved out a pretty lounge with port-hole windows, leather sofas, coir matting, timber frames, even a piano. Bedrooms are scattered about, some above the sitting room, others in the main house. All are pretty, with padded bedheads, seaside colours, crisp white linen, super bathrooms; if you want the best view in town, splash out on the Mayflower suite. Don't miss the blue flag beach at Dovercourt for exhilarating walks, or the Electric Palace, the second oldest cinema in Britain.

Rooms	14: 13 twins/doubles, 1 suite.
Price	£117-£215. Suite £190. Singles from £92.
Meals	2 course lunch from £20. Sunday lunch £29. Dinner à la carte £25-£40.
Closed	Never.
Directions	M25 junc. 28, A12 to Colchester bypass, then A120 to Harwich. Head for quay. Hotel opposite pier.

Paul & Geraldine Milsom
The Pier at Harwich,
The Quay, Harwich CO12 3HH

Tel +44 (0)1255 241212
Email pier@milsomhotels.com
Web www.milsomhotels.com

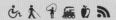

Tudor Farmhouse Hotel

This gorgeous small hotel sits on the edge of the Forest of Dean, a magical world of woodland walks, medieval castles, meandering rivers and bleating sheep. You're in the middle of a tiny village with lush views from a pretty garden – stone walls, postage-stamp lawn, a couple of cottages forming a courtyard. Inside, an airy elegance mixes with exposed stone walls and original timber frames, the house bearing testament to its Tudor roots. Bedrooms are lovely, some smaller, others huge, but all have smart fabrics, robes in fine bathrooms and super-comfy beds. They are scattered about, a few in the main house, others with exposed stone walls in pretty outbuildings; the loft suite is exceptional and comes with a claw-foot bath and an enormous glass shower. But it's not just style, there's plenty of substance, with fabulous food in the chic little restaurant, perhaps smoked salmon mousse, rare-breed beef, treacle tart with stout ice-cream. There are home-laid eggs for breakfast, too. Don't miss Puzzle Wood or Clearwell Caves. You can kayak on the Wye or join a guide and forage in the forest.

Rooms	21: 14 doubles, 3 twins, 2 four-posters, 2 suites.
Price	£95-£170. Suites £190-£210. Singles from £85.
Meals	Lunch from £6.95. Sunday lunch from £14.50. Dinner, 3 courses, £30-£40.
Closed	2-9 January.
Directions	South from Monmouth on A466. Clearwell signed left after 3 miles.

Colin & Hari Fell
Tudor Farmhouse Hotel,
High Street, Clearwell GL16 8JS

Tel +44 (0)1594 833046
Email info@tudorfarmhousehotel.co.uk
Web www.tudorfarmhousehotel.co.uk

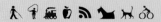

Three Choirs Vineyards

England's answer to the Napa Valley. After 15 years of tilling the soil (very sandy, good drainage), Thomas's 75 acres of Gloucestershire hillside now produce 300,000 bottles a year. There are regular tastings, a shop in which to buy a bottle or two, and paths that weave through the vines – a perfect stroll after a good meal. What's more, three fabulous lodges wait down by the lake, all with decks and walls of glass. You'll find claw-foot baths and comfy beds, so camp out in grand savannah style and listen to the woodpeckers. Rooms up at the restaurant are smart and spacious with terraces that overlook the vineyard. They come with padded bedheads, walls of colour, leather armchairs, flat-screen TVs and good little bathrooms. Finally, the restaurant: claret walls, an open fire, lovely views. Excellent food waits, perhaps goat cheese soufflé with beetroot crisps, spiced monkfish with mango purée, sticky toffee pudding with cinnamon ice-cream. World wines are on the list, but you'll plump for something from the vines that surround you; there's a microbrewery, too. Wonderful. *Minimum two nights at weekends.*

Rooms	11: 9 doubles, 2 twins.
Price	£135-£195. Singles from £105. Dinner, B&B from £105 p.p. (min. 2 nights).
Meals	Lunch from £7.50. Dinner à la carte about £35.
Closed	Christmas & New Year.
Directions	From Newent north on B4215 for about 1.5 miles. Follow brown signs to vineyard.

Thomas Shaw
Three Choirs Vineyards,
Castle Tump, Newent GL18 1LS

Tel +44 (0)1531 890223
Email info@threechoirs.com
Web www.three-choirs-vineyards.co.uk

Beaumont House

Fan and Alan have lived all over the world and came back to England to open the sort of hotel they like to stay in themselves. It's a very friendly place, nothing is too much trouble. Add a few luxuries into the mix – stylish bedrooms, excellent breakfasts, an honesty bar in the airy sitting room – and you have a great base for all things Cheltenham. Spotless bedrooms come over three floors. Some are simpler, others more extravagant, but all have lovely bathrooms and every budget will be happy here. Compact, airy doubles on the lower ground floor are perfect for short stays. Rooms above are bigger, some with striking design. One has an African theme, another has far-eastern wood carvings, you find vast headboards, smart furniture and flat-screen TVs. You breakfast in an elegant dining room, perhaps freshly made porridge, American pancakes, smoked haddock, the full cooked works. Good restaurants wait in town (you get live jazz at Daffodil's on Monday nights). As for Cheltenham, it has festivals coming out of its ears: folk, jazz, food, science, music, literature and horses. Brilliant. *Sofabed available.*

Rooms	16: 9 doubles, 2 twins/doubles, 2 singles, 1 family room, 2 suites.
Price	£89-£190. Suites £165-£249. Singles from £69.
Meals	Restaurants within walking distance. Room service Monday-Thursday eves.
Closed	Rarely.
Directions	Leave one-way system in centre of town for Stroud (south) on A46. Straight ahead, through lights and right at 1st mini-roundabout. On left after 500m.

Alan & Fan Bishop
Beaumont House,
56 Shurdington Road,
Cheltenham GL53 OJE

Tel	+44 (0)1242 223311
Email	reservations@bhhotel.co.uk
Web	www.bhhotel.co.uk

The Montpellier Chapter

The Montpellier Chapter offers what lots of us want: loads of style, attractive prices, excellent service from staff who care. It mixes old-fashioned hospitality (you are met in reception and shown to your room) with new technology (you browse the wine list on an iPad). More than anything else, it's a great place to be as it fills with happy locals who bring an infectious buzz. Follow your nose and find a library bar, a Victorian conservatory and a funky interior courtyard for breakfast in good weather. The style is contemporary, the building is a grand Victorian townhouse that's been meticulously restored. Bedrooms – some big, others smaller – spoil you all the way with super-comfy beds, an excess of technology and bathrooms that take your breath away. You get iPods full of local info, Nespresso coffee machines, even a complimentary mini-bar. Excellent comfort food waits in the restaurant, perhaps scallops cooked with garlic and herbs, Shepherd's pie with swede mash, tarte tatin with crème chantilly. And there's an electric car to whisk you around town.

Rooms	61: 55 doubles, 5 twins/doubles, 1 suite.
Price	£140-£245. Suite £400.
Meals	Bar lunch from £7. Restaurant lunch & dinner £12.50-£15. À la carte from £25.
Closed	Never.
Directions	Leave one-way system to the west, joining St George's Road, signed M5 north. Second left and hotel on right at top.

Barry Watson
The Montpellier Chapter,
Bayshill Road, Montpellier,
Cheltenham GL50 3AS

Tel +44 (0)1242 527788
Email vickyprice@chapterhotels.com
Web www.chapterhotels.com

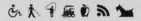

The Wheatsheaf

The Wheatsheaf stands at the vanguard of a cool new movement: the village local reborn in country-house style. It's a winning formula with locals and travellers flocking in for a heady mix of laid-back informality and chic English style. The inn stands between pretty hills in this ancient wool village on the Fosse Way. Inside, happy young staff flit about, throwing logs on the fire, ferrying food to diners, or simply stopping for a chat. Downstairs, you find armchairs in front of smouldering fires, noble portraits on panelled walls, cool tunes playing in the background. Outside, a smart courtyard garden draws a crowd in summer, so much so it has its own bar; English ales, jugs of Pimms and lovely wines all wait. Back inside, beautiful bedrooms come as standard, some bigger than others, all fully loaded with comfort and style. Expect period colours, Hypnos beds, Bang & Olufsen TVs, then spectacular bathrooms with beautiful baths and/or power showers. As for the food, you feast on lovely local fare, perhaps devilled kidneys, coq au vin, pear and almond tart. Don't miss it.

Rooms	14 doubles.
Price	£130-£200. Extra bed £25 child, £50 adult.
Meals	Continental breakfast included; cooked extras £5-£12. Lunch from £9. Dinner, 3 courses, about £30.
Closed	Never.
Directions	In village centre, off A429 between Stow & Burford.

Sam & Georgina Pearman
The Wheatsheaf,
West End, Northleach,
Cheltenham GL54 3EZ

Tel	+44 (0)1451 860244
Email	reservations@cotswoldswheatsheaf.com
Web	www.cotswoldswheatsheaf.com

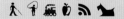

Wesley House Restaurant

A 15th-century timber-framed house on Winchcombe's ancient high street; John Wesley stayed in 1755, hence the name. Not satisfied with one excellent restaurant, Matthew has opened another next door. The elder statesman comes in traditional style with sofas in front of a roaring fire, candles flickering on smartly dressed tables and a conservatory for delicious breakfasts with views of town and country. Next door, the young upstart is unashamedly contemporary with a smoked-glass bar, faux zebra-skinned stools and hidden alcoves. Both buildings shine with original architecture: timber frames, beamed ceilings, stone flags and stripped boards. Quirky bedrooms up in the eaves tend to be cosy, one has a balcony with views over rooftops to field and hill. All come in a warm country style with good beds, pretty fabrics, small showers, smart carpets and wonky floors. Back downstairs, dig into food as simple or rich as you want, anything from fishcakes or a good burger to a three-course feast. The Cotswolds Way skirts the town, so bring your walking boots.

Rooms	5: 3 doubles, 1 twin, 1 twin/double.
Price	£90-£100. Singles from £65. Dinner, B&B (obligatory Sat) from £92.50 p.p.
Meals	Bar & grill: lunch & dinner from £9.50 (Not Sun or Mon). Restaurant: lunch from £14.50, dinner £20-£25 or £39.50 on Sat. Not Sun nights (except B&B).
Closed	Boxing Day.
Directions	From Cheltenham B4632 to Winchcombe. Restaurant on right. Drop off luggage, parking nearby.

Matthew Brown
Wesley House Restaurant,
High Street, Winchcombe,
Cheltenham GL54 5LJ

Tel +44 (0)1242 602366
Email enquiries@wesleyhouse.co.uk
Web www.wesleyhouse.co.uk

Horse & Groom

A happy pub informally run with lovely food, stylish interiors and wines and beers for all. It stands at the top of the hill with views on one side that pour over the Cotswolds. Inside, stripped floors, open fires and the odd stone wall give a smart rustic feel. Outside you can sit under the shade of damson trees and watch chefs gather eggs from the coop or carrots from the kitchen garden. Uncluttered bedrooms are nicely plush and come in contemporary country-house style with beautiful linen, pretty art, a padded window seat or two. One room is huge, the garden room opens onto the terrace, and those at the front are soundproofed to minimise noise from the road. This is a hive of youthful endeavour with two brothers at the helm. Will cooks, Tom pours the ales (or Cotswold vodka), and a cheery conviviality flows. Delicious food waits. Most is sourced within thirty miles and it's much prized by canny locals, so come for fish soup, pork and chorizo meatballs, Granny G's unmissable toffee meringue. Breakfast is a feast with homemade croissants, local milk in bottles and blocks of patted butter. *Minimum two nights at weekends.*

Rooms	5 doubles.
Price	£120-£170. Singles from £80.
Meals	Lunch from £4.75. Dinner, 3 courses, £25-£30. Not Sunday night.
Closed	Christmas Day & New Year's Eve.
Directions	West from Moreton-in-Marsh on A44. Climb hill in Bourton-on-the-Hill; pub at top on left. Moreton-in-Marsh railway station 2 miles away.

Tom & Will Greenstock
Horse & Groom,
Bourton-on-the-Hill,
Moreton-in-Marsh GL56 9AQ

Tel +44 (0)1386 700413
Email greenstocks@horseandgroom.info
Web www.horseandgroom.info

Lower Brook House

This village is a Cotswold gem, saved from tourist hordes by roads too narrow for coaches. Lower Brook is no less alluring, a great example of a small 21st-century country-house hotel. It was built in 1624 to house workers from one of the 12 silk mills that made Blockley rich. Step in and find the past on display: flagged floors, mullioned windows, timber-framed walls. Logs smoulder in a huge inglenook in winter, while excellent bedrooms (one is small) come in crisp country-house style with pretty fabrics, pristine linen and bowls of fresh fruit. One has a very fancy bathroom, most overlook the garden, views fly up the hill. Outside, roses ramble on golden walls, colour bursts from beds in summer and a tiny lawn runs down to a shaded terrace for afternoon tea in good weather. Walks start from the front door, so bring your boots. A well-priced supper menu is available in the evenings – confit of pork belly, fillet of salmon, rib-eye steak; there are good local gastro pubs, too. Breakfast treats include smoothies, croissants and freshly squeezed orange juice. *Minimum two nights at weekends.*

Rooms	6: 3 doubles, 2 twins, 1 four-poster.
Price	£80-£190.
Meals	Dinner £15-£30.
Closed	Christmas.
Directions	A44 west from Moreton-in-Marsh. At top of hill in Bourton-on-the-Hill, right, signed Blockley. Down hill to village; on right.

Julian & Anna Ebbutt
Lower Brook House,
Lower Street, Blockley,
Moreton-in-Marsh GL56 9DS

Tel +44 (0)1386 700286
Email info@lowerbrookhouse.com
Web www.lowerbrookhouse.com

Seagrave Arms

A cute little Cotswold inn. The ingredients are simple: lovely Georgian interiors, delicious local food and super rooms with honest prices. Inside, ancient flagstones lead through to the bar; you'll find a roaring fire, local ales, window seats and half-panelled walls. Next door is the charming little restaurant, where you dig into the freshest food. The Seagrave is a founding member of the Sustainable Restaurant Association, and 90% of its meat and vegetables come from local farms. Bedrooms are scattered about, some in the main house, others in the converted stables (dog-friendly). They may differ in size, but all have the same cool style with Farrow & Ball colours, crisp white linen and excellent bathrooms with REN lotions. You'll find a sofa if there's room, perhaps a double-ended bath. Spin back down for some lovely food – in summer you decant onto a gravelled terrace and small lawned garden – perhaps Windrush Valley goat cheese tart, Madgetts Farm duck with star anise, rhubarb crumble and clotted cream ice-cream. The Cotswold Way is close, a good way to atone.

Rooms	9: 8 doubles, 1 suite.
Price	£95-£125. Suite £125-£150.
Meals	Lunch from £5.95. Dinner, 3 courses, about £30. Not Monday.
Closed	Never.
Directions	Leave A44 at Broadway for B4632 towards Stratford-upon-Avon. In village.

Kevin & Sue Davies
Seagrave Arms,
Friday Street, Weston Subedge,
Chipping Campden GL55 6QH

Tel +44 (0)1386 840192
Email info@seagravearms.co.uk
Web www.seagravearms.co.uk

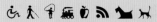

The Cotswold House Hotel & Spa

A deeply cool hotel – fabulous gardens, wonderful art, bedrooms that pack a beautiful punch. It stands on the high street in one of the Cotswolds prettiest villages, an ornament in golden stone with a wool-packers hall that dates to 1340. As for the hotel, it stretches back through stunning gardens to a smart spa with treatment rooms, a hammam, even a hydrotherapy pool. There's a croquet lawn, a beautiful terrace, deep borders packed with colour, deckchairs and sun loungers scattered about. Inside, a clipped elegance runs throughout: a pillared entrance hall, a restaurant filled with contemporary art, an airy brasserie that's open all day. Bedrooms spoil you rotten. Huge beds have shimmering throws, you get Bang & Olufsen TVs, armchairs or sofas, then seriously fancy bathrooms. A couple have Italian stone baths, another a shower for two. As for the suites, some have open fires or hot tubs on private terraces. Lovely food waits downstairs, perhaps salmon fishcakes, a good steak, a plate of local cheeses. Don't miss Broadway Tower for extraordinary views. *Minimum stay two nights at weekends.*

Rooms	30: 11 doubles, 10 twins/doubles, 6 suites, 3 cottage rooms.
Price	£220-£280. Suites £350-£500. Singles from £190.
Meals	Lunch from £6. Dinner: brasserie from £12.50; dining room, 5 courses, £55.
Closed	Never.
Directions	From Oxford, A44 north for Evesham. 5 miles after Moreton-in-Marsh, right on B4081 to Chipping Campden. Hotel in square by town hall.

Emma Dall
The Cotswold House Hotel & Spa,
The Square,
Chipping Campden GL55 6AN

Tel +44 (0)1386 840330
Email reservations@cotswoldhouse.com
Web www.cotswoldhouse.com

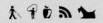

Chewton Glen

Chewton Glen is one of England's loveliest country-house hotels. It opened in 1964 with eight bedrooms and even though it now has 70, it remains delightfully intimate. Fifty years of evolution have brought a pillared swimming pool, a hydrotherapy spa, a golf course and a tennis centre. It recently added 12 treehouse suites, which sit peacefully in their own valley with hot tubs on balconies and wood-burners waiting inside. As for the hotel, beauty waits at every turn: stately sitting rooms, roaring fires, busts and oils, a bar that opens onto a sun-trapping terrace. Bedrooms are the best. Some come in country-house style, but most have a contemporary feel. Expect marble bathrooms, private balconies, designer fabrics, faultless housekeeping. Outside, four gardeners tend 130 acres of lawns and woodland, with a kitchen garden that helps the restaurant, so you'll eat well; perhaps Dorset crab, Devon duck, Charantais melon soup. You can atone in style: a walk on the beach, mountain biking in the New Forest, croquet on the lawn in summer. Hard to beat.
Minimum two nights at weekends.

Rooms	70: 5 doubles, 30 twins/doubles, 23 suites, 12 treehouses.
Price	£325-£685. Suites £610-£1,580. Treehouses £700-£1,450.
Meals	Breakfast: £21-£26. Lunch, 3 courses, £25. Sunday lunch £39.50. Dinner, 3 courses, £55-£65. Tasting menu £70. Light meals available throughout day.
Closed	Never.
Directions	A337 west from Lymington. Through New Milton for Christchurch. Right at r'bout, signed Walkford. Right again; hotel on right.

Andrew Stembridge
Chewton Glen,
Christchurch Road,
New Milton BH25 6QS

Tel +44 (0)1425 275341
Email reservations@chewtonglen.com
Web www.chewtonglen.com

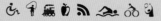

The Mill at Gordleton

A 400-year-old mill that sits in two acres of English country garden with Avon Water tumbling over the weir; mallards, lampreys, Indian runners and leaping trout all call it home. It's an idyllic spot, the terrace perfect for summer suppers, with the stream brushing past below. Inside: low ceilings, wonky walls, busts and mirrors, jars of shells. Colour tumbles from pretty fabrics, a fire roars in reception, a panelled bar serves pre-dinner drinks. Bedrooms are full of character. One is above the wheelhouse and comes with mind-your-head beams. You get pretty throws, sheets and blankets, bowls of fruit. Three rooms have watery views (you can fall asleep to the sound of the river), two have small sitting rooms, most have fancy new bathrooms, and while a lane passes outside, you are more likely to be woken by birdsong. Downstairs, the size of the restaurant bears testament to its popularity. The seven chefs use the best produce: look forward to tiger prawns with lemon grass, Hampshire pork braised in cider, an irresistible passion fruit soufflé. The coast is close.
Minimum two nights at weekends April-October.

Rooms	8: 3 doubles, 3 twins/doubles, 2 suites.
Price	£150-£195. Suites £150-£275. Singles from £115.
Meals	Lunch from £6.95. Sunday lunch from £21.50. Dinner £22.50-£27.50; à la carte about £40.
Closed	Christmas Day.
Directions	South from Brockenhurst on A337 for 4 miles. After 2nd roundabout 1st right, signed Hordle. On right after 2 miles.

Liz Cottingham
The Mill at Gordleton,
Silver Street, Sway,
Lymington SO41 6DJ
Tel +44 (0)1590 682219
Email info@themillatgordleton.co.uk
Web www.themillatgordleton.co.uk

The Montagu Arms Hotel

Beaulieu, an ancient royal hunting ground, was gifted to Cistercian monks by King John in 1204. Their abbey took 40 years to build and you can see its ruins in the nearby grounds of Palace House, seat of the Montagu family since 1538. As for the village, its tiny high street is a hotchpotch of 17th-century timber-framed houses that totter by the tidal estuary drinking in the view. The hotel dates to 1742, but was re-modelled in 1925 and interiors have an Edwardian country-house feel. You'll find roaring fires, parquet flooring, a library bar and a courtyard garden, where you can eat in summer. Traditional bedrooms vary in size, but all come with pretty fabrics, period furniture, good bathrooms, a sofa if there's room. Downstairs, a Michelin star in the dining room brings with it some fabulous food, so try Dover sole with brown shrimps, saddle of roe deer with parsnip purée, praline soufflé with dark chocolate ice-cream. There's a gastro pub if you want something lighter: local fish pie, great steaks, ham and chips with poached eggs from resident hens. Beautiful walks start from the front door. *Minimum two nights at weekends.*

Rooms	22: 9 doubles, 3 twins/doubles, 4 four-posters, 6 suites.
Price	£143-£258. Suites £233-£348. Singles from £129. Dinner, B&B from £121.50 p.p.
Meals	Lunch £6.50-£25. Sunday lunch £29.50. Dinner, 3 courses, £70 (not Monday nights in main restaurant).
Closed	Never.
Directions	South from M27, junc. 1 to Lyndhurst on A337, then B3056 for Beaulieu. Left into village and hotel on right.

Sunil Kanjanghat
The Montagu Arms Hotel,
Palace Lane, Beaulieu,
Brockenhurst SO42 7ZL

Tel	+44 (0)1590 612324
Email	reservations@montaguarmshotel.co.uk
Web	www.montaguarmshotel.co.uk

The Woolpack Inn

It's hard to fault this cool little inn. It's one of those rare places that ticks every box: friendly locals, pretty interiors, super food, lovely rooms. It stands blissfully lost in deepest Hampshire in the smallest hamlet in Britain. Its brick and flint exterior dates to 1880 and views from the front shoot across fields to a distant church; there are terraces at the front and the side, perfect for a pint in summer. Inside, you find a clean, contemporary take on a traditional English inn. A fire roars, there are warm colours, rugs on stone floors and the wine cellar is on display behind a wall of glass. Up in the restaurant, rustic charm is the order of the day with lots of wood, smart booths and candles everywhere, and the food is excellent, too, perhaps crispy fried squid, shoulder of lamb, honey and lemon tart. Bedrooms in the old skittle alley are great value. Expect exposed walls, the odd beam, Farrow & Ball colours and excellent bathrooms. There's a wood-fired oven on the terrace for pizza in summer, while Sunday lunch is madly popular – don't forget to book. Winchester is close.

Rooms	8: 6 doubles. 2-bedroom suite sharing 1 bathroom (same party bookings only).
Price	£95-£120. Suite £170.
Meals	Lunch & dinner £5.95-£30. Sunday lunch from £13.95.
Closed	Never.
Directions	On B3046 between Alresford & Basingstoke, 4 miles north of Alresford.

Andrew Cooper
The Woolpack Inn,
Totford, Northington,
Alresford SO24 9TJ

Tel +44 (0)1962 734184
Email info@thewoolpackinn.co.uk
Web www.thewoolpackinn.co.uk

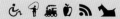

Castle House

Hereford's loveliest hotel stands 200 paces from the city's magnificent 11th-century cathedral, home to the Mappa Mundi. It's English to its core with a beautiful garden that overlooks what remains of the old castle's moat; in summer you can eat out here watching ducks glide by. Inside, the lap of luxury waits: a fine staircase, painted panelling, a delicious restaurant for the best food in town. Big bedrooms are lavish. Those in the main house are more traditional (the top-floor suite runs all the way along the front of the house); those in the townhouse (a 30-second stroll) are distinctly 21st century. All have a smart country-house feel with beautiful fabrics, super-comfy beds, crisp white linen, excellent bathrooms. Seriously good food, much from the owner's nearby farm, waits in the restaurant, perhaps goats' cheese ravioli, pan-fried sea bass, rhubarb mousse with ginger ice-cream. You can atone with a stroll along the river Wye, which runs through the park behind. Pop-up opera, guided walks and Evensong in the cathedral... and don't miss the Three Choirs Festival in July.

Rooms	Main house: 1 double, 11 suites, 4 singles. Townhouse: 3 doubles, 5 suites.
Price	£150-£190. Suites £195-£230. Singles from £130.
Meals	Lunch from £5. Dinner, 3 courses, about £35. Sunday lunch from £18.50
Closed	Never.
Directions	Follow signs to Hereford city centre, then City Centre east. Right off Bath St into Union St, through St Peters Sq to Owen's St, then right into St Ethelbert St. Hotel on left as road veers right.

Michelle Marriott-Lodge
Castle House,
Castle Street,
Hereford HR1 2NW

Tel	+44 (0)1432 356321
Email	info@castlehse.co.uk
Web	www.castlehse.co.uk

Wilton Court Restaurant with Rooms

A Grade-II listed house with a Grade-I listed mulberry tree; its berries are turned into sorbets and pies. The house dates to 1510 and looks across the lane to the river Wye: herons dive, otters swim, kingfishers nest. Roses ramble outside, happy guests potter within. This is a small, intimate hotel with pretty rooms, tasty food and owners that care. Bedrooms upstairs come in different shapes and sizes, but all have a nice fresh style. Those at the front have watery views, William Morris wallpaper, lots of space, perhaps a four-poster. A couple of rooms are small (as is their price), but, along with several others, have recently been refurbished. Expect warm colours, a wall of paper, white bathrooms and sofas in the bigger rooms. Back downstairs there's a wood-burner in the panelled bar, so stop for a pre-dinner drink, then hop across to the conservatory restaurant for some tasty food, perhaps seared king prawns, Barbary duck, and a silken cider panna cotta with apple crisp. A small garden across the lane drops down to the river for summer sundowners. Ross is a five-minute stroll.
Minimum two nights at weekends.

Rooms	10: 4 doubles, 5 twins/doubles, 1 family room.
Price	£125-£175. Family room £155-£195. Singles from £100. Dinner, B&B from £65 p.p. (min. 2 nights).
Meals	Lunch from £12.75. Sunday lunch £16.95-£18.95. Dinner, 3 courses, about £35. 7-course tasting menu £52.50.
Closed	First 2 weeks of January.
Directions	South into Ross at A40/A49 Wilton roundabout. 1st right into Wilton Lane. Hotel on right.

Roger & Helen Wynn
Wilton Court Restaurant with Rooms,
Wilton Lane, Wilton,
Ross-on-Wye HR9 6AQ

Tel +44 (0)1989 562569
Email info@wiltoncourthotel.com
Web www.wiltoncourthotel.com

Glewstone Court Country House Hotel & Restaurant

Those in search of the small and friendly will love it here. The staff are great, many have been here for yonks, and Bill and Christine run it all with great style, instinctively disregarding the bland new world in favour of a more colourful landscape. Their realm is this attractive country house filled with an eclectic collection of art and antiques. Eastern rugs cover stripped wood floors, resident dogs snooze in front of the fire, guests gather in the drawing room bar to eat, drink and relax. Outside, there's croquet on the lawn in the shade of an ancient cedar of Lebanon, while back inside a fine Regency staircase spirals up to a galleried landing. Warmly comfortable bedrooms await, tea trays come laden with homemade biscuits. Two bedrooms are huge, those at the front have long views across the Wye Valley to the Forest of Dean, those at the back overlook cherry orchards. Christine's fabulous food, seasonal and mostly local – Hereford beef, Marches lamb – is served at lunch and dinner every day with traditional Sunday lunch popular with locals. The Brecon Beacons and the Cotswolds are close. *One-night Saturday bookings not always accepted.*

Rooms	9: 7 doubles, 1 single, 1 suite.
Price	£125-£140. Suite £150. Singles from £85.
Meals	Lunch from £14. Dinner, 3 courses, about £30. Sunday lunch £21.
Closed	25-27 December.
Directions	From Ross-on-Wye A40 towards Monmouth. Right 1 mile south of Wilton r'bout for Glewstone. Hotel on left after 0.5 miles.

Christine & Bill Reeve-Tucker
Glewstone Court Country House Hotel,
Glewstone, Ross-on-Wye HR9 6AW

Tel +44 (0)1989 770367
Email info@glewstonecourt.com
Web www.glewstonecourt.com

The George Hotel

The George is a kingly retreat; Charles II stayed in 1671 and you can sleep in his room with its panelling and high ceilings. The house, a grand mansion in the middle of tiny Yarmouth, has stupendous views of the Solent; Admiral Sir Robert Holmes took full advantage when in residence, nipping off to sack passing ships. These days traditional interiors mix with contemporary flourishes. Ancient panelling and stone flags come as standard in the old house, but push on past the crackling fire in the bar to find an airy brasserie that opens onto the terrace. You can eat here in summer, next to the castle walls, with sailboats zipping past – a perfect spot for black truffles and scrambled eggs, New Forest venison with peppercorn butter, fig tart with honey and almond ice-cream. Bedrooms come in country-house style, some with crowns above the bed, others with fabulous views. Two rooms have balconies that overlook the water, but smaller rooms at the back have the same homely style. Head off to Osborne House, Cowes for the regatta or The Needles for magical walks. *Minimum two nights at weekends.*

Rooms	19: 17 twins/doubles, 2 singles.
Price	£190-£287. Singles from £99.
Meals	Lunch from £15. Dinner, 3 courses, about £40.
Closed	Rarely.
Directions	Lymington ferry to Yarmouth, then follow signs to town centre.

Jeremy Willcock
The George Hotel,
Quay Street, Yarmouth PO41 0PE

Tel +44 (0)1983 760331
Email res@thegeorge.co.uk
Web www.thegeorge.co.uk

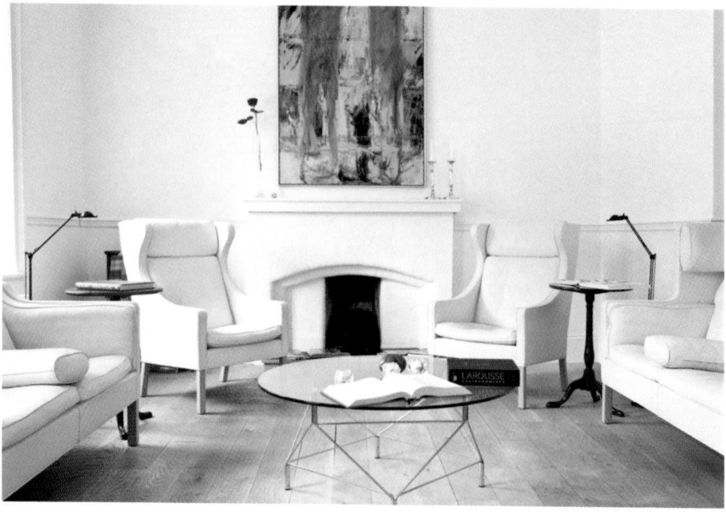

Hillside

A lovely small hotel with a cool Scandinavian feel that stands at the foot of forested hills with fine views over Ventnor and out to sea. Outside, five and a half acres of lawn, field and woodland with beehives, Hebridean sheep, red squirrels and white doves; there's an extensive kitchen garden, too, that provides much for the table. Inside, a pristine wonderland in white. There's a cosy bar with books, newspapers and a wood-burner, a sitting room/gallery with Danish leather sofas, a conservatory that opens onto a manicured terrace, and an airy restaurant with great art on the walls. Spotless bedrooms upstairs have a smart, uncluttered feel with comfy beds, vintage throws, more good art and lovely bathrooms. Those at the front look out to sea. Back downstairs, tasty food flies from the kitchen, with homemade bread and home-grown vegetables. The menu is French – frogs' legs with garlic, guinea fowl with savoy cabbage, lemon crème brûlée. Hillside also has an open-kitchen bistro in town, so you can make the most of two culinary worlds. Beaches, gardens and the coastal path wait. *Minimum two nights at weekends.*

Rooms	14: 6 doubles, 1 twin, 2 twins/doubles, 3 singles, 2 apartments.
Price	£150. Singles from £75. Dinner, B&B from £99 p.p.
Meals	Lunch from £5. Dinner, 3 courses, £28.
Closed	Never.
Directions	South to Ventnor on A3055, then right (on approach to town) onto B3277. Past tennis courts, up hill, on right.

Gert Bach
Hillside,
151 Mitchell Avenue,
Ventnor PO38 1DR

Tel	+44 (0)1983 852271
Email	mail@hillsideventnor.co.uk
Web	www.hillsideventnor.co.uk

Hever Castle Luxury Bed & Breakfast

Hever is out of this world, a magical slice of English DNA. This 14th-century moated castle was home to Anne Boleyn, second wife to Henry VIII, mother of Elizabeth I. It is one of those places that thrills at every turn. It has all the regal trimmings: 625 acres of green and pleasant land, fabulous formal gardens, a 38-acre lake you can walk around. You stay in the Astor Wing, built in Tudor style in 1903; gorgeous bedrooms, recently refurbished, are fit for a king. Expect period colours, panelled walls, perhaps a golden chaise longue or a glimpse of the castle through leaded windows. Lots have pretty wallpaper, one has a vaulted ceiling, several have four-poster beds, while bigger rooms have sofas. Bathrooms are predictably divine, some with claw-foot baths, others with walk-in power showers; a few have both. But don't linger; entrance to the castle and gardens is included in your very attractive price. You can boat on the lake, have picnic dinners, they even host the odd spot of jousting. There's golf, too, and a good pub in the village for dinner. Unbeatable.

Rooms	18: 13 doubles, 3 twins, 2 singles.
Price	£150-£195. Singles from £99. Price includes admission to castle & grounds.
Meals	Picnic lunches by arrangement. Restaurants within 0.25 miles.
Closed	Rarely.
Directions	Castle signed west out of Edenbridge.

Roland Smith
Hever Castle Luxury Bed & Breakfast,
Hever,
Edenbridge TN8 7NG

Tel +44 (0)1732 861800
Email stay@hevercastle.co.uk
Web www.hevercastle.co.uk

The Tunbridge Wells Hotel

Charles I put Tunbridge Wells on the map when he came to take the waters in 1630. By the end of the century the town had flourished and the great and good gathered to stroll along the Pantiles, the colonnaded terraces in the middle of town. They remain every bit as lovely today, with pavement cafés, antique shops, the odd concert and a weekly farmers' market. Hogging the limelight is this newly-refurbished hotel, which spills onto the terrace outside, a lovely spot to eat in summer. Inside, you find a buzzing brasserie that will make you think you've crossed the channel: clumps of lampshades hang from the ceilings, French art is crammed on the walls, a happy vibe runs throughout. The food is excellent, French to its core, perhaps lobster bisque, coq au vin, then tarte tatin, all of which you wash down with impeccable French wines. Bedrooms above have a simple elegance: warm colours, smart beds, pretty furniture, lovely prices. Good bathrooms have power showers, some a roll-top bath, one of which is in the room. The Downs wait across the road to work off any excess so come to make merry.

Rooms	20: 15 twins/doubles, 1 single, 2 suites, 2 family rooms for 4.
Price	£109-£129. Suites £169-£179. Family rooms £139. Singles from £85.
Meals	Continental breakfast included, cooked dishes from £3.50. Lunch & dinner £5-£30.
Closed	Never.
Directions	Sent on booking.

Julian Leefe-Griffiths
The Tunbridge Wells Hotel,
58 The Pantilles,
Tunbridge Wells TN2 5TD

Tel	+44 (0)1892 530501
Email	info@thetunbridgewellshotel.com
Web	www.thetunbridgewellshotel.com

Cloth Hall Oast

Sweep up the rhododendron-lined drive to this immaculate Kentish oast house and barn. For 40 years Mrs Morgan lived in the 15th-century manor next door where she tended both guests and garden; now she has turned her perfectionist's eye upon these five acres. There are well-groomed lawns, a carp-filled pond, pergola, summer house, heated pool and flower beds full of colour. In fine weather enjoy breakfast on the deck overlooking the pond. Light shimmers through swathes of glass in the dining room; there are off-white walls and pale beams that soar from floor to rafter. Mrs Morgan is a charming and courteous hostess and is always nearby to lend a helping hand. There are three bedrooms for guests: a four-poster on the ground floor, a family room and a queen-size double on the first. Colours are soft, fabrics are frilled but nothing is busy or overdone; you are spoiled with good bathrooms and fine mattresses, crisp linen, flowered chintz… and a Michelin starred restaurant in the village. Return to the guests' sitting room made snug by a log fire on winter nights. *No credit cards.*

Rooms	3: 1 double, 1 four-poster, 1 family room for 3.
Price	£90-£125.
Meals	Dinner from £25, by arrangement. Pub & restaurant 1 mile.
Closed	Christmas.
Directions	Leave village with windmill on left, taking Golford Road east for Tenterden. After a mile right, before cemetery. Signed right.

Katherine Morgan
Cloth Hall Oast,
Course Horn Lane,
Cranbrook TN17 3NR

Tel +44 (0)1580 712220
Email clothhalloast@aol.com
Web www.clothhalloast.co.uk

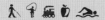

Elvey Farm

This ancient farmhouse stands in six acres of blissful peace, half a mile up a private drive. It's a deeply rural position, a nostalgic sweep back to old England. White roses run riot on red walls, a thick vine shades the veranda, trim lawns run up to colourful borders. Inside you find timber frames at every turn, but the feel is airy and contemporary with smart furniture sitting amid stripped boards and old beams. Bedrooms come in similar vein. The two in the main house are big and family-friendly, while those in the stable block have chunky beds, small sitting rooms and excellent wet rooms; two have slipper baths. Best of all are two seriously cool new rooms in the granary. Expect timber-framed walls in state-of-the-art bathrooms and massive beds under original rafters; one room comes with a hot tub in a secret garden. As for the restaurant, locally sourced Kentish fare offers delicious rustic treats: hunter's pâté, slow-roasted pork, tarte tatin with honeycomb ice-cream. The Greensand Way runs through the grounds, Leeds Castle is close, *The Darling Buds of May* was filmed in the village.

Rooms	11: 4 doubles, 7 suites.
Price	£105-£245. Singles from £85. Dinner, B&B from £74.50 p.p.
Meals	Dinner, 3 courses, about £30. Sunday lunch from £12.95.
Closed	Never.
Directions	M20 junc. 8; A20 to Lenham. At Charing r'bout 3rd exit for A20 Ashford. Right at lights to Pluckley. Bypass village, down hill, right at pub, right and right again.

Jeff Moody & Simon Peek
Elvey Farm,
Pluckley,
Ashford TN27 0SU

Tel	+44 (0)1233 840442
Email	bookings@elveyfarm.co.uk
Web	www.elveyfarm.co.uk

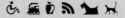

Wife of Bath

With Canterbury on your doorstep, you'd guess this restaurant took its name from Chaucer's famous tale, but the wife in question belonged to the original owner, whom he met in Bath. Named in her honour it opened in 1963 to great acclaim, one of the first restaurants with rooms to appear in the country. Over the years it has reinvented itself several times, always keeping its reputation for fabulous food; current chef, Robert Hymers, has been at the helm for 25 years. Georgian interiors have warm colours, timber frames, the odd roll of fancy wallpaper. There's a bar for cocktails, after which you are whisked through to feast on super food, perhaps smoked salmon mousse, fillet of beef poached in red wine, apple crumble with Calvados sorbet. Pretty bedrooms are well-priced, some in the main house, two in a cottage behind, thus good for families. All have crisp linen, warm colours, the odd beam and bathrobes. This ancient village is steeped in history and worth exploring, while Canterbury cathedral waits up the road. Ashford is close for Eurostar, but breakfast is excellent, so don't book an early train!

Rooms	5: 3 doubles, 1 twin, 1 four-poster.
Price	£95-£115.
Meals	Afternoon tea from £9.50. Lunch £17-£20. Sunday lunch from £20. Dinner, 3 courses, £27.50-£40. Not Sunday night, Monday, or Tuesday lunch.
Closed	Sunday & Monday nights.
Directions	M20 junc. 10, then A2070 & immediately right for Wye. Follow signs for 3 miles into Wye. Left in village; on left.

Mark Rankin
Wife of Bath,
4 Upper Bridge Street, Wye,
Ashford TN25 5AF

Tel +44 (0)1233 812232
Email relax@thewifeofbath.com
Web www.thewifeofbath.com

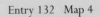

The Relish

It's not just the super-comfy interiors that make The Relish such a tempting port of call. There's a sense of generosity here: a drink on the house each night in the sitting room; tea and cakes on tap all day; free internet throughout. This is a grand 1850s merchant's house on the posh side of town with warmly contemporary interiors; wind up the cast-iron staircase to find bedrooms that make you smile. Hypnos beds with padded headboards wear crisp white linen and pretty throws. You get a sense of space, a sofa if there's room, big mirrors and fabulous bathrooms. All are great value for money. Downstairs there are candles on the mantelpieces above an open fire, stripped wooden floors and padded benches in the dining room; in summer, you can decamp onto the terrace for breakfast, a four-acre communal garden stretching out beyond. You're one street back from Folkestone's cliff-top front for huge sea views; steps lead down to smart gardens and the promenade. There are takeaway breakfasts for early Eurostar departures and a local restaurant guide in every room. *Minimum two nights at weekends in summer.*

Rooms	10: 9 doubles, 1 single.
Price	£98-£150. Singles from £75.
Meals	Restaurants nearby.
Closed	22 December-2 January.
Directions	In centre of town, from Langholm Gardens, head west on Sandgate Road. 1st right into Augusta Gardens/Trinity Gardens. Hotel on right.

Anton Gerber
The Relish,
4 Augusta Gardens,
Folkestone CT20 2RR

Tel +44 (0)1303 850952
Email reservations@hotelrelish.co.uk
Web www.hotelrelish.co.uk

Wallett's Court Country House Hotel & Spa

A fabulous position at the end of England, with sweeping fields heading south towards white cliffs; you can follow paths across to a lighthouse for rather good views. The hotel stands opposite a Norman church on land gifted by William the Conqueror to his brother Odo. The current building dates from 1627, but recent additions include an indoor swimming pool which opens onto the garden, and tree-hidden cabins for treatments. Eight acres of grounds include lush lawns, a tennis court, boules pitch and climbing frame. Timber-framed interiors display contemporary art on ancient brick walls, a fire roars in a sitting room bar and sublime food waits in the whitewashed restaurant – perhaps Shetland scallops, honey-glazed duck, a delicious banana tarte tatin. Bedrooms are scattered about, some grandly traditional with four-posters in the main house, simpler and quieter in the outbuildings; the suites above the pool come in contemporary style. Canterbury cathedral, Sandwich golf course and Dover Castle are close. *Dinner, B&B only on Saturday nights.*

Rooms	16: 12 twins/doubles, 4 suites.
Price	£95-£170.
Meals	Afternoon tea from £8.95. Sunday lunch from £16.95. Dinner, 3 courses, £39.95.
Closed	Rarely.
Directions	From Dover A2 & A20, then A258 towards Deal. Right, signed St Margaret's at Cliffe. House 1 mile on right, signed.

Chris, Lea & Gavin Oakley
Wallett's Court Country House Hotel & Spa,
Dover Road, Westcliffe,
Dover CT15 6EW

Tel +44 (0)1304 852424
Email mail@wallettscourt.com
Web www.wallettscourthotelspa.com

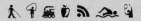

The White Cliffs Hotel & Trading Co.

You're lost in the last folds of England with the beach at the bottom of the hill and the White Cliffs of Dover soaring above, so climb up for views that stretch across to France. This pretty weatherboard hotel stands a mile back from the water with a fine Norman church across the road that's shielded by a curtain of lush trees. Inside, airy interiors come with stripped floors, sandblasted beams, contemporary art and an open fire in the sitting room/bar. Best of all is the walled garden with climbing roses, colourful borders and a trim lawn that plays host to Sunday lunch in summer. Bedrooms are all over the place. Those in the main house are bigger and more sophisticated, and come in bold colours with silky curtains, gilt mirrors and the odd four-poster. Garden rooms are altogether more simple, but good value for money. Expect summer colours, wooden beds, trim carpets and crisp linen. In the restaurant there's meat from Kent, fish from local waters and a children's menu, too. Dover Castle and Sandwich are close and you can use the pool and spa at Wallett's Court, the other half of Gavin's empire.

Rooms	15: 4 doubles, 1 triple, 1 four-poster. Mews cottages: 4 doubles, 1 twin, 2 singles, 2 family suites for 4.
Price	£109-£119. Family suites £139-£169. Singles from £79.
Meals	Lunch from £4.95. Dinner, 3 courses, £25-£30.
Closed	Rarely.
Directions	M20/A20 into Dover, then A2 north. At roundabout, right for Deal, then right again for St Margaret's. Right in village; hotel on left.

Chris, Lea & Gavin Oakley
The White Cliffs Hotel & Trading Co.,
High Street, St Margaret's-at-Cliffe,
Dover CT15 6AT

Tel	+44 (0)1304 852229
Email	mail@thewhitecliffs.com
Web	www.thewhitecliffs.com

The Marquis at Alkham

Lying in the Alkham Valley, the Marquis has the feel of deep country – you'd never think you were minutes from the motorway or Dover's bustling port or the Channel Tunnel at Folkestone (you can be in Paris is less than three hours). Instead, footpaths lead off to rolling downland, cricket graces the green in summer and lofty white cliffs stand a few miles west. As for this 200-year-old village pub, it's now a chic bolthole, a restaurant with rooms with a smart new look. You find whitewashed walls, contemporary art and leather sofas in the bar, then timber-framed walls, exposed red brick and stripped boards in the elegant restaurant. As for the food, it's exceptional stuff, some foraged, nearly all local, and the menu evolves with the seasons, so you might find garlic panna cotta with honey-soused vegetables, Godmersham hare with forest-fresh chestnuts, pear and meadowsweet soufflé. Ten stylish rooms come with contemporary wallpapers, big beds, crisp linen, plasma-screen TVs and espresso machines. Fancy bathrooms have monsoon showers; one has a bath in the room. Canterbury and Sandwich are close, too.

Rooms	10: 6 doubles, 3 twins/doubles, 1 suite.
Price	£89-£249. Suite £189-£279. Singles from £69.50. Dinner, B&B from £74.50 p.p.
Meals	Lunch from £9.50. Sunday lunch from £14.50. Dinner, 3 courses, about £40. Tasting menu £55.
Closed	Rarely.
Directions	M20 for Dover, A20 1st exit, then south for 100m on A260. 1st left for Alkham. In village after three miles.

Ben Walton
The Marquis at Alkham,
Alkham Valley Road, Alkham,
Dover CT15 7DF

Tel	+44 (0)1304 873410
Email	info@themarquisatalkham.co.uk
Web	www.themarquisatalkham.co.uk

The Royal Harbour Hotel

A delightfully quirky townhouse hotel that stands on a Georgian crescent with magnificent views of harbour and sea. Simplicity, elegance and eccentricity go hand in hand. The sitting room is wonderful with stripped floors, gorgeous armchairs, a crackling fire and an honesty bar. Beautiful things abound: a roll-top desk, super art, potted palms, a miniature orange tree bearing fruit. There are binoculars with which to scan the high seas (Ramsgate was home to the Commander of the Channel Fleet), books by the hundred for a good read (Dickens's *Bleak House* is up the road in Broadstairs) and a library of DVDs for the telly in your room. Bedrooms at the front are tiny, but have the view, those at the back are bigger and quieter. The suite has a coal fire and French windows that open onto tiny balconies. You get crisp linen, duck down pillows and excellent shower rooms. Breakfast is a leisurely feast with cured hams from James's brother, a Rick Stein food hero; there's a barbecue in the courtyard garden that guests can use in summer. *Minimum stay two nights at weekends in high season.*

Rooms	19: 14 doubles, 2 singles, 2 family rooms, 1 suite.
Price	£99-£139. Suite £200-£220. Singles from £79.
Meals	Restaurants in town.
Closed	Rarely.
Directions	M2, A299, then A256 into Ramsgate. Follow signs for town centre, pick up coast on right. On left as road drops down hill. Off-street parking.

James Thomas
The Royal Harbour Hotel,
10-11 Nelson Crescent,
Ramsgate CT11 9JF

Tel +44 (0)1843 591514
Email info@royalharbourhotel.co.uk
Web www.royalharbourhotel.co.uk

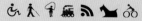

Read's Restaurant

A sublime country-house restaurant with rooms, Read's stands in five acres of lawned grounds with a half-acre kitchen garden that supplies much for the table. Inside, you find warm elegance at every turn. There's a sitting room bar for pre-dinner drinks, then a couple of beautiful dining rooms where you eat at smartly clothed tables surrounded by ornamental fireplaces and lots of good art. As for the food, it's some of the best in Kent. David and Rona came here 33 years ago, and locals and travellers come for their Michelin-starred delights: a hot soufflé of Montgomery Cheddar on a bed of smoked haddock, local venison with pickled pears and walnut croquettes, a chestnut and whisky parfait with toasted hazelnuts and Seville orange curd meringues. The bedrooms are just as good – country-house splendour in spades. Expect decanters of sherry, Roberts radios, huge beds dressed in crisp white linen, wonderful bathrooms with robes to pad about in. Canterbury, Whitstable, and Leeds Castle are close, as is Rochester for all things Dickens.

Rooms	6: 5 doubles, 1 twin/double.
Price	£165-£195. Dinner, B&B from £135 p.p.
Meals	Lunch £25. Dinner £60.
Closed	1st week in January, 1st 2 weeks in September.
Directions	M2, junc. 7, then A2 west into Faversham. Past petrol station and signed left after 400m.

David & Rona Pitchford
Read's Restaurant,
Macknade Manor, Canterbury Road,
Faversham ME13 8XE

Tel +44 (0)1795 535344
Email enquiries@reads.com
Web www.reads.com

The Spread Eagle

If you're on a budget, but want something special, you'll find it here. The Spread Eagle is one of those rare places that scores ten out of ten on all counts. Its position on the banks of the Ribble is dreamy, the pub itself is a small-scale pleasure dome, its fabulous bedrooms are an absolute steal. It's predictably popular with locals and walkers, who come for tasty food, well-kept ales, and helpful staff. Inside: Farrow & Ball colours, sofas and settles, roaring fires, flagstones and beams. The dining room comes with library wallpaper, but you can eat whatever you want wherever you want, perhaps pressed ham hock terrine, steak and stilton pudding, pear tarte tatin with cider sorbet. Lovely bedrooms have colour and style, pretty linen, big beds and fat mattresses. Some have river views, all have fancy showers, one has a bathtub in the room. You're in the glorious Ribble valley, on the edge of the Yorkshire Dales: Malham is close for walking, Settle for antiques. There's a film club, pie nights, zumba classes – it all happens here. To quote a reader: 'I couldn't fault anything.' Wonderful.

Rooms	7: 4 doubles, 2 twins/doubles, 1 suite.
Price	£85-£105. Suite £135. Singles from £70. Dinner, B&B from £72.50 p.p.
Meals	Lunch & bar meals from £8.95. Dinner from £9.95. Sunday lunch from £14.95.
Closed	Never.
Directions	A59 north past Clitheroe. Sawley & Sawley Abbey signed left after 2 miles.

Greig & Natalie Barnes
The Spread Eagle,
Sawley, Clitheroe BB7 4NH

Tel +44 (0)1200 441202
Email spread.eagle@zen.co.uk
Web www.spreadeaglesawley.co.uk

The Castle Hotel

Lincoln, a medieval powerhouse, has been at the centre of British life for 2,000 years. Romans, Vikings and Normans ruled here, the cathedral is one of the finest in Europe, an original copy of *Magna Carta* sits in its castle. As for the hotel, it's a great base from which to explore the city. It stands in the old town with views to the front of the castle's enormous walls and the cathedral's towers soaring two streets east. Paul and Saera renovated from top to toe, rescuing it from neglect. Now there's an airy bar in reception, an attractive restaurant for fancy food and a clutch of bedrooms waiting above. Expect contemporary colours, smart fabrics, padded bedheads, excellent bathrooms. Lincoln's wonders wait: the castle and its dungeon, the jaw-dropping cathedral, then Steep Hill (old-world charm with lots of tearooms) which leads down to Brayford Pool, where you can sit on café terraces and watch the world go by. The Christmas market in early December is one of the best in Britain. Come by train, it's only two hours from London.

Rooms	18: 16 twins/doubles, 1 single, 1 suite.
Price	£110-£130. Suite £140. Singles from £90. Dinner, B&B from £90 p.p.
Meals	Lunch & bar from meals £10. Dinner £30-£35.
Closed	Rarely.
Directions	Sent on booking.

Paul Catlow & Saera Ahmad
The Castle Hotel,
Westgate, Lincoln LN1 3AS

Tel	+44 (0)1522 538801
Email	info@castlehotel.net
Web	www.castlehotel.net

The William Cecil

Two minutes from the A1, yards from the gates of the magnificent Burghley estate, the William Cecil opened its doors in July 2011. Although more lavish than sister-pub the Bull and Swan just down the hill, the striking stone building still displays Hillbrooke Hotels' signature blend of quirkiness and splendour. A sweeping staircase leads to cosy country-house bedrooms, individually designed by Christine Boswell, with big comfy beds, bold fabrics, eclectic furnishings from Rajhasthan and fabulous bathrooms; the best have roll-top tubs and vast walk-in showers. Extra touches include organic vodkas by the bed. Downstairs, informality reigns. The food is local, fresh and delicious, with seasonal delights that include game from the Burghley estate. You might find pan-seared king scallops, breast of Gressingham duck with confit leg and cherry and port reduction, then a lemongrass sorbet with fresh mint. Walk it all off with a stroll into Stamford or explore the vast estate: you can reach it via the garden gate. The jewel in Stamford's crown – and great value, too.

Rooms	27: 20 doubles, 7 twins/doubles.
Price	£125.
Meals	Lunch from £6.50. Dinner from £12. Sunday lunch, 3 courses, £24.50.
Closed	Never.
Directions	Sent on booking.

Dominic Bishop
The William Cecil,
St Martins, Stamford PE9 2LJ

Tel +44 (0)1780 750070
Email enquiries@thewilliamcecil.co.uk
Web www.thewilliamcecil.co.uk

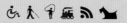

Magpies Restaurant Horncastle

This is a charming restaurant with rooms in a little-known corner of rural England and it's a huge treat to stay. It's a family affair and delightfully homespun – a warm welcome, no airs and graces, just remarkable food and lovely rooms. Andrew is self-taught and follows his nose to extraordinary flavours – a mere glance at one of his menus is enough to make you hungry. Caroline runs front of house with unpretentious charm, somehow managing to whisk up the puddings, too. Lunch and dinner are both irresistible, as is afternoon tea, a feast of scrumptious cakes, Stilton scones and red velvet cupcakes. As for the main event, you sit with a drink and some delicious nibbles, then wrestle over what to choose, plumping perhaps for escabeche of red mullet, partridge stuffed with chestnut and foie gras, dark chocolate terrine with Turkish Delight sorbet. Bedrooms above are lovely: pretty colours, comfy beds, fabulous bathrooms; they're also a steal. As for Horncastle, once famous for its medieval horse fair, it's now popular for its Christmas markets and the Viking Way. Don't miss Lincoln cathedral.

Rooms	3: 2 doubles, 1 twin/double.
Price	£110-£130. Singles from £70.
Meals	Lunch from £20. Dinner £39-£45. Not Monday, Tuesday or Saturday lunch.
Closed	First 2 weeks in January.
Directions	East into Horncastle on A158. Across junction with A153 and on right after 400m.

Caroline & Andrew Gilbert
Magpies Restaurant Horncastle,
71-73 East Street,
Horncastle LN9 6AA
Tel +44 (0)1507 527004
Web www.magpiesresturant.co.uk

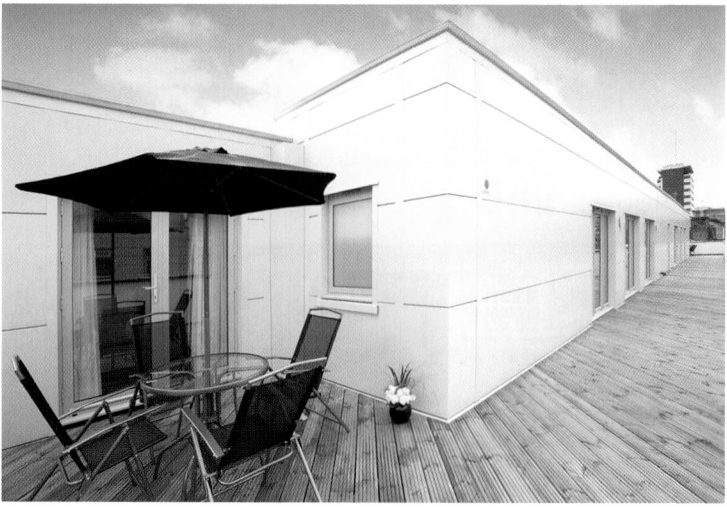

SACO Holborn - Lamb's Conduit St

Lamb's Conduit Street is cool, quirky and pedestrianised with a sprinkling of cafés and restaurants, including the mayor of London's favourite eaterie – and the legendary bookshop Persephone. A recent refurbishment has made these serviced apartments a great central base. You get the equivalent of a hotel suite and find super-cool kitchens thrown in for free. Sparkling top-floor apartments open onto vast decked terraces while those below have walls of glass overlooking the street. It's all a big surprise, given the utilitarian 60s exterior: there's space and style, with open-plan living rooms, excellent bathrooms, comfy bedrooms and lots of appealing extras such as washing machines, dishwashers and flat-screen TVs. And the reception staff are great. The building stands directly opposite Great Ormond Street Hospital and it's quiet at night, devoid of the crowds. It's also brilliantly central: you can walk to St Paul's, Oxford Street and the British Museum. Waitrose for shopping and Russell Square for the tube are both a step away. *Long-stay rates available.*

Rooms	36 apartments for 2, 4 or 6.
Price	Apartments £201-£462.
Meals	Self-catered. Restaurants nearby.
Closed	Never.
Directions	Train: Liverpool Street. Tube: Russell Square. Bus: 19, 38, 55, 243. Private parking from £15 a day.

Tim Ripman
SACO Holborn,
Spens House, 72-84 Lamb's Conduit St,
Holborn, London WC1N 3LT

Tel	+44 (0)20 7269 9930
Email	london@sacoapartments.com
Web	www.sacoapartments.com/london

22 York Street

This Regency townhouse in W1 is not your average London residence and it defies most attempts to pigeonhole it. There may be ten bedrooms, but you should still expect the feel of home. Michael and Liz try hard to keep things friendly and informal. This might explain the salsa dancing lessons that once broke out at breakfast, a convivial meal taken communally around a curved wooden table in the big, bright kitchen/dining room. Elsewhere, there's usually something to catch your eye, be it the red-lipped oil painting outside the dining room or a pair of old riding boots on the landing. Wooden floors run throughout, there's a first-floor sitting room with sofas, books and backgammon, then a lower-ground sitting room with a computer guests can use. Well-priced bedrooms are pretty without being fussy or overly ornate. Expect good beds, silk eiderdowns, white bathrooms, perhaps a walnut desk or an oak chest. Marylebone High Street, Regent's Park, and Madame Tussauds are all close, as is 221B Baker Street and Lord's for cricket. Hundreds of restaurants wait on your doorstep. A very friendly place.

Rooms	10: 5 doubles, 2 twins, 3 singles.
Price	£129. Singles from £90.
Meals	Continental breakfast included. Pubs/restaurants nearby.
Closed	Never.
Directions	Train: Paddington (to Heathrow). Tube: Baker Street (2-minute walk). Bus: 2, 13, 30, 74, 82, 113, 139, 274. Parking: £25 a day, off-street.

Michael & Liz Callis
22 York Street,
Marylebone, London W1U 6PX
Tel +44 (0)20 7224 2990
Email mc@22yorkstreet.co.uk
Web www.22yorkstreet.co.uk

Lime Tree Hotel

You'll be hard pressed to find better value in the centre of town. The Lime Tree – two elegant Georgian townhouses – stands less than a mile from Buckingham Palace, with Westminster, Sloane Square and Piccadilly easy strolls. Add warm interiors, kind owners and one of the capital's loveliest pubs waiting round the corner and you've unearthed a London gem. There's Cole & Son wallpaper in the airy dining room, so dig into an excellent breakfast (included in the price), then drop into the tiny sitting room next door for guide books and a computer for guests to use. Rooms – one on the ground floor with doors onto the garden and the quietest at the back – are just the ticket: smart without being lavish. Expect warm colours, crisp linen, pretty wallpaper and excellent bathrooms (most have super showers). Those at the front on the first floor have high ceilings and fine windows, those at the top (a few stairs!) are cosy in the eaves. Charlotte and Matt are hands-on and will point you in the right direction. Don't miss the Thomas Cubitt pub (50 paces from the front door) for seriously good food. *Minimum two nights at weekends.*

Rooms	25: 11 doubles, 4 triples, 4 twins, 5 singles, 1 family room.
Price	£155-£180. Triples £195. Family room £215. Singles from £99.
Meals	Restaurants nearby.
Closed	Never.
Directions	Train: Victoria (to Gatwick). Tube: Victoria or Sloane Square. Bus: 11, 24, 38, 52, 73, C1. Parking: £34 a day off-street.

Charlotte & Matt Goodsall
Lime Tree Hotel,
135 Ebury Street,
London SW1W 9QU

Tel	+44 (0)20 7730 8191
Email	info@limetreehotel.co.uk
Web	www.limetreehotel.co.uk

The Troubadour

Bob Dylan played here in the 60s, so did Jimi Hendrix, Joni Mitchell and the Rolling Stones. The Troubadour is a slice of old London cool, a quirky coffee house/bar in Earls Court with a magical garden and a small club in the basement where bands play most nights. Outside, pavement tables make the best of the weather; inside, rows of teapots elegantly adorn the windows, as they have since the bar opened in 1954. The ceiling drips with musical instruments, you find tables and booths, the odd pew. The kitchen is open all day (if you wear a hat on Tuesday nights, pudding is free), so try deep-fried calamari or rib-eye steak; in summer, you can eat in the garden. Next door, above their fabulous wine shop, two charming suites wait at the top of the house with views of London rooftops. Expect big colour, super beds, an alcoholic fridge, a small sofabed in front of a flat-screen TV. Both have kitchens, too; wake before 9am and make your own breakfast, or come down after for bacon and eggs served late into the afternoon. "Character pours out of every hidden cupboard," says a guest. Brilliant.

Rooms	2 suites.
Price	£175-£225. Singles from £160.
Meals	Continental breakfast included; cooked extras from £4.50. Lunch & dinner £5-£25.
Closed	25-26 December; 1 January.
Directions	Tube: Earl's Court or West Brompton (both 5-minute walk). Bus: 74, 328, 430, C1, C3. Car parks £35 a day.

Simon & Susie Thornhill
The Troubadour,
263-267 Old Brompton Road,
London SW5 9JA

Tel +44 (0)20 7370 1434
Email susie@troubadour.co.uk
Web www.troubadour.co.uk

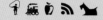

Temple Lodge Club

Temple Lodge, once home to the painter Sir Frank Brangwyn, is sandwiched between a courtyard and a lushly landscaped garden. The peace is remarkable making it a very restful place – simple yet human and warmly comfortable – an extremely nourishing experience. Michael and a small devoted team run it with quiet energy. You breakfast overlooking the garden, there are newspapers to browse, a library instead of TVs. Bedrooms make you smile, with crisp linen, garden views, good books, excellent prints. They're surprisingly stylish – clean, uncluttered with a hint of country chic – and exceptional value for money (book well in advance!). Only two rooms have their own bathrooms and loo; if you don't mind that, you'll be delighted. The Thames passes by at the end of the road, the Riverside Studios are close for theatre and film, and the Gate Vegetarian Restaurant is ten paces across the courtyard. It's a well-known eatery and was Brangwyn's studio, hence the enormous artist's window. The house is a non-denominational Christian centre with two services a week, which you may take or leave as you choose.

Rooms	11: 3 doubles, all en suite, one with separate wc; 2 twins, 5 twins/doubles, sharing 2 baths and 1 shower; 1 double, private bath.
Price	£88-£102. Singles from £64.
Meals	Continental breakfast included. Vegetarian restaurant across courtyard.
Closed	Never.
Directions	Tube: Hammersmith (5-minute walk). Bus: 9, 10, 27, 295.

Michael Beaumont
Temple Lodge Club,
51 Queen Caroline Street,
Hammersmith, London W6 9QL

Tel +44 (0)20 8748 8388
Email templelodgeclub@btconnect.com
Web www.templelodgeclub.com

Congham Hall

This is a lovely old Georgian merchant's house set in 30 acres of parkland, but it's also a cool little spa hotel with an indoor pool and treatment rooms, a perfect blend of old and new. Outside, three gardeners grow flowers for the house, vegetables for the kitchen and keep the gardens looking utterly lovely. Inside, a recent refurbishment has brought contemporary elegance into this smart country house. There's an open fire and beautiful art in the sitting room, a cool little bar with low-hanging lampshades, then an airy dining room for tasty food, perhaps Norfolk asparagus with a soft poached egg, Breckland duck with carrots and parsnips, lemon panna cotta with raspberry sorbet. After which you'll need to atone, so grab a robe from your room and roast away in the sauna before jumping in the pool for a few lengths; some might prefer the hot tub on the terrace. Bedrooms are lovely. Those in the house are more traditional, those in the courtyard have doors onto private terraces. Sandringham is close, as is the North Norfolk coast. Children are very welcome and have their own menu.

Rooms	26: 25 twins/doubles, 1 suite.
Price	£125-£245. Suite £250-£270.
Meals	Lunch from £6.50. Dinner £12.95-£40. Afternoon tea from £8.75.
Closed	Rarely.
Directions	A10 to King's Lynn, then A149 north. At second roundabout, take A148 east for 500m, then right for Grimston. Hotel signed.

Julie Woodhouse
Congham Hall,
Grimston, King's Lynn PE32 1AH

Tel +44 (0)1485 600250
Email info@conghamhallhotel.co.uk
Web www.conghamhallhotel.co.uk

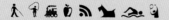

Gin Trap Inn

An actor and a lawyer run this old English Inn. Steve and Cindy left London for the quiet life and haven't stopped since, adding a bright airy conservatory dining room at the back and giving the garden a haircut. The Gin Trap dates to 1667, while the horse chestnut tree that shades the front took root in the 19th century; a conker championship is in the offing. A smart whitewashed exterior gives way to a beamed locals' bar with a crackling fire and the original dining room in Farrow & Ball hues. Upstairs, you find three delightful bedrooms in smart country style. Two have big bathrooms with claw-foot baths and separate showers, all come with timber frames, cushioned window seats, Jane Churchill fabrics and the odd chandelier; walkers will find great comfort here. Come down for delicious food: Thornham oysters, shoulder of lamb, a plate of local cheeses. (Breakfasts are just as good.) Ringstead – a pretty village lost in the country – is two miles inland from the coastal road, thus peaceful at night. You're on the Peddars Way, Sandringham is close and fabulous sandy beaches beckon.

Rooms	3 doubles.
Price	£78-£120. Singles from £39.
Meals	Lunch from £4. Dinner, 3 courses, £20-£25.
Closed	Rarely.
Directions	North from King's Lynn on A149. Ringstead signed right in Heacham. Pub on right in village.

Steve Knowles & Cindy Cook
Gin Trap Inn,
6 High Street, Ringstead,
Hunstanton PE36 5JU

Tel +44 (0)1485 525264
Email thegintrap@hotmail.co.uk
Web www.gintrapinn.co.uk

The White Horse

You strike gold at The White Horse. For a start, you get one of the best views on the North Norfolk coast – a long, cool sweep over tidal marshes to Scolt Head Island. But it's not just the proximity of the water that elates: the inn, its pleasant rooms and its fish-abundant menus score top marks. Follow your nose and find a sunken garden at the front, a locals' bar for billiards, a couple of sofas for a game of Scrabble, and a conservatory/dining room for the freshest fish. Best of all is the sun-trapping terrace; eat out here in summer. Walkers pass, sea birds swoop, sail boats glide off into the sunset. At high tide the water laps at the garden edge, at low tide fishermen harvest mussels and oysters from the bay. Inside, the feel is smart without being stuffy: stripped boards, open fires, seaside chic with sunny colours. Neat carpeted bedrooms come in seascape colours and bathrooms are spotless. In the main building some have fabulous views, those in the garden open onto flower-filled terraces. The coastal path passes directly outside. *Minimum stay two nights at weekends. Extra beds £30. Cots £5. Dogs £10.*

Rooms	15: 11 doubles, 4 twins.
Price	£95-£170.
Meals	Lunch & bar meals from £9.95. Dinner from £12.
Closed	Never.
Directions	Midway between Hunstanton & Wells-next-the-Sea on A149.

Cliff & James Nye
The White Horse,
Brancaster Staithe PE31 8BY

Tel +44 (0)1485 210262
Email reception@whitehorsebrancaster.co.uk
Web www.whitehorsebrancaster.co.uk

The Hoste

Nelson was a local, now it's farmers and film stars who jostle at the bar. In its 300-year history the Hoste has been a court house, a livestock market and a brothel. These days it's a Norfolk institution, a default destination for those in search of a little luxury. It's all things to all men: a fabulous restaurant, a conservatory café, a beautiful country pub. Inside, stylish interiors come as standard with warm colours, panelled walls and beautiful art everywhere. Best of all, it never stands still. The airy new garden room hums with happy guests, a fine spot for breakfast with a wall of glass that opens onto a lawned terrace. Elsewhere, four new bedrooms are predictably lovely, like all rooms at the Hoste, each refurbished every five years. You get sofas, four-posters, sleigh beds and fabulous bathrooms, you can even sleep in a railway carriage over at Railway House. As for the food, it's as local as possible, perhaps Brancaster oysters, Norfolk rib-eye, treacle tart with blood orange ice-cream. There's a beauty spa, live jazz and a magical coastline for windswept walks.

Rooms	64: 54 twins/doubles, 1 train carriage, 9 cottages.
Price	£130-£230. Train carriage £170-£230. Cottages £160-£200. Singles from £110. Dinner, B&B from £85 p.p.
Meals	Lunch from £6. Dinner, 3 courses, from £25. Sunday lunch from £14.
Closed	Never.
Directions	On B1155 for Burnham Market. By green & church in village centre.

Iris Rillaerts
The Hoste,
The Green, Burnham Market,
King's Lynn PE31 8HD

Tel +44 (0)1328 738777
Email reception@thehoste.com
Web www.thehoste.com

The Mulberry Tree

Attleborough is mentioned in the Domesday Book. Its weekly market is 800 years old, its monastery suffered at the hands of Henry VIII and a fire swept through in 1559. These days it's a sleepy English country town with a good line in street names: Defunct Passage, Surrogate Precinct and Thieves Lane all bring a smile. It's also well-positioned for Norwich, Snetterton, Thetford Forest, even Bury St Edmunds and Cambridge, making The Mulberry Tree a great little base for minor explorations. Airy interiors come in Farrow & Ball colours with stripped floors, big mirrors and contemporary art on the walls. There's a buzzing bar for local ales, a restaurant for super food and a terrace for sunny days. Best of all are the nicely priced rooms. Expect big beds, crisp linen, padded heads, flat-screen TVs. Willow twigs stand six feet high, mirrors lean against the wall, there are cushioned wicker chairs and excellent tongue-and-groove bathrooms. Back downstairs, try Suffolk ham, free-range eggs and hand-cut chips in the bar, or slip into the restaurant for a three-course feast. Perfect for those who want to explore.

Rooms	7: 6 doubles, 1 twin/double.
Price	£105. Singles from £78.
Meals	Lunch from £7.95. Dinner, 3 courses, £25-£30.
Closed	Sundays & Christmas.
Directions	On one-way system around town centre at junction with Station Road.

Philip & Victoria Milligan
The Mulberry Tree,
Station Road, Attleborough NR17 2AS

Tel +44 (0)1953 452124
Email relax@the-mulberry-tree.co.uk
Web www.the-mulberry-tree.co.uk

Joiners Arms

A cool little inn with fantastic rooms up on the Northumberland coast. You're half a mile back from the sea, where a string of beaches stretch north from Embleton to Bamburgh. As for the Joiners, a recent facelift has propelled it firmly into the 21st-century. Downstairs, you find a funky mix of raw panelling and old stone walls, with low-hanging lamps above the bar and a coal fire smouldering away. There are stripped floors, tables in bay windows, local ales, then cakes on the counter you can't resist. The restaurant comes in chic cabin style with raw wood walls and green leather banquettes. Bedrooms don't hold back. Expect antler chandeliers, low-slung French beds, double-ended baths in the corner of most rooms. Some have Juliet balconies, others exposed brickwork, all have rich colours, flat-screen TVs and robes in fabulous bathrooms. Outside, Alnwick Castle, Holy Island, the magical coast and beautiful hills all wait. As for the food, come home to tasty gastro fare, perhaps smoked haddock chowder, a delicious Northumbrian steak, sticky toffee pudding with ginger ice-cream.

Rooms	5 doubles.
Price	£140-£155. Dinner, B&B from £80 p.p.
Meals	Lunch from £4.95. Dinner, 3 courses, £25-£30.
Closed	Never.
Directions	A9 north from Alnwick for 4 miles, then right onto B6347 for Newton-by-the-Sea. On left in village.

Robin Freer
Joiners Arms,
Newton-by-the-Sea NE66 3AE

Tel	+44 (0)1665 576112
Email	info@joiners-arms.com
Web	www.joiners-arms.com

Eshott Hall

An utterly gorgeous Palladian mansion set in 35 acres of medieval woodlands and pasture. Wisteria fans out at the front, there's an ancient fernery, paths that weave past rare trees, an extremely productive kitchen garden. Inside is equally grand, and all the better for a recent refurbishment. You find Corinthian columns and a fine ornate ceiling in the drawing room, a roaring fire and leather sofas in the striking library, then a panelled dining room from which you may spot the odd deer tucking into the garden roses. Nip up the stairs, passing a stained-glass window designed by William Morris, and find a clutch of light-filled bedrooms. A couple come with free-standing baths in the room, others have high ceilings, garden views, perhaps a sofa or a four-poster bed. Chic bathrooms have natural stone, white robes and spoiling oils. There's tennis in the garden, peace at every turn, then white beaches, Hadrian's Wall, Holy Island and Alnwick Castle. Come back for a good dinner, perhaps potted Craster crab, Ingram Valley lamb, pear tarte tatin with mascarpone ice-cream. Fabulous.

Rooms	11 twins/doubles.
Price	£125-£250. Singles from £90. Dinner, B&B from £95 p.p.
Meals	Lunch from £6. Dinner, 3 courses, about £35. Sunday lunch from £17.50.
Closed	Never.
Directions	East off A1 7 miles north of Morpeth, 9 miles south of Alnwick, at Eshott signpost. Hall gates approx. 1 mile down lane.

Annabel Garven
Eshott Hall,
Eshott, Morpeth NE65 9EN
Tel +44 (0)1670 787454
Email info@eshotthall.co.uk
Web www.eshotthall.co.uk

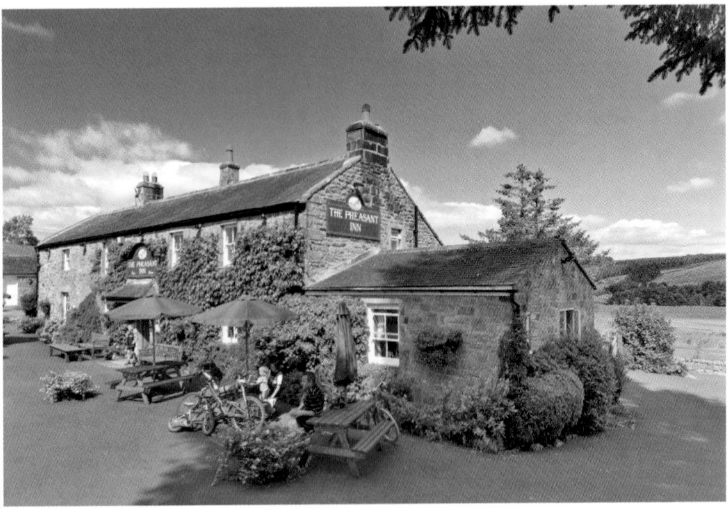

The Pheasant Inn

A super little inn lost in beautiful country, the kind you hope to chance upon. The Kershaws run it with great passion and an instinctive understanding of its traditions. The bars are wonderful. Brass beer taps glow, 100-year old photos of the local community hang on stone walls, the clock above the fire keeps perfect time. Fires burn, bowler hats and saddles pop up here and there, varnished ceilings shine. House ales are expertly kept, Timothy Taylor's and Wylam waiting for thirsty souls. Fruit and vegetables come from the garden, while Robin's lovely food hits the spot perfectly, perhaps twice-baked cheese soufflé, slow-roasted Northumberland lamb, brioche and marmalade bread and butter pudding; as for Sunday lunch, *The Observer* voted it 'Best in the North'. Bedrooms in the old hay barn are light and airy, cute and cosy, great value for money. You're in the Northumberland National Park – no traffic jams, not too much hurry. You can sail on the lake, cycle round it or take to the hills and walk. For £10 you can also gaze into the universe at the Kielder Observatory (best in winter). Brilliant. *Minimum two nights at weekends.*

Rooms	8: 4 doubles, 3 twins, 1 family room.
Price	£75-£95. Family room £90-£130. Singles from £65. Dinner, B&B from £70 p.p.
Meals	Bar meals from £8.95. Dinner, 3 courses, £18-£22.
Closed	25-27 December. Monday & Tuesday November-March.
Directions	From Bellingham follow signs west to Kielder Water & Falstone for 9 miles. Hotel on left, 1 mile short of Kielder Water.

Walter, Irene & Robin Kershaw
The Pheasant Inn,
Stannersburn,
Hexham NE48 1DD

Tel +44 (0)1434 240382
Email stay@thepheasantinn.com
Web www.thepheasantinn.com

Hart's Nottingham

A small enclave of good things. You're on the smart side of town at the end of a cul-de-sac, thus remarkably quiet. You're also at the top of the hill and close to the castle with exceptional views that sweep south for ten miles; at night, a carpet of light sparkles. Inside, cool lines and travertine marble greet you in reception. Bedrooms are excellent, not huge, but perfectly adequate and extremely well designed. All come with wide-screen TVs, Bose sound systems, super little bathrooms and king-size beds wrapped in crisp white cotton. Those on the ground floor open onto a fine garden, each with a terrace where you can breakfast in good weather; rooms on higher floors have better views (six overlook the courtyard). A cool little bar, the hub of the hotel, is open for breakfast, lunch and dinner, but Hart's Restaurant across the courtyard offers fabulous food, perhaps pan-fried wood pigeon with blackberries, free-range chicken with wild garlic, tarte tatin with caramel ice-cream. There's a private car park for hotel guests and a small gym for those who must.

Rooms	32: 29 doubles, 1 family room, 2 suites.
Price	£125-£175. Suites £265.
Meals	Continental breakfast £9, full English £14. Bar snacks from £3.50. Lunch from £14.95. Dinner, 3 courses, from £24.
Closed	Never.
Directions	M1 junc. 24, then follow signs for city centre and Nottingham Castle. Left into Park Row from Maid Marian Way. Hotel on left at top of hill. Parking £8.50/night.

Adam Worthington
Hart's Nottingham,
Standard Hill, Park Row,
Nottingham NG1 6GN

Tel +44 (0)115 988 1900
Email reception@hartshotel.co.uk
Web www.hartsnottingham.co.uk

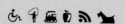

Langar Hall

Langar Hall is one of the most engaging and delightful places in this book – reason enough to come to Nottinghamshire. Imogen's exquisite style and natural joie de vivre make this a mecca for those in search of a warm, country-house atmosphere. The house sits at the top of a hardly noticeable hill in glorious parkland, bang next door to the church. Imo's family came over 150 years ago, building on the site of Admiral Lord Howe's burned-down home. Much of what fills the house arrived then and it's easy to feel intoxicated by beautiful things: statues and busts, a pillared dining room, ancient tomes in overflowing bookshelves, an eclectic collection of oil paintings. Bedrooms are wonderful, some resplendent with antiques, others with fabrics draped from beams or trompe l'œil panelling. Heavenly food, simply prepared for healthy eating, is a special treat. Come for Langar lamb, fish from Brixham, game from Belvoir Castle and garden-grown vegetables. In the grounds: medieval fishponds, canals, a den-like adventure play area and, once a year, Shakespeare on the lawn.

Rooms	12: 7 doubles, 2 twins, 1 four-poster, 1 suite, 1 chalet for 2.
Price	£100-£199. Suite £199. Chalet £100-£199.
Meals	Lunch from £18.50. Dinner, 3 courses, £25-£35.
Closed	Never.
Directions	From Nottingham A52 towards Grantham. Right, signed Cropwell Bishop, then straight on for 5 miles. House next to church on edge of village, signed.

Imogen Skirving
Langar Hall,
Church Lane, Langar,
Nottingham NG13 9HG

Tel	+44 (0)1949 860559
Email	info@langarhall.co.uk
Web	www.langarhall.com

The Feathered Nest Country Inn

The village is tiny, the view is fantastic, the bar is lively, the rooms are a treat. This 300-year-old malthouse had a recent facelift and now shines. Interiors mix all the old originals – stone walls, timber frames, beamed ceilings, open fires – with a contemporary, rustic style. The net result is an extremely attractive country inn, one of the best in the south. Downstairs, one room flows into another. Beautiful bay windows, roaring fires, saddled bar stools, green leather armchairs – everywhere you go something lovely catches the eye, not least the view – the best in the Cotswolds; it will draw you to the terrace where quilted fields run to a distant ridge. You get beds of lavender, swathes of lawn, a vegetable garden that serves the kitchen. Bedrooms upstairs are gorgeous. One is enormous, two have the view, beds are dressed in crisp linen. Most have power showers, one has a claw-foot bath, all have robes. There are coffee machines and iPod docks, too. Super food waits downstairs: Old Spot terrine, Fairford chicken, rhubarb and champagne jelly. *Minimum two nights at weekends.*

Rooms	4: 3 doubles, 1 family room.
Price	£150-£200. Singles from £105. Family room £175. Cots £15. Under 12s in family room, £30.
Meals	Lunch & dinner £6.50-£30. Not Sunday eve.
Closed	Mondays (except Bank Holidays).
Directions	North from Burford on A424 for Stow-on-the-Wold. After 4 miles right for Nether Westcote. In village.

Tony & Amanda Timmer
The Feathered Nest Country Inn,
Nether Westcote,
Chipping Norton OX7 6SD

Tel +44 (0)1993 833030
Email reservations@thefeatherednestinn.co.uk
Web www.thefeatherednestinn.co.uk

The Kingham Plough

You don't expect to find locals clamouring for a table in a country pub on a cold Tuesday in February, but different rules apply at the Kingham Plough. Emily, once junior sous chef at the famous Fat Duck in Bray, is now doing her own thing and it would seem the locals approve. You eat in the tithe barn, now a splendid dining room, with ceilings open to ancient rafters and excellent art on the walls. Attentive staff bring sublime food. Dig into game broth with pheasant dumplings, fabulous lamb hotpot with crispy kale, and hot chocolate fondant with blood orange sorbet. Interiors elsewhere are equally pretty, all the result of a delightful refurbishment. There's a piano by the fire in the locals' bar, a terrace outside for summer dining, fruit trees, herbs and lavender in the garden. Bedrooms, three of which are small, have honest prices and come with super-comfy beds, flat-screen TVs, smart carpets, white linen, the odd beam; one has a claw-foot bath. Arrive by train, straight from London, to be met by a bus that delivers you to the front door. The Daylesford Organic farm shop/café is close. *Minimum two nights at weekends. Travel cot available.*

Rooms	7 twins/doubles.
Price	£90-£130. Singles from £75.
Meals	Lunch from £15. Bar meals from £5. Dinner, 3 courses, about £30. Sunday lunch from £17.
Closed	Christmas Day.
Directions	In village, off B4450, between Chipping Norton & Stow-on-the-Wold.

Emily Watkins & Miles Lampson
The Kingham Plough,
The Green, Kingham,
Chipping Norton OX7 6YD

Tel	+44 (0)1608 658327
Email	book@thekinghamplough.co.uk
Web	www.thekinghamplough.co.uk

The Kings Head Inn

The sort of inn that defines this country: a 16th-century cider house made of ancient stone that sits on the green in a Cotswold village with free-range hens strutting their stuff and a family of ducks bathing in the pond. Inside, locals gather to chew the cud, scoff great food and wash it down with a cleansing ale. The fire burns all year, you get low ceilings, painted stone walls, country rugs on flagstone floors. Bedrooms, all different, are scattered about; all are well priced. Those in the main house have more character, those in the courtyard are bigger (and quieter). You'll find painted wood, lots of colour, pretty fabrics, spotless bathrooms; most have great views, too. Breakfast and supper are taken in a pretty dining room (exposed stone walls, pale wood tables), while you can lunch by the fire in the bar on Cornish scallops, steak and ale pie, then a plate of British cheeses. There are lovely unpompous touches like jugs of cow parsley in the loo, and loads to do: antiques in Stow, golf at Burford, walking and riding through gorgeous terrain. The front terrace teems with life in summer.

Rooms	12: 10 doubles, 2 twins/doubles.
Price	£95-£135. Singles from £70.
Meals	Lunch from £7.50. Dinner from £9.50. Sunday lunch, 3 courses, £30.
Closed	Never.
Directions	East out of Stow-on-the-Wold on A436, then right onto B4450 for Bledington. Pub in village on green.

Archie & Nicola Orr-Ewing
The Kings Head Inn,
The Green, Bledington,
Chipping Norton OX7 6XQ

Tel +44 (0)1608 658365
Email info@kingsheadinn.net
Web www.kingsheadinn.net

The Feathers Hotel

Woodstock is hard to beat, its golden cottages stitched together seamlessly. It's intrinsically linked to Blenheim Palace, one of Britain's finest houses, seat of the Dukes of Marlborough, birthplace of Winston Churchill. You can stroll up in five minutes, drop your jaw, then return to this wonderfully indulging hotel. It sits serenely on the high street with a carriage arch leading to a courtyard where in summer you sip your Pimms; just heavenly. Inside, a total refurbishment has poured in colour and style. You get old stone walls, parquet flooring, a roaring wood-burner, ancient windows that flood the place with light. Bedrooms are dreamy, big or small, with beautiful fabrics, lovely beds, mohair throws, delicious wallpapers. Some have sofas, all come with robes in gorgeous bathrooms. Back downstairs, the bar has over 100 varieties of gin – there's even a tasting menu with a different shot at each course. They'll help you wash down some wonderful food, perhaps Cornish mackerel with Daikon root and a toffee tasting of Valrhona chocolate with coconut, wasabi, ginger and sesame. Oxford is close. *Minimum two nights at weekends in summer.*

Rooms	21: 13 doubles, 3 twins/doubles, 5 suites.
Price	£169-£229. Suites £259-£319. Singles from £129.
Meals	Lunch from £5. Dinner £39.95-£49.95 (not Sunday eve).
Closed	Never.
Directions	North from Oxford on A44. In Woodstock left after traffic lights & hotel on left.

Luc Morel
The Feathers Hotel,
Market Street,
Woodstock OX20 1SX

Tel +44 (0)1993 812291
Email enquiries@feathers.co.uk
Web www.feathers.co.uk

Kings Arms Hotel

The Kings Arms stands in the middle of Woodstock, part inn, part chic hotel, part super little restaurant. The big draw here is Blenheim Palace – childhood home to Winston Churchill and one of the country's loveliest buildings. This brings a varied crowd to the bar, tourists from all over the world as well as die-hard locals, who come for the lovely food, the happy vibe and the half-price champagne on Wednesday nights. Inside, old and new combine as airy open-plan interiors drift from one room to another. Downstairs, you find boarded floors and an open fire in the bar, then an airy dining room with gilded mirrors and logs piled high in alcoves. Lovely, uncluttered bedrooms ramble about upstairs, all recently refurbished. Expect lime-white walls, mango wood beds, smart new carpets and lovely art. A couple are huge, most overlook the village, several have fancy new bathrooms. Equally up-to-date are the menus downstairs, so don't miss the irresistible food, perhaps crayfish cocktail, slow-roasted duck, lemon curd brûlée with honey shortbread. Bicester Village and Oxford are both close. *Children over 12 welcome.*

Rooms	15 doubles.
Price	£150. Singles from £80. Dinner, B&B from £100 p.p.
Meals	Lunch from £8.75. Dinner, 3 courses, £20-£30.
Closed	Never.
Directions	In Woodstock on A44 at corner of Market Street in town centre.

David & Sara Sykes
Kings Arms Hotel,
19 Market Street,
Woodstock OX20 1SU

Tel +44 (0)1993 813636
Email stay@kingshotelwoodstock.co.uk
Web www.kingshotelwoodstock.co.uk

The Swan

Free-range bantams strut in the garden, a pint of Hooky waits at the bar. This lovely old pub sits in glorious country with the river Windrush passing ten paces from the front door and the village cricket pitch waiting beyond. It started life as a water mill and stands on the Devonshire estate, hence all the pictures of the Mitford sisters hanging on the walls. Outside, wisteria wanders along golden stone and creepers blush red in the autumn sun. Interiors are delicious: low ceilings, open fires, beautiful windows, stone walls. Over the years thirsty feet have worn grooves into 400-year-old flagstones, so follow in their footsteps and stop for a drink at the bar, then eat from a seasonal menu that brims with local produce: curried sweet potato soup, Foxbury Farm chargrilled steak, dark chocolate and ginger pot. Doors in the conservatory restaurant open onto the garden terrace in fine weather. Bedrooms in the old forge hit the spot: very pretty, nicely priced, super-comfy beds. Expect 15th-century walls, 21st-century interior design and a pink chaise longue in the suite. Burford is close.

Rooms	6: 4 doubles, 1 twin, 1 suite.
Price	£110-£130. Suite £150-£180. Singles from £70.
Meals	Lunch & bar meals from £7.50. Dinner from £12. Sunday lunch, 3 courses, £30.
Closed	Christmas Day & Boxing Day.
Directions	West from Oxford on A40 for Cheltenham/Burford. Past Witney & village signed right at 1st r'bout.

Archie & Nicola Orr-Ewing
The Swan,
Swinbrook,
Burford OX18 4DY

Tel	+44 (0)1993 823339
Email	info@theswanswinbrook.co.uk
Web	www.theswanswinbrook.co.uk

Burford House

Burford was made rich by 14th-century mill owners. Its golden high street slips downhill to the river Windrush, where paths lead out into glorious country, passing a church that dates to Norman times; Cromwell held a band of Levellers here in 1649 and their murals survive inside. Halfway up the hill, this 17th-century timber-framed house stands bang in the middle of town. Interiors sweep you back to the soft elegance of old England: a couple of cosy sitting rooms, a whispering wood-burner, exposed stone walls, a courtyard for summer dining. Slip into the restaurant and find Farrow & Ball colours, freshly cut flowers, rugs on wood boards, theatre posters on the wall. The food is delicious so come for ham hock terrine, a trio of Cotswold lamb, a plate of rhubarb puddings. Bedrooms are delightful, two across the courtyard in the coach house. Some have oak beams, others a claw-foot bath. All come with super beds, woollen blankets and robes in good bathrooms; those at the back have rooftop views. Wake on Sunday to the sound of pealing bells. *Minimum two nights at weekends during summer. Children's beds available.*

Rooms	7: 3 doubles, 3 twins/doubles, 1 suite.
Price	£145-£200. Suite £145-£300. Singles from £125. Child bed available in all rooms.
Meals	Light lunch from £4.95. Dinner (Wednesday-Saturday) about £35 per person (if pre-booked, £30 per person).
Closed	Rarely.
Directions	In centre of Burford, halfway down hill. Free on-street parking, free public car park nearby.

Ian Hawkins
Burford House,
99 High Street,
Burford OX18 4QA

Tel	+44 (0)1993 823151
Email	stay@burfordhouse.co.uk
Web	www.burfordhouse.co.uk

The Trout at Tadpole Bridge

A 17th-century Cotswold inn on the banks of the Thames; pick up a pint, drift into the garden, watch the world float by. Inside you find all the trimmings of a lovely old pub: timber frames, exposed stone walls, a wood-burner to keep things toasty, local ales on tap at the bar. Logs are piled high in alcoves, good art hangs on the walls, pretty rugs cover old flagstones. Delicious food flies from the kitchen – anything from posh fish and chips or steak and ale pie to rack of lamb with a rosemary crust or Gressingham duck with ginger purée. Bedrooms at the back are away from the crowd; three open onto a small courtyard where wild roses ramble. You get smart fabrics, trim carpets, monsoon showers (one room has a claw-foot bath), DVD players, flat-screen TVs and a library of films. Sleigh beds, brass beds, smartly upholstered armchairs... one room even has a roof terrace. You can watch boats pass from the breakfast table, feast on local sausages, tuck into homemade marmalade courtesy of Helen's mum. Oxford is close, there are maps for walkers, you can even get married in the garden. *Minimum two nights at weekends May-October.*

Rooms	6: 2 doubles, 3 twins/doubles, 1 suite.
Price	£130. Suite £160. Singles from £85.
Meals	Lunch & dinner £10.95-£19. Sunday lunch from £11.95.
Closed	Christmas Day & Boxing Day.
Directions	A420 southwest from Oxford for Swindon. After 13 miles right for Tadpole Bridge. Pub on right by bridge.

Gareth & Helen Pugh
The Trout at Tadpole Bridge,
Buckland Marsh, Faringdon SN7 8RF

Tel +44 (0)1367 870382
Email info@troutinn.co.uk
Web www.trout-inn.co.uk

Old Parsonage Hotel

A country house in the city, with a lively bar for a drop of champagne, a rooftop terrace for afternoon tea and a hidden garden where you can sit in the shade and listen to the bells of St Giles. Logs smoulder in the original stone fireplace, the daily papers wait by an ancient window and an extensive collection of exquisite art hangs on the walls. You feast in the restaurant on meat from the owner's Oxfordshire farm or fish from the Channel Islands, then retire to warm stylish bedrooms which are scattered all over the place – some at the front (where Oscar Wilde entertained lavishly when he was sent down), others at the back in a sympathetic extension where some suites have French windows onto tiny balconies and a couple of the less-expensive rooms open onto private terraces. Expect Vi-Spring mattresses, flat-screen TVs, crisp white linen, spotless bathrooms. Daily walking tours led by an art historian are 'on the house', while the hotel can book a punt on the Cherwell, then pack you a picnic, so glide effortlessly past spire and meadow before tying up for lunch. *Minimum two nights at weekends.*

Rooms	35: 33 twins/doubles, 2 suites for 3.
Price	£146-£270. Suites £307-£440.
Meals	Breakfast £12.95-£14. Lunch & dinner £10-£45.
Closed	Never.
Directions	From A40 ring road, south onto Banbury Road; thro' Summertown and hotel on right just before St Giles church.

Rebecca Mofford
Old Parsonage Hotel,
1 Banbury Road, Oxford OX2 6NN
Tel +44 (0)1865 310210
Email info@oldparsonage-hotel.co.uk
Web www.oldparsonage-hotel.co.uk

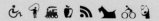

Old Bank Hotel

You're in the heart of old Oxford. Stroll south past Corpus Christi to Christ Church meadows, head north for the Radcliffe Camera and the Bodleian Library. Back at the Old Bank, contemporary elegance comes with an important collection of modern art and photography. It adorns most walls, even in bedrooms, and catalogues can be perused. Downstairs the old tiller's hall is now a vibrant bar/brasserie with arched windows giving views onto the high street; come for cocktails before a convivial meal (fish from the Channel Islands, meat from the owner's farm). Bedrooms upstairs are exemplary: fine beds, piles of cushions, Denon CD players, flat-screen TVs. Bigger rooms have sofas, you get robes in super bathrooms, there's free broadband access throughout. Service is friendly and serene: curtains are pleated, beds are turned down, the daily papers delivered to your door. There's room service, too. Breakfast is served in the tiller's hall or on the deck in the courtyard in summer. Off-street parking is priceless, daily walking tours led by an art historian are free for guests. *Minimum two nights at weekends.*

Rooms	42: 29 doubles, 12 twins, 1 suite.
Price	£134-£390. Suite £305-£500.
Meals	Breakfast £3.50-£14.50. Lunch & dinner £10-£30.
Closed	Never.
Directions	Cross Magdalen Bridge for city centre. Straight through 1st set of lights, then left into Merton St. Follow road right; 1st right into Magpie Lane. Car park 2nd right.

Ben Truesdale
Old Bank Hotel,
92-94 High Street,
Oxford OX1 4BJ

Tel +44 (0)1865 799599
Email info@oldbank-hotel.co.uk
Web www.oldbank-hotel.co.uk

Hambleton Hall Hotel & Restaurant

A sublime country house, one of the loveliest in England. The position here is matchless. The house stands on a tiny peninsular that juts into Rutland Water. You can sail on it or cycle around it, then come back to the undisputed wonders of Hambleton: sofas by the fire in the panelled hall, a pillared bar in red for cocktails, a Michelin star in the dining room. French windows in the sitting room (beautiful art, fresh flowers, the daily papers) open onto fine gardens. Expect clipped lawns and gravel paths, a formal parterre garden that bursts with summer colour and a walled swimming pool with views over grazing parkland to the water. Bedrooms are the very best. Hand-stitched Italian linen, mirrored armoires, Roberts radios, fabulous marble bathrooms; Stefa's eye for fabrics, some of which coat the walls, is faultless. The Pavilion, a supremely comfortable two-bedroom suite, has its own terrace. Polish the day off with incredible food, perhaps breast of wood pigeon, fallow venison with Asian pear, passion fruit soufflé with banana sorbet. Don't miss the hotel's bakery up the road. Irreproachable.

Rooms	16: 15 twins/doubles, 1 suite.
Price	£255-£430. Suite £400-£630. Singles from £195.
Meals	Lunch from £24.50. Sunday lunch £45. Dinner, 3 courses, £65. Tasting menu £72.
Closed	Never.
Directions	From A1, A606 west towards Oakham for about 8 miles, then left, signed Hambleton. In village bear left and hotel signed right.

Tim & Stefa Hart
Hambleton Hall Hotel & Restaurant,
Ketton Road, Hambleton,
Oakham LE15 8TH

Tel +44 (0)1572 756991
Email hotel@hambletonhall.com
Web www.hambletonhall.com

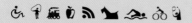

The Olive Branch

A lovely pub in a sleepy Rutland village, where bridle paths lead out across peaceful fields. The inn dates to the 17th century and is built of Clipsham stone. Inside, a warm, informal rustic chic hits the spot perfectly; come for open fires, old beams, exposed stone walls and choir stalls in the bar. Chalk boards on tables in the restaurant reveal the names of the evening's diners, while the food – seared scallops with black pudding fritter, slow-roast pork belly with creamed leeks and apple sauce – elates. As do the hampers that you can whisk away for picnics in the country. Bedrooms in Beech House across the lane are impeccable. Three have terraces, one has a free-standing bath, all come with crisp linen, pretty beds, Roberts radios, real coffee. Super breakfasts – smoothies, boiled eggs and soldiers, the full cooked works – are served in a smartly renovated barn, with flames leaping in the wood-burner. The front garden fills in summer, the sloe gin comes from local berries, and Newark is close for the biggest antiques market in Europe. A total gem. *Ask about cookery demos.*

Rooms	6: 5 doubles, 1 family suite.
Price	£115-£195. Singles from £97.50.
Meals	Bar meals £10.50. Dinner from £14.50. Sunday lunch £24.95.
Closed	Rarely.
Directions	A1 5 miles north of Stamford, then exit onto B668. Right & right again for Clipsham. In village (Beech House across the road from The Olive Branch).

Ben Jones & Sean Hope
The Olive Branch,
Main Street, Clipsham,
Oakham LE15 7SH

Tel +44 (0)1780 410355
Email info@theolivebranchpub.com
Web www.theolivebranchpub.com

Soulton Hall

There's been a house on this land since 1066, but Soulton goes back to 1430, a fortified house that was home to the first Protestant mayor of London. It stands magnificently in 500 acres of pasture and woodland, yours to roam. It's a family affair: John farms, Ann looks after the house. Climb the steps, slip through a spectacular stone doorway, arrive in the hall, sink in a sofa in front of a fire. Potter about and find an attractive dining room and a cosy bar, but it's the bedrooms in the main house that leave the big impression. You'll find them up an old oak staircase (and you glimpse a section of original wattle and daub on your way up). Four grand country-house bedrooms wait. They come with timber frames, mullioned windows, the odd panelled wall and polished floors; three have fancy bathrooms. It's all splendidly regal, and while simpler bedrooms are also available, it's worth bagging one of these. Back downstairs, you eat in style, perhaps carrot and coriander soup, lemon sorbet with sparkling wine, chicken cooked with hazelnuts and cream, sticky toffee pudding.

Rooms	7: 3 doubles, 1 twin/double. Carriage House: 2 doubles. Garden room: 1 four-poster.
Price	£110-£150.
Meals	Dinner, 4 courses, £38.50.
Closed	Rarely.
Directions	North from Shrewsbury on A49. Left in Prees Green onto B5065 for Wem. House on left after two miles.

Ann & John Ashton
Soulton Hall,
Shrewsbury SY4 5RS
Tel +44 (0)1939 232786
Email enquiries@soultonhall.co.uk
Web www.soultonhall.co.uk

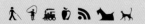

Draper's Hall

Shrewsbury, an old market town, was the birthplace of Charles Darwin, but it made its money from wool, hence this fine old medieval building, the Drapers' Guildhall. It dates to 1440 and stands quietly in the middle of town. Its original façade gives way to beautiful timber-framed interiors and you eat in its magnificent hall with vast paintings hanging from original panelling. Further back, the bar stands in what was the kitchen; the inglenook fireplace is now flanked by piles of wood; it doesn't take long to sink into one of its comfy sofas. It's a happy little place, with Nigel and Sharon looking after their guests with an easy informality. Bedrooms, all upstairs, are deeply comfortable: sumptuous 'Walnut' with a gilt mirror and smart blue wallpaper; 'Lime', a sleek, bijou, contemporary suite; 'Teal', the swish top-floor apartment with antique brass bed, sitting area, sweet children's bedroom. Back downstairs, there's great food in the hall, perhaps seared scallops, pot au feu, caramelised figs with goats' cheese curd. Shrewsbury waits, its castle, abbey and river walks.
Parking available close by: arrange when booking (£4-£6 overnight).

Rooms	5: 3 doubles, 2 suites.
Price	£145. Suites £155. Singles from £95.
Meals	Lunch from £6. Sunday lunch from £14. Afternoon tea from £12.50. Dinner £25-£30.
Closed	Rarely.
Directions	Sent on booking.

Nigel & Sharon Huxley
Draper's Hall,
10 St Marys Place,
Shrewsbury SY1 1DZ

Tel +44 (0)1743 344679
Email goodfood@drapershallrestaurant.co.uk
Web www.drapershallrestaurant.co.uk

Sebastian's

This lovely little restaurant with rooms occupies an old merchant's house that dates from 1640. Michelle and Mark have been at the helm for 23 years cooking up a fine reputation – not only for their delicious food, but for the quirky, old-world interiors in which they serve it. Step off the street to find huge beams, timber frames, half panelling and stripped floors. In between you get smartly clothed tables, fairy lights and candles, exotic screens and fresh flowers. Old posters of the Orient Express hang on the walls (Mark supplies the train with canapés and desserts). Back in the restaurant there are sofas in front of a cavernous fire that smoulders from morning to night in winter. Here you drool over the menu before digging into fabulous food, perhaps scallop ravioli with lemon grass and ginger, loin of lamb with a goats' cheese tart, limoncello mousse. Six delightful rooms wait, two in the main house (timber frames, lots of colour), four off the courtyard (comfy sofas, lovely bathrooms). Montgomery, the prettiest town in Wales, is close.

Rooms	6: 5 doubles, 1 twin/double.
Price	£75. Singles from £65.
Meals	Continental breakfast £6.95, full English £11.95. Dinner £19.95–£39.50.
Closed	Rarely.
Directions	In middle of Oswestry on B4580.

Michelle & Mark Sebastian Fisher
Sebastian's,
45 Willow Street,
Oswestry SY11 1AQ

Tel +44 (0)1691 655444
Email sebastians.rest@virgin.net
Web www.sebastians-hotel.com

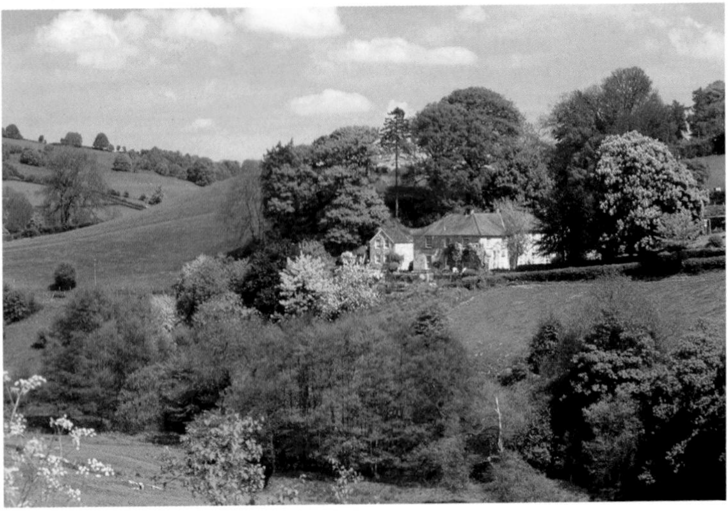

Pen-y-Dyffryn Country Hotel

In a blissful valley lost to the world, this small, traditional country house sparkles on the side of a peaceful hill. To the front, beyond the stone terraces lush with aubretia, fields tumble down to a stream that marks the border with Wales. Daffodils erupt in spring, the lawns are scattered with deckchairs in summer, paths lead onto the hill for excellent walks. Colourful interiors are attractive: Laura Ashley wallpaper and an open fire in the quirky bar; shuttered windows and super food in the restaurant; the daily papers and a good collection of art in the sitting room. Bedrooms are stylish without being grand. Most have great views, one has a French sleigh bed, a couple have jacuzzi baths for two. Four rooms are dog-friendly and have their own patios. You get crisp white linen, silky curtains, padded bedheads. There's super food, too: Shetland mussels, Welsh beef, a plate of local cheese; the smoked haddock at breakfast is divine. Offa's Dyke and Powis Castle are close. Spa treatments are available in your room; perfect after a long walk in the hills. *Minimum two nights at weekends.*

Rooms	12: 8 doubles, 4 twins.
Price	£114-£166. Singles from £86.
Meals	Light lunch (for residents) by arrangement. Dinner £30-£37.
Closed	Rarely.
Directions	From A5 head to Oswestry. Leave town on B4580, signed Llansilin. Hotel 3 miles up. Approach Rhydycroesau, left at town sign, first right.

Miles & Audrey Hunter
Pen-y-Dyffryn Country Hotel,
Rhydycroesau, Oswestry SY10 7JD

Tel	+44 (0)1691 653700
Email	stay@peny.co.uk
Web	www.peny.co.uk

The Castle Hotel

This thriving medieval market town sits amid some of the loveliest country in the land, a launch pad for walkers and cyclists, with Offa's Dyke, Long Mynd and the Kerry Ridgeway all close. After a day in the hills what better than to roll back down to this quirky hotel for a night of genteel carousing. You'll find heaps of country comforts: hearty food, an impeccable pint, cosy rooms with honest prices. Downstairs, there's a coal fire in the pretty snug, oak panelling in the breakfast room, and Millie the short-haired dachshund who patrols the corridors with aplomb. Spotless bedrooms upstairs have good beds, warm colours, flat-screen TVs, an armchair if there's room. Some are up in the eaves, several have views of the Shropshire hills, two are seriously fancy. Back downstairs you find the sort of food you hanker for after a day in the open air, perhaps broccoli and stilton soup, beef and ale pie, sticky toffee pudding (all for a song). Don't miss the hugely popular real ale festival in July, the beer drinker's equivalent of Glastonbury. There's a lovely garden, too, perfect for sundowners in summer.

Rooms	10: 7 doubles, 1 twin, 2 family rooms.
Price	£85-£130. Singles from £60. Dinner, B&B from £70 p.p.
Meals	Lunch from £4.50. Dinner, 3 courses, about £25.
Closed	Christmas Day.
Directions	At top of hill in town, off A488.

Henry Hunter
The Castle Hotel,
Bishops Castle SY9 5BN

Tel	+44 (0)1588 638403
Email	stay@thecastlehotelbishopscastle.co.uk
Web	www.thecastlehotelbishopscastle.co.uk

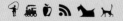

The Swan

The Swan is gorgeous, a contemporary take on a village local. It's part of a new wave of cool little pubs that open all day and do so much more than serve a good pint. The locals love it. They come for breakfast, pop in to buy a loaf of bread, then return for afternoon tea and raid the cake stands. It's set back from the road, with a sprinkling of tables and chairs on the pavement in French-café style. Interiors mix old and new brilliantly. You get Farrow & Ball colours and cool lamps hanging above the bar, then lovely old rugs on boarded floors and a wood-burner to keep things toasty. Push inland and find an airy restaurant open to the rafters that overlooks the garden. Here you dig into Tom Blake's fabulous food (he's ex-River Cottage), anything from a Cornish crab sandwich with lemon mayo to a three-course feast, maybe Wye valley asparagus, Wedmore lamb chops, bitter chocolate mousse with chocolate cookies. Bedrooms are lovely. Two have fancy baths in the room, you get vintage French furniture, iPod docks, colourful throws and walk-in power showers. Glastonbury is close, as are the Mendips.

Rooms	6: 4 doubles, 2 twins/doubles.
Price	£85-£120. Extra bed £20. Cots available.
Meals	Lunch from £5. Dinner, 3 courses, about £25. Sunday lunch from £14. Bar meals only Sun night.
Closed	Rarely.
Directions	M5, junc. 22, then B3139 to Wedmore. In village.

Cassia Stevens
The Swan,
Cheddar Road,
Wedmore BS28 4EQ

Tel +44 (0)1934 710337
Email info@theswanwedmore.com
Web www.theswanwedmore.com

The Talbot Inn at Mells

A timeless village – ancient church, manor house, unspoilt stone cottages – with this 15th-century coaching inn hogging the limelight. It's an absolute stunner, with huge oak doors that lead into a cobbled courtyard, where life gathers in good weather. There's a tithe-barn sitting room with big sofas and a Sunday cinema, then the Coach House Grill, where you eat at weekends under hanging beams. As for the main house, it's a warren of ancient passageways, nooks and crannies and low doorways – the décor may be contemporary, but the past lives on. You'll find rugs on wood floors, crackling log fires, a lovely bar for a pint of Butcombe, then cosy rooms where you dig into tasty food, perhaps leek and potato soup, lemon sole with greens and beets, apple and rosemary tarte tatin. Bedrooms are the best, some small, others huge with claw-foot baths beside modern four-posters. Nothing is too much trouble for the spoiling staff. There's a colourful garden, then further afield some great local walking, so bring your boots. The First World War poet, Siegfried Sassoon, is buried in the churchyard. *Minimum stay two nights at weekends.*

Rooms	8 doubles.
Price	£95-£150.
Meals	Lunch & dinner £5-£30. Sunday lunch, 2 courses, £15.
Closed	Never.
Directions	From Frome A362 for Radstock; Left turn for Mells. At mini-roundabout take right to Mells. After 1 mile turn right to Mells.

Matt Greenlees
The Talbot Inn at Mells,
Selwood Street, Mells,
Frome BA11 3PN

Tel +44 (0)1373 812254
Email info@talbotinn.com
Web www.talbotinn.com

At The Chapel

Every now and then you walk into a small hotel and immediately know you've struck gold. That's what happens here. You cross the threshold and suddenly your pleasure receptors erupt in delight. At the front, you find an intoxicating wine shop on one side, then an irresistible bakery on the other (if you stay, they leave freshly baked croissants outside your room in the morning, a pre-breakfast snack). Back downstairs your eyes draw you through to an enormous room. This is an old Baptist chapel that Catherine and Ahmed bought ten years ago; the chapel itself, now a restaurant/café/art gallery/theatre was once their sitting room. You get white walls, vast windows, contemporary art and a rather cool bar. The food is perfect, nothing too posh, just seriously tasty stuff: fabulous pizza, fish from Lyme Bay, an ambrosial baked aubergine with parmesan and basil. Outside, a gorgeous terrace looks over the town to green hills; above, fabulous bedrooms come with flawless white marble bathrooms. We've run out of space, so come to see for yourself; expect something very special.

Rooms	8: 6 doubles, 2 suites.
Price	£100-£150. Suites £200-£250.
Meals	Breakfast from £2.50. Lunch & dinner £5-£35.
Closed	Rarely.
Directions	Bruton is 5 miles north of the A303 at Wincanton. On high street.

Catherine Butler & Ahmed Sidki
At The Chapel,
High Street, Bruton BA10 0AE

Tel	+44 (0)1749 814070
Email	mail@atthechapel.co.uk
Web	www.atthechapel.co.uk

The Pilgrims Restaurant

Medieval pilgrims in search of King Arthur's tomb would stop here for sustenance before heading out across the marshes on their way to Glastonbury abbey. These days, the food, the welcome and the rooms are all so lovely you're more likely to suffer a crisis of faith and stay put. Jools is to blame – his food is far too good to miss, good enough to alter the DNA of these walls – the Pilgrims has recently morphed into a restaurant with rooms by popular demand. All the lovely old stuff survives – stone walls, timber frames, panelled walls and a couple of sofas in front of the fire. Tables in the restaurant are nicely spaced apart, the lighting is subtle, the service hits the spot. As for the food, expect local ingredients cooked to perfection, perhaps Lyme Bay scallops, rack of local lamb, Somerset rhubarb crumble. Five lovely bedrooms wait in the old skittle alley. Three have cathedral ceilings, all come with exposed stone walls, flat-screen TVs and crisp linen on good beds. As for the bathrooms, expect double-ended baths, separate power showers, fluffy robes. Wells and Glastonbury are close.

Rooms	5: 4 doubles, 1 twin/double.
Price	£60-£120.
Meals	Lunch from £8. Dinner, 3 courses, about £30. Sunday lunch £19. Not Monday.
Closed	Rarely.
Directions	On B3153 between Castle Cary & Somerton. In village by traffic lights.

Julian & Sally Mitchison
The Pilgrims Restaurant,
Lovington, Castle Cary BA7 7PT
Tel +44 (0)1963 240597
Email jools@thepilgrimsatlovington.co.uk
Web www.thepilgrimsatlovington.co.uk

The Queens Arms

Stride across rolling fields, feast on Corton Denham lamb, retire to a perfect room. Buried down several Dorset/Somerset border lanes, Gordon and Jeanette Reid's 18th-century stone pub has an elegant exterior – more country gentleman's house than pub. The bar, with its rug-strewn flagstones and bare boards, pew benches, deep sofas and crackling fire, is most charming. In the dining room – big mirrors on terracotta walls, new china on old tables – robust British dishes are distinguished by fresh ingredients from local suppliers. Try pheasant, pigeon and black pudding terrine, followed by monkfish with chive velouté... then make room for a comforting crumble. Bedrooms are beautifully designed in soothing colours, and all have lovely views over the village and surrounding hills. New coach house rooms are super, too: underfloor heating, crisp linen and down duvets, brass and sleigh beds, iPod docks and immaculate wet rooms. Expect Moor Queen's Revival on tap, homemade pork pies on the bar, Black Spot bacon at breakfast, and stunning walks from the front door. *Dogs welcome in ground-floor bedroom.*

Rooms	8: 6 doubles, 2 twins/doubles.
Price	£85-£120. Singles from £80.
Meals	Lunch from £6.50. Dinner, 3 courses £25-£33.
Closed	Never.
Directions	From A303 take Chapel Cross turning. Through South Cadbury, then next left & follow signs to Corton Denham. Pub at end of village on right.

Gordon & Jeanette Reid
The Queens Arms,
Corton Denham,
Sherborne DT9 4LR

Tel	+44 (0)1963 220317
Email	relax@thequeensarms.com
Web	www.thequeensarms.com

Little Barwick House

A dreamy restaurant with rooms, lost in the hills three miles south of Yeovil. Tim and Emma rolled west ten years ago and have gathered a legion of fans who come to feast on their ambrosial food. The small Georgian country house stands in three acres of peace. A curtain of trees shields it from the outside world, horses graze in the paddock below and afternoon tea is served in the garden in summer, to the sound of birdsong. Inside, graceful interiors flood with light thanks to fine windows that run along the front. There's an open fire in the bar, eclectic reading in the sitting room, and hessian-style carpets in the high-ceilinged dining room. Upstairs, super bedrooms hit the spot with warm colours, silk curtains and a country-house feel. Dinner is the main event: heaven in three courses. Everything is homemade and cooked by Tim and Emma, an equal partnership in the kitchen. Try twice-baked cheese soufflé, pan-fried fillet of Cornish sea bass, apple strudel with calvados ice-cream. A treat. *One-night weekend bookings not always accepted.*

Rooms	6: 4 doubles, 2 twins.
Price	£210-£260. Price includes dinner for two.
Meals	Lunch £23.95-£27.95 (not Tues). Dinner included; non-residents £43.95.
Closed	Sunday & Monday. 2 weeks in January.
Directions	From Yeovil A37 south for Dorchester; left at 1st r'bout. Down hill, past church, left in village and house on left after 200m.

Emma & Tim Ford
Little Barwick House,
Rexes Hollow Lane, Barwick,
Yeovil BA22 9TD
Tel +44 (0)1935 423902
Email reservations@barwick7.fsnet.co.uk
Web www.littlebarwickhouse.co.uk

Lord Poulett Arms

In a ravishing village, an idyllic inn, French at heart and quietly groovy. Part pub, part country house, with walls painted in reds and greens and old rugs covering flagged floors, the Lord Poulett gives a glimpse of a 21st-century dream local, where classical design fuses with earthy rusticity. A fire burns on both sides of the chimney in the dining room; on one side you can sink into leather armchairs, on the other you can eat under beams at antique oak tables while candles flicker. Take refuge with the daily papers on the sofa in the locals' bar or head past a pile of logs at the back door and discover an informal French garden of box and bay trees, with a piste for boules and a creeper-shaded terrace. Bedrooms upstairs come in funky country-house style, with fancy flock wallpaper, perhaps crushed velvet curtains, a small chandelier or a carved-wood bed. Two rooms have slipper baths behind screens in the room; two have claw-foot baths in bathrooms one step across the landing; Roberts radios add to the fun. Delicious food includes summer barbecues, Sunday roasts and the full works at breakfast.

Rooms	4: 2 doubles, both en suite. 2 doubles, each with separate bath.
Price	£85-£95. Singles from £60.
Meals	Lunch from £5.50. Dinner, 3 courses, £25-£30.
Closed	Never.
Directions	A303, then A356 south for Crewkerne. Right for West Chinnock. Through village, 1st left for Hinton St George. Pub on right in village.

Steve & Michelle Hill
Lord Poulett Arms,
High Street,
Hinton St George TA17 8SE

Tel	+44 (0)1460 73149
Email	reservations@lordpoulettarms.com
Web	www.lordpoulettarms.com

The Devonshire Arms

A lively English village with a well-kept green; the old school house stands to the south, the church to the east and the post office to the west. The inn (due north) is over 400 years old and was once a hunting lodge for the Dukes of Devonshire; a rather smart pillared porch survives at the front. These days open-plan interiors are warmly contemporary with high ceilings, shiny blond floorboards and fresh flowers everywhere. Hop onto brown leather stools at the bar and order a pint of Moor Revival, or sink into sofas in front of the fire and crack open a bottle of wine. In summer, life spills onto the terrace at the front, the courtyard at the back and the lawned garden beyond. Super bedrooms run along at the front; all are a good size, but those at each end are huge. You get fresh light rooms, natural flooring, crisp white linen and freeview TV. Two have free-standing baths, some have compact showers. Delicious food is on tap in the restaurant – chargrilled scallops, slow-cooked lamb, passion fruit crème brûlée – so take to the nearby Somerset levels and walk off your indulgence in style.

Rooms	9 doubles.
Price	£90-£135.
Meals	Lunch from £6.95. Dinner £11.50-£18.95.
Closed	Rarely.
Directions	A303, then north on B3165, through Martock to Long Sutton. On village green.

Philip & Sheila Mepham
The Devonshire Arms,
Long Sutton,
Langport TA10 9LP

Tel +44 (0)1458 241271
Email mail@thedevonshirearms.com
Web www.thedevonshirearms.com

Farmers Arms

A lovely inn lost in peaceful hills on the Somerset Levels – a great base for a night or two of affordable luxury. Outside, cockerels crow, cows graze and glorious views from the beer garden drift downhill for a couple of miles – a perfect spot for a pint in summer. Inside, you'll find friendly natives, sofas in front of an open fire and a timber-framed bar, where one airy room rolls into another giving a sense of space and light. There are beamed ceilings, tongue-and-groove panelling, logs piled high in the alcoves. Bedrooms – some big, some huge – are just the ticket. They come with whitewashed walls, cast-iron beds, varnished floors, power showers or double-ended baths. One has a daybed, others have sofas, another has a private courtyard. Delicious food flies from the kitchen, perhaps half a pint of Atlantic prawns, West Country lamb with dauphinoise potatoes, orange and mango cheesecake; in summer you can eat in a courtyard garden. There are local stables if you want to ride and great walking, so bring your boots. Five berths for camper vans wait above the beer garden, too. *Well-behaved dogs welcome.*

Rooms	5: 4 doubles, 1 twin/double.
Price	£75-£125. Singles from £75.
Meals	Lunch & dinner £5-£35.
Closed	Never.
Directions	M5 junc. 25, then south on A358. On dual carriageway, right, signed West Hatch. Follow signs to RSPCA centre up hill for two miles. Signed on left.

Alison Perris
Farmers Arms,
West Hatch, Taunton TA3 5RS

Tel +44 (0)1823 480980
Email farmersarmswh@gmail.com
Web www.farmersarmssomerset.co.uk

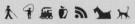

The Castle at Taunton

A Saxon castle stood on this land 1,300 years ago. Its fortunes fluctuated with the centuries and it fell into disrepair, but when the hotel rose from its ashes in 1830, it was crenellated in keeping with the old battlements around it (now the museum). The best spot to appreciate all this is the garden, once the Norman keep. These days, a 200-year-old wisteria roams across the front wall, quite some sight in full bloom. As for the interior, you spin through revolving doors to find tapestries hanging in the hall and grandfather clocks that chime on the hour. It's as if you've entered a gentleman's club, but much of the hotel has a contemporary feel: the ever-busy brasserie, the smart grill room, the cool little bar for a pre-dinner snifter, nooks and crannies to hide away in. Best of all is the music. Five weekends a year are given over to chamber music with musicians from across the globe flying in to perform. Country-house bedrooms come with pretty fabrics, the odd antique, huge beds dressed in white linen. The cricket ground is a short stroll, Exmoor and the Somerset Levels are close. *Children under ten free when sharing parents' room.*

Rooms	44: 27 twins/doubles, 12 singles, 5 garden rooms.
Price	£155-£200. Singles from £99.
Meals	Lunch & dinner £15-£34.
Closed	Never.
Directions	M5 junc. 25 or 26, then centre of town. In town, pick up brown signs to hotel and follow them in.

Marc MacCloskey
The Castle at Taunton,
Castle Green, Taunton TA1 1NF
Tel +44 (0)1823 272671
Email reception@the-castle-hotel.com
Web www.the-castle-hotel.com

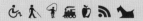

Combe House Hotel

A country lane winds up to this hotel, which basks peacefully in the first folds of the Quantocks. Woodlands rise, a stream pours past and paths lead out for uplifting walks, though with the recent addition of a couple of treatments rooms and a hot tub, you might want to stay put. The hotel, an old mill, dates back to the 17th century and couldn't be in better hands; Gareth and Catherine came to look after the place and have done just that. Outside, free-range chickens stroll around a very productive kitchen garden, while inside you find airy interiors, smart carpets, a wood-burner in the inglenook, the odd exposed wall. Sofas take the strain in the sitting room, armchairs do the job in the bar and you eat under beams in the restaurant, where seriously good local food does the trick: seared scallops with cauliflower purée, Exmoor lamb with dauphinoise potatoes, passion fruit brûlée with mango sorbet. Bedrooms have all been refurbished. Expect a contemporary country style with warm colours, silky throws, flat-screen TVs, and robes in super new bathrooms. There are deer on the hill, too.

Rooms	15: 11 twins/doubles, 2 singles, 2 suites.
Price	£95-£150. Suites £165. Singles from £65. Dinner, B&B from £80 p.p.
Meals	Lunch from £5.50. Sunday lunch from £16. Dinner, 3 courses, about £30.
Closed	Never.
Directions	From Bridgwater A39 to Minehead. At Holford left at Plough Inn; follow lane thro' village. Bear left at fork signed Holford Combe; on right.

Gareth & Catherine Weed
Combe House Hotel,
Holford, Bridgwater TA5 1RZ

Tel +44 (0)1278 741382
Email enquiries@combehouse.co.uk
Web www.combehouse.co.uk

The Oaks Hotel

Another old-school charmer. This Edwardian house sits above the village, a winning position on the side of the hill. A beautiful garden wraps around you; views to the front shoot out to sea, those to the side skim over rooftops and land on Exmoor hills. Tim and Anne do it all themselves and practise the art of old-fashioned hospitality with great flair: they stop to chat, carry bags, ply you with tea and cake on arrival. Logs smoulder on the fire in the hall, hot coals glow in the sitting room. There's a snug bar, parquet flooring, floral fabrics, masses of books. Spotless bedrooms, all with sea views, are lovely: deeply comfy, lots of colour, great value for money. You get bowls of fruit, crisp white linen, fluffy bathrobes and Roberts radios; most have sofas, while beds are turned down every evening. As for dinner, Anne whisks up a four-course feast, perhaps smoked duck and almond salad, Cornish crab cakes with lime and ginger, Somerset pork with prunes and sherry, hot treacle tart with marmalade ice-cream. Exmoor, the coast and Dunster Castle all wait.

Rooms	7: 6 twins/doubles, 1 double.
Price	£155-£175. Dinner, B&B from £115 p.p.
Meals	Dinner, 4 courses, £37.50.
Closed	November-April.
Directions	A39 west to Porlock. Keep left down hill into village and hotel on left after 200m.

Anne & Tim Riley
The Oaks Hotel,
Porlock TA24 8ES

Tel +44 (0)1643 862265
Email info@oakshotel.co.uk
Web www.oakshotel.co.uk

The Culbone

This lovely little restaurant with rooms has glorious views that stretch for miles across these mighty moors. You can walk straight out – the path to Robber's Bridge cuts through the garden. Mark and Jack are part of their community: sourcing their food from nearby farms; giving locals land for an allotment; offering jobs to those who live here. After a day on the moors, come home to comfy sofas by the wood-burner and, of course, Jack's wonderful food (great value) – anything from a spectacular Toulouse sausage sandwich to grilled sea bass with harissa and fennel. If eating the food isn't enough, Jack runs a cookery school and will teach you how prepare his dishes; he'll even take you down to the farm, into the forest to forage or along to the river to fish: total immersion! Back at the inn you find whitewashed walls and contemporary furniture, then pretty bedrooms (not huge) with lots of comfort, thoughtful touches, the occasional shiny bedspread. One opens onto its own terrace, another has extra special views across the moors. And dogs are made most welcome.

Rooms	5: 4 doubles, 1 twin/double.
Price	£85-£125. Dinner, B&B from £65 p.p.
Meals	Lunch from £6.50. Dinner, 3 courses, £25-£35.
Closed	Never.
Directions	West from Porlock on A39 and on right after 5 miles.

Mark Sanders & Jack Scarterfield
The Culbone,
Porlock, Minehead TA24 8JW
Tel +44 (0)1643 862259
Email mark@pipspubs.com
Web www.theculbone.com

Cross Lane House

A medieval farmhouse in a National Trust village, where a 500-year-old bridge sweeps you across to ancient woodland. Outside, a cobbled courtyard leads up to a hay barn that's open on one side – not a bad spot for breakfast in good weather. Inside, original panelling is the big architectural draw, but Max and Andrew's lovely design gives a warm country-house feel, making this an intimate bolthole in which to linger. You'll find a sitting room packed with beautiful things – books galore, a wood-burner, sofas and armchairs to take the strain. There's a spy hole in the panelling, some ancient graffiti, too, then a pretty dining room with candles and low ceilings for nicely priced food, perhaps scallops with wild garlic, chicken wrapped in prosciutto, lemon tart with amaretto cream. Bedrooms upstairs are deeply satisfying: lovely beds, bowls of fruit, timber frames, super bathrooms. One is smaller, two are bigger, the family suite comes with a separate bedroom for children (or adults). Expect Roberts radios, Cowshed oils, a sofa if there's room. Exmoor waits. The road passes quietly at night. *Minimum two nights at weekends.*

Rooms	3: 2 doubles, 1 suite (1 double, 1 twin).
Price	£120-£145. Suite £120-£160. Singles from £100.
Meals	Lunch from £6 (Thur-Sat). Dinner £23.50-£27.50. Sunday lunch £18-£24.
Closed	January.
Directions	A39 west from Minehead. On right after 5 miles, 1 mile before Porlock.

Max Lawrence & Andrew Stinson
Cross Lane House,
Allerford, Minehead TA24 8HW
Tel +44 (0)1643 863276
Email max@crosslanehouse.com
Web www.crosslanehouse.com

Netherstowe House

This quirky hotel is full of surprises, not least its wonderful bedrooms that are an absolute steal, but also for its peculiar location on the edge of a 1970s housing estate. If the latter puts you off, don't let it – the house is hidden by fine beech hedging and once up the drive you forget the outside world. Inside you fall immediately under the spell of some rather eccentric interiors that mix country-house style with 19th-century colonial overtones. You'll find varnished wood floors, roaring fires, erupting tropical plants, the odd chandelier. Gorgeous bedrooms are great value for money and come in an elegant clean style: beautiful beds, cool colours, old armoires. Bathrooms are fabulous. If you want something more contemporary, nip across the courtyard to the serviced apartments. They have fancy kitchens but breakfast is included and the hotel is yours to roam. As for the food, it's served in a couple of smart dining rooms, perhaps wild mushroom risotto, slow-cooked spicy pork belly, roast pineapple with mango salsa. There are good steaks in the colourful cellar bistro, too.

Rooms	9 + 8: 7 doubles, 1 twin, 1 suite. Garden: 8 apartments for 4, with kitchens.
Price	£95-£145. Suite £195. Apartments £120.
Meals	Lunch from £19.95. Dinner, 3 courses, about £30.
Closed	26 December-2 January.
Directions	Sent on booking.

Ben Heathcote
Netherstowe House,
Netherstowe Lane,
Lichfield WS13 6AY

Tel +44 (0)1543 254270
Email info@netherstowehouse.com
Web www.netherstowehouse.com

The Bildeston Crown

A 15th-century village inn owned by the local farmer – his roast rib of beef on Sundays is hard to beat. Outside, there's a terrace overlooking the village, then a small courtyard for a pint in the sun. Inside, timber frames, sagging ceilings and heavy beams are all original. A contemporary feel runs throughout with bold colours, comfy sofas and big art on the walls. There's an open fire in the pretty bar, a good spot for afternoon tea, but the big draw here is the restaurant with Suffolk lamb, Red Poll beef and Nedging pork all from the fields around you; vegetables come from the farm's kitchen garden, too. A couple of menus run side by side: one for dishes like fish pie or chargrilled steak, then another for fancier food altogether, perhaps duck consommé, Suffolk venison, chocolate fondant with vanilla ice-cream (an eight-course tasting menu is an extension of the à la carte). Upstairs, lovely bedrooms wait. One has a four-poster, another comes in black with a funky bath, all have robes in good bathrooms. Bury St Edmunds, medieval Lavenham and the Suffolk coast are close.

Rooms	12: 10 doubles, 2 twins.
Price	£100-£195. Singles from £70.
Meals	Bar meals (lunch & dinner) from £12. Dinner, 3-course set menu, £25; à la carte about £45; tasting menu £70. Sunday lunch from £17.
Closed	Never.
Directions	A12 junc. 31, then B1070 to Hadleigh. A1141 north, then B1115 into village & on right.

Alice Gibbons
The Bildeston Crown,
104 High Street, Bildeston,
Lavenham IP7 7EB

Tel +44 (0)1449 740510
Email reception@thebildestoncrown.com
Web www.thebildestoncrown.com

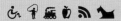

The Swan at Lavenham

The Swan is ancient, 600 years old, a spectacular tangle of medieval timber and sagging beams. Recently refurbished in epic style, you get the impression it has never looked better. Inside, fires roar, ceilings soar and the loveliest staff weave through the mix delivering sinful plates of afternoon tea or cocktails before supper. Potter about and find a minstrel's gallery in the vaulted dining room, a fabulous old bar that was a favourite haunt of WWII airmen, then a lawned courtyard garden, where you can stop for a glass of Pimms in summer. Bedrooms are lovely, some vast with four-posters and timber-framed walls, others more contemporary with cool colours and good sofas. All have super-comfy beds, crisp white linen, sparkling bathrooms and fluffy robes; bowls of fruit come as standard, beds are turned down during dinner. Elsewhere, there's a 14th-century hall for private dinners and weddings, and you can eat in an open-plan brasserie if you want something lighter. Finally, medieval Lavenham is a sight to behold; don't miss it. *Minimum two nights at weekends. Some on-site parking. Ask about special offers.*

Rooms	45: 32 twins/doubles, 2 four-posters, 1 single, 10 suites.
Price	£195-£250. Suites £290-£350. Singles from £105. Dinner, B&B from £122.50 p.p.
Meals	Lunch, 2 courses, from £16.95. Dinner, 3 courses £35.95. Brasserie, 2 courses, from £16.
Closed	Never.
Directions	10 miles south of Bury St Edmunds; 15 miles north of Colchester. On High Street in village.

Ingo Wiangke
The Swan at Lavenham,
High Street, Lavenham CO10 9QA

Tel +44 (0)1787 247477
Email info@theswanatlavenham.co.uk
Web www.theswanatlavenham.co.uk

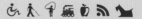

The Great House

Lavenham is a Suffolk gem, a medieval wool town trapped in aspic. The Great House stands across the market place from the Guildhall, its Georgian façade giving way to airy 15th-century interiors, where timber frames and old beams mix with contemporary colours and varnished wood floors. The poet Stephen Spender and his brother Humphrey – famous artist and photographer – once lived here and the house became a meeting place for artists, but these days it's the ambrosial food that draws the crowd. French to its core – the cheese board must qualify as one of the best in Britain – so dig into something delicious, perhaps venison, pistachio and sultana terrine, sea bass served with olives and white wine, then tarte tatin with cinnamon ice-cream. Fabulous bedrooms – all recently refurbished in lavish style – come with delicious bed linen, suede sofas, coffee machines, and robes in magnificent bathrooms. Four are huge, but even the tiniest is a dream. One has a regal four-poster, another has a 14th-century fireplace in its bathroom. All come with an array of gadgets: hi-fi, surround-sound, flat-screen TV... *Minimum stay two nights at weekends.*

Rooms	5: 4 doubles, 1 twin/double.
Price	£95-£195. Dinner, B&B from £112.50 p.p.
Meals	Breakfast £10-£15. Lunch from £18.50 (not Mon/Tues). Dinner £33.50 (not Sun/Mon).
Closed	First 4 weeks in January; 2 weeks in summer.
Directions	A1141 to Lavenham. At High Street 1st right after The Swan or up Lady Street into Market Place. On-site parking.

Régis & Martine Crépy
The Great House,
Market Place, Lavenham,
Sudbury CO10 9QZ

Tel +44 (0)1787 247431
Email info@greathouse.co.uk
Web www.greathouse.co.uk

The Crown

Everything here is good: a lovely country pub, a very pretty village, a sublime position in Constable country. The Crown dates back to 1560 and has old beams and timber frames, but the country interiors have youthful good looks – tongue-and-groove bars, terracotta-tiled floors, a fancy wine cellar that stands behind a wall of glass, rugs and settles, the daily papers, leather armchairs in front of a wood-burner. Four ales wait at the bar, 30 wines come by the glass and seasonal food has a local following; try buck rarebit with fried quail's eggs, confit of Blythburgh pork with honey and apricots, steamed marmalade pudding with custard. In summer you can eat on the terrace. Airy bedrooms – peacefully hidden away at the bottom of the garden – are exemplary, with bathrooms as good as they get. There are excellent beds, lovely linen, underfloor heating, a dash of colour. All have armchairs or sofas, three have French windows that open onto private terraces. Outside, fields stretch off to a distant ridge, birds soar high in the sky. A great place to eat, sleep and potter.

Rooms	11: 10 doubles, 1 suite.
Price	£130-£210. Suite £185-£225. Singles from £95.
Meals	Lunch & dinner £5-£25.
Closed	Rarely.
Directions	North from Colchester on A134, then B1087 east into Stoke-by-Nayland. Right at T-junction; pub on left.

Richard Sunderland
The Crown,
Park Street, Stoke-by-Nayland,
Colchester CO6 4SE

Tel	+44 (0)1206 262001
Email	enquiries@crowninn.net
Web	www.crowninn.net

Kesgrave Hall

This Georgian mansion sits in 38 acres of woodland and was built for an MP in 1812. It served as home to US airmen during WWII, becoming a prep school shortly after. Refurbished in 2008, it was an instant hit with locals, who love the style, the food and the informal vibe, and despite its country-house good looks, it is almost a restaurant with rooms, the emphasis firmly on the food. Inside, you find Wellington boots in the entrance hall, high ceilings in the huge sitting room, stripped boards in the humming bistro and doors that open onto a terrace in summer. Excellent bedrooms have lots of style. One is huge and comes with a faux leopard-skin sofa and free-standing bath. The others might not be quite as wild, but they're lovely nonetheless, some in the eaves, others in beautifully refurbished outbuildings. Expect warm colours, crisp linen, good lighting and fancy bathrooms. Back downstairs tasty bistro food flies from the kitchen, perhaps goats' cheese panna cotta, cottage pie with red cabbage, pear tart with rosemary and vanilla ice-cream. Suffolk's magical coast waits.

Rooms	23: 10 doubles, 7 twins/doubles, 6 suites.
Price	£125-£230. Suites £275-£300.
Meals	Breakfast £10-£16. Lunch & dinner, 3 courses, £25-£30.
Closed	Never.
Directions	Skirt Ipswich to the south on A14, then head north on A12. Left at 4th roundabout; signed right after 0.25 miles.

Oliver Richards
Kesgrave Hall,
Hall Road,
Kesgrave, Ipswich IP5 2PU

Tel +44 (0)1473 333741
Email reception@kesgravehall.com
Web www.milsomhotels.com

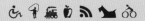

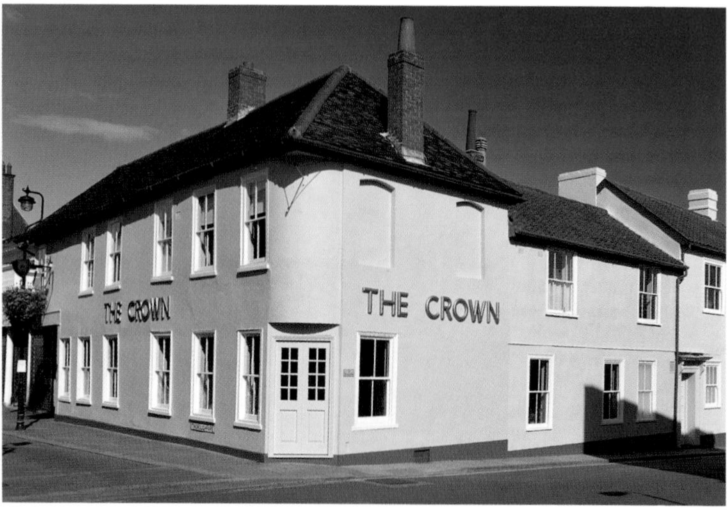

The Crown at Woodbridge

This cool little inn in the middle of Woodbridge slopes down Quay Street, its rainbow of pastel colours now a landmark in town. Inside, open-plan interiors flood with light courtesy of a glass ceiling. A Windermere skiff hangs above the bar, you find painted panelling, comfy sofas, slate floors and a wood-burner roaring in the fireplace. Dining rooms sprawl, one in red, another in pale olive; you get leather banquettes, contemporary art, the odd window seat. Beautiful bedrooms upstairs vary in size, but all have the same smart feel: cool colours, duck down duvets, padded headboards, Hypnos beds. You'll find panels of entwined willow, pitchforks hanging on the wall, super bathrooms that go the whole hog. Back downstairs, Stephen's rustic food is the big draw, perhaps potted shoulder of venison with walnuts and sloe jelly, steamed mussels in white wine and garlic, toffee apple tart with vanilla ice-cream. As for breakfast, everything is brought to your table: poached fruits, flagons of juice, the best sausages in Suffolk. Don't miss Snape Maltings, Sutton Hoo or the Aldeburgh food festival in October.

Rooms	10: 8 twins/doubles, 2 family rooms.
Price	£120-£160. Singles from £95.
Meals	Lunch & dinner £6-£30. Sunday lunch from £12.50.
Closed	Never.
Directions	A12 north from Ipswich, then B1438 into town. Pass station & left into Quay St. On right.

Stephen David
The Crown at Woodbridge,
Thoroughfare, Woodbridge IP12 1AD

Tel +44 (0)1394 384242
Email info@thecrownatwoodbridge.co.uk
Web www.thecrownatwoodbridge.co.uk

The Crown & Castle

Orford is unbeatable, a sleepy Suffolk village blissfully marooned at the end of the road. River, beach and forest wait, as does the Crown & Castle, a fabulous English hostelry where the art of hospitality is practised with great flair. The inn stands in the shadow of Orford's 12th-century castle. The feel is warm and airy with stripped floorboards, open fires, eclectic art and candles at night. Rooms come with Vi-Spring beds, super bathrooms, lovely fabrics, the odd armchair. Four in the main house have watery views, the suite is stunning, the garden rooms big and light, the courtyard rooms (the latest addition) utterly sublime. All have crisp white linen, TVs, DVDs and digital radios. Wellington boots wait at the back door, so pull on a pair and explore Rendlesham Forest or hop on a boat and chug over to Orfordness. Ambrosial food awaits your return, perhaps seared squid with coriander and garlic, slow-cooked pork belly with a shellfish broth, crushed pistachio meringue with a chocolate ice-cream sundae. A great place to wash up for a few lazy days. Sutton Hoo is close. Very dog-friendly. *Minimum two nights dinner, B&B at weekends.*

Rooms	21: 18 doubles, 2 twins, 1 suite.
Price	£130-£190. Suite £245. Dinner, B&B from £99.50 p.p.
Meals	Lunch from £8.50. À la carte dinner around £35.
Closed	Never.
Directions	A12 north from Ipswich, A1152 east to Woodbridge, then B1084 into Orford. Right in square for castle. On left.

David & Ruth Watson
The Crown & Castle,
Orford, Woodbridge IP12 2LJ

Tel +44 (0)1394 450205
Email info@crownandcastle.co.uk
Web www.crownandcastle.co.uk

The Old Rectory

A small country house full of beautiful things. The welcome, the food, the style, the bedrooms, all hit the spot. You're in three acres of orchards and lawns, with a vegetable garden that supplies much for the table and a small band of chickens that provide eggs for breakfast. Inside, fat sofas sit by a smouldering fire, beautiful art hangs on the walls, an honesty bar helps you unwind. It's a little like being at a house party – friendly and informal with other people doing all the hard work. In winter you breakfast in the chic dining room with logs crackling on the fire; in summer you decant to the stone-flagged conservatory that opens onto the terrace. Lovely bedrooms have warm colours, pretty furniture, smart bathrooms, the odd sofa. One is up in the eaves, two open onto the garden. As for the food, it's simply delicious, maybe parsnip soup, rack of lamb, apple tart and caramel ice-cream. Lunch is served once a month with everything you eat coming from the garden. Snape Maltings and Sutton Hoo are close. A very happy house; bring your friends and have the place to yourself. *Minimum two nights at weekends April-October.*

Rooms	7: 6 doubles, 1 twin/double.
Price	£95-£145. Singles from £75.
Meals	Dinner, 3 courses, £28. Mon, Wed & Fri only (except for parties of 8 or more).
Closed	Rarely.
Directions	North from Woodbridge on A12 for 8 miles, then right onto B1078. In village, over railway line; house on right just before church.

Michael & Sally Ball
The Old Rectory,
Station Road, Campsea Ashe,
Woodbridge IP13 0PU

Tel +44 (0)1728 746524
Email mail@theoldrectorysuffolk.com
Web www.theoldrectorysuffolk.com

Wentworth Hotel

The Wentworth has the loveliest position in town, the beach literally a pebble's throw from the garden, the sea rolling east under a vast sky. Inside, fires smoulder, clocks chime and seaside elegance abounds. It's all terrifically English, with vintage wallpapers, kind local staff and an elegant bar that opens onto a terrace garden. The restaurant looks out to sea, spilling onto a sunken terrace in summer for views of passing boats. Delicious English fare flies from the kitchen: stilton soup, breast of guinea fowl, lemon posset with raspberries and shortbread. The hotel has been in the same family since 1920 and old-fashioned values mix harmoniously with interiors that are refreshed often to keep things sparkling. Spotless bedrooms are deeply comfy, those at the front have huge sea views (and binoculars). Expect warm colours, wicker armchairs, padded headboards and comfortable beds. Bathrooms, all refurbished, are excellent. Sofas galore in the sitting room, but you may want to spurn them to walk by the sea. Joyce Grenfell was a regular. The Snape Maltings are close. *Minimum two nights at weekends.*

Rooms	35: 24 twins/doubles, 4 singles. Darfield House: 7 doubles.
Price	£140-£220. Singles from £85. Dinner, B&B from £70 p.p.
Meals	Bar meals from £5. Lunch from £12. Dinner, 3 courses, £18.50-£24.
Closed	Never.
Directions	A12 north from Ipswich, then A1094 for Aldeburgh. Past church, down hill, left at x-roads; hotel on right.

Michael Pritt
Wentworth Hotel,
Wentworth Road,
Aldeburgh IP15 5BD

Tel +44 (0)1728 452312
Email stay@wentworth-aldeburgh.com
Web www.wentworth-aldeburgh.com

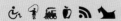

The Brudenell Hotel

The Brudenell stands bang on the beach in one of England's loveliest seaside towns. It makes the most of its view: a dining terrace at the front runs the length of the building; a glass-fronted restaurant swims in light; an elegant sitting room looks the right way. The hotel mixes a contemporary style and an informal feel. You'll find coastal art, sunny colours, driftwood sculptures on display. Beautiful bedrooms come in different shapes and sizes. Those at the back look onto open country and river marsh, those at the front have hypnotic views of sea and sky. A chic style runs throughout: seaside colours, good fabrics, blond wood furniture, sofas if there's room; bathrooms are excellent. Back downstairs the open-plan brasserie is the hub of the hotel. It serves good comfort food with lots of fish on the menu, but you can always grab a burger or a steak if that's what you want. Try crispy fried goats' cheese, Harwich crab tart, sticky toffee pudding with clotted cream. Elsewhere, there are beach towels, deckchairs or golf up the road at Thorpeness, and on clear nights the starry sky will amaze you. *Minimum two nights at weekends.*

Rooms	44: 12 doubles, 30 twins/doubles, 2 singles.
Price	£150-£325. Singles from £80.
Meals	Lunch from £5. Dinner, 3 courses, about £30.
Closed	Never.
Directions	A1094 into Aldeburgh. Right at T-junction, down high street, last left in village before car park & yacht club.

Garth Wray
The Brudenell Hotel,
The Parade,
Aldeburgh IP15 5BU

Tel	+44 (0)1728 452071
Email	info@brudenellhotel.co.uk
Web	www.brudenellhotel.co.uk

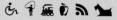

The Westleton Crown

This is one of England's oldest coaching inns, with 800 years of continuous service under its belt. It stands in a village two miles inland from the sea at Dunwich, with Westleton Heath running east towards Minsmere Bird Sanctuary. Inside, you find the best of old and new. A recent refurbishment has introduced Farrow & Ball colours, leather sofas and a tongue-and-groove bar, and they mix harmoniously with panelled walls, stripped floors and ancient beams. Weave around and find nooks and crannies in which to hide, flames flickering in an open fire, a huge map on the wall for walkers. You can eat wherever you want, and a conservatory/breakfast room opens onto a terraced garden for summer barbecues. Fish comes straight off the boats at Lowestoft, local butchers provide local meat. Bedrooms are scattered about – between the inn and the car park annexe – and come in cool lime-white with comfy beds, crisp linen, flat-screen TVs. Super bathrooms are fitted out in Fired Earth, and some have claw-foot baths. Aldeburgh and Southwold are close by. *Minimum two nights at weekends.*

Rooms	34: 26 doubles, 2 twins, 1 single, 2 family rooms, 3 suites.
Price	£95-£180. Suites £185-£215. Singles from £90.
Meals	Lunch & dinner from £5.50. Sunday lunch from £14.95.
Closed	Never.
Directions	A12 north from Ipswich. Right at Yoxford onto B1122, then left for Westleton on B1125. On right in village.

Gareth Clarke
The Westleton Crown,
The Street, Westleton,
Saxmundham IP17 3AD

Tel +44 (0)1728 648777
Email info@westletoncrown.co.uk
Web www.westletoncrown.co.uk

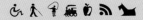

The Anchor

The Anchor is one of those wonderful places that has resisted the urge to be precious. This is a cool little seaside inn where relaxed informality reigns; kids are welcome, staff are lovely, dogs fall asleep in the bar. You're 500m back from the sea with a vast sky hovering above and waves breaking in the distance. Outside, a big terrace fills with happy locals in summer, while a lawned garden stretches off towards the water. Inside, a beautiful simplicity abounds – Cape Cod meets English country local. You'll find books everywhere, wonderful art, then roaring fires, scrubbed pine tables, old leather benches and painted tongue-and-groove. Sophie's local food is the big draw, perhaps cheese soufflé with caramelised onions, roast cod with lentils and chorizo, then banana fritters with toffee sauce. Bedrooms are great value; those in the house are simpler, while the fabulous garden chalet suites have just been superbly refurbished. They're big, airy and open onto terraces that overlook the garden. Mark's menu of bottled beers is exceptional, as is the night sky. Unmissable. *10% discount to Sawday's readers.*

Rooms	10 doubles.
Price	£100-£150.
Meals	Lunch from £5.25. Dinner, 3 courses, about £30. Sunday lunch, 2 courses, £20.
Closed	Never.
Directions	From A12 south of Southwold, B1387 to Walberswick.

Mark & Sophie Dorber
The Anchor,
Main Street, Walberswick,
Southwold IP18 6UA

Tel +44 (0)1502 722112
Email info@anchoratwalberswick.com
Web www.anchoratwalberswick.com

The Swan House

Once a 16th-century tavern, now a 21st-century pleasure dome, Swan House is a magical little place – quirky, intimate, deeply beautiful. It sits opposite a 14th-century church, the river Waveney passing below. In summer life spills onto the pedestrianised Walk; in winter you sink into sofas in front of the fire. Interiors are perfect: timber frames, ancient walls, beamed ceilings, striking colours. It's a tiny place which adds greatly to its charm. A movie plays in the front hall every day, you get fresh flowers and lovely art everywhere. One restaurant comes in red with pretty rugs and logs in the alcove; the other doubles as a gallery and has a fine oval table. Faultless bedrooms mix low ceilings, contemporary panelling, creaky floorboards and piles of books. Two have open fires, one a mezzanine for children, another a small balcony; all have magnificent bathrooms. Breakfast is extraordinary, one delicious course after another: Irish tea loaf, hams and cheese, plates of fruit, the full cooked works. Dinner is equally splendid: fresh mussels, confit of duck, amaretto ice-cream. One of the best. *Minimum stay two nights at weekends. Children over six welcome.*

Rooms	5: 4 doubles, 1 family room.
Price	£90-£145. Family room £140-£165.
Meals	Lunch from £6. Dinner, table d'hôte, £14-£17.50; à la carte, £25-£35. Sunday lunch from £14.
Closed	Never.
Directions	In centre of town at foot of clock tower. Car parks nearby.

Roland Blunk & Camela Sabatini
The Swan House,
By the tower,
Beccles NR34 9HE

Tel +44 (0)1502 713474
Email info@swan-house.com
Web www.swan-house.com

Halfway Bridge Inn

Fancy visiting Petworth House or walking the South Downs? You've come to the perfect place. With the Crab & Lobster at Sidlesham thriving, Sam Bakose has worked his magic on this mellow old coaching inn deep in polo country, just back from the A272. A series of spruced-up rooms comes with cosy corners and split levels, the bar with a modern look, the rest more traditional: scrubbed tables, crackling fires, fat candles. Thirsts are quenched by local Langham and Long Man beers and 25 wines by the glass, and the food is a satisfying mix of traditional and modern British, the menus evolving with the seasons. Tuck into moules frites at the bar or pork belly and black pudding terrine, or baked bream with clam and caper butter – just leave room for prune and armagnac tart. For summer there's a sheltered patio with posh tables and brollies. A hundred yards away, over the lane, are seven super rooms in the long, low Cowdray barns, with old beams and panelling, rustic brickwork and flat-screen TVs, local artwork, new carpets, soft furnishings and deep beds. *Two-night minimum stay at weekends.*

Rooms	7: 6 doubles, 1 suite.
Price	£120-£150. Suite £170-£190. Singles from £80 (Sun-Thurs).
Meals	Lunch & dinner £14.50-£28. Bar meals £6.50-£12.50.
Closed	Never.
Directions	On A272 halfway between Midhurst & Petworth.

Sam Bakose
Halfway Bridge Inn,
Halfway Bridge,
Petworth GU28 9BP

Tel	+44 (0)1798 861281
Email	enquiries@halfwaybridge.co.uk
Web	www.halfwaybridge.co.uk

Park House Hotel & Spa

A blissful pocket of rural Sussex. Park House sits in 12 acres of glorious English gardens with quilted fields circling the grounds and the South Downs rising beyond. Potter about outside and find a croquet lawn, a grass tennis court and a six-hole golf course that slips into the country. Fine shrubberies burst with colour while Wellington boots wait at the front door for long country walks. You may prefer to stay put; the newest addition is its fabulous spa. It comes with a very swanky indoor pool to go with its outside partner, four treatment rooms, a sauna and steam room, then a proper gym and a terraced bar for lazy afternoons. As for the house, it's just as good. Beautiful interiors abound mixing country-house style with contemporary colours. The pavilion bar overlooks the gardens, you breakfast in the conservatory or out on the terrace, there are flagstones in reception, the daily papers in the sitting room, great food in the dining room. Gorgeous bedrooms are the final luxury: heavenly beds, big country views, fancy bathrooms, iMac TVs. Exceptional. *Special rates for Goodwood.*

Rooms	20 + 1: 10 twins/doubles, 6 doubles, 4 family suites. Self-catering cottage for 2-4.
Price	£160-£224. Family suites & cottage £230-£360.
Meals	Lunch, 2 courses, from £20.95. Afternoon tea £19.95. Dinner, 3 courses, £37.50.
Closed	Rarely.
Directions	South from Midhurst on A286. At sharp left bend, right (straight ahead), signed Bepton. Hotel on left after 2 miles.

Rebecca Coonan
Park House Hotel & Spa,
Bepton, Midhurst GU29 0JB

Tel +44 (0)1730 819000
Email reservations@parkhousehotel.com
Web www.parkhousehotel.com

The Royal Oak Inn

This pretty inn sits in a sleepy Sussex village with the South Downs rising above and the coast at the Whitterings waiting below. Inside, an attractive rusticity prevails: stripped floors, low ceilings and the odd racing print (the inn was once part of the Goodwood estate). There's a small bar for a pint in front of an open fire, but these days it's a mostly dining pub, the restaurant spreading itself far and wide, through the conservatory and out onto the terrace in summer. A small army of chefs conjure up irresistible food, perhaps Selsey crab mousse with a Vermouth foam, roast guinea fowl with a prune terrine, whisky Mac jelly with cinnamon oats. Elegant bedrooms are sprinkled about, some in garden cottages, others upstairs. All come in contemporary style with smart fabrics, leather armchairs, comfy beds and good bathrooms. CD players, plasma screens, and DVD libraries keep you amused. Staff are attentive, complimentary newspapers arrive with breakfast. The South Downs are all about, Goodwood is a mile up the road, Chichester Theatre and Bosham are close. *Minimum two nights at weekends.*

Rooms	8: 3 twins/doubles, 2 doubles, 3 suites.
Price	£110-£190. Suites £180-£280. Singles from £85.
Meals	Lunch from £7.95. Dinner, 3 courses, about £35. Sunday lunch £25-£29.
Closed	Never.
Directions	From Chichester A286 for Midhurst. First right at first mini roundabout into E. Lavant. Down hill, past village green, over bridge, pub 200m on left. Car park opposite.

Charles Ullmann
The Royal Oak Inn,
Pook Lane, East Lavant,
Chichester PO18 0AX

Tel +44 (0)1243 527434
Email rooms@royaloakeastlavant.co.uk
Web www.royaloakeastlavant.co.uk

The Crab & Lobster

This tiny arrowhead of land south of Chichester is something of a time warp, more 1940s than 21st century. The Crab & Lobster is older still – 350 years at last count. It sits on Pagham Harbour, a tidal marsh that teems with preening birds. Outside, you find a smart whitewashed exterior and a small garden for dreamy views across grazing fields to the water. Inside, a glittering refurbishment comes in contemporary style with Farrow & Ball colours, flagstone floors, blond wood furniture, suede armchairs and a smouldering fire. Big mirrors reflect the light, candles flicker in the evening. Upstairs, four super rooms come in duck-egg blue with crisp white linen, flat-screen TVs and gorgeous little bathrooms. Three have views of the water, one is up in the eaves and has a telescope to scan the high seas. There's much to explore: Bosham, where King Canute tried to turn back the waves; Fishbourne, for its imperious Roman palace; the Witterings, for sand dunes and miles of beach. Don't forget dinner, perhaps fresh calamari, Barbary duck, marmalade bread and butter pudding. *Minimum two nights at weekends.*

Rooms	5: 4 doubles, 1 cottage.
Price	£145. Cottage £230.
Meals	Lunch from £10.50. Bar meals from £6.50. Dinner from £16.95. Sunday lunch, 2-3 courses, £24-£35.
Closed	Never.
Directions	Mill Lane is off B2145 Chichester to Selsey road, just south of Sidlesham. Pub close to Pagham Harbour.

Sam Bakose
The Crab & Lobster,
Mill Lane, Sidlesham,
Chichester PO20 7NB

Tel +44 (0)1243 641233
Email enquiries@crab-lobster.co.uk
Web www.crab-lobster.co.uk

Burpham Country House & Brasserie

Come for old England in the foothills of the South Downs. Woodpeckers and warblers live in the woods, the church was built in 1167 and when you potter south to Arundel, its magnificent castle looms across the fields. The road runs out in the village and the house stands quietly, with colour tumbling from stone walls and a lawned terrace in front of a Victorian veranda. Originally a Georgian hunting lodge, it served as a vicarage to Tickner Edwardes, the great apiarist, who fought in Gallipoli; John Ruskin knew the house, too. Inside, comfortable interiors are stylish without being style-led. There's an airy sitting room bar, a panelled restaurant for local food, and a brick-and-flint conservatory that opens onto a croquet lawn. Spotless bedrooms are good value for money, some big, some smaller, all with crisp linen and flat-screen TVs; most have country views. Collared doves nest in the garden, swans winter on the Arundel wetlands and Alfred the Great extended this ridge 1,200 years ago to defend England from the Vikings. There's cricket in summer, too. *Minimum two nights at weekends April-October. Dogs by arrangement.*

Rooms	9: 5 doubles, 4 twins/doubles.
Price	£85-£145.
Meals	Lunch from £10 (Wed-Sat). Sunday lunch from £18. Dinner, 2 courses, £16 (mid-week only), or à la carte £25-£30 (not Sun or Mon).
Closed	Rarely.
Directions	A27 east from Arundel, past station, then left for Burpham. Straight ahead for 2.5 miles; on left.

Jacqueline & Steve Penticost
Burpham Country House,
Burpham,
Arundel BN18 9RJ

Tel	+44 (0)1903 882160
Email	info@burphamcountryhouse.com
Web	www.burphamcountryhouse.com

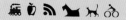

The Bull

Stepping into The Bull is like travelling back in time to Dickensian England; little seems to have changed in 200 years. Electricity has been introduced, but even that is rationed on aesthetic grounds; as a result, light plays beautifully amid old timbers. Elsewhere, fires roar, beams sag, candles twinkle, tankards dangle. You might call it 'nostalgic interior design', but whatever it is, the locals love it; the place was packed on a Sunday afternoon in late January. Well-kept ales are on tap in the bar, excellent food flies from the kitchen, perhaps caramelised parsnip and apple soup, a magnificent plate of rare roast beef, then chilled white chocolate and vanilla fondue. Upstairs, four pretty rooms await (two larger, two above the bar) with more planned. You may find timber-framed walls, leather sleigh beds or statues of eastern deities, while the 21st century delivers digital radios, contemporary art and very good compact bathrooms. Bring walking boots or mountain bikes and take to the high trails on the South Downs National Park, which rise beyond the village. Brighton is close.

Rooms	4: 3 doubles, 1 twin/double.
Price	£80-£120.
Meals	Lunch from £5.50. Dinner, 3 courses, about £30.
Closed	Never.
Directions	Leave A23 just north of Brighton for Pyecombe. North on A273, then west for Ditchling on B2112. In centre of village at crossroads.

Dominic Worrall
The Bull,
2 High Street, Ditchling,
Hassocks BN6 8TA

Tel +44 (0)1273 843147
Email info@thebullditchling.com
Web www.thebullditchling.com

The Griffin Inn

A proper inn, one of the best, a community local that draws a well-heeled and devoted crowd. The occasional touch of scruffiness makes it almost perfect; fancy designers need not apply. The Pullan family run it with huge passion. You get cosy open fires, 400-year-old beams, oak panelling, settles, red carpets, prints on the walls... this inn has aged beautifully. There's a lively bar, a small club room for racing on Saturdays and two cricket teams playing in summer. Bedrooms are tremendous value for money, full of uncluttered country-inn elegance: uneven floors, lovely old furniture, soft coloured walls, free-standing Victorian baths, huge shower heads, crisp linen, fluffy bathrobes, handmade soaps. Rooms in the coach house are quieter, those in next-door Griffin House quieter still. Seasonal menus include fresh fish from Rye and Fletching lamb. On Sundays in summer they lay on a spit-roast barbecue in the garden, with ten-mile views stretching across Pooh Bear's Ashdown Forest to Sheffield Park. Not to be missed. *Minimum two nights bank holiday weekends.*

Rooms	13: 6 doubles, 7 four-posters.
Price	£85-£145. Singles from £60 (Sun-Thur).
Meals	Bar meals from £6.50. Dinner, 3 courses, £30-£40.
Closed	25 December.
Directions	From East Grinstead A22 south, right at Nutley for Fletching. On for 2 miles into village.

Nigel & James Pullan
The Griffin Inn,
Fletching, Uckfield TN22 3SS

Tel +44 (0)1825 722890
Email info@thegriffininn.co.uk
Web www.thegriffininn.co.uk

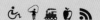

Newick Park Hotel & Country Estate

A heavenly country house that thrills at every turn. The setting – 255 acres of parkland, river, lake and gardens – is spectacular; come in winter and you may wake to find a ribbon of mist entangled in a distant ridge of trees. Inside, majestic interiors elate, be it sagging bookshelves in a panelled study, Doric columns in a glittering drawing room or roaring fires in a sofa-strewn hall. You get all the aristocratic fixtures and fittings – grand pianos, plaster mouldings, a bar that sits in an elegant alcove – while views from the terrace run down to a lake. Oils hang on walls, chandeliers dangle above. Country-house bedrooms fit the bill: lush linen, thick floral fabrics, marble bathrooms with robes and lotions, views to the front of nothing but country; some are the size of a London flat. A two-acre walled garden provides much for the table, so don't miss exceptional food, perhaps a hen's egg with Serrano ham, pheasant from the woods around you, Earl Grey tea parfait. Peacocks roam outside, the Ashdown Forest is close for Pooh sticks.

Rooms	16 twins/doubles.
Price	£165-£285. Singles from £125.
Meals	Lunch from £17.50. Dinner £42.50.
Closed	Never.
Directions	From Newick village turn off the green & follow signs to Newick Park for 1 mile until T-junction. Turn left; after 300m, entrance on right.

Andrew Hawkes
Newick Park Hotel,
Newick, Lewes BN8 4SB
Tel +44 (0)1825 723633
Email bookings@newickpark.co.uk
Web www.newickpark.co.uk

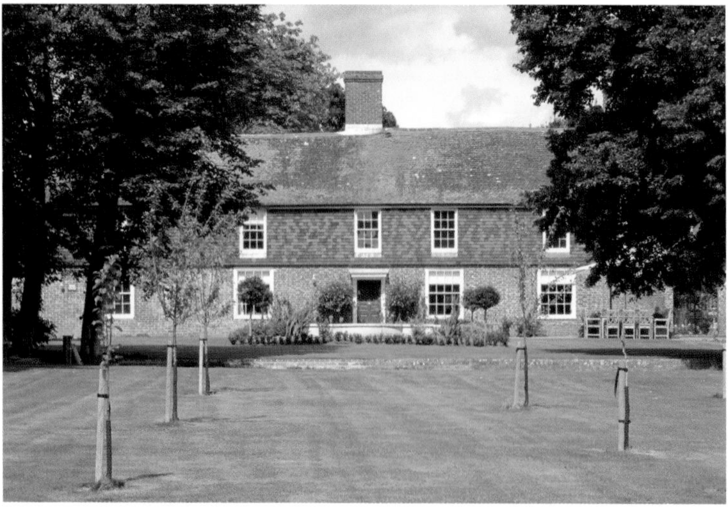

Chilverbridge House

Nick and Nina's stunning 17th-century farmhouse stands in seven lovely acres overlooking the South Downs; you'll find sweeping lawns, an iris-fringed pond and access to Arlington Reservoir Nature Reserve. As for the once-dilapidated Old Granary and Coach House, a magical restoration has produced five gorgeous bedrooms, a big hit with the Glyndebourne set. They come in fine style with balconies or private patios onto the garden. You get beautiful beds, goose down duvets and plump pillows, then Colefax & Fowler fabrics, delicious antiques and lots of high-tech gadgetry. Bathrooms are the best, all with baths, walk-in showers and thick bathrobes. In summer, you breakfast like a king on the terrace with views of the Wilmington Long Man. At other times you eat at linen-clothed tables by the fire in the low-ceilinged dining room. Beachy Head, Cuckmere Haven and Pevensey Castle all wait, as do the South Downs for magical walking. Come by train, Nick picks you up from the village station. A brilliant bolthole with a raft of good restaurants waiting close by. *Children over 12 welcome in high season.*

Rooms	5: 4 doubles, 1 twin/double.
Price	£120-£185. Singles from £95 (low season Sun-Thurs).
Meals	Restaurants within 1 mile. Dinner, 3 courses, £45 by arrangement.
Closed	Rarely.
Directions	Sent on booking.

Nick & Nina Keats
Chilverbridge House,
Chilver Bridge Road,
Arlington BN26 6SB

Tel +44 (0)7748 395327
Email chilverbridge@chilverbridgehouse.com
Web www.chilverbridgehouse.com

Wingrove House

If you need proof that small hotels are infinitely lovelier than their big brothers, here's the evidence. This gorgeous bolthole stands at the end of a pretty village with an ancient church on one side and the South Downs Way passing on the other. At the front a small walled garden leads up to a stone terrace, a great spot to linger in summer; in winter you grab a sofa in front of the wood-burner and roast away in the cool little sitting room bar (wood floors, interesting art, chic colonial feel). Upstairs, delicious bedrooms have smart fabrics, vibrant colours, iPod docks and fancy bathrooms. Two at the front open onto a veranda, the biggest at the back overlooks the churchyard (the bell chimes rarely). There's lots to do. Great walks start from the front door with Cuckmere Haven, Friston Forest and Beachy Head all within range, so work up an appetite, then return to feast on excellent local food, perhaps potted South Coast crab, Sussex lamb with garlic and rosemary, French lemon tart with local raspberry sorbet. Come by train and Nick will pick you up from the station. Brilliant.

Rooms	5 doubles.
Price	£95-£175.
Meals	Lunch from £10 (Sat and Sun only). Dinner, 3 courses, £28-£32.
Closed	Rarely.
Directions	M23, A23, then A27 east from Brighton. Past Berwick, then south at r'bout for Alfriston. In village on left.

Nicholas Denyer
Wingrove House,
High Street, Alfriston,
Polegate BN26 5TD

Tel +44 (0)1323 870276
Email info@wingrovehousealfriston.com
Web www.wingrovehousealfriston.com

The Tiger Inn

The Tiger sits on a village green that has hardly changed in 50 years and in summer life spills onto the terrace to soak up an English sun. It's all part of a large estate that hugs the coast from Beachy Head to Cuckmere Haven with Birling Gap in between; some of the best coastal walking in the south lies on your doorstep. Back at the inn a fabulous renovation has breathed new life into old bones. Downstairs has bags of character with low beams, stone floors, ancient settles and a roaring fire. Beer brewed on the estate pours from the tap, so try a pint of Legless Rambler before digging into hearty food – Beachy Head beer battered catch of the day, sausage and mash with a sweet onion gravy, treacle tart with vanilla ice-cream. Five country-house bedrooms are the big surprise. Find beautiful fabrics, padded bedheads, funky bathrooms, the odd beam. Beds are dressed with lambswool throws, warm colours hang on the walls. Back outside, white cliffs wait, as do the South Downs. Finally, Arthur Conan Doyle knew the village and a blue plaque on one of the cottages suggests Sherlock Holmes retired here.

Rooms	5: 4 doubles, 1 twin.
Price	£110-£120.
Meals	Lunch & dinner from £8.95. Sunday lunch, 3 courses, around £20.
Closed	Never.
Directions	West from Eastbourne on A259. Left in village. Parking on right near village hall.

Jacques Pienaar
The Tiger Inn,
The Green, East Dean,
Eastbourne BN20 0DA

Tel +44 (0)1323 423209
Email tiger@beachyhead.org.uk
Web www.beachyhead.org.uk

Belle Tout Lighthouse

On top of a white cliff, a fabulous lighthouse with rather good views. To your left, Beachy Head, to your right, Birling Gap – it's a magical position with the South Downs rolling into the English Channel. As for the lighthouse, it dates to 1832, was recently moved backwards 57 feet to stop it crumbling into the sea and featured prominently in the BBC's production of *The Life and Loves of a She-Devil*. It re-opened in 2010 after a splendid renovation as a lovely little B&B hotel. Bedrooms are rather wonderful: not huge, but most with double-aspect windows that bring the outside in. You find white walls to soak up the light, fantastic views of rolling hills, pretty fabrics, lovely linen, the odd exposed brick wall; shower rooms are small but sweet, and one room has a bath. Ian's legendary breakfasts are served on high with views of sea and cliff. There's a fabulous sitting room up here, too, where guests gather each night before climbing up to explore the lantern room. You'll eat well in the village pub, magnificent walking waits. *Minimum stay two nights. Over 15s welcome.*

Rooms	6 doubles.
Price	£145-£220. Singles from £101.50.
Meals	Pub/restaurant within 1 mile.
Closed	Christmas & New Year.
Directions	A259 to East Dean, then south for Beachy Head. Keep left at Birling Gap and on right above sea.

Ian Noall
Belle Tout Lighthouse,
Beachy Head Road, Beachy Head,
Eastbourne BN20 0AE

Tel +44 (0)1323 423185
Email info@belletout.co.uk
Web www.belletout.co.uk

Strand House

Strand House was built in 1425 and originally stood on Winchelsea harbour, though the sea was reclaimed long ago and marshland now runs off to the coast. You can walk down after breakfast, a great way to atone for your bacon and eggs. Back at the house, cosy interiors come with low ceilings, timber frames and ancient beams, all of which give an intimate feel. You'll find warm reds and yellows, sofas galore, a wood-burner in the sitting room and an honesty bar where you help yourself. It's a homespun affair: Hugh cooks breakfast, Mary conjures up delicious dinners: grilled goats' cheese with red onion marmalade, Dover sole with a lemon butter, rhubarb and ginger crumble. Attractive bedrooms are warm and colourful and a couple are small; one has an ancient four-poster, some have wonky floors, all have beamed ceilings, good linen, comfy beds. Tall people are better off with ground-floor rooms as low ceilings are de rigueur on upper floors; all rooms have compact bathrooms. The house, once a workhouse, was painted by Turner and Millais. A short walk through the woods leads up to the village. *Dogs £7.50.*

Rooms	13: 8 doubles, 1 twin/double, 3 triples, 1 suite.
Price	£70-£180. Singles from £60.
Meals	Dinner, 3 courses, £34.50.
Closed	Rarely.
Directions	A259 west from Rye for 2 miles. House on the left at foot of hill, opposite Bridge Inn pub.

Mary Sullivan & Hugh Davie
Strand House,
Tanyards Lane, Winchelsea,
Rye TN36 4JT

Tel	+44 (0)1797 226276
Email	info@thestrandhouse.co.uk
Web	www.thestrandhouse.co.uk

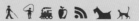

Jeake's House

Rye is utterly gorgeous, one of those lovely English country towns that's been around for centuries, but has never lost its looks. The same is true of Jeake's House. It's spent 300 years on this peaceful cobbled street in the old town accruing a colourful past as a wool store, a school, and the home of American poet Conrad Potter Aiken. Inside: timber frames, ancient beams and smartly carpeted corridors that weave along to cosy bedrooms, the latter generously furnished, deeply comfortable and excellent value for money. Some have four-posters, all have rich fabrics, one has a telly concealed in the wood-burner. The galleried dining room – once an old Baptist chapel, now painted deep red – is full of busts, books, clocks and mirrors – a fine setting for a full English breakfast. There's also a lovely cosy honesty bar, where a fire burns in winter. Outside, you'll find art galleries, antiques shops, old churches and river walks. All this would be blossom in the wind without Jenny, whose natural friendliness has created a winning atmosphere. Don't miss it. *Children over eight welcome.*

Rooms	11: 1 double, 7 twins/doubles, 3 suites.
Price	£90-£116. Suites £126-£140. Singles from £79.
Meals	Restaurants within walking distance.
Closed	Never.
Directions	From centre of Rye on A268, left off High St onto West St, then 1st right into Mermaid St. House on left. Private car park, £3 a day for guests.

Jenny Hadfield
Jeake's House,
Mermaid Street,
Rye TN31 7ET

Tel	+44 (0)1797 222828
Email	stay@jeakeshouse.com
Web	www.jeakeshouse.com

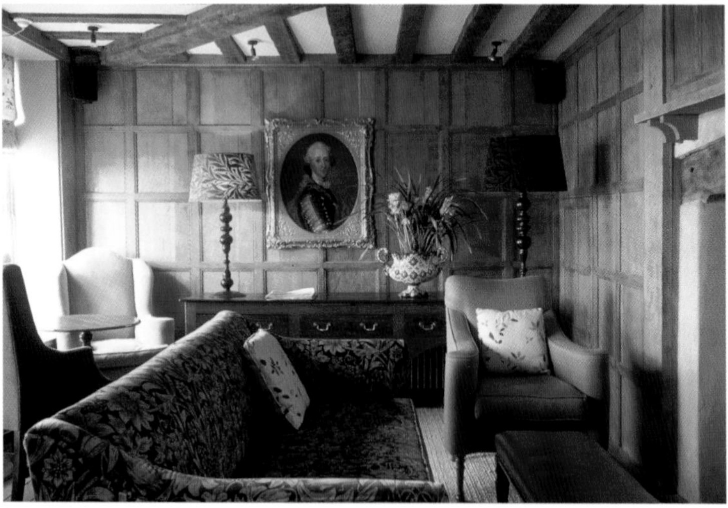

The George in Rye

Ancient Rye has a big history. It's a reclaimed island, a Cinque Port which held its own army. Henry James lived here, too, and the oldest church clock in England chimes at the top of the hill. The George stands serenely on the cobbled high street. Built in 1575 from reclaimed ships' timbers, its exposed beams and panelled walls remain on display. Inside, beautiful interiors mix contemporary and classical styles to great effect – expect Jane Austen in the 21st century. There's a roaring fire in the bar, screen prints of the Beatles on the walls in reception, a first-floor ballroom with a minstrels' gallery. Gorgeous bedrooms come in all shapes and sizes – make sure you check – but chic fabrics, Frette linen and Vi-Spring mattresses are standard, as are cashmere covers on hot water bottles. Finally, excellent brasserie-style food waits in the lovely new George Grill restaurant – perhaps Spanish charcuterie, half a lobster, treacle tart and stem ginger ice-cream; you can wash it all back with delicious wines, some English. Festivals abound: scallops in February, art in September.

Rooms	34: 8 doubles, 21 twins/doubles, 5 suites.
Price	£135-£195. Suites £295-£325. Singles from £95.
Meals	Lunch & dinner from £12.95.
Closed	Never.
Directions	Follow signs up hill into town centre. Through arch; hotel on left, below church. 24-hour parking 5 minutes down hill.

Alex & Katie Clarke
The George in Rye,
98 High Street,
Rye TN31 7JT

Tel +44 (0)1797 222114
Email stay@thegeorgeinrye.com
Web www.thegeorgeinrye.com

The Gallivant Hotel

A boutique motel, a diner with rooms – friendly and stylish with excellent food. It stands across the road from Camber Sands, miles of beach that's popular with sand surfers, beach cricketers and sun worshipers alike. However, the beach will act as an interlude to events at the hotel – the big draw here is some seriously good food. The head chef worked alongside Marco Pierre White and Christophe Novelli, the sous chef spent a year at the French Laundry before working for Tom Aikens. They use the freshest local ingredients and once you've had a nibble you'll find yourself coming back for more, perhaps a posh fish finger sandwich at lunch, then a slap-up dinner of garlic mussels, salt-marsh lamb and a stupendous pear tarte tatin. You eat in a cool little brasserie – think beach chic with stripped wood floors, coastal art and a driftwood terrace for breakfast in the sun. Bedrooms have a similar style: seaside colours, comfy beds, good bathrooms, a sofa if there's room; you get flat-screen TVs and DVD players, too. Cookery courses can be arranged. Don't miss Derek Jarman's cottage at Dungeness. *Minimum two nights at weekends.*

Rooms	20: 16 doubles, 4 suites.
Price	£115-£170. Suites £135-£170.
Meals	Lunch from £12.50. Dinner, 3 courses, about £30.
Closed	Rarely.
Directions	A259 east from Rye, then B2075 for Camber & Lydd. On left after 2 miles.

Mark O'Reilly
The Gallivant Hotel,
New Lydd Road, Camber,
Rye TN31 7RB

Tel +44 (0)1797 225057
Email enquiries@thegallivanthotel.com
Web www.thegallivanthotel.com

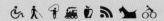

The Howard Arms

The Howard buzzes with good-humoured babble as well-kept beer flows from the flagstoned bar. Logs crackle contentedly in a vast open fire; a blackboard menu scales the wall above; a dining room at the far end has unexpected elegance, with great swathes of bold colour and some noble paintings. Gorgeous bedrooms are set discreetly apart from the joyful throng, mixing period style and modern luxury beautifully: one with a painted antique headboard and bleached beams, another more folksy, while the five newer rooms in the annexe come in more contemporary style with fancy bathrooms. All are individual, all huge by pub standards. The village is a surprise, too, literally tucked under a lone hill, with an unusual church surrounded by orchards and an extended village green. Round off an idyllic walk amid buzzing bees and wild flowers with a meal at the inn, perhaps salmon trio with celeriac remoulade and orange dressing, then beef, ale and mustard pie before spiced pear and apple flapjack crumble. From a menu with seasonal local produce, the food is inventive, upmarket and very good.

Rooms	8: 5 doubles, 3 twins/doubles.
Price	£100-£145. Singles from £75.
Meals	Lunch from £4.50. Dinner from £10.50
Closed	Never.
Directions	From south take A429 Fosse Way through Moreton-in-Marsh. After 5 miles left to Ilmington.

Grant Owen
The Howard Arms,
Lower Green, Ilmington,
Shipston-on-Stour CV36 4LT
Tel +44 (0)1608 682226
Email info@howardarms.com
Web www.howardarms.com

The Bell

A lively inn on the Alscot estate with gardens that run down to a small river – rugs and picnic hampers are available, so you can decamp in good weather. There's a pretty courtyard terrace, too, with wicker armchairs and sofas, not a bad spot for a pint of home-brewed ale. Inside, you find that happy mix of old and new – low beamed ceilings and exposed brick walls, then cool colours and the odd sofa. There are armchairs in front of the fire, a cute sail-shaded conservatory, live music on the last Friday of the month. There's good food, too, with lamb and beef straight from the estate; you might find duck liver pâté, sea bream with saffron, caramel and chocolate cheesecake. Bedrooms are scattered about, some in the main house, a new batch in the converted barn that flanks the terrace. They vary in size (two are small), but all have comfort and style with smart fabrics, crisp linen and sofas or armchairs if there's room. The suites are enormous with exposed beams and fabulous bathrooms. A road passes to the front, quietly at night. Stratford waits up the road for all things Shakespeare.

Rooms	9: 5 doubles, 2 twins, 2 suites.
Price	£95-£140. Suites £145-£165. Singles from £65 (Sunday-Thursday).
Meals	Bar meals from £7. Main courses from £13 (not Sunday night except bank holidays). Sunday lunch, 3 courses, £25.
Closed	Never.
Directions	On A3400 in Alderminster.

Ken Taylor
The Bell,
Shipston Road, Alderminster,
Stratford-upon-Avon CV37 8NY

Tel +44 (0)1789 450414
Email info@thebellald.co.uk
Web www.thebellald.co.uk

Methuen Arms Hotel

Built around the remains of a 14th-century nunnery, converted into a brewery and coaching inn in 1608, and with an impressive Georgian façade, the Methuen has history in spades. Restyled as a boutique inn following a sympathetic restoration, its doors swung open in November 2010 to reveal a stunning interior. From a grand tiled hallway a sweeping staircase leads to a dozen ultra-stylish rooms, those in the former nunnery oozing character with wonky beams and other fascinating features. All have colourful headboards on big beds, wonderfully upholstered armchairs, funky rugs and some rather swish bathrooms, the best with roll-top tubs and walk-in showers. Back downstairs are rugs on stone and wood floors, crackling logs in old stone fireplaces, glowing candles on tables and vintage photos of Corsham; the traditional bar and informal dining rooms are truly inviting. A seasonal modern British menu is a further enticement, so tuck into pasta with game ragù, fish pie, or lamb marinated in oregano and garlic. This grand almost Tardis-like inn promises more rooms in 2012.

Rooms	12: 10 doubles, 1 twin/double, 1 family room.
Price	£140-£170. Family room £140-£220. Singles from £90.
Meals	Lunch from £5.95. Early supper £18.50-£21.50. Dinner, 3 courses, about £30. Sunday lunch from £14.95.
Closed	Never.
Directions	M4 junc. 17, then A350 south & A4 west. B3353 south into Corsham. On left.

Martin & Debbie Still
Methuen Arms Hotel,
2 High Street,
Corsham SN13 0HB

Tel +44 (0)1249 717060
Email info@themethuenarms.com
Web www.themethuenarms.com

The Muddy Duck

In 1125 Cluniac monks founded a monastery in the village; this venerable building was their sleeping quarters. It turned into an alehouse in the 19th-century to satisfy the miners who dug Bath stone from under these hills. These days, it's a gorgeous old inn with an ancient wisteria gracing the stone courtyard at the front, then a smart terraced garden with views across open farmland behind. Inside, old and new mix gracefully: wooden floors, the odd beam and half-panelled walls, then red leather bar stools, armchairs in front of the fire and low-hanging lamps in the restaurant. The bar plays host to a colourful cast of farmers and shoot parties, who come for a pint of Butcombe and some great food. Three bedrooms in the house vary in size. All have warm colours, comfy beds and robes in good bathrooms, but the suite is huge with a sofa in front of an open fire and a claw-foot bath in the room. Two new suites wait beyond the car park with smart bathrooms, snug sitting rooms and small terraces, too. Don't miss the food, perhaps grilled sardines, local duck, honey panna cotta. Bath is close.

Rooms	5: 2 doubles, 3 suites.
Price	£95-£150. Suites £195.
Meals	Lunch from £4.95. Dinner, 3 courses, about £30.
Closed	Never.
Directions	M4 junction 18, then A46/A4 to Bathford. South on A363 for two miles, then left for Monkton Farleigh. Left at x-roads and on left.

Joe Holden
The Muddy Duck,
Monkton Farleigh,
Bradford-on-Avon BA15 2QH

Tel +44 (0)1225 858705
Email joe.holden@themuddyduckbath.co.uk
Web www.themuddyduckbath.co.uk

The Lamb at Hindon

The Lamb has been serving ale on Hindon's high street for 800 years. It is a yard of England's finest cloth, a place where shooting parties come for lunch, and farmers meet to chew the cud. Step inside and find huge oak settles, heavy old beams, then deep red walls and roaring fires. A clipped Georgian country elegance lingers; you almost expect Mr Darcy to walk in, give a tormented sigh, then turn on his heels and vanish. There are flagstone floors and stripped wooden boards, window seats and gilded mirrors; old oils entwined in willow hang on the walls, a bookshelf is stuffed with aged tomes of poetry. At night, candles come out, as do some serious whiskies, and in the restaurant you can feast on ham hock and foie gras ballotine, game pie or Dover sole, then local cheeses. Revamped bedrooms come with mahogany furniture, rich colours, tartan throws, the odd four-poster, and some rather smart bathrooms. Splash out and stay in one of the cosy new rooms in the converted coach house. Fishing can be arranged, or you can shoot off to Stonehenge, Stourhead, Salisbury or Bath. *Minimum two night stay April-September.*

Rooms	19: 10 doubles, 2 twins/doubles, 4 four-posters, 3 suites.
Price	£75-£135. Suites £100-£165.
Meals	Lunch & dinner £5-£25.
Closed	Never.
Directions	M3, A303 & signed left at bottom of steep hill 2 miles east of junction with A350.

Bernice Gallagher
The Lamb at Hindon,
High Street, Hindon,
Salisbury SP3 6DP

Tel	+44 (0)1747 820573
Email	reservations@lambathindon.co.uk
Web	www.lambathindon.co.uk

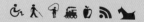

The Beckford Arms

A country-house inn on the Fonthill estate – you sweep in under the Triumphal Arch. Outside, a pretty half-acre garden for hammocks in the trees, parasols on the terrace and a church spire soaring beyond. Georgian interiors are no less lovely. There's a drawing room with facing sofas in front of a roaring fire; a restaurant with a wall of glass that opens onto the terrace; a bar with parquet flooring for an excellent local pint. Follow your nose and chance upon the odd chandelier, roaming wisteria and a rather grand mahogany table in the private dining room. Bedrooms are small but perfectly formed with prices to match: white walls, the best linen, sisal matting, super bathrooms. If you want something bigger try the pavilions on the estate; former guests include Byron and Nelson, though we doubt they had it so good (small kitchens, claw-foot baths, chic country style). As for the food, it's lovely stuff, perhaps marrow fritters with lemon mayo, local partridge with bread sauce, chocolate bread and butter pudding. There are film nights most Sundays, the cricket team comes to celebrate.

Rooms	10: 7 doubles, 2 pavilions, 1 twin/double.
Price	£95-£120. Pavilions £150-£175.
Meals	Dinner about £30.
Closed	Never.
Directions	On the road between Tisbury & Hindon, 3 miles south of A303 (Fonthill exit).

Charlie Luxton
The Beckford Arms,
Fonthill Gifford, Tisbury,
Salisbury SP3 6PX

Tel +44 (0)1747 870385
Email info@beckfordarms.com
Web www.beckfordarms.com

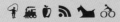

Howard's House

In a gorgeous English village, a wormhole back in time, this Grade-II listed house dates from 1623 and comes with fine gardens in front of fields that sweep uphill to a ridge of old oak. You can walk straight out, so bring your boots. Inside, airy country-house interiors come with exquisite arched windows, flagstones in reception and the odd beam. Deep sofas, fresh flowers and the morning papers wait in the sitting room, where a fire crackles on cold days. When the sun shines, doors open onto a very pretty terrace for breakfasting. Elegant bedrooms mix old and new to great effect. They're not overly plush, but deeply comfortable with warm colours, mullioned windows, bowls of fruit and a sofa if there's room. Expect oak headboards, pretty fabrics, robes in good bathrooms. Spin downstairs for dinner – perhaps fillet of sea bass with parsnip purée, Scottish beef with roasted shallots, apple crème caramel with a calvados jelly – then climb back up to find your bed turned down. Salisbury, Stonehenge and the gardens at Stourhead are all close.

Rooms	9: 6 doubles, 1 twin/double, 1 four-poster, 1 family room.
Price	£190-£210. Singles from £120.
Meals	Lunch £29.50. Dinner £29.50; à la carte £45. 6-course tasting menu £60.
Closed	Rarely.
Directions	A30 from Salisbury, B3089 west to Teffont. There, left at sharp right-hand bend following brown hotel sign. Entrance on right after 0.5 miles.

Noele Thompson & Simon Greenwood
Howard's House,
Teffont Evias, Salisbury SP3 5RJ

Tel +44 (0)1722 716392
Email enq@howardshousehotel.co.uk
Web www.howardshousehotel.co.uk

The Cottage in the Wood & Outlook Restaurant

A nine-mile ridge runs above the hotel – fabulous walks lead through light-dappled trees. Come back for afternoon tea on the terrace and sip your Earl Grey amid 30-mile views that stretch off to distant Cotswold hills. And while the view is utterly magical, so is this delightfully welcoming hotel. The décor isn't cutting-edge, but nor would you want it to be. Here is a hotel where the old-fashioned art of hotel keeping is practised with flair. The service is charming, the sort you only get with a passionate family at the helm and a battalion of long-standing staff to back them up. Mix in ambrosial food in a restaurant that drinks in the view and you have a winning combination for those who seek solid comforts, not fly-by-night fashions. Rooms are split between the main house (simple and traditional), the cottage (cosy low ceilings, warm and snug) and the Pinnacles (nice and spacious, pretty colours, super bathrooms, the odd balcony). All have crisp linen and woollen blankets, floral fabrics, flat-screen TVs and DVD players. A pretty garden adds the colour. Hard to beat.

Rooms	30: 24 doubles, 5 twins/doubles, 1 four-poster.
Price	£99-£198. Singles £79-£121. Dinner, B&B from £66 p.p. (min. 2 nights).
Meals	Lunch from £5.45. Sunday lunch £23.95. Dinner, 3 courses, £25-£40. Packed lunch £8.95.
Closed	Never.
Directions	M5 junc. 7, then A449 through Gt Malvern. In Malvern Wells 3rd right after Railway pub. Signed.

John & Sue Pattin
The Cottage in the Wood &
Outlook Restaurant,
Holywell Road, Malvern WR14 4LG

Tel	+44 (0)1684 588860
Email	reception@cottageinthewood.co.uk
Web	www.cottageinthewood.co.uk

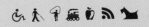

Estbek House

A super find on the Whitby coast. This is a quietly elegant restaurant with rooms ten paces from the beach at Sandsend. It's small, intimate and very welcoming. Tim cooks brilliantly, David talks you through his exceptional wine list and passes on the local news. Cliffs rise to the north, the beach runs away to the south, East Beck river passes directly opposite, ducks waddle across the road. There's a terrace at the front for drinks in summer and a small bar on the lower ground, where you can watch Tim at work in his kitchen. Upstairs, two dining rooms swim in seaside light and come with stripped floors, old radiators and crisp white tablecloths. Grab a window seat for watery views and dig into fresh Whitby crab with avocado and mango salad, local lamb with rhubarb compote, apricot tarte tatin. Bedrooms – bigger on the first floor, smaller on the second – have painted panelling, crisp white linen, colourful throws and shuttered windows. Breakfast is delicious – David's mum makes the marmalade. There are cliff walks, the moors to discover and you can follow the river upstream to Mulgrave Castle.

Rooms	5: 4 doubles, 1 twin/double.
Price	£120-£150. Singles from £80.
Meals	Dinner, 3 courses, about £35.
Closed	Occasionally.
Directions	North from Whitby on A174 to Sandsend. On left in village by bridge.

David Cross & Tim Lawrence
Estbek House,
Eastrow, Sandsend, Whitby YO21 3SU

Tel +44 (0)1947 893424
Email info@estbekhouse.co.uk
Web www.estbekhouse.co.uk

The Talbot Hotel

A 17th-century hunting lodge on the Fitzwilliam estate, not far from Castle Howard. It stands on the edge of town with Malton's streets on one side and big views over field and river on the other. Inside, two fires burn in the drawing room, you find fresh flowers, lovely art, the daily papers and cavernous sofas. There's a bar that drops down to an airy conservatory, then a country-house restaurant that could double as a ballroom. It's headed up by TV chef James Martin and is making quite a name for itself – regulars love the excellent Yorkshire produce, perhaps local wood pigeon with parsnip purée, beer-braised beef with wild garlic, buttermilk panna cotta with Yorkshire rhubarb. Lovely bedrooms have smart floral fabrics, pale wool carpets and botanical prints on the walls. Bigger rooms have sofas, several have the view, bathrooms are gorgeous and come with robes. You're well positioned for York, the Moors, coastal walks and Castle Howard. Malton, a historic market town, makes the most of its natural larder with a popular farmers' market every other Saturday and a fabulous food festival in May. *Minimum stay two nights at weekends.*

Rooms	26: 23 doubles, 3 suites.
Price	£99-£205. Suites £199-£295. Dinner, B&B from £102.50 p.p.
Meals	Dinner £33-£39. Bar meals from £9. Sunday lunch from £20.
Closed	Rarely.
Directions	A64 north from York, then B2148 into Malton. Keep right in town and on right after half a mile.

Jeremy du Plessis
The Talbot Hotel,
45-47 Yorkersgate, Malton YO17 7AJ

Tel +44 (0)1653 639096
Email reservations@talbotmalton.co.uk
Web www.talbotmalton.co.uk

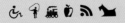

The White Swan Inn

A dreamy old inn that stands on Market Place, where farmers set up shop on the first Thursday of the month. The exterior is 16th century and flower baskets hang from its mellow stone walls. Inside, you find a seriously pretty world: stripped floors, open fires, a tiny bar, beautiful windows. The restaurant is at the back – the heart and soul of the inn – with delicious food flying from the kitchen, perhaps Whitby fishcakes, rack of spring lamb, glazed lemon tart with blood-orange sorbet. Excellent bedrooms are scattered about. Those in the main house have padded bedheads, delicious linen, Osborne & Little fabrics and flat-screen TV/DVDs; bathrooms have robes and Bath House oils. Rooms in the courtyard tend to be bigger and come in crisp contemporary style with black-and-white screen prints, mohair blankets and York stone bathrooms. You'll also find the Bothy here, a cool little residents' sitting room, with a huge open fire and cathedral ceilings. The moors are all around: fabulous walking, Castle Howard and Whitby all wait. *Children sharing parents' room £20. Pets £12.50. Minimum two nights some weekends.*

Rooms	21: 14 doubles, 4 twins/doubles, 3 suites.
Price	£139-£200. Suites £149-£239. Singles from £105.
Meals	Lunch from £5.25. Dinner £13.95-£27.95. Sunday lunch from £12.95.
Closed	Never.
Directions	From North A170 to Pickering. Entering town left at traffic lights, then 1st right into Market Place. On left.

Victor & Marion Buchanan
The White Swan Inn,
Market Place,
Pickering YO18 7AA

Tel	+44 (0)1751 472288
Email	welcome@white-swan.co.uk
Web	www.white-swan.co.uk

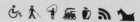

The Pheasant

Jacquie's eye for interior design has recently turned the Pheasant into a small-scale pleasure dome. It sits above the village pond with a terrace for drinks in the sun, but the drawing room is utterly gorgeous, so you may well choose to hole up inside. You'll find elegant sofas, walls of books, an open fire, flowers everywhere. Cool, earthy tones run throughout, there's a smart bar, padded window seats, candles flickering at night. Outside, a converted stone barn is home to a pretty swimming pool and you can potter across in bathrobes for a dip. Beautiful bedrooms are scattered about. There's a suite in the garden with a decked terrace, then a couple of lovely family rooms with bunk beds for kids. Those in the main house are no less beautiful: cool colours, chic fabrics, the odd four-poster, padded bedheads. Best of all is the food, perhaps hand-dived scallops with Yorkshire rhubarb, roasted wood pigeon with wild garlic risotto, lime tart with banana sorbet. Castle Howard for *Brideshead* fans and the Moors for walkers both wait. You can self-cater in three gorgeous cottages, too.

Rooms	15 + 3: 11 doubles, 1 single, 2 family rooms, 1 suite. 3 self-catering cottages.
Price	£155. Suite £200. Cottages £150 (£700 p.w.). Singles from £78. Dinner, B&B from £110 p.p.
Meals	Light lunches from £6. Dinner, 3 courses, about £40. 7-course tasting menu £65.
Closed	Never.
Directions	Leave Helmsley to the east on A170. First right for Harome; hotel in village.

Jacquie Pern & Peter Neville
The Pheasant,
Harome,
Helmsley YO62 5JG

Tel +44 (0)1439 771241
Email reservations@thepheasanthotel.com
Web www.thepheasanthotel.com

The Black Swan at Oldstead

A sparkling country inn or a Michelin-starred restaurant with rooms – take your pick. Outside, a grass terrace shaded by cherry trees gives views of field and ridge, a perfect spot for a pint in summer. Inside, a bar of matchless elegance: a fire primed for combustion, 400-year-old flagstones, a couple of gorgeous bay windows, candelabra hanging from the ceiling. The inn is built into the side of a hill with stairs that lead up to a country-house restaurant, where smart rugs cover golden floorboards and cream walls make the most of the light. And the food is what you've come for. The Banks family has farmed here for generations and much of what you eat comes straight from local fields. It's ambrosial stuff, immaculately presented, perhaps scallops with mussels and salsify, lamb three ways with basil and olive, apple tart with almonds and crème Anglaise. Four sublime bedrooms wait in a low stone building next door. Expect beautiful beds, white linen, oak armoires, fabulous bathrooms (one has a copper bath). Each room opens onto a peaceful terrace, and they'll even bring you a whisky before dinner.

Rooms	4 doubles.
Price	£270-£330. Price includes dinner for two.
Meals	Lunch: £25-£50 (not Mon-Wed). Dinner included. Non residents: early bird set menu £25 (not Sat); à la carte £40-£50; 7-course tasting menu £70.
Closed	First 2 weeks in January.
Directions	A19 from Thirsk; left to Thirkleby & Coxwold, then left for Byland Abbey; follow signs left for Oldstead.

The Banks Family
The Black Swan at Oldstead,
Oldstead, York YO61 4BL

Tel +44 (0)1347 868387
Email enquiries@blackswanoldstead.co.uk
Web www.blackswanoldstead.co.uk

The Grange Hotel

York Minster is imperious, the oldest Gothic cathedral in northern Europe; its Great East Window is the largest piece of medieval stained glass in the world and a Roman column stands outside the West Door. All around is the feel of Dickensian London. The Minster stands less than half a mile from the front door of this extremely comfortable Regency townhouse – a five-minute stroll after bacon and eggs. A country-house elegance runs throughout: marble pillars in a flagged entrance hall, an open fire in the cosy morning room and a first-floor drawing room that opens onto a small balcony. Bedrooms come in different shapes and sizes with smart florals, mahogany dressers, period colours and good bathrooms. The more expensive rooms are seriously plush, with high beds and swathes of silky curtain. York racecourse brings in a happy crowd. There are deep red walls and leather chairs in the super-smart Ivy Restaurant. You can also eat downstairs in the vaulted brasserie, where steaks are the order of the day.
Minimum two nights at weekends.

Rooms	36: 14 doubles, 18 twins/doubles, 3 singles, 1 suite.
Price	£137-£235. Suites £284. Singles from £123.
Meals	Lunch from £10. Dinner, 3 courses, £30-£35 (early bird discount).
Closed	Never.
Directions	South into York from ring road on A19. On right after two miles, 500m north of York Minster.

Steven Hodgkinson
The Grange Hotel,
1 Clifton, York YO30 6AA

Tel	+44 (0)1904 644744
Email	info@grangehotel.co.uk
Web	www.grangehotel.co.uk

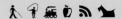

The Bijou

Great prices, an easy style and ever-present owners are the hallmarks of this smart B&B hotel close to the centre of town. Outside, a small, manicured garden leads up to a Victorian stone townhouse; inside, a clean contemporary feel runs throughout. Gill and Stephen (he's ex-Hotel du Vin) renovated completely; out with the woodchip and swirly carpets, in with stripped boards and faux zebra-skin rugs. There's a cool little sitting room with an open fire, a computer for guests to use, and an honesty bar on tap all day. Bedrooms mix leather bedheads, airy colours, Cole & Son wallpaper and orange stools. Excellent bathrooms, most compact, have smart creamy ceramics, you get waffle robes, hot water bottles, flat-screen TVs and double glazing (the house is set back from the road). Two rooms in the coach house are good for small groups. Breakfast is a leisurely feast: freshly-squeezed orange juice, eggs and bacon from a local farm, homemade breads and muesli. Don't miss the Stray (the vast common that wraps up the town) or Betty's for afternoon tea. Good restaurants wait, too.

Rooms	10: 8 doubles, 1 twin, 1 single.
Price	£85-£110. Singles from £65.
Meals	Restaurants within walking distance.
Closed	23-30 December.
Directions	A61 north into town, following signs for Ripon. Past Betty's Teashop, down hill, back up, past Cairn Hotel. Signed on left.

Stephen & Gill Watson
The Bijou,
17 Ripon Road, Harrogate HG1 2JL
Tel +44 (0)1423 567974
Email info@thebijou.co.uk
Web www.thebijou.co.uk

Gallon House

Rick and Sue's gorgeous B&B is a perennial Sawday favourite. It's like a mini luxury hotel, and if you come with friends and take the whole place, you have canapés and champagne 'on the house' before dinner. As for Gallon, it sits on top of a hill with a most wonderful view to behold: a medieval castle tottering on one side, a spectacular railway bridge passing on the other. Below, the river Nidd sparkles, so nip down ancient steps and hire a boat or follow the water into the country. Back at home, walls of glass bring in the view. There's Lloyd Loom wicker in the conservatory, an open fire in the beautiful sitting room, stripped floors and cool colours in the dining room. Best of all is the sun terrace – Knaresborough's Royal Box – with parasols, pots of colour and deckchairs to take the strain. Bedrooms are warmly stylish, not too big, but spoiling nonetheless, with bathrobes and white towels, crisp linen and soft colours. Two have the view, two have showers in the actual room. As for Rick's slow food, expect the best, perhaps wild mushroom tart, free-range chicken, pear and almond tart. *No credit cards.*

Rooms	3: 2 doubles, 1 twin.
Price	£120. Singles from £85.
Meals	Dinner, 3 courses, £36, by arrangement.
Closed	Christmas & New Year.
Directions	A1(M) junc. 47, A59 west for 3 miles. Climb hill into Knaresborough. Left into Market Place at Barclays bank; 1st right into Kirkgate; on left.

Sue & Rick Hodgson
Gallon House,
47 Kirkgate, Knaresborough HG5 8BZ

Tel +44 (0)1423 862102
Email gallon-house@ntlworld.com
Web www.gallon-house.co.uk

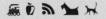

Devonshire Fell Hotel

You're high on the hill with huge views of Wharfdale: mountains rise, the river roars and in summer you can watch the cricket team toil on the pitch below. Up at this rather cool hotel there's a plant-festooned terrace and a trim lawn for sunbathing (people do). Inside, funky interiors are the order of the day. A lilac bar comes with halogen lighting and leather sofas; wander on and find stripped floors, Designers Guild fabrics and a warming wood-burner. There's a sense of space, too, with one room flowing into another, the bar, restaurant and conservatory united by an open-plan feel. Expect splashes of colour, padded bedheads and beautiful upholstery in the bedrooms; those at the front have stupendous views. You get big TVs, DVD players, a sofa if there's room; tongue-and-groove bathrooms come with robes and fluffy towels. Back downstairs, delicious food is served informally in the bar, perhaps a haddock burger with tartare sauce and crushed peas. In the restaurant try Lishman black pudding; honey roast duck; vanilla crème brûlée with strawberries. There are movie nights and the walking is heavenly.

Rooms	12: 6 doubles, 4 twins, 2 suites.
Price	£129-£219. Suites £209-£259.
Meals	Lunch from £4.50. Dinner £26-£32.
Closed	Never.
Directions	From Harrogate A59 west for 15 miles, then right onto B6160, signed Burnsall & Bolton Abbey. Hotel on the edge of the village.

Stephane Leyreloup
Devonshire Fell Hotel,
Burnsall, Skipton BD23 6BT

Tel +44 (0)1756 729000
Email res@devonshirehotels.co.uk
Web www.devonshirefell.co.uk

The Tempest Arms

A 16th-century ale house three miles west of Skipton with great prices, friendly staff and an easy style. Inside you find stone walls and open fires, six ales on tap at the bar and a smart beamed restaurant. An airy open-plan feel runs throughout with sofas and armchairs strategically placed in front of a fire that burns on both sides. Delicious traditional food is a big draw – the inn is packed for dinner most nights. You can eat wherever you want, so grab a seat and dig into mussels in a white wine sauce, Bolton Abbey lamb with roasted vegetables, treacle tart with pink grapefruit sorbet. Bedrooms are a steal. Those in the main house are simpler, those next door in two stone houses are quietly indulging. You get crisp linen, neutral colours, slate bathrooms and flat-screen TVs. Some have views of the fells, the suites are large and worth the money, a couple have decks with hot tubs to soak in. The Dales are on your doorstep, this is a good base for walkers. Skipton, a proper Yorkshire market town, is worth a look. Hard to fault for the price. Children and dogs are welcome.

Rooms	21: 9 twins/doubles, 12 suites.
Price	£90. Suites £110-£165. Singles from £70. Extra beds £12.99.
Meals	Lunch & bar meals from £8.95. Dinner from £14.95.
Closed	Never.
Directions	A56 west from Skipton. Signed left after two miles.

Martin & Veronica Clarkson
The Tempest Arms,
Elslack, Skipton BD23 3AY
Tel +44 (0)1282 842450
Email info@tempestarms.co.uk
Web www.tempestarms.co.uk

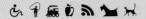

The Traddock

A northern outpost of country-house charm, beautiful inside and out. It's a family affair and those looking for a friendly base from which to explore the Dales will find it here. You enter through a wonderful drawing room – crackling fire, pretty art, the daily papers, cavernous sofas. Follow your nose and find polished wood in the dining room, panelled walls in the breakfast room, then William Morris wallpaper in the sitting room bar, where you can sip a pint of Skipton ale while playing a game of Scrabble. Bedrooms are just the ticket, some coolly contemporary, others deliciously traditional with family antiques and the odd claw-foot bath. Those on the second floor are cosy in the eaves, all have fresh fruit, homemade shortbread and Dales views. Elsewhere, a white-washed sitting room that opens onto the garden and a rug-strewn restaurant for fabulous local food, perhaps Whitby crab, slow-roasted pork, raspberry and white chocolate soufflé. Spectacular walks start at the front door, there are cycle tracks and some extraordinary caves – one is bigger than St Paul's. Brilliant. *Minimum two nights at weekends March-November. Dogs £5.*

Rooms	11: 7 doubles, 1 twin/double, 1 single, 2 family rooms.
Price	£95-£195. Singles from £85. Dinner, B&B from £80 p.p.
Meals	Lunch from £9.50. Dinner, 3 courses, around £30.
Closed	Never.
Directions	0.75 miles off the A65, midway between Kirkby Lonsdale & Skipton, 4 miles north-west of Settle.

Paul Reynolds
The Traddock,
Austwick, Settle LA2 8BY

Tel +44 (0)1524 251224
Email info@thetraddock.co.uk
Web www.thetraddock.co.uk

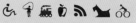

Yorebridge House

This rather chic boutique hotel stands just outside the village with views of rising fells on one side and the valley shooting off to Hawes on the other. It was built in 1850 for a headmaster (big house, tiny school, the latter now four lovely rooms), then snapped up by the Yorkshire Dales National Park to act as their HQ. Outside, five acres of grounds are bounded by two rivers, with fishing rights if you want to try your luck. Inside, beautiful interiors are just the ticket. You'll find leather sofas in the sitting room, where 1920s school photos adorn the walls, then oak floors and an open fire in the relaxed bar. Beautiful bedrooms are scattered about. Two in the school house have hot tubs on terraces (one overlooks the river). Those in the main house are just as good with fabulous fabrics, cool colours, Bang & Olufsen TVs, magnificent bathrooms (one has a bath in the room). Great food waits in the orangery restaurant, perhaps mackerel pâté, roast rump of lamb, Yorkshire Blue cheesecake with malt crumb. Outside, the Dales wait, so bring walking boots and bikes.

Rooms	13: 9 doubles, 2 twins/doubles, 2 suites.
Price	£200-£240. Suites £250-£285.
Meals	Lunch from £6.50. Dinner, 3 courses, about £40.
Closed	Never.
Directions	East from Hawes on A684. In Bainbridge bear left at Rose & Crown for Askrig. On right after 400m.

David & Charlotte Reilly
Yorebridge House,
Bainbridge DL8 3EE

Tel +44 (0)1969 652060
Email enquiries@yorebridgehouse.co.uk
Web www.yorebridgehouse.co.uk

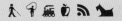

The Burgoyne Hotel

The Burgoyne is one of the loveliest places to stay in the Dales. The view from the front is imperious, a smooth sweep three miles south off to Swaledale; half a dozen benches on the village green look the right way. Inside, the past lives on: an elegant drawing room with a crackling fire where you gather for drinks before dinner; a restaurant in racing green where you feast on delicious Yorkshire-sourced food: hot asparagus wrapped in smoked salmon; Gressingham duck with apple mash and orange liqueur; vanilla panna cotta with red berry coulis. Julia and Mo, who arrived in 2011, are here to keep the traditions alive, updating as they go. Bedrooms come in country-house style: colourful fabrics, excellent beds, thick white linen, a sofa if there's room. A four-poster occupies the old snooker room, all but one room has the view. There are maps for walkers, fishing can be arranged. As for Reeth, it's a gorgeous old traditional village, mentioned in the Domesday Book, with a market every Friday and the best grouse moors in Britain. Dogs are welcome, too.

Rooms	8: 3 doubles, 1 twin, 1 four-poster, 1 suite, all en suite. 2 twins with separate bathrooms.
Price	£140-£195. Suite £210. Singles from £112.50.
Meals	Dinner, 4 courses, £39.
Closed	Monday-Thursday in January.
Directions	From Richmond A6108, then B6270 to Reeth. Hotel on north side of village green.

Julia & Mo Usman
The Burgoyne Hotel,
Reeth, Richmond DL11 6SN
Tel +44 (0)1748 884292
Email enquiries@theburgoyne.co.uk
Web www.theburgoyne.co.uk

Swinton Park

Swinton is utterly glorious, a fabulous old pile that flaunts its beauty with rash abandon. It stands in 200 acres of parkland, part of a 20,000-acre estate. You get the full aristocratic works: five lakes and a huge kitchen garden outside, then stately interiors at every turn within. Expect marble pillars, varnished wood floors, vast arched windows, roaring fires. The drawing room is stupendous, a little like the salon of a 17th-century French château, but the dining room is equally impressive, its magnificent ceiling worth the trip alone. The main corridor is an art gallery, there's a bar in the old chapel, a hugely popular cookery school in the old stables, a small spa, too. Bedrooms come in grand style: plush fabrics, huge beds, marble bathrooms, decanters of complimentary gin and whisky. One of the suites occupies the turret, some rooms have sublime views over Home Lake, a couple interconnect, so perfect for families. As for the food, game from the estate and vegetables from the garden are plentiful, while hampers can be left in bothies for walkers wanting a rather good lunch. Magnificent.

Rooms	31: 25 twins/doubles, 6 suites.
Price	£195-£380. Suites £330-£555. Dinner, B&B from £132.50 p.p.
Meals	Lunch from £25.95. Dinner £52. Tasting menu £60.
Closed	Never.
Directions	A1(M), Junc. 50, follow signs to Masham on road that runs parallel to motorway. After 3 miles, left onto B6267 to Masham. Hotel signed in village, 1 mile south-west, past golf course.

Mark & Felicity Cunliffe-Lister
Swinton Park,
Swinton, Ripon HG4 4JH

Tel +44 (0)1765 680900
Email reservations@swintonpark.com
Web www.swintonpark.com

The White Bear Hotel

At five o'clock on a Friday evening there's only one place to be in town: the tap room at the White Bear, spiritual home of Theakston's beer. The great and the good gather to mark the end of the week, the odd pint is sunk, the air is thick with gossip. Interior design is strictly 19th century – red leather, polished brass, a crackling fire. Elsewhere: a country-house dining room in salmon pink; a handsome public bar with stripped floorboards; a flower-festooned terrace for lunch in the sun. 21st-century luxury comes courtesy of excellent bedrooms. They occupy the old Lightfoot brewery, but don't expect nostalgia here. The style is contemporary, with beautiful fabrics, warm colours, sumptuous beds and cutting-edge bathrooms; some have views across town and the vast penthouse is open to the rafters. There's a courtyard for guests, a sitting room, too; staff will bring drinks if you want privacy and peace. As for dinner, delicious comfort food waits in the restaurant: smoked salmon, steak and ale pie, treacle sponge pudding. The Dales are all around.

Rooms	14: 13 twins/doubles, 1 suite.
Price	£110-£120. Suite £200-£220.
Meals	Lunch from £4.95. Dinner, 3 courses, about £30.
Closed	Never.
Directions	North from Ripon on A6108. In Masham up hill (for Leyburn). Right at crest of hill. Signed.

Sue Thomas
The White Bear Hotel,
Wellgarth, Masham, Ripon HG4 4EN
Tel +44 (0)1765 689319
Email sue@whitebearmasham.co.uk
Web www.thewhitebearhotel.co.uk

Channel Islands

Photo: istockphoto.com

The Georgian House

Holly's family have been holidaying in Alderney for more than 30 years, now she's come back to take over this treasure of an hotel. Along with her charming young team, they've turned it into the beating heart of the island. Step off the cobbled high street straight into a traditional, cosy bar; grab a bite here or something more extravagant in the light-strewn dining room that opens out to the pretty garden. Vegetables and salad come from their own allotment, the butter is vivid yellow and meat and fish is as local as can be: try the divine head-to-toe pork dish (great for sharing) or a zingy chilli squid. Upstairs four quaint bedrooms, all en suite, are pretty and pristine with locally made soaps and views across the road to the town. The 100-seater cinema opposite shows arthouse films on reels, during the interval you wander over to The Georgian for a drink. The hotel is packed with locals and visitors alike, and rightly so; there are barbecues, bands, taster evenings, and a blissful atmosphere. Old forts and stunning beaches wait, so hire bikes and explore the island. And book early.

Rooms	4: 2 doubles, 2 twins/doubles.
Price	£70-£95. Singles from £45.
Meals	Light lunch from £6. Dinner, 3 courses, £25-£30.
Closed	Mid-January to mid-March.
Directions	Sent on booking. Airport pick-ups.

Holly Fisher
The Georgian House,
Victoria Street, Alderney GY9 3UF

Tel +44 (0)1481 822471
Email info@georgianalderney.com
Web www.georgianalderney.com

White House Hotel

Herm is unique, a tiny island run benignly by the 40 souls lucky enough to live on it. They keep things blissfully simple: no cars, no TVs, just a magical world of field and sky, a perfect place to escape the city. A coastal path rings the island; high cliffs to the south, sandy beaches to the north, cattle grazing the hills between. You get fabulous views at every turn – shimmering islands, pristine waters, yachts and ferries zipping about. There are beach cafés, succulent gardens, an ancient church, even a tavern. Kids love it, so do parents, and the self-catering cottages are extremely popular. As for the hotel, it lingers happily in an elegant past, a great base from which to enjoy the island. You'll find open fires, delicious four-course dinners, a tennis court, a pool to keep you cool. Spotless bedrooms are scattered about, some in the village's colour-washed cottages, others with balconies in the hotel. Several come in contemporary style with fancy bathrooms, but most are warmly traditional as befits the setting. Expect pretty colours, padded headboards and watery views.

Rooms	40 + 20: 28 twins/doubles, 2 singles, 10 family rooms. 20 self-catering cottages.
Price	£148-£208. Cottage rooms £128-£168. Singles from £64. Self-catering cottages £273-£1,288 per week.
Meals	Lunch from £5. Dinner, 4 courses, £28.50.
Closed	November-Easter.
Directions	Via Guernsey. Trident ferries leave from the harbour at St Peter Port 8 times a day in summer (£11 return).

Siôn Dobson Jones
White House Hotel,
Herm Island GY1 3HR

Tel +44 (0)1481 750075
Email hotel@herm.com
Web www.herm.com

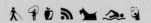

Photo left: The Wheatsheaf, Gloucesterhire, entry 111
Photo right: At the Chapel, Somerset, entry 185

Scotland

Photo: Grants at Craigellachie, Highland, entry 273

Darroch Learg Hotel

The country here is glorious – river, forest, mountain, sky – so walk by Loch Muick, climb Lochnagar, fish the Dee or drop down to Braemar for the Highland Games. Swing back to Darroch Learg and find nothing but good things. This is a smart family-run hotel firmly rooted in a graceful past: an old country house with roaring fires, polished brass, Zoffany wallpaper and ambrosial food in a much-admired restaurant. Ever-present Nigel and Fiona look after guests with great aplomb and many return year after year. Everything is just as it should be: tartan fabrics on the walls in the hall, Canadian pitch pine windows and doors, fabulous views sweeping south across Balmoral forest. Bedrooms upstairs come in different shapes and sizes; all have warmth and comfort in spades. Big grand rooms at the front thrill with padded window seats, wallpapered bathrooms, old oak furniture, perhaps a four-poster bed. Spotlessly cosy rooms in the eaves are equally lovely, just not quite as big. You get warm colours, pretty furniture, crisp white linen and bathrobes to pad about in. A perfect highland retreat.

Rooms	12: 10 twins/doubles, 2 doubles.
Price	£140-£250. Dinner, B&B (obligatory at weekends) from £105 p.p.
Meals	Sunday lunch £24. Dinner £45.
Closed	Christmas & last 3 weeks in January.
Directions	From Perth A93 north to Ballater. Entering village hotel 1st building on left above road.

Nigel & Fiona Franks
Darroch Learg Hotel,
56 Braemar Road, Ballater AB35 5UX

Tel	+44 (0)1339 755443
Email	enquiries@darrochlearg.co.uk
Web	www.darrochlearg.co.uk

The Kilberry Inn

It's a little like *Local Hero*, a patch of heaven in the middle of nowhere with vast skies, forested hills and the Sound of Jura pouring past. As for the Kilberry, it stands on the road in this tiny village (cars pass at the rate of one an hour). Outside, the phone box is soon to become the smallest whisky bar in the world. Inside, oodles of rustic charm, with Farrow & Ball colours, exposed stone walls and an open fire that burns most nights. Half-bottles of champagne wait at the bar, as do local ales and excellent malts. In summer life spills onto the roadside for lunch in the sun. And the food here is the big draw. Clare's cooking is some of the best on the west coast, perhaps mussels and surf clams cooked in white wine, rack of hill lamb marinated in honey, then mocha brûlée with coffee ice-cream. Spotless bedrooms have pretty colours, comfy beds, robes in compact shower rooms. Two are bigger; one has a sitting room, another a hot tub on a private terrace. Elsewhere, sandy beaches, standing stones and golf at Machrihanish. Worth the detour.
Minimum two nights at weekends July/Aug.

Rooms	5: 1 suite, 4 doubles.
Price	£210. Price includes dinner for two.
Meals	Lunch from £15. 3-course, à la carte dinner included; non-residents about £35.
Closed	Mondays. January & February. Sunday-Thursday in November & December.
Directions	A83 south from Lochgilphead for 3 miles, then right onto B8024 for 16 miles. In village on left.

Clare Johnson & David Wilson
The Kilberry Inn,
Kilberry, Tarbert PA29 6YD
Tel +44 (0)1880 770223
Email relax@kilberryinn.com
Web www.kilberryinn.com

The Creggans Inn

The real James Bond once owned this hotel – Sir Fitzroy MacLean was one of a cast of characters on whom Ian Fleming modelled his hero; the fact the Royal Navy regularly send their big ships into Loch Fyne on exercise is purely coincidental. These days, life at the inn is decidedly restful. Views from the front stretch for miles, the loch eventually giving way to the distant peaks of the Kintyre peninsular. Inside, an airy elegance has spread far and wide. Downstairs, sofas and armchairs are liberally scattered about, there's a locals' bar which doubles as the clubhouse for the village shinty team, then picture windows in the smart restaurant, where you dig into super local fare – perhaps grilled goats' cheese, breast of guinea fowl, chocolate and hazelnut parfait – while watching the sun set over the hills. Traditional country-house bedrooms are lovely: warm colours, pretty fabrics, delicate wallpapers, padded bedheads; most have loch views. There's lots to do: castles and gardens, boat trips and golf, hills for cyclists and walkers. All this an hour and a half from hip Glasgow.

Rooms	14: 4 doubles, 9 twins/doubles, 1 suite.
Price	£120-£180. Suite £160-£220. Singles from £85. Dinner, B&B from £80 p.p.
Meals	Bar: lunch & dinner from £4.25. Restaurant: 4-course table d'hôte menu £37.
Closed	Never.
Directions	From Glasgow, A82 to Tarbert, A83 towards Inverary for 13 miles, then left on A815 to Strachur (10 miles). Hotel on left before village.

Archie & Gillian MacLellan
The Creggans Inn,
Loch Fyne, Strachur,
Cairndow PA27 8BX

Tel	+44 (0)1369 860279
Email	info@creggans-inn.co.uk
Web	www.creggans-inn.co.uk

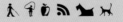

The Manor House

A 1780 dower house for the Dukes of Argyll – their cottage by the sea – built of local stone, high on the hill, with long views over Oban harbour to the Isle of Mull. A smart and proper place, not one to bow to the fads of fashion: sea views from the lawn, cherry trees in the courtyard garden, a fire roaring in the drawing room, a beautiful tiled floor in the entrance hall and an elegant bay window in the dining room that catches the eye. Bedrooms tend to be small, but they're also rather pretty and come in warm colours – blues, reds, yellows, greens – with fresh flowers, crisp linen, bowls of fruit and piles of towels in good bathrooms; those that look seaward have binoculars with which to scour the horizon. Try Loch Fyne kippers for breakfast, salmon for lunch and, if you've room, rack of lamb for supper; there's excellent home baking, too. Ferries leave for the islands from the bottom of the hill – see them depart from the hotel garden. At the top, overlooking Oban, watch the day's close from McCaig's Folly; sunsets here are really special. *Children over 12 welcome.*

Rooms	11: 9 doubles, 2 twins.
Price	£115-£225. Dinner, B&B from £87.50 p.p.
Meals	Lunch from £8.50. Dinner £39.
Closed	Christmas.
Directions	In Oban follow signs to ferry. Hotel on right 0.5 miles after ferry turn-off, signed.

Gregor MacKinnon
The Manor House,
Gallanach Road,
Oban PA34 4LS
Tel +44 (0)1631 562087
Email info@manorhouseoban.com
Web www.manorhouseoban.com

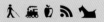

The Airds Hotel & Restaurant

This smart country-house hotel on the Appin peninsular stands above Loch Linnhe with views across the water to the Morvern Mountains. It started life in 1750, an inn for passengers taking the paddle steamers up to the Caledonian canal. These days, it's one of the loveliest places to stay on the West Coast, its whitewashed exterior giving no hint of the wonders within. You enter through a small conservatory, then find yourself in a world of smouldering fires, freshly cut flowers, beautiful wallpapers and sofas by the dozen. Bedrooms pack a lovely punch – warm colours, smart fabrics, Frette linen for Vi-Spring beds, sparkling marble bathrooms with Italian robes. Those at the front have the view, bigger rooms have sofas, some at the back have terraces, all spoil you rotten. Best of all is the ambrosial food, perhaps seared scallops with pickled cauliflower, lemon sole with parsley mousse, banana soufflé with passion fruit ice-cream. Outside, there's a garden for croquet and afternoon tea with views of water and mountains. The loveliest staff look after you all the way. Brilliant. *Check website for seasonal offers.*

Rooms	11 + 1: 8 twins/doubles, 3 suites. Self-catering cottage for 2.
Price	£290-£418. Suites £385-£495. Price includes dinner for two. Self-catering cottage £575-£875 p.w.
Meals	Lunch from £7. Dinner, 5 courses, included; non-residents £55. Tasting menu £75. Sunday lunch £18.95.
Closed	Monday & Tuesday November to January.
Directions	A82 north for Fort William, then A828 south for Oban. Right for Port Appin after 12 miles. On left after 2 miles.

Shaun & Jenny McKivragan
The Airds Hotel & Restaurant,
Port Appin,
Appin PA38 4DF

Tel	+44 (0)1631 730236
Email	airds@airds-hotel.com
Web	www.airds-hotel.com

Kilmeny

Islay is fabulous – easy to get to, seriously pretty, lots to do. It's home to famous whisky distilleries, plays host to 60,000 geese every winter, has spectacular sandy beaches that stretch for miles. You can walk in the hills and spot red deer, or jump in a kayak and glide past seal colonies. As for Kilmeny, it's the perfect island base, part farmhouse B&B, part stylish hotel. It sits in 300 acres of beautiful silence. Blair (from Jura) and Margaret (Islay through and through) have been here for 41 years (they don't look old enough!). Blair runs sheep and cattle (you can wander freely, even help during lambing), while Margaret has perfected the art of spoiling guests rotten. She plies you with tea and cake on arrival, serves a mean breakfast in the pretty dining room, she'll even cook a three-course feast in the evening, perhaps smoked salmon, local lamb, raspberry and almond crumble. Rooms are gorgeous with beautiful beds, delicious fabrics, sofas or armchairs, slipper baths in wonderful bathrooms. As for Islay, Blair and Margaret will share all their secrets, so come to explore. *No credit cards.*

Rooms	5: 4 twins/doubles, 1 suite.
Price	£135. Suite £155. Singles from £90.
Meals	Dinner, £35, by arrangement.
Closed	Mid-October to Easter.
Directions	3 miles west from Port Askaig on A846. Signed left.

Margaret & Blair Rozga
Kilmeny,
Ballygrant,
Isle of Islay PA45 7QW

Tel +44 (0)1496 840668
Email info@kilmeny.co.uk
Web www.kilmeny.co.uk

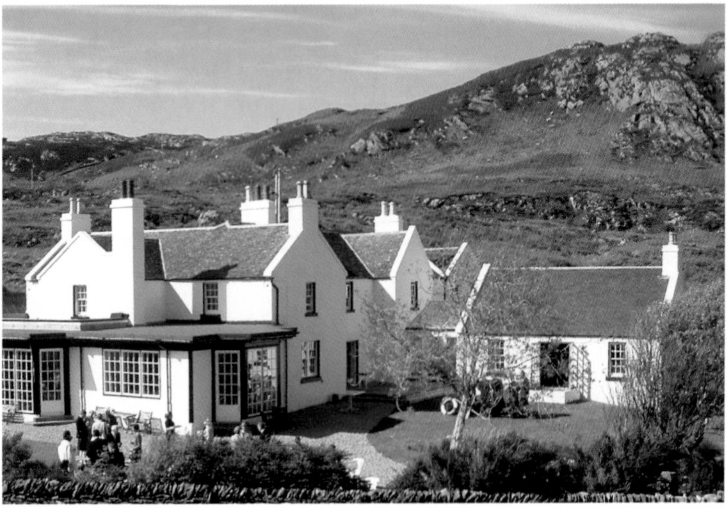

The Colonsay

Another fabulous Hebridean island, a perfect place to escape the world. Wander at will and find wild flowers in the machair, a golf course tended by sheep and huge sandy beaches across which cows roam. Wildlife is ever present, from a small colony of wild goats to a rich migratory bird population; the odd golden eagle soars overhead, too. At low tide the sands of the south give access to Oronsay. The island's 14th-century priory was one of Scotland's finest and amid impressive ruins its ornate stone cross still stands. As for the hotel, it's a splendid base and brims with an easy style – airy interiors, stripped floors, fires everywhere, friendly staff. There's a locals' bar for a pint (and a brewery on the island), a pretty sitting room packed with books, a dining room for super food, a decked terrace for drinks in the sun. Bedrooms have local art, warm colours, lovely fabrics and the best beds; some have sea views, all have good bathrooms. Spin around on bikes, search for standing stones, lie in the sun and stare at the sky. There's a festival in May for all things Colonsay. Wonderful.

Rooms	9: 4 doubles, 3 twins, 1 single, 1 family room.
Price	£85-£145. Singles from £70.
Meals	Lunch from £4.50. Packed lunch £7. Bar meals from £11.50. Dinner, 3 courses, about £25.
Closed	November, January (after New Year) & February.
Directions	Calmac ferries from Oban or Kennacraig (not Tue) or Hebridean Airways (Tue & Thur). Hotel on right, half a mile up road from jetty.

Jane Howard
The Colonsay,
Scalasaig,
Isle of Colonsay PA61 7YP

Tel +44 (0)1951 200316
Email hotel@colonsayestate.co.uk
Web www.colonsayestate.co.uk

Glengorm Castle

Few places defy overstatement, but Glengorm does so with ease. It stands in 5,000 acres at the top of Mull with views that stretch across miles of water to Coll and the Uists, Barra and Rhum. Directly in front the land falls away, rolls over lush pasture, then tumbles into the sea. Sheep graze by the hundred, birds play in the sky. Believe it or not, despite the grandeur, this is a B&B, a family home with children and dogs pottering about. The informality is infectious, you feel immediately at home. First you bounce up a four-mile drive, then you step into a vast hall, where sofas wait in front of the fire and big art hangs on the walls. An oak staircase sweeps you up to fabulous country-house rooms (three have the view). You get warm colours, antique furniture, sofas if there's room, excellent bathrooms. Elsewhere: a panelled library for guests to use with a selection of whiskies 'on the house', a vast kitchen garden and magnificent coastal paths. Breakfast is a feast. There's a farm shop and café, so stop for lunch. Good restaurants wait in Tobermory.

Rooms	5: 3 doubles, 1 four-poster, all en suite. 1 twin/double with separate bath.
Price	£130-£210.
Meals	Restaurants 5 miles.
Closed	Castle closed Christmas & New Year.
Directions	North to Tobermory on A848. Straight over roundabout (not right for town). Over x-roads after half a mile and straight ahead for four miles to castle.

Tom & Marjorie Nelson
Glengorm Castle,
Tobermory,
Isle of Mull PA75 6QE

Tel +44 (0)1688 302321
Email enquiries@glengormcastle.co.uk
Web www.glengormcastle.co.uk

Tiroran House

The setting is magnificent – 17 acres of lush gardens rolling down to Loch Scridian with the Ross of Mull rising beyond. Otters and dolphins pass by, red deer visit the garden. As for this welcoming 1850 shooting lodge, you'll be hard pressed to find a more comfortable island base, so it's no surprise to discover it was recently voted 'Best Country House Hotel in Scotland'. There are fires in the drawing rooms, fresh flowers everywhere, games to be played, books to be read. Big airy bedrooms hit the spot: crisp linen on pretty beds, beautiful fabrics and the odd chaise longue, watery views and silence guaranteed. You eat in a smart dining room. The food is exceptional with much from the island or waters around it, perhaps hand-dived scallops, local venison, dark chocolate and salted caramel tart. You're bang in the middle of Mull with loads to do: Tobermory, the prettiest town in the Hebrides; Calgary and its magical beach; day trips to Iona with its famous monastery; boat trips to Fingal's Cave. Come back for afternoon tea – it's as good as the Ritz.

Rooms	10: 5 doubles, 5 twins/doubles.
Price	£175-£220.
Meals	Dinner, 4 courses, £48.
Closed	Rarely.
Directions	From Craignure or Fishnish car ferries, A849 for Bunessan & Iona car ferry. Right onto B8035 for Gruline. After 4 miles left at converted church. House 1 mile further.

Laurence & Katie Mackay
Tiroran House,
Isle of Mull PA69 6ES

Tel +44 (0)1681 705232
Email info@tiroran.com
Web www.tiroran.com

Cavens

The Solway Firth is a magical spot; overlooked by many, those who come have this patch of heaven to themselves. You swoop down from Dumfries through glorious country, then crest a hill and there it is, vast tracts of tidal sands with a huge sky above. It's a magnet for birdlife, the rich pickings of low tide too tempting to refuse. As for this 1752 shooting lodge, it stands in 20 acres of sweeping lawns, native woodlands and sprawling fields. Inside, elegant interiors come as standard. Two lovely sitting rooms are decked out with busts and oils, golden sofas, smouldering fires, a baby grand piano; in summer, you slip onto the terrace for afternoon tea. Country-house bedrooms have garden views, period furniture, bowls of fruit. One is smaller, others big with room for sofas. One has a stunning bathroom, another has an en suite sunroom. Back downstairs you feast on Angus's delicious food in the smart yellow restaurant, perhaps scallops with lime and Vermouth, Galloway pork in a mustard sauce, lemon panna cotta. There are gardens aplenty and golf at spectacular Southerness. Dogs are very welcome.

Rooms	5: 4 doubles, 1 twin.
Price	£100-£190.
Meals	Dinner, 3-course market menu, £25. Packed lunch available.
Closed	Never.
Directions	From Dumfries A710 to Kirkbean (12 miles). Signed in village on left.

Jane & Angus Fordyce
Cavens,
Kirkbean, Dumfries DG2 8AA
Tel +44 (0)1387 880234
Email enquiries@cavens.com
Web www.cavens.com

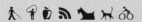

Knockinaam Lodge

Lawns run down to the Irish sea, roe deer come to eat the roses, sunsets turn the sky red. This exceptional 1869 shooting lodge is nothing short of glorious: a Michelin star in the dining room, 150 malts in the bar and a level of service you rarely find in such far-flung corners of the realm. There's history, too. Churchill once stayed and you can sleep in his elegant room, read his books and climb the same steps into an ancient bath. Elsewhere, immaculate country-house interiors abound: gorgeous bedrooms, the very best bathrooms, a morning room where the scent of flowers mingles with wood smoke. Outside: cliff walks, nesting peregrine falcons and a rock pool. When it's stormy, waves crash all around. Trees stand guard high on the hill, their branches buffeted by the wind, while bluebells carpet the hills in spring. John Buchan knew the house and described it in *The Thirty-Nine Steps* as the house to which Hannay fled. Remote, beguiling, utterly spoiling – grand old Knockinaam is simply unmissable.

Rooms	10: 4 doubles, 5 twins/doubles, 1 family room.
Price	£285-£440. Family room £340-£440. Price includes dinner for two.
Meals	Lunch, by arrangement, £30-£40. Dinner, 5 courses, included; non-residents £60.
Closed	Never.
Directions	From A77 or A75 pick up signs to Portpatrick. West from Lochans on A77, then left after 2 miles, signed. Follow signs for 3 miles to hotel.

David & Sian Ibbotson
Knockinaam Lodge,
Portpatrick, Stranraer DG9 9AD

Tel	+44 (0)1776 810471
Email	reservations@knockinaamlodge.com
Web	www.knockinaamlodge.com

Trigony House Hotel

A small, welcoming, family-run hotel: Adam and Jan are doing their own thing without fuss. Expect delicious home-cooked food, comfortable bedrooms and a lovely garden to roam – look out for rare red squirrels. The house dates back to 1700, a shooting lodge for the local castle. Inside: Japanese oak panelling in the hall, a wood-burner in the sitting room and an open fire in the dining room; doors open onto the terrace for al fresco dinners in summer. Adam cooks extremely good rustic fare, perhaps crab tart, local venison, rhubarb and hazelnut crumble; there's a small, organic kitchen garden that provides much for the table in summer. Bedrooms vary in size and style, some with pretty fabrics, golden throws and summer colours: many are dog-friendly too. One has its own conservatory/sitting room which opens onto a private lawn, but even the simpler rooms have flat-screen TVs with DVDs; there's a film library downstairs. Falconry, riding and fishing can be arranged, even vintage car hire. Fill up with a cooked breakfast – one of the best – then head west into the hills for fabulous countryside.

Rooms	9: 4 doubles, 4 twins/doubles, 1 suite.
Price	£90-£130. Suite £155. Singles from £80. Dinner, B&B from £75 p.p.
Meals	Lunch from £5. Dinner, 3 courses from £30.
Closed	24-26 December.
Directions	North from Dumfries on A76; through Closeburn; signed left after 1 mile.

Adam & Jan Moore
Trigony House Hotel,
Closeburn, Thornhill DG3 5EZ

Tel +44 (0)1848 331211
Email info@trigonyhotel.co.uk
Web www.countryhousehotelscotland.com

Brooks Hotel Edinburgh

Carla and Andrew's third hotel sticks to a simple philosophy: great prices, stylish interiors, happy staff, a central position in town. It is exactly what lots of us want – boutique on a budget – and with Edinburgh's magnetic pull, it's likely to be a big hit. It stands in the West End, a mile from the castle (there are umbrellas at the front door in case it rains). Interiors have been completely renovated. There are sofas, great art and an honesty bar in the sitting room, then doors onto an attractive courtyard, where tables and chairs wait for summer. Back inside, you get a good breakfast in the dining room with lots of choice, too: smoked salmon and scrambled eggs, the full cooked works, even boiled eggs and soldiers. Rooms vary in size, but not style. There's a lift to whizz you up, then Cole & Son wallpapers, Farrow & Ball paints, goose down duvets on pocket-sprung mattresses. You get free WiFi, iPod docks, flat-screen TVs and DVD players. Compact bathrooms have big power showers. Edinburgh waits outside: castle, parliament, cathedral and palace, even the odd bar and restaurant.

Rooms	46: 43 doubles, 3 family rooms.
Price	£59-£149. Family rooms £99-£169. Singles from £55.
Meals	Restaurants nearby.
Closed	Never.
Directions	Sent on booking.

Carla & Andrew Brooks
Brooks Hotel Edinburgh,
70-72 Grove Street,
Edinburgh EH3 8AP

Tel +44 (0)131 228 2323
Email info@brooksedinburgh.com
Web www.brooksedinburgh.com

21212

21212 is the new jewel in Edinburgh's crown. Paul left his Michelin star down south, bought this Georgian townhouse, spent a small fortune converting it into a 21st-century pleasure dome, then opened for business and won back his star. The house stands at the top of a hill with long views north towards the Firth of Forth. It's bang in the centre of town with Arthur's Seat and Princes Street both close by. Inside, contemporary splendour waits. High ceilings and vast windows come as standard, but wander at will and find a chic first-floor drawing room, cherubs on the wall, busts and statues all over the place, even a private dining pod made of white leather. Stunning bedrooms have enormous beds, cool colours, fat sofas and iPod docks. Those at the front have the view, all have robes in magnificent bathrooms. As for the restaurant: the kitchen is on display behind a wall of glass and the food it produces is heavenly, perhaps fillet of beef with apricots and thyme, Gloucestershire Old Spot with white asparagus, saffron-poached pineapple baked in a caramelised lemon curd. Out of this world.

Rooms	4 doubles.
Price	£95-£325.
Meals	Lunch from £28. Dinner from £48.
Closed	Rarely.
Directions	A720 ring road, then A702/A7 into town. Right at T-junc. at Balmoral Hotel, then immediately left with flow. Right at second r'about and 1st right. On right.

Paul Kitching & Katie O'Brien
21212,
3 Royal Terrace,
Edinburgh EH7 5AB
Tel +44 (0)131 523 1030
Email reservations@21212restaurant.co.uk
Web www.21212restaurant.co.uk

23 Mayfield

Edinburgh – the most beautiful city in Scotland and therefore in Britain. Those who come to gaze on its glory will enjoy this spoiling B&B hotel that stands in the shadow of Arthur's Seat. Built in 1868, it was home to a coffee merchant and comes with plaster-moulded ceilings and a stained-glass window on the landing. There's an airy dining room for excellent breakfasts (toasted muffins with hand-picked mushrooms, peat-smoked haddock with poached eggs), then a sitting room with Chesterfields where you can browse a collection of guide books or surf the net on the house computer. Super bedrooms have excellent prices. Some come with high ceilings and shuttered windows, most with travertine marble bathrooms, all have period colours, panelled walls and good beds with excellent linen. You get iPod docks, Bose technology and classical CDs, and the family room comes with a Nintendo Wii. There's good art throughout; a history of Scotland is framed on the landing. A short bus ride zips you into town, there's off-street parking and loads of local eateries. You can hire bikes, too. *Minimum two nights at weekends.*

Rooms	9: 4 twins/doubles, 1 triple, 3 four-posters, 1 family room.
Price	£80-£175. Singles from £65.
Meals	Restaurants within half a mile.
Closed	24-26 December.
Directions	A720 bypass, then north onto A722 for Edinburgh. Right onto A721 at T-junction with traffic lights. Over x-roads with main flow, under railway bridge, on right.

Ross Birnie
23 Mayfield,
23 Mayfield Gardens,
Edinburgh EH9 2BX
Tel +44 (0)131 667 5806
Email info@23mayfield.co.uk
Web www.23mayfield.co.uk

94DR

Close to Holyrood and Arthur's Seat, this super-friendly designer B&B is not only popular for its contemporary style, but for Paul and John, who treat guests like friends and make sure you see the best of their city. A traditional Victorian exterior gives no hint of the cool interiors that await within. You find original floor tiles and ornate ceilings intact, but other than that it's a clean sweep: deep charcoal downstairs; pure white above. There's a sitting room with iPads in case you want to book a restaurant, an honesty bar, an espresso machine and lots of handy guide books. Upstairs, stylish, well-priced bedrooms wait. Some are big with claw-foot baths, others smaller with walk-in power showers. All come with comfy beds, bath robes, beautiful linen and contemporary Scottish art. The family suite (two rooms) has bunk beds and a PlayStation for kids. Delicious breakfasts are served in a conservatory overlooking the back garden, a memorable feast orchestrated by Paul, with lively conversation that travels the world. Majestic Edinburgh is yours to explore. *Minimum two nights at weekends.*

Rooms	6: 3 doubles, 2 suites, 1 family room (1 double, 1 bunk room).
Price	£100-£145. Suites £125-£160. Singles from £80.
Meals	Restaurants within 0.5 miles.
Closed	2-15 January.
Directions	Sent on booking.

John MacEwan & Paul Lightfoot
94DR,
94 Dalkeith Road,
Edinburgh EH16 5AF

Tel +44 (0)131 662 9265
Email stay@94dr.com
Web www.94dr.com

The Peat Inn

The Peat Inn has been around for 300 years. It's a Scottish institution, a national treasure, and when it changes hands (very rarely), people take note. Geoffrey and Katherine took it on five years ago and have already made their mark: a Michelin star landed here in 2010. It is divided in two: restaurant and rooms, though the latter are suites, not rooms. You get wonderful beds dressed in crisp white linen, pretty colours that soak up the light, decanters of sherry, bowls of fruit, sofas from which to watch the telly. Not that you'll have time for that. You'll be over in the restaurant digging into some of the best food in Scotland. The scene is suitably theatrical: three rooms beautifully lit, tables spaced out generously. As for the food, ambrosial delights await: wild leek soup with a poached duck egg, roast rump of lamb with a red pepper compote, pavé of chocolate with pistachio. You can eat à la carte, try the menu du jour or feast on a six-course tasting menu (the cheese course is a soufflé!); all are well priced. As for the staff, you won't find better. St Andrews is close.

Rooms	8 suites.
Price	£185-£195.
Meals	Lunch from £19. Dinner: menu du jour £45; à la carte £55-£58. 6-course tasting menu £65 (or £115 with wine flights).
Closed	Rooms & restaurant closed Sunday & Monday; also 24-26 December & 1 week in January.
Directions	From Edinburgh A90 north, then A92 for Dundee. Right onto A91 and into Cupar. There, B940 for Crail to inn.

Geoffrey & Katherine Smeddle
The Peat Inn,
Peat Inn,
Cupar KY15 5LH
Tel +44 (0)1334 840206
Email stay@thepeatinn.co.uk
Web www.thepeatinn.co.uk

15 Glasgow

This is a seriously smart Glasgow address – bang in the middle of town, yet beautifully insulated from it. The house, a Victorian gem, stands on an attractive square with communal gardens running through. Inside, the feel is distinctly contemporary, though you still get a pair of Corinthian pillars and the original mosaic entrance hall. Shane and Laura spent a year renovating; while technically you're in a B&B, these interiors are as good as any boutique hotel. Downstairs there's a vast sitting room with a couple of sofas in front of a fire; bedrooms upstairs are no less generous. Those at the back are large, the suites at the front are enormous. All come with huge beds, crisp white linen, handmade bedheads and robes in seriously fancy bathrooms. Suites have a few added extras: big sofas, beautiful windows, one has a double-ended bath overlooking the square. Breakfast is brought to you whenever you want. As for Glasgow, you'll find great restaurants close to home. Try Crab Shakk for serious seafood, then head to Ben Nevis for a wee dram; folk musicians play most nights.

Rooms	5: 2 doubles, 1 twin/double, 2 suites.
Price	£120. Suites £150.
Meals	Restaurants on your doorstep.
Closed	Never.
Directions	West into Glasgow on M8. Exit at junc. 18 for Charing X (outside lane), then double back at lights. 1st left, 1st left, 1st left (really). Follow square round to house.

Shane & Laura McKenzie
15 Glasgow,
15 Woodside Place,
Glasgow G3 7QL

Tel +44 (0)141 332 1263
Email info@15glasgow.com
Web www.15glasgow.com

The Lime Tree

The Lime Tree – a hotel/art gallery – is a Mackintosh manse. It dates to 1850, while the tree itself, sublime on the front lawn, was planted in 1700, the year the town was settled. Inside you find a small, stylish world – stripped floors in the hall, bold colours on the walls, open fires scattered around, beautiful windows for views of Loch Linnhe. David – a mountain guide who also paints – has a fabulous map room, but if you want to do more than walk, you've come to the right place; climbing, cragging, mountain biking, kayaking and diving can all be arranged. Airy bedrooms are lovely – oatmeal carpets, crisp white linen, good art and flat-screen TVs. You get neat little bathrooms, white walls to soak up the light and those at the front have watery views. Downstairs, drift through to the gallery and see what's on (when the Royal Geographical Society came, they had a full-scale copy of Ernest Shackleton's boat on the front lawn). There's a rustic bistro, too, the best place to eat in town, perhaps homemade soups, slow-cooked lamb, sticky toffee pudding. Ben Nevis is close.

Rooms	9: 3 doubles, 1 twin, 5 family rooms.
Price	£80-£130. Singles from £60.
Meals	Dinner £27.95-£29.95.
Closed	Rarely.
Directions	North to Fort William on A82. Hotel on right at 1st roundabout in town.

David Wilson
The Lime Tree,
Achintore Road,
Fort William PH33 6RQ

Tel +44 (0)1397 701806
Email info@limetreefortwilliam.co.uk
Web www.limetreefortwilliam.co.uk

Kilcamb Lodge Hotel & Restaurant

A stupendous setting, with Loch Sunart at the end of the garden and Glas Bheinn rising beyond. Kilcamb has all the ingredients of the perfect country house: a drawing room with a roaring fire; an elegant dining room for excellent food; super-comfy bedrooms that don't shy from colour; views that feed the soul. The feel here is shipwreck-chic; the 12-acre garden has half a mile of shore. Stroll to the water's edge and look for dolphins, otters and seals. Ducks and geese fly by, and if you're lucky you'll see eagles. Back inside, you'll find stained-glass windows on the landing, flowers in the bedrooms, and a laid-back lounge bar and brasserie. Or dress up for a five-course dinner and feast on king scallops with pea purée and Stornaway black pudding, roasted loin of Argyll lamb with apricot mousse, goats' cheese mash with caper and mint butter, and banana crème brûlée. Bedrooms, some new, come in two styles: contemporary or traditional. Expect big beds, smart white towels and shiny bathrooms. Kind staff go the extra mile. *Minimum two nights at weekends in May.*

Rooms	10: 7 doubles, 3 suites.
Price	£190-£295. Suites £290-£375. Price includes dinner for two.
Meals	Lunch from £8.50. Dinner included; non-residents £49.50.
Closed	January. Limited opening November & February.
Directions	From Fort William A82 south for 10 miles to Corran ferry, then A861 to Strontian. Hotel west of village on left, signed. A830 & A861 from Fort William takes an hour longer.

David & Sally Ruthven-Fox
Kilcamb Lodge Hotel & Restaurant,
Strontian,
Acharacle PH36 4HY

Tel	+44 (0)1967 402257
Email	enquiries@kilcamblodge.co.uk
Web	www.kilcamblodge.co.uk

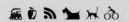

Doune

You arrive by boat – there's no road in – a ferry across to Knoydart, the last great wilderness in Britain. You'll find mountains, sea and beach – a thrilling landscape of boundless peace and ever-changing light. Guillemots race across the water, dolphins and seals come to play, the Sound of Sleat shoots across to Skye. As for Doune, it's a tiny community of happily shipwrecked souls, who rescued this land from ruin; Martin, Jane and Liz look after you with instinctive generosity. The dining room is the hub, pine-clad from top to toe, with a stove to keep you warm and a couple of fiddles for the odd ceilidh. The food is delicious – crab from the bay, roast lamb from the hill, chocolate tart with homemade ice-cream. Bedrooms along the veranda are delightfully simple – pine clad with mezzanine bunks for children, hooks for clothes, armchairs for watching the weather; compact shower rooms sparkle. The walking is magnificent, boat trips can be arranged, the night sky will astound you. There's a lodge for groups, too. A very special place, miss it at your peril. *Boat pick-up Tues & Sat. Minimum three nights. 15% off weekly stays.*

Rooms	4: 3 family rooms (mezzanine beds for children); 1 single with separate shower. Catered lodge for 12 (shared washrooms).
Price	£160 for two including all meals. Singles £68. Children aged 2-12 £32. 15% off weekly stays.
Meals	All meals included. Dinner, £30, for non-residents.
Closed	October-Easter.
Directions	Park in Mallaig; the boat will collect you at an agreed time.

Martin & Jane Davies
Doune,
Knoydart, Mallaig PH41 4PL
Tel +44 (0)1687 462667
Email martin@doune-knoydart.co.uk
Web www.doune-knoydart.co.uk

Grants at Craigellachie

An old factor's house on the banks of Loch Duich with the Five Sisters of Kintail flaunting their beauty to the south; three are munros, views from the top are spectacular. This is a great little base for Highland flings – quirky, homespun, lovely owners. There's lots to do: Glenelg, Applecross and Skye are on your doorstep, Loch Ness is within easy reach, Dornie Castle (the one on the water you see on TV) is on the other side of the loch. After a day pottering through magical landscapes, come home to this cute restaurant with rooms. It's a tiny operation. Tony and Liz do it all themselves: cook, clean, polish and shine, chat to guests after delicious breakfasts, point you in the right direction. There are four rooms, two in the main house (small but sweet, warm colours, fine for a night), then two out back, smarter altogether with neutral colours, lovely linen, robes in fancy bathrooms. One is a suite (with a small kitchen), both have decked terraces. As for Tony's lovely food, don't expect to go hungry. You might have hand-dived scallops and thyme, Glenelg lamb with rosemary, whisky panna cotta. *Wine tasting and food & wine-matching courses available.*

Rooms	4: 2 doubles, 1 twin, 1 suite.
Price	£100-£145. Suite £155-£185. Singles from £70. Dinner, B&B from £82.50 p.p.
Meals	Dinner, 3 courses, about £35. Not Sunday or Monday.
Closed	Mid-November to mid-February.
Directions	A87 north from Invergarry to Shiel Bridge. Left in village for Glenelg. First right down to Loch Duich. On left in village.

Tony & Liz Taylor
Grants at Craigellachie,
Ratagan, Glenshiel, Kyle IV40 8HP

Tel +44 (0)1599 511331
Email info@housebytheloch.co.uk
Web www.housebytheloch.co.uk

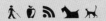

The Torridon

You're in the middle of nowhere, but you wouldn't be anywhere else. Mountains rise, red deer roam, sea eagles and otters patrol high and low. This 1887 shooting lodge was built for the Earl of Lovelace and stands in 58 acres that roll down to the shores of Upper Loch Torridon. Inside, sparkling interiors thrill: a huge fire in the panelled hall, a zodiac ceiling in the drawing room, 350 malts in the pitch pine bar. Huge windows pull in the view, while canny walkers pour off the hills to recover in luxury. Fabulous bedrooms are hard to fault, some big, others bigger. A super-smart contemporary style runs throughout: cool colours, padded headboards, exquisite linen, magnificent bathrooms; one has a shower in a turret. Outside, cattle graze in the fields, while the two-acre kitchen garden is a work of art in itself. It provides much for the table, so feast on fresh food sublimely cooked: pan-roasted monkfish, Highland beef with a red wine jus, apple tarte tatin with butterscotch ice-cream. You can scale Liathach or take to the sea in a kayak. Fantastic.

Rooms	18 + 1: 12 doubles, 2 twins, 4 suites. 1 self-catering boathouse.
Price	£230-£435. Suites £230-£465. Boathouse £925-£1,425 p.w.
Meals	Lunch from £5.95. Dinner, 5 courses, £55.
Closed	January.
Directions	A9 to Inverness, A835 to Garve, A832 to Kinlochewe, A896 to Annat (not Torridon). Signed on south shore.

Daniel & Rohaise Rose-Bristow
The Torridon,
Annat, By Achnasheen IV22 2EY

Tel +44 (0)1445 791242
Email info@thetorridon.com
Web www.thetorridon.com

Tigh an Eilean Hotel

Head north from the Kyle of Lochalsh and you leave the world behind, plunging into magnificent wilderness, a wonderland of natural beauty that rolls north for a hundred miles. On your left Hebridean seas sparkle, on your right mountains soar. Villages dot the coast, few as pretty as Sheildaig, which sits on the water, each house drinking in the view. Bang in the middle you find this friendly bolthole, an old-school charmer with warm interiors and lovely food. Inside, an appealing simplicity has taken root. It's cosy, not fancy, with sofas in front of the wood-burner, an honesty bar for guests, binoculars with which to scan the high seas. You'll find a couple of sitting rooms, maps and bird books, then homely bedrooms with colourful fabrics and crisp linen. Those at the front have the view, none have TVs, all have baths. There's lots to do – boat trips, gardens to visit, mountains to climb, day trips to Applecross and Skye. Return for a good dinner, either in the restaurant (more formal) or in the bistro (pizza, steak, seafood stew). There's a pub, too, where local fiddles occasionally fly.

Rooms	10: 6 twins/doubles, 3 singles, 1 family room.
Price	£120-£150. Singles from £75.
Meals	Lunch & dinner in Coastal Kitchen from £8. Dinner, 4 courses, in restaurant £42.50. Packed lunches on request.
Closed	January.
Directions	On loch front in centre of Shieldaig.

Christopher & Cathryn Field
Tigh an Eilean Hotel,
Shieldaig, Strathcarron IV54 8XN

Tel	+44 (0)1520 755251
Email	tighaneilean@keme.co.uk
Web	www.tighaneilean.co.uk

Mackay's Rooms

This is the north-west corner of Britain and it's utterly magical: huge skies, sandy beaches, aquamarine seas, cliffs and caves. You drive – or cycle – for mile upon mile with mountains soaring into the heavens and ridges sliding into the sea. If you like big, remote landscapes, you'll love it here; what's more, you'll pretty much have it to yourself. Mackay's – they have the shop, the bunkhouse and the garage, too – is the only place to stay in town, its earthy colours mixing with stone walls, open fires and stripped floors to great effect. Bedrooms (some big, others smaller) are extremely comfy. They come with big wooden beds and crisp white linen, while Fiona, a textiles graduate, has a fine eye for fabrics and upholstery. You also get excellent bathrooms, iPod docks, flat-screen TVs and DVD players. Breakfast sets you up for the day – grilled grapefruit, whisky porridge, venison sausages, local eggs – so head east to the beach, west for great golf or catch the ferry across to Cape Wrath and scan the sea for whales. There's surfing for the brave and the beautiful.

Rooms	7 + 4: 6 doubles, 1 twin. 4 self-catering cottages.
Price	£125-£165. Singles from £110. Cottages £800-£1,600 per week.
Meals	Restaurants in village.
Closed	October-April. Cottages open all year.
Directions	A838 north from Rhiconich. After 19 miles enter Durness village. Mackay's is on right-hand side opposite memorial.

Fiona Mackay
Mackay's Rooms,
Durine, Durness,
Lairg IV27 4PN

Tel	+44 (0)1971 511202
Email	stay@visitdurness.com
Web	www.visitdurness.com

Ullinish Country Lodge

This sparkling Georgian farmhouse stands on the magical west coast under a vast sky. Mighty views stretch across Loch Harport to the Cuillin mountains beyond. Samuel Johnson stayed on his famous tour, though you can bet your bottom dollar he didn't eat as well as you will. Pam and Brian came to add to Skye's gastronomic reputation and have done just that, serving up some of the best food on the island. Inside, warm interiors come with tartan carpets in the hall and leather sofas in front of the sitting room fire. Bedrooms upstairs have huge mahogany beds, stately colours, silky crowns and watery views. You'll find claw-foot baths and flat-screen TVs, too. As for dinner, expect the best, perhaps Isle of Skye langoustine, fillet of Mallaig skate, then banana soufflé with warm chocolate sauce. Outside, the tidal island of Oronsay waits. Dolphins and whales pass by, sea eagles patrol the skies, there are standing stones and iron age remains. Finally, the famous Talisker distillery at Carbost stands on the far side of the loch, so drop in for a tour and a wee dram. *Over 16s welcome.*

Rooms	6: 5 doubles, 1 twin.
Price	£110-£160. Singles from £80.
Meals	Dinner, 4 courses, £48.
Closed	24 December to end of January.
Directions	North from Skye bridge on A87, then A863 for Dunvegan. Thro' Struan and signed left after 250m. House on right after 1 mile.

Brian & Pam Howard
Ullinish Country Lodge,
Ullinish, Struan,
Isle of Skye IV56 8FD

Tel +44 (0)1470 572214
Email enquiries@ullinish-country-lodge.co.uk
Web www.theisleofskye.co.uk

Greshornish House

On its own private peninsular, hidden away from the rest of Skye, this 18th-century country house stands in ten acres of peace directly above the sea. Outside, free-range chickens nip across the croquet lawn, while down at the loch seals and otters splash about in the water. As for the house, it's a great island base and Neil and Rosemary look after guests with infectious charm. Step inside and find a sofa'd bar that doubles as reception, an open fire crackling in the drawing room and a grand piano in the billiard room, where walls of books surround you. Upstairs, lovely big bedrooms have a smart homely feel. Two at the front have the view, all have warm colours, fresh flowers, usually a sofa. One is enormous, another has a claw-foot bath, two have fancy showers. Back downstairs, seriously tasty food waits in the dining room (candlelit tables, claret-red walls), so work up an appetite on one of Skye's mountains, then return for a feast, perhaps oak-smoked salmon, tomato and fennel soup, delicious Scotch beef or Lochaber venison, chocolate and hazelnut terrine. Wonderful. *Minimum stay two nights. Dogs allowed in some bedrooms.*

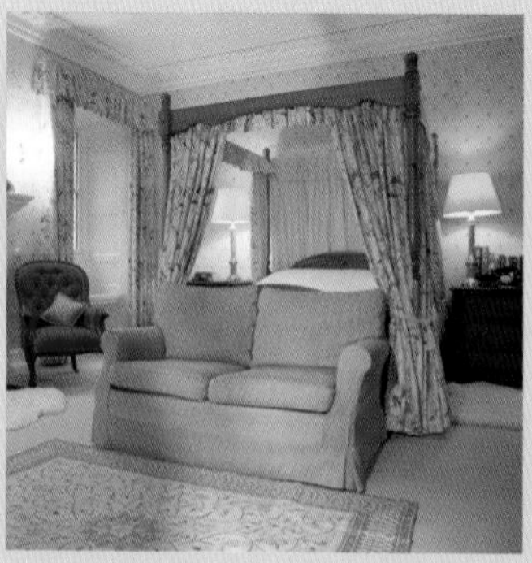

Rooms	6: 2 twins/doubles, 2 four-posters, 2 family rooms.
Price	£130-£185. Family rooms £130-£235. Singles from £95.
Meals	Dinner £38-£45. Packed lunch £10.
Closed	November-March.
Directions	A87 through Portree, then west on A850 for Dunvegan. Signed right after 10 miles (1 mile west of Edinbane). 2.5 miles down single track road to hotel.

Neil & Rosemary Colquhoun
Greshornish House,
Edinbane, Portree,
Isle of Skye IV51 9PN

Tel	+44 (0)1470 582266
Email	info@greshornishhouse.com
Web	www.greshornishhouse.com

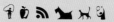

The Glenview

Small is beautiful at The Glenview. This delicious little restaurant with rooms started life in 1890 as a croft. Once the village shop, it has recently fallen into excellent hands. Simon and Kirsty are young and full of life. They love Skye, and have refurbished brilliantly. You find daffodils in the flower beds, logs in the porch, painted floorboards and maps on the wall. The style – a warm, rustic simplicity with a contemporary folksy edge – fits the mood perfectly. The dining room doubles as an art gallery, you can roast away in front of the wood-burner in the sitting room, there are games to be played, books to be read, tales to be told. Rooms are excellent: warm and cosy (though not small) with smart carpets, fresh flowers and eclectic furniture. Then there's the food – seasonal fruits and organic Skye bacon for breakfasts, while Simon sure cooks a mean dinner, perhaps, hand-dived scallops, roast local venison, rhubarb and sticky toffee pudding with praline ice-cream. There's loads to see: the Old Man of Storr, the Kilt Rock waterfall, even dinosaur footprints on Staffin beach. Fabulous.

Rooms	5: 4 doubles, 1 twin.
Price	£90-£120. Singles from £75.
Meals	Dinner £29-£35.
Closed	Sunday & Monday. December-January.
Directions	North from Portree on A855. Signed on left in dip in village.

Simon & Kirsty Faulds
The Glenview,
Culnacnoc,
Isle of Skye IV51 9JH
Tel +44 (0)1470 562248
Email enquiries@glenviewskye.co.uk
Web www.glenviewskye.co.uk

Viewfield House Hotel

This old ancestral pile stands high above Portree Bay with fine views tumbling down to the Sound of Rassay below. Twenty acres of mature gardens and woodland wrap around you, with croquet on the lawn and a hill to climb for 360° views of peak and sea. As for this grand Victorian factor's house, expect a few aristocratic fixtures and fittings: hunting trophies in the hall, cases filled with curios, a grand piano and open fire in the drawing room, Sanderson wallpaper in the dining room. Family oils hang on the walls, you'll find wood carvings from distant lands and a flurry of antiques, all of which blend grandeur with touches of humour. Upstairs a warren of bedrooms wait. Most are big, some are vast, all come in country-house style with lovely fabrics, crisply laundered sheets and sea views from those at the front. Dive into Skye – wildlife, mountains, sea lochs and castles all wait, as do a couple of distilleries. Suppers are on tap – tomato and basil soup, lamb noisettes, chocolate and almond cake with vanilla sauce; there's Highland porridge for breakfast, too. Fantastic.

Rooms	11: 8 twins/doubles, 2 singles, all en suite. 1 double with separate bath.
Price	£116-£150. Singles from £58.
Meals	Dinner, 3 courses, £25. Packed lunch £7.
Closed	Mid-October to Easter.
Directions	On A87, coming from south, driveway entrance on left just before the Portree filling station.

Hugh Macdonald
Viewfield House Hotel,
Viewfield Road, Portree,
Isle of Skye IV51 9EU

Tel	+44 (0)1478 612217
Email	info@viewfieldhouse.com
Web	www.viewfieldhouse.com

Culdearn House

Grantown is a great base for Highland flings. You can fish the Spey, jump on the whisky trail, check out a raft of castles, even ski in Aviemore. Loch Ness is close, as is Royal Deeside, there's golf everywhere and the walking is divine; in short, expect to be busy. As for Culdrean, it stands in a row of five identical houses that were built in 1860 by Lord Seafield, one for each of his daughters. These days it's a small, intimate hotel where William and Sonia look after guests with much kindness. There's an open fire and facing sofas in the pretty sitting room, panelled windows and a marble fireplace in the dining room, then a batch of smart homely bedrooms that offer the sort of comfort you'd want after a day in the hills. You get decanters of sherry, super beds, pretty furniture, and bathrooms that are scrupulously clean. Back downstairs, William looks after a tempting wine list and 60 malts, while Sonia whisks up delicious four-course dinners: game terrine with poached pear marmalade, elderflower sorbet or mushroom soup, local lamb in a plum and port jus, dark chocolate torte – a treat.

Rooms	6: 4 doubles, 1 twin, 1 twin/double.
Price	£138-£158. Singles from £69. Dinner, B&B from £100 p.p.
Meals	Dinner, 4 courses, £39.50.
Closed	Never.
Directions	North into Grantown from A95. Left at 30 mph sign & house directly ahead.

Sonia & William Marshall
Culdearn House,
Woodlands Terrace,
Grantown on Spey PH26 3JU

Tel +44 (0)1479 872106
Email enquiries@culdearn.com
Web www.culdearn.com

Dalmunzie House

Dalmunzie is quite some sight, an ancient hunting lodge lost to the world in one of Scotland's most dramatic landscapes. You're cradled by mountains in a vast valley; it's as good a spot as any to escape the world. Surprisingly, you're not that remote – Perth is a mere 30 miles south – but the sense of solitude is magnificent, as is the view. As for the hotel, you potter up a one-mile drive to find a small enclave of friendly souls. Interiors are just the ticket: warm, cosy and quietly grand. You find sofas in front of open fires, a smart restaurant for delicious Scottish food, a snug bar for a good malt, a breakfast room with a big view. Country-house bedrooms have colour and style. Some are grand, others simpler, several have ancient claw-foot baths. There's loads to do: fantastic walking, mountain bike trails, royal Deeside, the Highland games at Braemar, even skiing up the road in winter. As for the tricky golf course, it was almost certainly laid out by Alister MacKenzie, who later designed Augusta National; the famous par three at Amen Corner is all but identical to the 7th here.

Rooms	17: 3 tower rooms, 5 four-posters, 7 doubles, 1 twin, 1 family room.
Price	£140-£240. Dinner, B&B from £85 p.p.
Meals	Lunch from £4.50. Packed lunch £10. Dinner, 4 courses, £45.
Closed	Rarely.
Directions	North from Blairgowrie on A93. Hotel signed left in Glenshee up 1-mile drive.

Nick Jefford & Jen Gleeson
Dalmunzie House,
Spittal O'Glenshee,
Blairgowrie PH10 7QG

Tel +44 (0)1250 885224
Email reservations@dalmunzie.com
Web www.dalmunzie.com

Killiecrankie House Hotel

No Highland fling would be complete without a night at Killiecrankie. Henrietta runs the place with great charm and has spent the last five years pouring in love and money; now it shines. Outside, gardens galore: one for roses, another for vegetables, and a fine herbaceous border. Further afield, you'll find much to please: Loch Tummel, Rannoch Moor and magnificent Glenshee, over which you tumble for the Highland Games at Braemar. Return to the indisputable comforts of a smart country hotel: tartan in the dining room, 52 malts at the bar, views at breakfast of red squirrels climbing garden trees. There's a snug sitting room where a fire burns in winter; in summer doors open onto the garden. Delightful bedrooms come in different shapes and sizes. All are smart with pretty linen, warm colours, chic fabrics and lovely views. Dinner is predictably delicious, perhaps pea and mint soup, Highland venison, sticky toffee pudding. There's porridge with cream and brown sugar for breakfast. Castles, hills and distilleries wait. A great wee place with staff who care.

Rooms	10: 3 doubles, 5 twins/doubles, 2 singles.
Price	£230-£280. Price includes dinner for two.
Meals	Lunch from £4.50. Dinner included; non-residents £42.
Closed	January-February.
Directions	A9 north of Pitlochry, then B8079, signed Killiecrankie. Straight ahead for 2 miles. Hotel on right, signed.

Henrietta Fergusson
Killiecrankie House Hotel,
Killiecrankie,
Pitlochry PH16 5LG

Tel +44 (0)1796 473220
Email enquiries@killiecrankiehotel.co.uk
Web www.killiecrankiehotel.co.uk

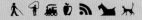

Craigatin House & Courtyard

Craigatin is one of those lovely places where beautiful rooms have attractive prices and hands-on owners go out of their way to make your stay special. It stands peacefully in two acres of manicured gardens on the northern shores of town; good restaurants are a short stroll. Smart stone exteriors give way to warmly contemporary interiors, where beautiful windows flood rooms with light. There are shutters in the breakfast room, which overflows into an enormous conservatory where sofas wait in front of a wood-burner and walls of glass open onto the garden. Big uncluttered bedrooms – some in the main house, others in converted stables – are super value for money. Expect Farrow & Ball colours, comfy beds, crisp white linen, padded bedheads and pretty shower rooms. Breakfast offers the full cooked works and tempting alternatives, perhaps smoked haddock omelettes or apple pancakes with grilled bacon and maple syrup. As for Pitlochry – gateway to the Highlands – it's a vibrant town with lots to do: castles and mountains, lochs and forests, its famous theatre festival. You're on the whisky trail, too. *Minimum two nights at weekends.*

Rooms	14: 11 doubles, 2 twins, 1 suite.
Price	£90-£100. Suite £117. Singles from £77.
Meals	Restaurants within walking distance.
Closed	Christmas.
Directions	A9 north to Pitlochry. Take 1st turn-off for town, up main street, past shops and signed on left.

Martin & Andrea Anderson
Craigatin House & Courtyard,
165 Atholl Road, Pitlochry PH16 5QL

Tel +44 (0)1796 472478
Email enquiries@craigatinhouse.co.uk
Web www.craigatinhouse.co.uk

Torrdarach House

You're high on the hill with big views south and lovely gardens to enjoy. It's a little like an Indian hill station, the big house sitting in blissful peace with the bustle of town a short stroll below. Struan and Louise came south from the far north and renovated completely: new bedrooms, new bathrooms, new everything. The result is this very friendly, super stylish, generously priced B&B. Inside you find an iPad in the hall instead of newspapers, then an airy sitting room that looks the right way; there are comfy sofas, lovely art, a whisky bar and binoculars to scan the hills. Delightful bedrooms come in the same happy style: neutral colours, smart fabrics, textured wallpaper, tartan bedheads. You get blond oak furniture, cute leather armchairs, jugs of iced water and flat-screen TVs; shower rooms are excellent. Downstairs, the glass-walled breakfast room overlooks the garden. Here you feast on local eggs, Wester Ross salmon and Speyside bacon; the porridge comes with a splash of whisky. Good golf, fabulous walking and the famous festival theatre all wait. *Minimum two nights at weekends.*

Rooms	6: 4 doubles, 2 twins/doubles.
Price	£88-£98. Singles from £78.
Meals	Pubs/restaurants 200m.
Closed	December-February.
Directions	North to Pitlochry on A9. In town, up high street, past shops, then 1st right into Larchwood Road. Up hill, keep left, then right into Golf Course Road. On right.

Struan & Louise Lothian
Torrdarach House,
Golf Course Road, Pitlochry PH16 5AU

Tel +44 (0)1796 472136
Email info@torrdarach.co.uk
Web www.torrdarach.co.uk

Kinnaird Estate

A magnificent 1770 mansion set in 6,000 acres of prime Perthshire countryside. The river Tay passes dramatically below, sheep and cattle graze contentedly, paths behind lead into the estate. The house is sublime from top to toe, grand yet welcoming, a place to feel at home. Most beautiful of all is the panelled drawing room with roaring fire, grand piano, beautiful art and sofas galore. The dining room has original murals, you breakfast in the company of the Maharaja of Jaipur (well, his portrait), there's a billiards room with fine views, a snug study, too. Big country-house bedrooms have vast beds, smart wallpapers and colourful fabrics. Those at the front get the view, several have fires, excellent bathrooms come with white robes. The estate owns a couple of world-class fishing beats, so come to try your luck; there's shooting in season, clays, too. Food is delicious (local meat, estate eggs) and you can bring your own wine. Staff are lovely. Five estate cottages tempt you to linger. Fabulous walking and the odd castle wait. House parties are welcome.

Rooms	8 + 5: 7 twins/doubles, 1 suite. 5 cottages for 2-8.
Price	£130-£150. Suite £180. Singles from £110. Cottages £300-£1,050 p.w.
Meals	Picnic lunch £10. Dinner, 3 courses, £35 (not Sunday or Monday).
Closed	February. Whole house bookings only for Christmas & New Year.
Directions	Leave A9 for B898 2 miles north of Dunkeld. On right after 6 miles.

Shannon Mulholland
Kinnaird Estate,
Dunkeld PH8 0LB

Tel	+44 (0)1796 482440
Email	reservations@kinnairdestate.com
Web	www.kinnairdestate.com

Fortingall Hotel

You're away from the crowds in one of Perthshire's loveliest glens – wild deer roam, buzzards nest, fishermen stand in silent rapture on the banks for the river Lyon. As for this lovely country-house hotel, it sits next to the village church in the shade of an ancient yew tree. In 1900 it was remodelled in Arts & Crafts style, as was the village, hence the thatched cottages. Inside, it's smart but not stuffy, with roaring fires, bold colours, country art, the odd grandfather clock. There's a grand piano in the sitting room, local art in the library, a half-panelled dining room with views up the valley, a cute locals' bar where farmers gather. Bedrooms upstairs have a fresh, country-house feel: padded bedheads, Glen Lyon tweed, sofas in the bigger rooms, spotless bathrooms; those at the front have the view. Back downstairs, you can eat in the dining room or the bar – duck terrine and fillet of beef one night, bangers and mash the next. You can fish, cycle, scale a couple of munros, play some golf or visit the smallest distillery in Scotland. Don't miss afternoon tea.

Rooms	11: 9 doubles, 2 twins.
Price	£165-£200. Singles from £110. Dinner, B&B from £145 p.p.
Meals	Lunch from £6.95. Dinner, 4 courses, £35. Bar meals from £9.95.
Closed	Rarely.
Directions	A9, A872 west to Aberfeldy, then B846 north. Left in Coshieville and on right after 3 miles.

Robbie & Mags Cairns
Fortingall Hotel,
Fortingall, Aberfeldy PH15 2NQ

Tel +44 (0)1887 830367
Email enquiries@fortingallhotel.com
Web www.fortingall.com

Monachyle Mhor

Monachyle is unique – a designer hotel on a remote hill farm that started life as a B&B. Today it's one of the coolest places to stay in Scotland and it's still run by the same family with the children at the helm. Dick farms, Melanie designs the magical rooms, Tom cooks some of the best food in Scotland. It sits in 2,000 acres of blissful silence at the end of the track with the Trossachs circling around you and Loch Voil shimming below. Sheep graze, buzzards swoop, the odd fisherman tries his luck. Inside, there's a cool little bar, a fire in the sitting room, then a slim restaurant that drinks in the view. Bedrooms ooze 21st-century chic: big beds, cool colours, fabulous design, hi-tech gadgets. Bathrooms are equally good, perhaps a deluge shower in a granite steam room or claw-foot baths with views down the glen. Loft-house suites are enormous, but the smaller rooms are lovely, too. Dinner is a five-course feast with beef, lamb, pork and venison all off the farm. Rob Roy lived in the glen, you can visit his grave. The hotel holds a festival in May – fabulous food and cool Scottish tunes.

Rooms	14: 9 twins/doubles, 5 suites.
Price	£195-£215. Suites £265.
Meals	Lunch from £5.50. Dinner £50. Sunday lunch £32.
Closed	Two weeks in January.
Directions	M9, junc. 11, then B824 and A84 north. Right for Balquhidder 6 miles north of Callander. 5 miles west along road & Loch Voil. Hotel on right, signed.

Tom Lewis
Monachyle Mhor,
Balquhidder, Lochearnhead FK19 8PQ

Tel	+44 (0)1877 384622
Email	monachyle@mhor.net
Web	www.mhor.net

Pilot Panther

The Pilot Panther is a classic 1950 showman's wagon originally built by The Coventry Steel Company, once renowned as the finest wagon makers in the country. Its journey has been long and rambling, but it has settled in a fine location in the grounds of Monachyle Mhor hotel. The views from your window are of the spectacular loch which seems to change with the weather and provide a new sight every day. Off the main living and sleeping area, which also has the wood-burner, oven and grill, is the double bunk room. The loos and shower are a minute's walk away at the hotel. The great walking and stunning views around the long loch will help you work up an appetite worthy of the hotel restaurant, an award-winning pilgrimage for Scottish foodies. Or you can arrange to have breakfast at the hotel and fuel up before you go. Rather handily, the family also manage the farm, fishery and bakery, which ensures that a good supply of very local produce goes onto the menu. The Panther is both an unusual way to stay at a heavenly hotel, and an experience in itself.
Minimum two nights. Book through Sawday's Canopy & Stars online or by phone.

Rooms	1 showman's wagon.
Price	£125.
Meals	BYO breakfast, or at hotel, £12.50. Dinner £50. Sunday lunch £32.
Closed	Never.
Directions	M9 junc. 11, then B824 and A84 north. Right for Balquhidder 6 miles north of Callander. Signed right after 5 miles.

Sawday's Canopy & Stars
Pilot Panther,
Mhor, Balquhidder FK19 8PQ

Tel +44 (0)1275 395447
Email enquiries@canopyandstars.co.uk
Web www.canopyandstars.co.uk/pilotpanther

Creagan House at Strathyre

Creagan is a delight – a small, traditional restaurant with rooms run with great passion by Gordon and Cherry. At its heart is Gordon's delicious food, which draws a devoted crowd, perhaps fillet of brill with plum and damson, local venison with a sloe gin and juniper sauce, then an apple, prune and almond flory with clotted cream. Food is local – meat and game from Perthshire, seafood from west-coast boats – and served on Skye pottery; some vegetables come from the garden. A snug sitting room doubles as a bar, where a good wine list and 50 malt whiskies wait; if you like a dram, you'll be happy here. Bedrooms fit the bill: warm and comfy with smart carpets, pretty colours, flat-screen TVs, a sofa if there's room. Breakfast is a treat; where else can you sit in a baronial dining room and read about the iconography of the toast rack while waiting for your bacon and eggs? No airs and graces, just the sort of attention you only get in small owner-run places. Hens, woodpeckers and red squirrels live in the garden. There are hills to climb, boat trips on lochs, secure storage for bikes. Very dog-friendly.

Rooms	5: 3 doubles, 1 twin, 1 four-poster.
Price	£130-£150. Singles from £75.
Meals	Dinner, 3 courses, £35.
Closed	Wednesday-Thursday. February.
Directions	From Stirling A84 north through Callander to Strathyre. Hotel 0.25 miles north of village on right.

Gordon & Cherry Gunn
Creagan House at Strathyre,
Callander FK18 8ND

Tel +44 (0)1877 384638
Email eatandstay@creaganhouse.co.uk
Web www.creaganhouse.co.uk

Barley Bree

A few miles north of Gleneagles, a super little restaurant with rooms that delivers what so many people want: stylish interiors, super food, excellent prices, a warm welcome. This is a small family-run affair. Fabrice is French and cooks sublimely, Alison, a Scot, looks after the wine. Their stage is Barley Bree – whisky soup to you and me – an 18th-century coaching inn that has recently had a facelift. Now a band of happy locals come for fabulous Scottish food cooked with predictable French flair, perhaps rabbit terrine with a wild garlic salad, fillet of halibut with spring onion mash, and cardamom cheesecake with chocolate ice-cream. The restaurant, nicely rustic, has a fire that burns on both sides, while in summer you decant onto a terrace for lunch in the sun. Upstairs, six lovely rooms come in neutral colours. You get crisp linen and comfy beds, then underfloor heating in excellent little shower rooms. One room is big and has a claw-foot bath. Head down to Gleneagles for a game of golf; the Ryder Cup comes through in 2014.
Ask about wedding receptions.

Rooms	6 twins/doubles.
Price	£105-£140. Singles from £70.
Meals	Lunch from £6. Dinner, 3 courses, about £40. Not Monday or Tuesday.
Closed	Christmas & New Year.
Directions	A9 north from Dunblane, then A822 for Muthill. In village on left before church.

Fabrice & Alison Bouteloup
Barley Bree,
6 Willoughby Street, Muthill PH5 2AB

Tel	+44 (0)1764 681451
Email	info@barleybree.com
Web	www.barleybree.com

Royal Hotel

The Royal is lovely – softly grand, intimate and welcoming, a country house in the middle of town. Queen Victoria once stayed, hence the name. It stands on the river Earn – its eponymous loch glistens five miles up stream – but you're brilliantly placed to strike out in all directions: Loch Tay, Pitlochry, The Trossachs and Perth are close. Those who linger fare rather well. You get a wall of books in an elegant sitting room where two fires burn; newspapers hang on poles, logs tumble from wicker baskets, sofas and armchairs are impeccably upholstered. There's a grandfather clock in the hall, rugs to cover stripped floors in a country-house bar, then walls festooned with beautiful art. You can eat all over the place, in the bar, in the conservatory or at smartly dressed tables in the elegant dining room, perhaps asparagus spears with a poached egg, breast of duck with cabbage and bacon, rhubarb sponge with vanilla ice-cream. Smart homely rooms have padded bedheads, crisp linen, mahogany dressers, gilt-framed mirrors. Bathrooms come with fluffy robes, one four-poster has a log fire.

Rooms	12: 8 doubles, 3 twins, 1 house.
Price	£140-£180. House £320. Self-catering from £320 (low season 2 nights).
Meals	Bar meals from £6.95. Dinner, 3 courses, £27.75.
Closed	Rarely.
Directions	A9 north of Dunblane, A822 thro' Braco, left onto B827. Left for town centre, over bridge, hotel on square.

Teresa Milsom
Royal Hotel,
Melville Square, Comrie,
Crieff PH6 2DN

Tel +44 (0)1764 679200
Email reception@royalhotel.co.uk
Web www.royalhotel.co.uk

Windlestraw Lodge

There are few better distractions in Scotland than following the river Tweed: fishing lines glisten in the sun, lambs bleat high on the hill, ospreys glide through the afternoon sky. This is the river which brought prosperity to Scotland, its mills a source of huge wealth in Victorian days. Windlestraw, a heavenly country house, stands in evidence; it was built as a wedding gift for a mill owner and sits on the side of a hill with timeless views down the valley. Outside, a copper beech shades the lawn; inside, a dazzling refurbishment elates. You get stripped floors, painted ceilings, roaring fires, a panelled dining room. Light pours in through windows at the front, gilt mirrors hang on walls, fat sofas encourage idleness. There are binoculars with which to scan the valley, a terrace for afternoon tea, a sitting room for a quiet snooze. Country-house bedrooms are sublime. An elegant contemporary style runs throughout, those at the front have lovely views, one has the coolest of bathrooms. Add to this Alan's fabulous food and you have a very special place. There's golf at Peebles. Not to be missed.

Rooms	5: 4 doubles, 1 twin.
Price	£150-£190. Singles from £95. Dinner, B&B from £120 p.p.
Meals	Lunch by arrangement. Supper, 3 courses, £30. Dinner, 4 courses, £45. Tasting menu £60.
Closed	Rarely.
Directions	East from Peebles on A72. Into Walkerburn; house signed left on western flank of town.

Julie & Alan Reid
Windlestraw Lodge,
Galashiels Road,
Walkerburn EH43 6AA

Tel +44 (0)1896 870636
Email reception@windlestraw.co.uk
Web www.windlestraw.co.uk

The Allanton Inn

Allanton, population 100. Welcome to the sleepy back of beyond, an untouched corner of the rural idyll that most people skip on their rush north. Well, there's no rush here, just patchwork fields, rolling hills and the river Tweed pottering off to the coast. As for this cute little inn, it's a great base from which to explore. The style is charming, the locals friendly, the prices lovely, the food a treat. It sits on the only street in town with a garden that backs onto open country; in summer you can have lunch in the sun while watching the farmer plough his fields. Inside, home-spun interiors have warmth, style and colour. There's an open-plan feel, the airy bar flowing into a half-panelled restaurant. You'll find a smouldering fire, good art, fresh flowers. Pretty rooms above come with good bathrooms, Farrow & Ball colours, padded bedheads and homemade biscuits. A couple are big, those at the back have the view. Super local food waits downstairs, perhaps hot smoked salmon, rack of local lamb, Tia Maria tiramisu. Local fishing is easy to arrange, there's golf and excellent walking, too.

Rooms	6: 2 doubles, 2 twins/doubles, 1 single, 1 family room.
Price	£75-£90. Family room £125. Singles from £50.
Meals	Lunch from £6.75. Dinner, 3 courses, £25-£35. Sunday lunch from £12.50.
Closed	Christmas.
Directions	West from Berwick on A6105, then left in Churnside onto B6437. On left in village.

William & Katerina Reynolds
The Allanton Inn,
Allanton, By Duns TD11 3JZ

Tel	+44 (0)1890 818260
Email	info@allantoninn.co.uk
Web	www.allantoninn.co.uk

Ballochneck

Donnie and Fiona's magical pile stands one mile up a private drive, soundproofed by 175 acres of lush Stirlingshire country. Swans nest on the lake in spring, which doubles as a curling pond in winter (you can), while sheep graze the fields and deer come to eat the rhododendrons. The house – still a home, albeit a grand one – dates to 1863 and was built for the Lord Provost of Glasgow. Inside you get all the aristocratic works – roaring fires, painted panelling, magical windows that bring in the view, wonderfully ornate ceilings – but Donnie and Fiona are the real stars; expect friendly banter, a few good stories and a trip to the top of the house where a full-size snooker tables stands amid purple walls. Vast bedrooms at the front have huge views, beautiful beds and acres of crisp linen; one has an open fire, while a claw-foot bath next door comes with candles and views down the valley. Delicious breakfasts are served in the panelled dining room with an open fire in winter. Stirling castle, Loch Lomond and the Trossacks are close, while Glasgow and Edinburgh are less than an hour by car. *Minimum two nights at weekends.*

Rooms	2 doubles, 1 with separate bathroom.
Price	£160.
Meals	Dinner, 4 courses, £35 by arrangement.
Closed	November-March.
Directions	M9 junc. 10, A84 west, B8075 south, then A811 for Buchlyvie. In village, right onto B835 for Aberfoyle. Over bridge, up to lodge house 200m on left. 1 mile up drive to house.

Donnie & Fiona Allan
Ballochneck,
Buchlyvie, Stirling FK8 3PA

Tel +44 (0)1360 850216
Email info@ballochneck.com
Web www.ballochneck.com

Langass Lodge

Vast skies, water everywhere, golden beaches that stretch for miles. Nothing prepares you for the epic majesty of the Uists, a place so infinitely beautiful you wonder why you've got it to yourself. As for Langass, an old shooting lodge, it makes a great base, not least because Amanda and Niall know the island inside out and can help you discover its secrets. The hotel sits in ten silent acres with paths that lead up to standing stones or down to the water. Inside, cosy interiors fit the bill perfectly: a roaring fire in the bar; watery views in the restaurant; doors onto a terrace for drinks in summer. Bedrooms – warmly traditional in the main house, nicely contemporary in the new wing – are super value for money. Expect comfy beds, crisp white linen, excellent bathrooms, lots of colour. As for the food, it's the best on the island, with game off the estate and seafood plucked fresh from the sea. There's loads to do: kayaking, walking, wild fishing, bird watching. The night sky is magnificent, as are the Northern Lights. Children and dogs are very welcome. Don't miss it.

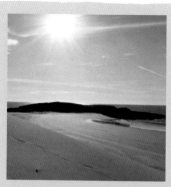

Rooms	11: 9 twins/doubles, 2 family suites for 4.
Price	£95-£145. Family suites £120-£160. Singles from £75.
Meals	Dinner in bar from £12.95; in restaurant £30-£36.
Closed	Never.
Directions	South from Lochmaddy on A867. Signed left after five miles.

Amanda & Niall Leveson Gower
Langass Lodge,
Langass,
North Uist HS6 5HA

Tel	+44 (0)1876 580285
Email	langasslodge@btconnect.com
Web	www.langasslodge.co.uk

Scarista House

All you need to know is this: Harris is one of the most beautiful places in the world. Beaches of white sand that stretch for a mile or two are not uncommon. If you bump into another soul, it will be a delightful coincidence, but you should not count on it. The water is turquoise, coconuts sometimes wash up on the beach. The view from Scarista is simple and magnificent: field, ridge, beach, water, sky. Patricia and Tim are the kindest people, quietly inspiring. Their home is island heaven: coal fires, rugs on painted floors, books everywhere, old oak furniture, a first-floor drawing room and fabulous Harris light. Homely bedrooms come in country-house style. The golf club has left a set of clubs by the front door in case you wish to play (the view from the first tee is one of the best in the game). A corncrake occasionally visits the garden. There are walking sticks and Wellington boots to help you up the odd hill. Kind local staff may speak Gaelic and the food is exceptional, maybe quail with an armagnac mousse, fillet of Stornoway halibut, orange marmalade tart. A perfect place.

Rooms	6: 2 doubles, 1 twin, 3 suites for 2.
Price	£190–£220. Suites £235. Singles from £137.
Meals	Dinner, 3 courses, £43. Packed lunch £7.50.
Closed	January–February.
Directions	From Tarbert A859 south, signed Rodel. Scarista 15 miles on left after golf course. W10 bus stops at gate.

Patricia & Tim Martin
Scarista House,
Scarista,
Isle of Harris HS3 3HX

Tel +44 (0)1859 550238
Email timandpatricia@scaristahouse.com
Web www.scaristahouse.com

Auberge Carnish

Scotland has a way of throwing up vast landscapes of staggering beauty and it's fair to say that Auberge Carnish sits bang in the middle of one of them. Outside, the endless acres of Uig Sands ebb and flow with the tide, a sight so strangely addictive you can sit and watch it all day. Atlantic storms pour through, an infinitely satisfying event, so cast yourself adrift on the wild west coast and walk in the dunes, comb the beach, or spin up the road to the famous standing stones at Callanish. And where else to stay than the lovely Auberge? It teeters above the water, gorging itself on the view – sea, sky and land, that's your lot. Inside, warm contemporary interiors wait. Bedrooms have cool colours, fabulous bathrooms, super-comfy beds, blond wood furniture. One has double-aspect views, another has doors onto a terrace. Downstairs, there's a wood-burner in the bar, then an airy restaurant with great views, where Richard serves up his tasty food, perhaps fresh langoustine, Lewis lamb, chocolate profiteroles with vanilla ice-cream. Come off season and you may see the Northern Lights.

Rooms	4: 3 doubles, 1 twin.
Price	£130-£150.
Meals	Dinner, £28.50-£34.50.
Closed	Never.
Directions	A859, A858 west, then B8011 for Uig. Through Ardroil, over Red River bridge and signed right.

Richard & Jo Leparoux
Auberge Carnish,
5 Carnish, Uig,
Isle of Lewis HS2 9EX

Tel +44 (0)1851 672459
Email stay@aubergecarnish.co.uk
Web www.aubergecarnish.co.uk

Photo: Tom Bell

Wales

Photo: istockphoto.com

Ty Mawr Country Hotel

Pretty rooms, attractive prices and delicious food make this super country house hard to resist. It's a very peaceful, tucked-away spot. You drive over the hills, drop into the village and wash up at this 16th-century stone house that glows in yellow. Outside, a sun-trapping terrace laps against a trim lawn, which in turn drops into a passing river. Gentle eccentricities abound: croquet hoops take the odd diversion, logs are piled high like giant beehives, a seat has been chiselled into a tree trunk. Inside, exposed stone walls, terracotta-tiled floors and low beamed ceilings give a warm country feel. There are fires everywhere – one in the sitting room, which overlooks the garden, another in the dining room that burns on both sides. Excellent bedrooms are all big. You get warm colours, big beds, crisp linen, good bathrooms. Some have sofas, all are dog-friendly, three overlook the garden. Back downstairs, the bar doubles as reception, and there's Welsh art on sale. Steve's cooking is the final treat: Cardigan Bay scallops, organic Welsh beef, calvados and cinnamon rice pudding. First class. *Children over ten welcome.*

Rooms	6: 4 doubles, 2 twins/doubles.
Price	£115-£130. Singles from £70. Dinner, B&B from £80 p.p.
Meals	Dinner £24-£29.
Closed	Rarely.
Directions	M4 west onto A48, then B4310 exit, for National Botanic Gardens. 6 miles north to Brechfa. In village centre.

Annabel & Steve Thomas
Ty Mawr Country Hotel,
Brechfa SA32 7RA

Tel +44 (0)1267 202332
Email info@wales-country-hotel.co.uk
Web www.wales-country-hotel.co.uk

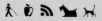

The Cors

A bohemian bolthole, one of the best. Nick is a cook, an artist and gardener, his two lush acres a perfect retreat in summer, so come to sip your Earl Grey while the river potters past. Gunnera, bamboo and tree ferns all flourish, so expect a little green-fingered theatre. Inside, a small, personal world of French inspiration – sit in the bar and be swept back to 1950s Paris. Doors open onto a Victorian veranda where roses and clematis ramble elegantly, perfect for pre-dinner drinks in summer. As for the food, you eat accompanied by cool tunes, with busts and paintings all around – perhaps at the front with garden views, or wrapped up behind in claret reds. It's a feast of local produce with an Italian twist: roasted figs with gorgonzola and Parma ham, Carmarthenshire chicken filled with spinach and mascarpone, then a zesty lemon tart. Bedrooms upstairs have a simple, chic style: rugs on bare boards, vintage William Morris wallpapers, pretty pine, bold colours – perfect for the price. Don't miss Laugharne for all things Dylan Thomas. *Minimum stay two nights in summer.*

Rooms	3 doubles.
Price	£80. Singles from £50.
Meals	Dinner, 3 courses, from £35 (Thur-Sat only). Sunday lunch from £17.
Closed	2 weeks in November.
Directions	A4066 south from St Clears for Laugharne. In village right at pub. Over bridge and on right.

Nick Priestland
The Cors,
Newbridge Road, Laugharne SA33 4SH

Tel	+44 (0)1994 427219
Email	nick@thecors.co.uk
Web	www.thecors.co.uk

Penbontbren

You're lost in lovely hills, yet only three miles from the sea. Not that you're going to stray far. These gorgeous suites don't just have wonderful prices, they're also addictive – this is a great spot to come and do nothing at all. Richard and Huw have thought it all through. You get crockery and cutlery, kettles and fridges, you're also encouraged to bring your own wine and to nip up to the farm shop for provisions for lunch. As for the suites, they have big beds, super bathrooms, sofas and armchairs in cosy sitting areas, and doors onto semi-private terraces – perfect for lunches in summer. Potter about and find iPod docks, flat-screen TVs, robes and White Company lotions. Breakfast is served in the big house – the full Welsh works. Incredibly, this was a caravan park once, all trace of which has vanished; in its place, field and sky, birdsong and sheep. Beaches, hills, Cardigan and magical St Davids all wait. Good local restaurants are on hand: lobster from the sea, lamb from the hills. A great place to unwind with discounts for longer stays. *Minimum two nights in high season.*

Rooms	5 + 1: 5 suites, 1 self-catering cottage for 7.
Price	£105-£120. Cottage £700-£995.
Meals	Restaurants within 3 miles.
Closed	Christmas.
Directions	Sent on booking.

Richard Morgan-Price
& Huw Thomas
Penbontbren,
Glynarthen, Llandysul SA44 6PE

Tel +44 (0)1239 810248
Email contact@penbontbren.com
Web www.penbontbren.com

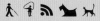

Harbourmaster

This is one of those fabulous places where everything hits the spot – the food, the views, the vibe, the style. The hotel stands on the town's quay with Cardigan Bay sparkling beyond. Inside you get that winning combination of seductive good looks, informal but attentive service and a menu overflowing with fresh local produce. The airy open-plan dining room/bar has stripped floors, local art, exposed walls and windows overlooking the harbour. Wind up the staircase to find super bedrooms that come with shuttered windows, lots of colour and quietly funky bathrooms. You get Welsh wool blankets, hot water bottles in winter, flat-screen TVs and DVD players, watery views and tide books. Fabulous suites in the Warehouse next door are worth splashing out on: they're big and stylish with excellent bathrooms. Back downstairs, there are local beers at the horseshoe bar, then great food that's informally served, perhaps half a dozen oysters, a pizza or a steak, Bakewell tart with almond ice-cream. There are bikes to borrow, cycle tracks that lead into the hills, coastal paths that head north and south. *Minimum two nights at weekends. Children over five welcome.*

Rooms	11: 4 doubles, 3 twins/doubles, 4 suites.
Price	£110-£175. Suites £120-£250. Singles from £65. Dinner, B&B from £90 p.p.
Meals	Lunch & bar meals from £6. Dinner, 3 courses, about £30. Sunday lunch £21.
Closed	Christmas Day.
Directions	A487 south from Aberystwyth. In Aberaeron right for the harbour. Hotel on waterfront.

Glyn & Menna Heulyn
Harbourmaster,
Pen Cei,
Aberaeron SA46 0BT

Tel +44 (0)1545 570755
Email info@harbour-master.com
Web www.harbour-master.com

Nanteos Mansion

A fabulous old manor house lost at the end of a one-mile drive, with a small lake, a Georgian walled garden and 25 acres of ancient woodland. Outside, four pillars stand at the front door; inside, sofas wait by a wood-burner in the hall. The house dates to 1731, but stands on medieval foundations; it is most famous for the Nanteos Cup, thought to be the Holy Grail, which was carried here by monks from Glastonbury Abbey. A magnificent renovation has recently bought the house back to life – electric-shock therapy performed by interior designers. Downstairs, there's a morning room, a smart bar, then an irresistible restaurant where you dig into delicious food, perhaps mackerel with a rhubarb compote, slow-roasted pork with a toffee apple sauce, dark chocolate mousse with white chocolate ice-cream. Bedrooms are dreamy: cool colours, fabulous bathrooms, lovely beds, wonderful art; the bridal suite is divine. There's loads to do: rivers to fish, mountains to climb, coastal paths to follow. Don't miss the music room (Wagner may have visited). You can self-cater in a cool mews house, too. Brilliant.

Rooms	14 + 1: 14 twins/doubles, 1 mews house.
Price	£180-£300. Mews house £500.
Meals	Lunch from £7.50. Dinner £32.50-£39.95. Sunday lunch from £23.50
Closed	Rarely.
Directions	Leaving Aberystwyth to the south, take A4120 Devil's Bridge Road, then immediately right onto B4340. House signed left after 1 mile.

Mark Rawlings-Lloyd
Nanteos Mansion,
Rhydyfelin, Aberystwyth SY23 4LU

Tel	+44 (0)1970 600522
Email	info@nanteos.com
Web	www.nanteos.com

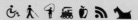

Escape Boutique B&B

A super-cool boutique B&B with fabulous rooms, attractive prices and some seriously lovely bathrooms. The house stands high on the hill, away from the crowds, a short stroll from the buzz of town and its two-mile sandy beach. This is a 19th-century mill owner's villa and its fine old windows, sparkling wood floors and enormous carved fireplace bear testament to Victorian roots. Other than that it's a clean sweep of funky interiors. Sam and Gaenor scoured Europe for the eclectic collection of colourful retro furniture that fills the rooms – orange swivel chairs, iconic G-plan sofas, beautiful beds wrapped in crisp white linen. Urban Cool, Retro Red, Modern Romance... take your pick. All come with flat-screen TVs, Blu-ray DVD players and iPod docks. Bathrooms are excellent: one room has a magnificent shower for two, another has a copper bath in the room. Downstairs, there's an honesty bar and a fire in the sitting room, while delicious breakfasts are served in the attractive dining room. Excellent restaurants wait in town: try Osborne's for a little glamour or the Seahorse for great fish. *Minimum two nights at weekends.*

Rooms	9: 8 doubles, 1 twin/double.
Price	£89-£140. Singles from £74.
Meals	Restaurants within walking distance.
Closed	Christmas.
Directions	A55 junc. 19, then A470 for Llandudno. On promenade, head west hugging the coast, then left at Belmont Hotel and house on right.

Sam Nayar & Gaenor Loftus
Escape Boutique B&B,
48 Church Walks, Llandudno LL30 2HL

Tel	+44 (0)1492 877776
Email	info@escapebandb.co.uk
Web	www.escapebandb.co.uk

Pentre Mawr Country House

The setting is beautiful, 190 acres of deep country at the end of a lane. The house isn't bad either. This is an old estate, which fell into ruin 80 years ago. It has been in Graham's family for 400 years, and he and Bre have done a fine job renovating the place. Outside, a lawn runs down to fields, Doric columns flank the front door. Inside is half B&B (informal, personal, very welcoming), half hotel (smart rooms, attentive service, a menu in the restaurant). Wander about and find a couple of sitting rooms, open fires, vast flagstones, a bust of Robert Napier. Bedrooms are scattered about. Big rooms in the main house have a country-house feel and spa baths for two; stylish suites in the gardener's cottage have hot tubs on private terraces; super-cool safari lodges in the garden flaunt faux leopard-skin throws and fabulous bathrooms. There's a sun-trapping courtyard with a small pool, tennis on the grass, a kitchen garden that's being teased back to life. And Bre cooks a fine dinner, perhaps smoked salmon, rack of lamb, bread and butter pudding. *Minimum two nights in hot tub suites & at weekends.*

Rooms	11: 3 doubles. Gardener's Cottage: 2 suites. Garden: 6 canvas safari lodges.
Price	£150-£210. Suites £180-£230. Dinner, B&B (obligatory Fri & Sat) from £100 p.p.
Meals	Dinner, 5 courses, £35.
Closed	Christmas.
Directions	A55, then A525 south to Denbigh. Left at second roundabout to Llandyrnog, then left at mini-roundabout onto B5429. 1st left; signed left after 0.5 miles.

Graham & Bre Carrington-Sykes
Pentre Mawr Country House,
Llandyrnog,
Denbigh LL16 4LA

Tel	+44 (0)1824 790732
Email	info@pentremawrcountryhouse.co.uk
Web	www.pentremawrcountryhouse.co.uk

The Hand at Llanarmon

Single-track lanes plunge you into the middle of nowhere. All around, lush valleys rise and fall, so pull on your boots and scale a mountain or find a river and jump into a canoe. Back at The Hand, a 16th-century drovers' inn, the pleasures of a traditional country local are hard to miss. A coal fire burns on the range in reception, a wood fire crackles under brass in the front bar and a wood-burner warms the lofty dining room. Expect exposed stone walls, low beamed ceilings, old pine settles and candles on the mantelpiece. There's a games room for darts and pool, a quiet sitting room for maps and books. Delicious food is popular with locals, so grab a table and enjoy seasonal menus – perhaps game broth, lamb casserole, then sticky toffee pudding. Bedrooms are just as they should be: not too fancy, cosy and warm, spotlessly clean with crisp white linen and good bathrooms. A very friendly place. Martin and Gaynor are full of quiet enthusiasm and have made their home warmly welcoming. John Ceiriog Hughes, who wrote *Bread of Heaven*, lived in this valley. Special indeed.

Rooms	13: 8 doubles, 4 twins, 1 suite.
Price	£90-£127. Singles from £52.50.
Meals	Lunch from £6.50. Sunday lunch £21. Dinner £12-£20.
Closed	Rarely.
Directions	Leave A5 south of Chirk for B4500. Llanarmon 11 miles on.

Gaynor & Martin De Luchi
The Hand at Llanarmon,
Llanarmon Dyffryn Ceiriog,
Llangollen LL20 7LD

Tel +44 (0)1691 600666
Email reception@thehandhotel.co.uk
Web www.thehandhotel.co.uk

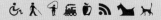

Y Meirionnydd

By day you explore the mighty wonders of Snowdonia, by night you return to this lovely small hotel and recover in style. It's one of those places that delivers just what you want; it's smart without being posh, the welcome is second to none, there's great food and the bedrooms are fantastic. You're in the middle of a small country town with a terrace at the front, so sit outside in summer and watch the world pass by. Inside, soft colours and warm lighting create a mellow feel. There's a cute bar with armchairs and games, an airy breakfast room for the full Welsh works, then a smart restaurant cut into the rock, which was once the county jail; the food is somewhat better than it was then, perhaps venison pâté with hot chillies, fillet of salmon with lime and ginger, fresh fruit crumble with lashings of cream. Bedrooms upstairs are gorgeous. Some are bigger than others, but all have the same style: clean lines, cool colours, huge beds, beautiful linen. You get the odd stone wall, an armchair if there's room, then super bathrooms. There's secure storage for bikes, too. *Minimum two nights at weekends.*

Rooms	5: 3 doubles, 2 twins/doubles.
Price	£75-£135. Singles from £60.
Meals	Dinner, 3 courses, £25. Not Sundays in low season.
Closed	One week at Christmas.
Directions	In centre of town on one-way system, off A470.

Marc Russell & Nick Banda
Y Meirionnydd,
Smithfield Square, Dolgellau LL40 1ES

Tel +44 (0)1341 422554
Email info@themeirionnydd.com
Web www.themeirionnydd.com

Penmaenuchaf Hall

The gardens are amazing – woodlands strewn with daffodils in spring, topiary on the upper lawn, a walled garden of tumbling colour. The position high on the hill is sublime, with the Mawdacch estuary carving imperiously through the valley below. The house has attitude, too. Built in 1865 for a Bolton cotton merchant, the smell of wood smoke greets you at the front door. In chilly weather, an open fire crackles in the half-panelled hall, where armchairs take the strain. The drawing room is even better with mullioned windows framing the view, a grand piano and cavernous sofas, country rugs on original wood floors. Steps illuminated by fairy lights lead up to the airy conservatory/dining room, where French windows open onto to a terrace for al fresco dining. Bedrooms come in traditional country-house style with a warm contemporary feel, ornamental fireplaces, padded window seats and comfy beds. Some rooms are huge, several have balconies, all have bathrooms that are more than adequate. There are 13 miles of river to fish, while Snowdon, Bala and Portmeirion are close. *Children over six welcome.*

Rooms	14: 7 doubles, 5 twins/doubles, 1 four-poster, 1 family room.
Price	£174-£268. Singles from £118.
Meals	Lunch from £6. Afternoon tea from £7.90. Dinner, 3 courses, £42.50.
Closed	Rarely.
Directions	From Dolgellau A493 west for about 1.5 miles. Entrance on left.

Mark Watson & Lorraine Fielding
Penmaenuchaf Hall,
Penmaenpool, Dolgellau LL40 1YB
Tel +44 (0)1341 422129
Email relax@penhall.co.uk
Web www.penhall.co.uk

Plas Bodegroes

Close to the end of the world and worth every second it takes to get here, inspirational Chris and Gunna's home is a temple of cool elegance, the food possibly the best in Wales. Fronted by an avenue of 200-year-old beech trees, this Georgian manor house is wrapped in climbing roses and wildly roaming wisteria. The veranda circles the house, as do long French windows that lighten every room, so pull up a chair and listen to birdsong. There's no formality here – come to relax and be yourself. Bedrooms are wonderful, the courtyard rooms especially good, where exposed wooden ceilings give the feel of a smart Scandinavian forest hideaway. Best of all is the dining room, almost a work of art in itself, cool and crisp with exceptional art on the walls – a great place to eat Chris's ambrosial food; try sea trout wrapped in Carmarthen ham, mountain lamb with rosemary jus, baked vanilla cheesecake with passion fruit sorbet. Don't miss the Lleyn Peninsula: sandy beaches, towering cliffs and country walks all wait. Snowdon and Portmeirion are close too.

Rooms	10: 8 doubles, 1 twin, 1 suite.
Price	£140-£180. Singles from £112.
Meals	Sunday lunch £22.50. Dinner £45. Not Sunday or Monday evenings.
Closed	December-February. Sunday & Monday throughout year.
Directions	From Pwllheli A497 towards Nefyn. House on left after 1 mile, signed.

Chris & Gunna Chown
Plas Bodegroes,
Efailnewydd, Pwllheli LL53 5TH

Tel +44 (0)1758 612363
Email gunna@bodegroes.co.uk
Web www.bodegroes.co.uk

Plas Dinas Country House

This is the family home of Lord Snowdon. It dates to the 1600s and stands in 15 acres with an avenue of oak that sweeps you up to the house. Princess Margaret stayed often and much of what fills the house belongs to the family: stunning chandeliers, oils by the score, gilt-framed mirrors – an Aladdin's cave of beautiful things. There's a baby grand piano in the drawing room, where you find smart wood floors, an honesty bar and a fire that roars, but potter about the house and find masses of memorabilia framed on the walls (make sure you visit the private dining room). Bedrooms are quite something, the past mixing gracefully with modern design. Nothing is left to chance, a constant programme of refurbishment sees to that. You get four-posters, classic colours, sumptuous fabrics, a sofa if there's room. Bathrooms are excellent, some with showers, others with free-standing baths. Back downstairs Andy's cooking hits the spot, perhaps smoked salmon mousse, lamb shank with mint and rosemary, then Baileys crème brûlée. Snowdon is close, as you'd expect. *Minimum two nights on bank holiday weekends.*

Rooms	9: 4 doubles, 3 twins/doubles, 2 four-posters.
Price	£129-£275. Singles from £99.
Meals	Dinner, 3 courses, £26-£30.
Closed	22 December-2 January.
Directions	South from Caernarfon on A487. Through Bontnewydd and signed right after half a mile at brow of shallow hill.

Andy & Julian Banner-Price
Plas Dinas Country House,
Bontnewydd, Caernarfon LL54 7YF

Tel +44 (0)1286 830214
Email info@plasdinas.co.uk
Web www.plasdinas.co.uk

The Bell at Skenfrith

The position here is magical: an ancient stone bridge, a magnificent valley, glorious hills rising behind, cows grazing in lush fields. It's a perfect spot, not least because providence has blessed it with this sublime inn, where crisply designed interiors ooze country chic. In summer doors fly open and life spills onto a stone terrace, where views of hill and wood are interrupted only by the odd chef pottering off to a productive and organic kitchen garden. Back inside, airy rooms come with slate floors, open fires and plump-cushioned armchairs in the locals' bar, but the emphasis is firmly on the food, with the kitchen turning out delicious fare, perhaps seared scallops with cauliflower purée, heather-roasted venison with chestnut gnocchi, marmalade soufflé with whisky ice-cream. Country-house bedrooms are as good as you'd expect: uncluttered and elegant, brimming with light, some beamed (mind your head!), all with fabulous bathrooms. All have sweet views, either of the kitchen garden or the river. Idyllic circular walks sweep you through blissful country. *Minimum two nights at weekends.*

Rooms	11: 5 doubles, 3 twins/doubles, 3 four-posters.
Price	£110-£220. Singles from £75.
Meals	Lunch from £18. Sunday lunch from £22. Dinner, 3 courses, around £35.
Closed	Tuesdays (November-March).
Directions	From Monmouth B4233 to Rockfield; B4347 north for 5 miles; right on B4521; Skenfrith 1 mile.

William & Janet Hutchings
The Bell at Skenfrith,
Skenfrith, Abergavenny NP7 8UH

Tel +44 (0)1600 750235
Email enquiries@skenfrith.co.uk
Web www.skenfrith.co.uk

Penally Abbey

A small country house high on the hill with views to the front of Carmarthen Bay. Caldy Island lies to the east, the road ends at the village green, a stroll across the golf course leads to the beach. Up at the house, a fine arched window by the grand piano frames the view perfectly, so sink into a Chesterfield in front of the fire and gaze out to sea. The house dates to 1790 and was once an abbey; St Deiniol's, a ruined 13th-century church, stands in the garden. There's a terrace for pre-dinner drinks, bluebells carpet the wood in May. Bedrooms are all different: grand four-posters with wild flock wallpaper in the main house; a simpler cottage feel in the coach house next door. Steve's gentle, unflappable manner is infectious and relaxing – don't expect to feel rushed. Elleen cooks in the French style, much of it picked up in the kitchen of a château many years ago, perhaps stilton and walnut mousse, haunch of venison with juniper berries, iced coffee Tia Maria. The Pembrokeshire coastal path passes by outside. Further afield, Narbeth, St Davids and Dylan Thomas country wait. *Minimum two nights at weekends during summer.*

Rooms	12: 5 doubles, 6 twins/doubles, 1 twin.
Price	£148-£184. Dinner, B&B from £99 p.p.
Meals	Dinner, 3 courses, £36.
Closed	Never.
Directions	From Tenby A4139 for Pembroke. Right into Penally after 1.5 miles. Hotel signed above village green. Train station 5-mins walk.

Steve & Elleen Warren
Penally Abbey,
Penally, Tenby SA70 7PY

Tel +44 (0)1834 843033
Email info@penally-abbey.com
Web www.penally-abbey.com

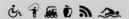

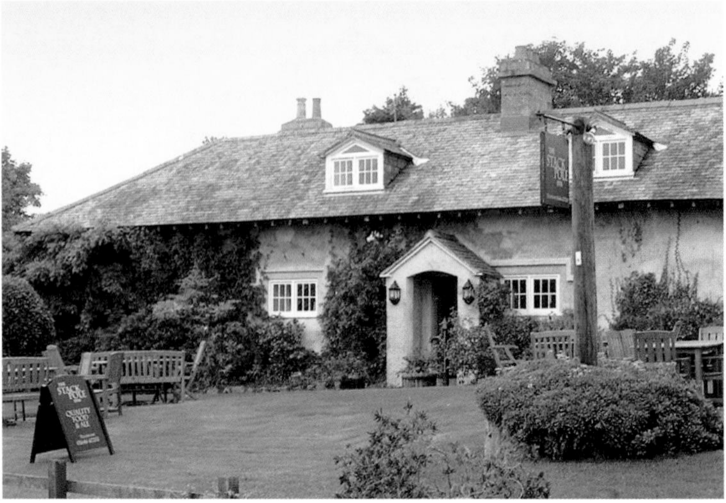

Stackpole Inn

This friendly inn is hard to fault. It sits in a quiet village drenched in honeysuckle with a fine garden at the front, a perfect spot for a drop of Welsh ale in summer. Wander further afield and you come to the sea at Barafundle Bay – a Pembrokeshire glory – where you can pick up the coastal path and follow it west past Stackpole Head to St Govan's Chapel. Stride back up to the inn and find interiors worthy of a country pub. There are smart red carpets, whitewashed walls, a hard-working wood-burner and obligatory beamed ceilings. Locals and visitors mingle in harmony, there are four hand pumps at the slate bar and tasty rustic cooking in the restaurant, perhaps deep-fried whitebait, rack of lamb, fresh raspberry brûlée. Super bedrooms are tremendous value for money and quietly positioned in a converted outbuilding. Two have sofabeds, two have velux windows for star gazing. All come in seaside colours with tongue-and-groove panelling, stripped floors, comfy beds, crisp linen and excellent bathrooms. Don't miss Pembroke Castle or the beach at Freshwater West.

Rooms	4: 2 twins/doubles, 2 family rooms.
Price	£90. Singles from £60.
Meals	Lunch from £5. Dinner, 3 courses, £25-£30 (not Sundays October-March). Sunday lunch, 3 courses, £18.95.
Closed	Rarely.
Directions	B4319 south from Pembroke for 3 miles, then left for Stackpole. Through Stackpole Cheriton, up hill, right at T-junction. On right.

Gary & Becky Evans
Stackpole Inn,
Stackpole, Pembroke SA71 5DF

Tel +44 (0)1646 672324
Email info@stackpoleinn.co.uk
Web www.stackpoleinn.co.uk

The Grove at Narberth

In the last couple of years the Grove has emerged as one of the loveliest places to stay in Wales – a cool country-house hotel with one foot in its Georgian past and the other in the contemporary present. It stands lost in Pembrokeshire's beautiful hills with big views to the front and a vast kitchen garden that provides much for the table. Inside, exquisitely refurbished Arts & Crafts interiors come as standard – an explosion of wood in the entrance hall, a roaring fire in the drawing room bar, and a smart restaurant for some of the best food in Wales, perhaps home-smoked salmon, local beef, pecan pie with roasted figs. Gorgeous bedrooms are split between the main house and converted outbuildings. All are divine, some are just bigger than others. Expect beautiful fabrics, cool wallpaper, crisp white linen and super-comfy beds. Bathrooms are equally spoiling with robes and heated floors. There's a parterre garden for lunch in summer and Wellington boots for those who want to walk; the coastal path is close. Don't miss Narberth, a pretty country town full of lovely shops. *Minimum two nights at weekends.*

Rooms	20: 14 doubles, 6 suites.
Price	£150-£260. Suites £250-£290.
Meals	Lunch £19-£22. Dinner, 3 courses, £49.
Closed	Never.
Directions	M4, then A48 & A40 west towards Haverfordwest. At A470 roundabout, take 1st exit to Narberth. Through town, down hill, then follow brown signs to hotel.

Neil Kedward & Zoe Agar
The Grove at Narberth,
Molleston, Narberth SA67 8BX
Tel +44 (0)1834 860915
Email info@thegrove-narberth.co.uk
Web www.thegrove-narberth.co.uk

Crug Glas

If you've never been to St Davids, know this: it is one of the most magical places in Britain. It sits in Pembroke's national park, has an imperious 12th-century cathedral, and is surrounded by magnificent coastline that's dotted with cliffs and vast sandy beaches. As for Janet's wonderful retreat, it's part chic hotel, part farmhouse B&B, stylish yet personal, a great place to stay. The house dates from 1120 and sits in 600 acres of arable and grazing land (they run cattle, grow cereals). Outside, you find lawns and a small copse sprinkled with bluebells, then field and sky, and that's about it. Inside, there's an honesty bar in the sitting room and a Welsh dresser in the dining room, where Janet serves delicious food: homemade soups, home-reared beef, chocolate mousse with clotted cream. Bedrooms are the big surprise: a vast four-poster, a copper bath, old armoires, beautiful fabrics. All have robes in fancy bathrooms, one room occupies much of the top floor, two beautiful suites in an old barn have exposed timbers and underfloor heating. The coast is close.

Rooms	7: 3 doubles, 1 twin/double, 3 suites.
Price	£115-£150. Suites £170-£185. Singles from £90.
Meals	Sunday lunch, £22.50. Afternoon tea from £12.50. Dinner, 3 courses, about £35.
Closed	22-27 December.
Directions	South from Fishguard on A487. Through Croes goch, then signed right after 2 miles.

Janet & Perkin Evans
Crug Glas,
Solva, Haverfordwest SA62 6XX

Tel +44 (0)1348 831302
Email janet@crugglas.plus.com
Web www.crug-glas.co.uk

Cnapan Restaurant & Hotel

Cnapan is a way of life – a family affair with two generations at work in harmony. Judith excels in the kitchen, Michael looks after the bar and son Oliver has returned to the fold to help them both. It is a very friendly place that ticks to its own beat with locals popping in to book tables and guests chatting in the bar before dinner. The house is cosy and traditionally home-spun – whitewashed stone walls and old pine settles in the dining room; comfy sofas and a wood-burner in the sitting room; a tiny telly in the bar for the odd game of rugby (the game of cnapan, rugby's precursor, originated in the town). There are maps for walkers, bird books, flower books, the daily papers, too. Spill into the garden in summer for pre-dinner drinks under the weeping willow, then tuck into Judith's delicious food: smoked salmon fishcakes, Preseli lamb, banoffee pie with espresso ice-cream. Comfy bedrooms, warmly simple, are good value for money; half have new showers, half are getting them soon. You're in the Pembrokeshire National Park; beaches and cliff-top coastal walks beckon. *Minimum two nights at weekends. Extra bath available.*

Rooms	5: 1 double, 3 twins, 1 family room.
Price	£90. Singles from £60. Extra child in family room £15.
Meals	Dinner £25-£30.
Closed	Christmas, January-February.
Directions	From Cardigan A487 to Newport. 1st pink house on right, 300m into Newport.

Michael, Judith & Oliver Cooper
Cnapan Restaurant & Hotel,
East Street, Newport SA42 0SY

Tel +44 (0)1239 820575
Email enquiry@cnapan.co.uk
Web www.cnapan.co.uk

Llys Meddyg

This fabulous restaurant with rooms has a bit of everything: cool rooms that pack a designer punch, super food in a sparkling restaurant, a cellar bar for drinks before dinner, a fabulous garden for summer treats. It's a very friendly place with charming staff on hand to help, and it draws in a local crowd who come for the seriously good food, perhaps mussel and saffron soup, rib of Welsh beef with hand-cut chips, cherry soufflé with pistachio ice-cream. You eat in style with a fire burning at one end of the restaurant and good art hanging on the walls. Excellent bedrooms are split between the main house (decidedly funky) and the mews behind (away from the road). All have the same fresh style: Farrow & Ball colours, good art, oak beds, fancy bathrooms with fluffy robes. Best of all is the back garden with a mountain-fed stream pouring past. In summer, a café/bistro opens up out here – coffee and cake or steak and chips – with doors that open onto the garden. Don't miss Pembrokeshire's fabulous coastal path for its windswept cliffs, sandy beaches and secluded coves.

Rooms	9: 4 doubles, 4 twins/doubles, 1 suite.
Price	£100-£180. Singles from £85.
Meals	Lunch from £7. Dinner from £14.
Closed	Rarely.
Directions	East from Fishguard on A487. On left in Newport towards eastern edge of town.

Louise & Edward Sykes
Llys Meddyg,
East Street, Newport SA42 0SY

Tel	+44 (0)1239 820008
Email	info@llysmeddyg.com
Web	www.llysmeddyg.com

Hammet House

Down a smart avenue of trees find a deliciously creeper-clad Georgian house set in eight acres along the banks of the river Teifi and gloriously young, energetic new owners, Owen and Philippa. The whole place is relaxed and grand at the same time: uncover a spacious open-plan bar and drawing room with a crackling fire, dark painted walls with vibrant contemporary furniture sitting happily with leather Chesterfields and splodges of vivid colours (lime, pink and orange). The restaurant is a calm space; choose between the full works from a Michelin-trained chef, or a bar menu of local produce: Pembrokeshire potatoes, homemade Welsh broth. There's a colourful den with TV for young escapees. All bedrooms (a work in progress so some better than others) are on the first floor and have handmade oak beds, white linen, dreamy mattresses; bathrooms are traditional and roomy with huge fluffy towels. Venture outside for smooth lawns, a dining terrace, fishing on the river. Grand walking is to be had in the Preseli hills, beaches are wild and woolly; this is an untrumpeted part of Wales and worth exploring.

Rooms	12: 10 doubles, 1 twin, 1 family room.
Price	£130-£175. Singles from £95. Children £25.
Meals	Dinner, 3 courses, about £35. Bar meals from £10.
Closed	Never.
Directions	Sent on booking.

Philippa & Owen Gale
Hammet House,
Llechryd, Cardigan SA43 2QA

Tel +44 (0)1239 682382
Email mail@hammethouse.co.uk
Web www.hammethouse.co.uk

Gliffaes Hotel

A charming country house above the river Usk, which pours through the valley below. In summer, the sitting room bar opens onto a large terrace, where you can sit in the sun and soak in the view – red kites circling above the water, sheep grazing majestic hills. You're in 35 peaceful acres of formal lawns and mature woodland. Inside, interiors pack a punch. Afternoon tea is laid out in a sitting room of panelled walls and family portraits, while logs crackle in a grand fireplace. This is a fishing hotel, one of the best, and fishermen often gather in the bar for tall tales and a quick drink at the end of the day. Eventually, they spin through to the restaurant and dig into seasonal food (the hotel is part of the Slow Food Movement) – goats' cheese soufflé, lemon sole, plum and cherry crumble... Bedrooms above are in country-house style with smart fabrics and carpets, all mod cons, a sofa if there's room; others are in the coach house annexe. Several have river views, a couple have small balconies, one has a claw-foot bath that overlooks the front lawn. *Minimum two nights at weekends.*

Rooms	23: 19 twins/doubles, 4 singles.
Price	£112-£265. Singles from £100. Dinner, B&B from £90 p.p.
Meals	Light lunches from £5. Sunday lunch £22-£29. Dinner, 3 courses, £42.
Closed	January.
Directions	From Crickhowell, A40 west for 2.5 miles. Signed left and on left after 1 mile.

James & Susie Suter
Gliffaes Hotel,
Gliffaes Road,
Crickhowell NP8 1RH

Tel +44 (0)1874 730371
Email calls@gliffaeshotel.com
Web www.gliffaeshotel.com

Peterstone Court

Sheep graze in fields to the front, a swimming pool shimmers by an 11th-century church, a sun-trapping dining terrace overlooks the river Usk, you can walk straight into sublime country. The house dates back to 1750 and has a panelled sitting room with an open fire, a cute little spa in the vaulted cellars, a brasserie/bar that overlooks the garden with views that shoot off to Pen y Fan, the highest peak in South Wales. Bedrooms mix country-house style with warm colours and eclectic furniture. Rooms in the old stables come over two floors and have a rustic feel. Those in the main house are grander, some with high-ceilings and four-poster beds, others with padded headboards and cavernous sofas; all have fine views. Downstairs, much of the food in the restaurant comes straight from the hotel's farm eight miles up the road (free-range chickens, mountain lamb, succulent pork), so dig into pressed ham hock with Welsh rarebit, roast duck with breaded hen's egg, coconut panna cotta with pineapple sorbet. Mountains wait so bring your boots and bikes. Brecon is close, too. *Minimum two nights at weekends. Ask about seasonal offers.*

Rooms	12: 3 doubles, 5 twins/doubles, 2 family rooms, 2 suites.
Price	£115-£165. Suites £215-£225. Singles from £100. Dinner, B&B from £87.50 p.p.
Meals	Lunch from £5. Dinner, 3 courses, £25-£35.
Closed	One week in January.
Directions	A40 west from Abergavenny for Brecon. Peterstone Court signed on left, two miles east of Brecon.

Sean Gerrard & Glyn & Jessica Bridgeman
Peterstone Court,
Llanhamlach, Brecon LD3 7YB

Tel +44 (0)1874 665387
Email info@peterstone-court.com
Web www.peterstone-court.com

The Felin Fach Griffin

It's quirky, homespun, and thrives on a mix of relaxed informality and colourful style. The low-ceilinged, timber-framed bar resembles the sitting room of a small hip country house, with squashy sofas in front of a fire that burns on both sides and backgammon waiting to be played. Painted stone walls throughout come in blocks of colour; on Sundays a musician plays. More informality in the restaurant, where stock pots simmer on an Aga; try cured salmon, shoulder of local lamb, Eve's pudding with cinnamon custard… delicious veggie options too. Bedrooms above are warmly simple with comfy beds wrapped in crisp linen, making this a must for those in search of a lovely billet near the mountains. There are framed photographs on the walls, the odd piece of mahogany furniture, good books, no TVs (unless you ask). Breakfast is served in the dining room; wallow with the papers, make your own toast. A main road passes outside, quietly at night, lanes lead into the hills, and an organic kitchen garden provides much for the table. Walk, ride, cycle, canoe, or head to Hay for books galore.

Rooms	7: 2 doubles, 2 twins/doubles, 2 four-posters, 1 family room.
Price	£115-£125. Four-posters £150-£165. Family room £160. Singles from £100. Dinner, B&B from £82.50 p.p.
Meals	Lunch from £18.50. Dinner about £30. Sunday lunch, 3 courses, £23.50.
Closed	Christmas Day & Eve (night). 4 days in January.
Directions	From Brecon A470 north to Felin Fach (4.5 miles). On left.

Charles & Edmund Inkin
The Felin Fach Griffin,
Felin Fach, Brecon LD3 0UB

Tel	+44 (0)1874 620111
Email	enquiries@felinfachgriffin.co.uk
Web	www.felinfachgriffin.co.uk

Llangoed Hall

Once home to fashion icon Laura Ashley, this Jacobean mansion was built on the site of the first Welsh parliament. It sits in the Wye Valley with shallow hills rising behind, a flawless rural retreat set in 17 acres of landscaped gardens. Outside, you find tennis and croquet, ducks and hens, an orchard and a maze, a vegetable garden that serves the kitchen. Inside, spectacular country-house interiors – even the hallways are things of beauty. There's a grand piano in the morning room, beautiful art in the sitting room, fires and fresh flowers everywhere, busts and stone flagging in the garden room. Country-house bedrooms have lovely fabrics, elegant colours, smartly-dressed beds and garden views. You'll find Roberts radios, decanters of sherry, bowls of fruit, perhaps a sofa at the foot of a four-poster. Bathrooms are divine; expect robes, deep baths and power showers. Delicious local fare waits in the panelled dining room, perhaps local asparagus with a poached pheasant's egg, Welsh lamb with wild garlic, chocolate fondant with cherry sorbet. Don't miss afternoon tea.

Rooms	23: 19 twins/doubles, 4 suites.
Price	£150-£275. Suites £300-£350.
Meals	Lunch from £6.50. Dinner, 3 courses, £55. Tasting menu £85. Sunday lunch £32.50.
Closed	Never.
Directions	From Brecon, A470 for Builth Wells for about 6 miles; left on A470 to Llyswen. Left in village at T-junc. Entrance 1.5 miles further on right.

Calum Milne
Llangoed Hall,
Llyswen, Brecon LD3 0YP

Tel +44 (0)1874 754525
Email enquiries@llangoedhall.com
Web www.llangoedhall.com

The Lake Country House & Spa

Deep in the silence of mid-Wales, an old-school country house that looks after you well. Fifty acres of lawns, lakes and ancient woodland wrap around you, there's a spa with an indoor pool, treatment rooms and a tennis court by the lake. Sit in a hot tub and watch guests fish for their supper, try your luck on the nine-hole golf course, saddle up nearby and take to the hills. Come home to afternoon tea in the big, elegant drawing room, where an archipelago of rugs warms a brightly polished wooden floor and chandeliers hang from the ceiling. The hotel opened over a hundred years ago and the leather-bound fishing logs date to 1894. A feel of the 1920s lingers. Fires come to life in front of your eyes, grand pianos and grandfather clocks sing their songs, snooker balls crash about in the distance. Dress for a delicious dinner – the atmosphere deserves it – then retire to cosseting bedrooms. Most are suites: those in the house are warmly traditional, those in the lodge softly contemporary. The London train takes four hours and stops in the village. Resident geese waddle.

Rooms	30: 6 twins/doubles, 24 suites.
Price	£195. Suites £240-£260. Singles from £145. Dinner, B&B (min. 2 nights) from £122.50 p.p.
Meals	Lunch, 3 courses, £22.50. Dinner, 4 courses, £38.50.
Closed	Never.
Directions	From Builth Wells A483 west for 7 miles to Garth. Signed from village.

Jean-Pierre Mifsud
The Lake Country House & Spa,
Llangammarch Wells LD4 4BS

Tel	+44 (0)1591 620202
Email	info@lakecountryhouse.co.uk
Web	www.lakecountryhouse.co.uk

Milebrook House Hotel

An old-school country hotel with three acres of gardens that run down to the river Teme. You'll find Wales on one bank and England on the other, so bring your wellies and wade across; the walking is magnificent. The house, once home to writer Wilfred Thesiger, is informally run by two generations of the Marsden family with Beryl and Rodney leading the way. Step inside and enter a world that's rooted in a delightful past: clocks tick, cats snooze, fires crackle, the odd champagne cork escapes its bondage. Beautiful art hangs on the walls, the sitting room is stuffed with books, the bar comes in country-house style and there's food to reckon with in the dining room – perhaps Cornish scallops with a pea purée, rack of Welsh lamb with fondant potatoes, glazed orange tart with mango and praline. A kitchen garden supplies much for the table. You can fish for trout, spot deer in the woods, play croquet on the lawn. Red kite, moorhens, kingfishers and herons live in the valley. Homely bedrooms do the trick, and Presteigne and Ludlow are close.

Minimum stay two nights at weekends. Children over eight welcome.

Rooms	10: 5 doubles, 4 twins, 1 family room.
Price	£136. Family room £161. Singles from £79. Dinner, B&B from £95 p.p. (min. 2 nights).
Meals	Lunch, 2 courses, £14.95 (not Monday). Dinner, 3 courses, £32.95.
Closed	Never.
Directions	From Ludlow A49 north, then left at Bromfield on A4113 towards Knighton for 10 miles. Hotel on right.

Rodney, Beryl & Joanne Marsden
Milebrook House Hotel,
Stanage, Knighton LD7 1LT

Tel +44 (0)1547 528632
Email hotel@milebrookhouse.co.uk
Web www.milebrookhouse.co.uk

Fairyhill

This lovely country house on the Gower sits in 24 acres of beautiful silence with a sun-trapping terrace at the back for lunch in summer. Potter about and find a walled garden, a stream-fed lake, free-range ducks and an ancient orchard. Inside, country-house interiors come fully loaded: smart fabrics, warm colours, deep sofas, the daily papers. There's an open fire in the bar, a grand piano in the sitting room, then delicious food in the restaurant, most locally sourced. Stylish bedrooms hit the spot. Most are big and fancy, a couple are small, but sweet. Some have painted beams, others a sofa or a wall of golden paper. Sparkling bathrooms, some with separate showers, have deep baths, white robes and fancy oils; if that's not enough, there's a treatment room, too. Outside, the Gower waits – wild heathland, rugged coastline, some of the best beaches in the land – so explore by day, then return for a good meal, perhaps scallops with cauliflower and chorizo, Gower lamb with gratin potatoes, baked honey and amaretto cheesecake. The wine list is one of the best in Wales, so don't expect to go thirsty. *Children over eight welcome.*

Rooms	8: 3 doubles, 5 twins/doubles.
Price	£180-£280. Singles from £160. Dinner, B&B from 135 p.p.
Meals	Lunch from £20. Dinner £35-£45.
Closed	First 3 weeks in January. Monday & Tuesday, November-March.
Directions	M4 junc. 47, A483 south, then A484 west to Gowerton and B4295 for Llanrhidian. Through Oldwalls, 1 mile up on left.

Andrew Hetherington & Paul Davies
Fairyhill,
Reynoldston, Gower Peninsula,
Swansea SA3 1BS

Tel +44 (0)1792 390139
Email postbox@fairyhill.net
Web www.fairyhill.net

Wheelchair-accessible

At least one bedroom and bathroom accessible for wheelchair users.

England

Bath & N.E. Somerset 1
Bristol 9
Cambridgeshire 12
Cornwall 16 •17 • 18 • 19 • 20 • 21 • 23 • 31 • 34 • 36
Cumbria 41 • 42 • 46 • 50 • 53 • 55 • 57
Devon 63 • 65 • 66 • 68 • 70 • 72 • 76
Dorset 90 • 91 • 92 • 95 • 99 • 101
Durham 102
Essex 103 • 106
Gloucestershire 108 • 110 • 115
Hampshire 117 • 120
Herefordshire 121
Isle of Wight 124
Kent 131 • 138 • 139
Lancashire 141
Lincolnshire 144 • 145
Norfolk 154 • 155 • 156
Northumberland 163
Nottinghamshire 164
Oxfordshire 169 • 173 • 174 • 175
Rutland 176 • 177
Somerset 186 • 187 • 192 • 193
Suffolk 198 • 199 • 201 • 202 • 206 • 207 • 208
Sussex 217 • 218 • 226
Warwickshire 227
Wiltshire 231
Worcestershire 234
Yorkshire 236 • 237 • 238 • 244 • 245 • 247

Scotland

Argyll & Bute 260
Edinburgh 264
Fife 268
Highland 274 • 280
Perth & Kinross 284 • 288 • 290
Western Isles 296 •

Wales

Ceredigion 302 • 303
Denbighshire 305 • 306
Pembrokeshire 312
Powys 319 • 323 • 324

Event hire

The whole building can be hired for an event.

England

Bath & N.E. Somerset 2 • 4
Brighton & Hove 5 • 6
Bristol 8
Buckinghamshire 10
Cambridgeshire 11 • 12 • 13 • 14
Cleveland 15
Cornwall 16 • 17 • 19 • 20 • 23 • 25 • 26 • 27 • 29 • 30 • 34 • 36 • 37 • 39 • 40
Cumbria 41 • 42 • 47 • 49 • 50 • 51 • 53 • 54 • 56 • 57 • 59
Derbyshire 60 • 61
Devon 64 • 65 • 66 • 67 • 68 • 70 • 72 • 73 • 76 • 77 • 79 • 82 • 84 • 85
Dorset 86 • 88 • 89 • 90 • 92 • 96 • 98 • 99 • 101
Essex 103 • 106
Gloucestershire 107 • 110 • 112 • 114 • 116
Hampshire 117 • 118 • 119
Herefordshire 121 • 122 • 123
Isle of Wight 124 • 125 • 126
Kent 128 • 129 • 131 • 132 •

Channel Islands

Scotland

Wales

Weddings

You can get married at these places.

England

Channel Islands

Scotland

Wales

Singles

Single room OR rooms let to single guests for half the double room rate, or under.

England

Channel Islands

Scotland

Wales

Horse riding

Riding can be arranged nearby.

England

Channel Islands

Scotland

Wales

For many years Alastair Sawday Publishing has been 'greening' the business in different ways. Our aim is to reduce our environmental footprint as far as possible and with almost everything we do we have environmental implications in mind. In recognition of our efforts we won a Business Commitment to the Environment Award in 2005, a Queen's Award for Enterprise in the Sustainable Development category in 2006, and the Independent Publishers Guild Environmental Award in 2008.

The buildings

Beautiful as they were, our old offices leaked heat, used electricity to heat water and rooms, flooded spaces with light to illuminate one person, and were not ours to alter.

So in 2005 we created our own eco offices by converting some old barns to create a low-emissions building. Heating and lighting the building, which houses over 30 employees, now produces only 0.28 tonnes of carbon dioxide per year – a reduction of 35%. Not bad when you compare this with the six tonnes emitted by the average UK household. We achieved this through a variety of innovative and energy-saving building techniques, some of which are described below.

Insulation By laying insulating board 90mm thick immediately under the roof tiles and on the floor, and lining the inside of the building with plastic sheeting, we are now insulated even for Arctic weather, and almost totally air-tight.

Heating We installed a wood pellet boiler from Austria in order to be largely fossil-fuel free. The heat is conveyed by water to all corners of the building via an underfloor system.

Water We installed a 6,000-litre tank to collect rainwater from the roofs. This is pumped back, via an ultra-violet filter, to lavatories, shower and basins. There are also two solar thermal panels on the roof providing heat to the one hot-water cylinder.

Lighting We have a mix of low-energy lighting – task lighting and up lighting – and have installed three sun pipes.

Electricity Our electricity has long come from the Good Energy Company and is 100% renewable.

Photo left: Tom Germain
Photo right: Jackie King

Materials Virtually all materials are non-toxic or natural, and our carpets are made from (80%) Herdwick sheep wool from National Trust farms in the Lake District.

Doors and windows Outside doors and new windows are wooden, double-glazed and beautifully constructed in Norway. Old windows have been double-glazed.

More greenery

Besides having a building we are proud of, and which is pretty impressive visually, too, we work in a number of other ways to reduce the company's overall environmental footprint.

- office travel is logged as part of a carbon sequestration programme, and money for compensatory tree planting donated to SCAD in India for a tree-planting and development project
- we avoid flying and take the train for business trips wherever possible
- car sharing and the use of a company pool car are part of company policy, with recycled cooking oil used in one car and LPG in the other
- organic and Fair Trade basic provisions are used in the staff kitchen and organic and/or local food is provided by the company at all in-house events
- green cleaning products are used throughout

However, becoming 'green' is a journey and, although we began long before most companies, we realise we still have a long way to go.

Sawday's
CANOPY
&STARS
A beautiful collection of treehouses, cabins, yurts, Gypsy caravans, wagons and more – across Britain, France, Spain and Portugal...
Everything you love about Sawday's, but outdoors.
+44 (0)1275 395447
www.canopyandstars.co.uk

ON
WHEELS
UP IN THE
TREES

Alastair Sawday has been publishing books for over 20 years, finding Special Places to Stay in Britain and abroad. All our properties are inspected by us and are chosen for their charm and individuality, and now with 17 titles to choose from there are plenty of places to explore. You can buy any of our books at a reader discount of 25%* on the RRP.

List of titles:	RRP	Discount price*
British Bed & Breakfast	£15.99	£11.99
Special Places to Stay in Britain for Garden Lovers	£19.99	£14.99
British Hotels and Inns	£15.99	£11.99
Pubs & Inns of England & Wales	£15.99	£11.99
Venues	£11.99	£8.99
Cotswolds	£9.99	£7.49
Wales	£9.99	£7.49
Dog-friendly Breaks in Britain	£14.99	£11.24
French Bed & Breakfast	£15.99	£11.99
French Self-Catering	£14.99	£9.74
French Châteaux & Hotels	£15.99	£11.99
Italy	£15.99	£11.99
Portugal	£12.99	£9.74
Spain	£15.99	£11.99
India	£11.99	£8.99
Go Slow England & Wales	£19.99	£14.99
Go Slow France	£19.99	£14.99

*postage and packaging is added to each order

How to order:

You can order online at the discounted price at: www.sawdays.co.uk/bookshop
or call: +44 (0)1275 395431

THE BECKFORD ARMS

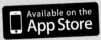

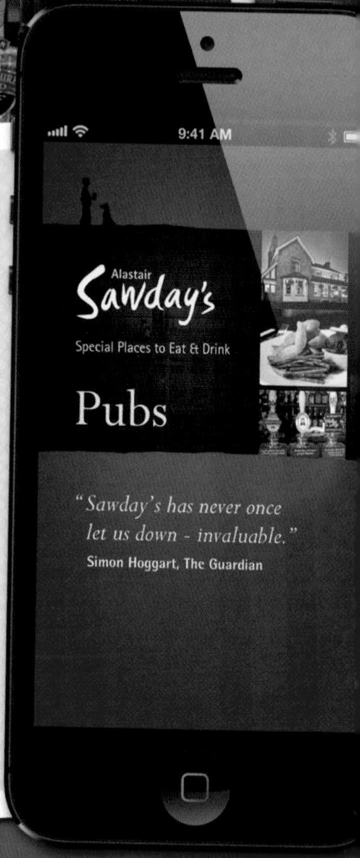
9:41 AM
Alastair Sawday's
Special Places to Eat & Drink
Pubs
"Sawday's has never once let us down - invaluable."
Simon Hoggart, The Guardian

We have indexed places under their MAIN postal town. See maps for clear positioning.

Photo: The Pheasant, Yorkshire, entry 238

1 Hotel

Dorset 2

3 ## Alexandra Hotel & Restaurant

4 Everything here is lovely, but the view is hard to beat, a clean sweep up the Jurassic coast towards Portland Bill. The hotel overlooks Lyme Bay; the only thing between you and it is the lawn. Below, the Cobb curls into the sea, the very spot where Meryl Streep withstood the crashing waves in *The French Lieutenant's Woman*. In summer, steamer chairs pepper the garden and guests fall asleep, book in hand, under an English sun. As for the hotel, it's just as good. Kathryn, ex-Firmdale, bought it from her mother and has refurbished brilliantly. You get stripped wood floors, windows everywhere, an airy bar for pre-dinner drinks, an attractive sitting room with plenty of books. The dining room could double as a ballroom, the conservatory brasserie opens onto a terrace; both provide excellent sustenance, perhaps Lyme Bay scallops, roast rump of Devon lamb, gingerbread pudding with vanilla ice-cream. Beautiful rooms hit the spot, most have the view. Expect super beds, padded headboards, robes in lovely bathrooms. Lyme, the beach and the fossil-ridden coast all wait.

5	Rooms	25: 19 twins/doubles, 2 singles, 3 family rooms, 1 apartment.
6	Price	£177-£225. Apartment £320. Singles from £85. Dinner, B&B from £120 p.p.
7	Meals	Lunch from £9.90. Afternoon tea from £6.50. Dinner, 3 courses, about £35. Sunday lunch from £19.50.
8	Closed	Rarely.
9	Directions	In Lyme Regis up hill on high street; keep left at bend; on left after 200m.

Kathryn Haskins
Alexandra Hotel & Restaurant,
Pound Street, Lyme Regis DT7 3HZ

Tel +44 (0)1297 442010
Email enquiries@hotelalexandra.co.uk
Web www.hotelalexandra.co.uk

10 

11 Entry 86 Map 2